TREATING THE ELDERLY WITH PSYCHOTHERAPY

TREATING THE ELDERLY WITH PSYCHOTHERAPY

The Scope for Change in Later Life

Edited by

Joel Sadavoy, M.D.

and

Molyn Leszcz, M.D.

INTERNATIONAL UNIVERSITIES PRESS, INC.
Madison   Connecticut

Library of Congress Cataloging-in-Publication Data

Treating the elderly with psychotherapy.

  Includes bibliographies and index.
  1. Geriatric psychiatry. 2. Psychotherapy.
I. Sadavoy, Joel, 1945-   . II. Leszcz, Molyn,
1952-   . [DNLM: 1. Mental Disorders—in old age.
2. Psychotherapy—in old age. WT 150 T7836]
RC451.4.A5T7 1987   618.97′68914   86-10487
ISBN 0-8236-6647-6

Manufactured in the United States of America

For my parents Belle and Ben Sadavoy, my wife Sharian and my children, Marion, Andrew, Beth, and Daniel.—J.S.

For my parents Saul and Clara, my wife Bonny and my children, Benjamin and Talia.—M.L.

CONTENTS

Foreword IRVIN D. YALOM   ix
Preface   xv
Acknowledgments   xxi
Contributors   xxiii

Part I   GENERAL PSYCHODYNAMIC
          PERSPECTIVES

  1. The Mourning-Liberation Process: Ideas on the
     Inner Life of the Older Adult
     GEORGE H. POLLOCK   3
  2. The Aged in Psychotherapy: Psychodynamic
     Contributions to the Treatment Process
     JEROME M. GRUNES   31
  3. Reflections on Psychotherapy with the Elderly
     MARTIN A. BEREZIN   45

Part II   MANIFESTATIONS OF
          PSYCHOPATHOLOGY

  4. Psychodynamics of Paranoid Phenomena in the
     Aged
     ADRIAN VERWOERDT   67
  5. The Impact of Massive Psychic Trauma and the
     Capacity to Grieve Effectively: Later Life Seque-
     lae
     HENRY KRYSTAL   95
  6. Exaggerated Helplessness Syndrome
     LAWRENCE BRESLAU   157

7. Character Disorders in the Elderly: An Overview
JOEL SADAVOY   175

Part III SPECIFIC PSYCHOTHERAPEUTIC
MODALITIES

8. Geriatric Psychotherapy: Beyond Crisis Management
RALPH J. KAHANA   233
9. Brief Psychotherapy with the Elderly: A Study of Process and Outcome
LAWRENCE W. LAZARUS and LESLEY GROVES   265
10. The Whole Grandfather: An Intergenerational Approach to Family Therapy
ETTA GINSBERG MCEWAN   295
11. Group Psychotherapy with the Elderly
MOLYN LESZCZ   325

Name Index   351
Subject Index   355

FOREWORD

Enter this book and you will jettison many venerable conceptions about the psychotherapeutic endeavor with the aged. Immerse yourself only briefly in these pages and it will no longer be possible to regard the psychotherapy of the aged as a low throttle, low challenge variant of adult psychotherapy—a form of therapy that requires unusual patience and limited goals and is based on the belief that aged patients are disillusioned, demoralized, possess inelastic resistive personality structures, and buffeted by calamitous, powerful environmental stresses—poverty, institutionalization, cognitive impairment and chronic physical illness.

Once the contributors to this volume have swept away these myths—myths spawned by contemporary ageism and by archaic psychoanalytic doctrines about human development—they then proceed to enlighten. The reader learns, for example, that the psychotherapy of the aged is no minor subspecialty enterprise. Keep in mind that more than one ninth of the population is over 65 (in fifty years it will be one fifth of the population). Furthermore, the percentage of individuals over 65 in therapy is likely to accelerate at a pace greater than that of the ageing of society. The proportion of individuals over 65 who sought psychotherapy in the past is unlikely to be a good indicator of the percentage who will seek it in the future. Tomorrow's aged will be better educated, more psychologically sophisticated, and more likely to have had psychotherapy at other points in life than the contemporary 65 year old cohort. Nor are the elderly poor or institutionalized: over two thirds of individuals over 65 own their homes free and clear and only five percent dwell in institutions. This volume informs us that many misconceptions about the aged have occurred because a disproportionate amount of medical and psychiatric literature has dealt with the institutionalized five percent.

Nor are the elderly untreatable. The idea that the elderly have rigid, inelastic, personality structures is the scion of a rigid, inelastic personality theory. Only now is this myth yielding to clinical experience and empirical evidence. This book emphasizes that it is the nature of the psychiatric disorder and not the age of the patient that is the crucial issue.

Patients always provide more material than therapy can assimilate. Dreams, reverie, daily problems and concerns, ruminations about the past soon overstuff the therapy hour. The therapist must perform a triage; he must focus on some material and discard the rest. But how to make that choice? It is important to keep in mind that, while expertise in the psychotherapy and psychodynamics of the young is often helpful, it does not necessarily generalize to the aged. There exist many psychodynamic concerns that are age specific and highly germane to the psychotherapy of the aged patient.

For example, consider this dream of a 70 year old patient: "I saw a large box with a curious shape. It was a square box on wheels. It was not a casket. It was black and shiny. It had only two windows, in the rear, and they were askew." A companion dream fragment the same night involved a vehicle with a fogged over rear window and rear view vision mirror. The therapist's understanding of the germane dynamics guides his mode of dream inquiry. In a younger patient, for example, I would have elected to focus upon the theme of the obscured rear vision, upon the patient's inability to understand some family secret that transpired in his childhood home. With this patient, it was far more profitable to direct the patient's attention to the lack of *front* windows. What lay ahead? Was there no future to be seen? This theme led into fertile areas: the patient was a writer obsessed, indeed tormented, by work and, for the first time, truly reached out to acknowledge the future. Could he really finish all three books upon which he was currently working? Perhaps it was time to accept limitations and to choose and to finish one book. This line of inquiry allowed the patient to discuss his conviction that he would die if he were to complete one of these books—that he was kept alive only by incessant work upon an unfinished book.

Of all age-specific dynamic themes, the contributors to this volume, above all, emphasize loss. The geriatric patient usually has endured extraordinary loss—loss of strength, power, prestige, recognition, physical ability, beauty, friends and affiliations, material wealth, intimacy, sexual opportunities, and occupation. But the most grievous loss of all is the loss of possibility. As possibility dwindles, the presence of death looms ever closer. (Heidegger defined death as "the impossibility for possibility"). Even the possibilities of defensive pathology are narrowed: the young have a vast range of methods to act out pathology (for example, drug abuse, sexual promiscuity, antisocial behavior, high risk sporting activities, workaholism) whereas the aged have only a few final common symptomatic pathways (for example, depression, hypochondriasis, paranoia, and angry or helpless demands upon caretakers).

Many aged patients are described as disillusioned: they have lost those illusions that provided them sustenance in the past. But which illusions have they lost? Is it not a good thing to abandon illusions and to embrace the firm trunk of reality? Perhaps old age is a time to live in time present relinquishing the illusions of time past. One abandons fantasies of ultimate success, recognition, justice, and redemption, and comes to terms with contingency and ordinariness—not "ordinary" in the base sense but in the human, existential sense. One understands that one has limits, that one is not outside of biological law, and must face the cosmic indifference of the universe. But is it possible to renounce illusion and not be mortally disillusioned? Was Camus always right when he said, "to begin to think is to begin to be undermined"? These are not abstract airy concerns; this volume emphasizes that they are concrete issues with which the geriatric psychotherapist must grapple in everyday practice.

Therapy can be conducted in any of a number of formats, but each format contains its own age-specific aspects. Group therapy, for example, is complicated by the group members' own prejudices against the aged. Those who harbor ageism stereotypes will ultimately arrive at the age where they discriminate against contemporaries and eventually against self. Family therapy of the geriatric patient, to take another example, raises such complex moral and clinical questions as "balancing the ledger." If a child cared for his aged parents, then can he not expect equivalent, "pay-back" care from his children? Must the child repay everything given by the parent? And then there is, of course, the question of the intergenerational legacy. Some families pass on the unfulfilled goals of the aged from one generation to the next, much like an olympic torch.

Virtually every contributor elucidates one or another aspect of countertransference. The treatment of the elderly bestirs the memory of our relationships to parents and grandparents. What does it mean to us to see former denizens who are now frail and helpless? To what extent does our sense of hopelessness or pessimism in treating the elderly reflect our personal dread of inexorable aging and death?

And do not forget the richness that we can obtain from treating the elderly. It has too often been said that this is the first generation in human history that has little to learn from the previous generation (and of course even less from more distant generations). This homily is an expression of a technocratic frame of reference that this volume does so much to correct. We may have nothing technical to learn from the previous generation but we can learn what it means when one struggles with life during this, the final phase of human development.

Irvin D. Yalom

PREFACE

Despite growing sophistication in diagnostic and therapeutic biological approaches to psychiatry, psychodynamic approaches still form an essential basis for the comprehensive understanding of individuals in emotional distress. This is particularly true for the geriatric patient, in whom the interplay of organic disease and functional emotional difficulty may induce a mechanistic, biological, and behavioral therapeutic attitude, that ignores the inner world of the older adult. In addition, psychodynamic understanding and psychotherapeutic approaches are of major value in responding to difficulties experienced around the older patient—his family, his interpersonal, and at times, his institutional milieu. This book is presented by the editors, to focus attention on the intrapsychic world of the aging individual, and on the development of late life psychopathology. The initial organizing impetus for this book grew out of a 1984 conference held in Toronto, Canada entitled, "The Scope for Change in Later Life."

As psychoanalytic thinking has dramatically expanded over the past 30 years, psychodynamic understanding of the aging process and the resultant therapeutic approaches, may now move to incorporate the valuable perspectives currently available. Particularly important developments have been advances in object relations theory and self psychology, both of which draw attention to the intrapsychic meaning of relationship and self-esteem, key psychological issues for the aging person, who may experience traumatic losses in both these spheres. Competent geriatric psychiatric treatment requires a synthesis of

xvi   TREATING THE ELDERLY WITH PSYCHOTHERAPY

both biological and psychotherapeutic approaches in order to deal with the full range of psychiatric problems in the elderly. Yet historically, there has been a special hopelessness attached to psychotherapeutic approaches with this age group. As a result, those who practice in this way, often feel isolated in their work and unaware of the fertile activity in this field. We hope that the contributions in this book will help to encourage realistic hopefulness about the scope for change in the elderly. A realistic, therapeutic perspective is necessary to counter the often expressed pessimism, shared not only by patients, families, and society, but also by therapists who view emotional disturbances, depression, disengagement, and demoralization in the elderly, as inevitable and immutable.

The editors are grateful to the contributors for presenting their work in a fashion which permits the practical application of complex theoretical constructs. The authors' clinical illustrations further crystalize the ideas they express. We hope, therefore, that this text will be useful to a wide range of health professionals dealing with the elderly. The book focuses on a spectrum of disorders and difficulties in both ambulatory, relatively intact individuals, and institutionalized and more severely impaired patients. A special emphasis has been placed on the understanding and management of the problems of the interdisciplinary team in dealing with the difficult elderly person who evokes difficult transference–countertransference reactions within certain milieus. General psychiatrists dealing with the elderly and those who use psychotherapeutic approaches, psychogeriatric consultants, as well as social workers, nurses, psychologists, and other members of the health care team may find the book of value.

The book is divided into three main sections. The first deals with general psychodynamic issues, providing an overview of theoretical, psychodynamic, and psychotherapeutic principles in the treatment of the aged patient. This section draws upon the wealth of experience and expertise of Drs. Pollock,

Grunes, and Berezin who address with warmth and wisdom several of the central issues of development, psychopathology, and psychotherapeutic treatment in this age group. The function of the mourning-liberation process throughout aging and the role and limits of empathy are key contributions in this section. The authors elaborate as well on the socioeconomic aspects of psychiatric treatment for the elderly person drawing attention to important ethical concerns. Dr. Berezin's contribution differs somewhat in that the editors have tried to take advantage of his broad perspective by encouraging him not only to write about his general views on psychotherapy with the elderly, but in addition, to critically review and discuss the concepts presented by Drs. Pollock, Grunes, Lazarus, and Kahana, much as he did at the "Scope for Change in Later Life" meeting.

Part II deals more specifically with four aspects of psychopathology which are especially relevant to the elderly: paranoid disorders, the effect of massive psychic trauma, the exaggerated helplessness syndrome, and character pathology. Dr. Verwoerdt's psychodynamic formulations of paranoid symptoms provide a basis for psychotherapeutic treatment approaches which augment the necessary biological management. Dr. Krystal has presented a challenging chapter, not only describing the aftereffects of massive psychic trauma, but using the insights derived from his extensive study of survivors, to elaborate a theory of the development of affect and affect tolerance throughout life. The role of affects in health and disease is relevant throughout the individual's development, but is especially important for the elderly, in whom the adaptation to earlier life traumata is frequently challenged by the specific assaults of aging. Difficulties in tolerating painful affect impair self-integration of painful experiences and events and block effective grieving, factors that shape the psychotherapeutic work as described in Part I of this book. Moreover, the editors have had a special interest in massive trauma as it manifests in the aging Holocaust survivor. As the survivors of other traumatic experiences age, such as the Vietnam veterans, these concepts will have yet broader application. Chapter 6, "Exaggerated Helplessness Syndrome" and Chapter 7, "Character Disorders in the Elderly: An Overview," are linked in that the syndrome described by Dr. Breslau is most often found in patients who have underlying character pathology. Both of these disorders are particularly important in institutional and residential settings which can intensify symptomatic behavior, by virtue of the tension created by persistent and ongoing engagement and enmeshment between patient and staff, as described by Dr. Sadavoy.

The final section of the book is devoted to specific approaches to treatment. Drs. Kahana and Lazarus address different types of individual work with geriatric patients. Dr. Kahana, in chapter 8, deals with the reality of many older people's lives, as a time of frequent change, adaptation, and potential crises. Dr. Kahana draws on his varied and extensive clinical experience to provide models for treating the elderly both at the time of crisis and beyond. Dr. Lazarus and his colleagues use data from ongoing studies on brief psychotherapy to highlight the clinical usefulness of this modality of therapy with the older person. This chapter describes and measures the process and outcome of brief psychotherapy. Scientific evaluation of the effectiveness of psychotherapy is an immediate challenge to the mental health field, and Dr. Lazarus's methodology will be of additional interest to researchers as well as clinicians. The elderly individual is particularly vulnerable to interpersonal isolation and loss of self-esteem, generated not only by the multiple and unavoidable crises of aging as they are experienced internally, but also through pathological and maladaptive interactions with his family and his environment. Ms. McEwan and Dr. Leszcz contribute chapters elaborating on family therapy and group therapy with the elderly. In both chapters, theoretical understanding is linked to practical, clinical interventions.

Understanding the inner life of the aging individual is a complex and challenging therapeutic task. We hope this volume achieves its purpose of aiding those who are seriously engaged in treating the elderly, by demonstrating psychodynamic and psychotherapeutic theories and techniques which can be practically applied on a clinical level.

Joel Sadavoy
Molyn Leszcz

ACKNOWLEDGMENTS

We would like to acknowledge with thanks two colleagues, Dr. Daniel Silver and Dr. Stanley E. Greben whose approach to and understanding of what is therapeutic about psychotherapy, has shaped and influenced our own work in many ways. We are grateful to the administration and staff of Baycrest Centre for Geriatric Care, for their continued support, in developing a stimulating clinical and academic setting. We are also deeply grateful to Malerie Feldman for her unending hard work and good cheer, two invaluable commodities in bringing this book from its original conceptualization to its final form.

CONTRIBUTORS

MARTIN A. BEREZIN, M.D.
Clinical Professor of Psychiatry, Emeritus, Harvard Medical School; Honorary President, Boston Society for Gerontologic Psychiatry, Boston, Massachusetts.

LAWRENCE BRESLAU, M.D.
Assistant Clinical Professor of Psychiatry, Case Western Reserve Medical School; Consultant, Menorah Park Jewish Home for the Aged, Beachwood, Ohio.

LESLEY GROVES, M.S.
Research Assistant, Rush-Presbyterian-St. Luke's Medical Center, Chicago, Illinois.

JEROME M. GRUNES, M.D.
Associate Professor of Psychiatry, Northwestern University Medical School; Psychoanalyst, Private Practice, Chicago, Illinois; Senior Consultant—Older Adult Project, Institute of Psychiatry, Northwestern Memorial Hospital, Illinois.

RALPH J. KAHANA, M.D.
Associate Clinical Professor, Harvard Medical School; Associate Psychiatrist, Beth Israel Hospital, Boston, Massachusetts; Co-editor Journal of Geriatric Psychiatry.

HENRY KRYSTAL, M.D.
Professor of Psychiatry, Michigan State University; Private Practice, Psychiatry and Psychoanalysis, Southfield, Michigan.

LAWRENCE W. LAZARUS, M.D.

Assistant Professor, Department of Psychiatry, Rush-Pres-byterian-St. Luke's Medical Center, Chicago, Illinois; Psychiatric Consultant to the Johnston R. Bowman Health Center for the Elderly, Illinois.

MOLYN LESZCZ, M.D.

Assistant Professor of Psychiatry, University of Toronto, Co-ordinator of Group Therapy, Baycrest Centre for Geriatric Care, Toronto; Staff Psychiatrist, Mount Sinai Hospital, Toronto, Ontario, Canada.

ETTA GINSBERG MCEWAN, M.S.W.

Director, Department of Social Work, Baycrest Hospital, Toronto, Canada.

GEORGE H. POLLOCK, M.D.

President, The Institute of Psychoanalysis, Chicago; Professor of Psychiatry, Northwestern University Medical Center; President, Center for Psychosocial Studies, Chicago, Illinois.

JOEL SADAVOY, M.D.

Head, Department of Psychiatry, Baycrest Centre for Geriatric Care, Toronto; Associate Professor of Psychiatry, University of Toronto; Consultant Psychiatrist, Mount Sinai Hospital, Toronto, Ontario, Canada.

ADRIAN VERWOERDT, M.D.

Professor of Psychiatry, Duke University, Durham, North Carolina; Director of Geropsychiatry, Duke University, Durham, North Carolina; Director, Geropsychiatric Institute, John Umstead Hospital, Butner, North Carolina.

Part I
GENERAL PSYCHODYNAMIC PERSPECTIVES

1

THE MOURNING-LIBERATION PROCESS: IDEAS ON THE INNER LIFE OF THE OLDER ADULT

George H. Pollock, M.D.

Introduction

Cicero, the famous Roman orator and philosopher wrote an essay entitled, "De Senectute", "On Old Age," in 44 B.C. The form chosen by Cicero is a dialogue, a form often used by both the Greeks and the Romans. In the essay, two younger men pose their questions to the wise elder, Marcus Procius Cato, aged 84, who shares his experiences and observations with them. The dialogue is like a play or even a dream in that the various speakers represent the author's personal points of view. Cicero (106–43 B.C.) wrote "On Old Age" at age 62, the year before he was killed, although the dialogue is set in Rome in the year 150 B.C. In this work, Cicero anticipates much later gerontological research. Grant notes in the introduction to his (1982) translation that, "Cicero's reflections on immortality come from the heart because of the recent death of his beloved daughter Tullia" (p. 212), who died in childbirth. Furthermore, since Cicero may also have been distressed at the idea of his impending retirement, he may have wanted to show that he was still very capable of writing about a most important human concern in a positive way.

Scipio, aged thirty-five, opens the conversation by saying to Cato: "I have never noticed that you find it wearisome
to be old. That is very different from most other old men,
who claim to find their age a heavier burden than Mount
Etna itself." Cato responds, "A person who lacks the means,
within himself, to live a good and happy life will find any
period of his existence wearisome. But rely for life's bless-
ings on your own resources, and you will not take a gloomy
view of any of the inevitable consequences of nature's laws.
Everyone hopes to attain an advanced age; yet when it comes
they all complain! . . . Old age, they protest, crept up on
them more rapidly than they had expected . . . who was to
blame for their mistaken forecast? For age does not steal
upon adults any faster than adulthood steals upon children . . . I follow and obey nature as a divine being. Now
since she has planned all the earlier divisions of our lives
excellently, she is not likely to make a bad playwright's mis-
take of skimping the last act. And a last act was inevitable.
There had to be a time of withering, of readiness to fall,
like the ripeness which comes to the fruits of the trees and
of the earth. But a wise man will face this prospect with
resignation, for resistance against nature is as pointless as
the battles of the giants against the gods" [Cicero, 44 B.C.,
pp. 214–215].

Aging and reactions to aging have always been a major
human concern. A most informative document prepared by the
American Association of Retired Persons and the Administration on Aging of the United States Department of Health and
Human Services, *A Profile of Older Americans: 1984*, points out
that persons 65 years or older numbered 27.4 million in 1983.
"They represented 11.7 percent of the U.S. population, about
one in every nine Americans. The number of older Americans
increased by 1.7 million or 6 percent since 1980, compared to
an increase of 3 percent for the under-65 population" (p. 1).
"Since 1900 the percentage of Americans 65 and over almost

tripled . . . and the number increased more than eight times" (p. 1). "The older population itself is getting older. In 1983 the 65–75 age group . . . was over seven times larger than in 1900, but the 75–84 group . . . was 11 times larger and the 85 + group . . . was 20 times larger" (p. 1). "In 1983, there were 16.4 million older women and 11.0 million older men, or a sex ratio of 149 women for every 100 men . . . the sex ratio increased to a high of 241 for persons 85 and older" (p. 1). It is anticipated that the older population is expected to continue to grow in the future and by 2030, there will be 65 million older persons, 2½ times their number in 1980. Furthermore, by the year 2000, persons 65 + are expected to represent 13 percent of the population, and this percentage may climb to 21.2 percent by 2030 (p. 2). These statistics are most impressive and clearly, social issues such as widowhood, living arrangements, geographic distribution, income and poverty, housing, employment and retirement, and health care (especially problems in mental and psychological health) need to be addressed. Most older persons have at least one chronic condition and many have multiple difficulties. "The most frequently occurring conditions for the elderly in 1981 were: arthritis (46 percent), hypertension (38 percent), hearing impairments and heart conditions (28 percent each), sinusitis (18 percent), visual impairments and orthopedic impairments (14 percent each), arteriosclerosis (10 percent), and diabetes (8 percent)" (p. 13). Although emotional and mental disorders per se do not appear in this list they constitute an important element in the reactions to stress and strain induced by ill-health, psychosocial disruptions, exit and entrance events, transitions, and the diffusing of structures which gave the individual support and boundaries. The same demographic patterns found in the United States are reflected world wide, and in other developed countries some of the socioeconomic problems related to an increased older population are similar to patterns observable in North America.

In 1980 there were approximately 600 physicians in the United States identified as geriatricians. It is estimated that by 1990, there will be a need for 9,000 geriatricians. Moeller (1985) has noted that even though older people utilize physicians and health services more than younger adults, they do not use them inappropriately and probably underutilize both health and social services. Most older persons living in the community, even though they have some chronic condition, have few serious limitations in their daily activities. However, "among all persons 65 years and older, approximately 10–15 percent have marked mental health problems, and about 25 percent have serious difficulties caring for their daily tasks" (Moeller, 1985, p. 13). This is especially true for individuals over 80 years of age, as the number of individuals in that age group with physical and mental difficulties nearly doubles in comparison to those between the ages of 65–80. Fiscal considerations also need to be actively examined. Dr. Moeller has noted "the means (public or private) of paying health care expenses has little effect on either the incidence of medical problems or death rates. Rather the organization of health services appears to be a critical variable in the quality of health care, and consequently planning becomes an essential aspect of the efficient delivery of a geriatric health system" (p. 13). How mental health fits into this system is a significant issue that needs to be addressed, despite apparent wishes to avoid or ignore it.

The problems of the elderly that mental health workers encounter professionally may include depression, paranoid reactions, anxiety reactions, and the fear of helplessness and isolation when there are no family or other available support systems. Elsewhere, the author has discussed the question of aging and the aged, and how this can be viewed as either normal development or pathology (Pollock, 1981a). Without a data base for normal development in the older years, it is too easy to equate aging adults and/or aged adults as incompetent, ill, or incoherent. This has been an incorrect inference based upon studies of the decompensated elderly, whose conditions have been extrapolated to all or most elderly, with the resultant perpetuation of the myths of mental illness in older adults.

An important distinction should be made between developmental states, namely, normative or normal developmental crises that are predictable, anticipatable, and universal, and catastrophic crises. The developmental crises can be traumatic without being overwhelming and usually the stress-strain they induce can be coped with by individuals who have sufficient "strength," "energy," and integration. Of course, some decompensations may occur and these may require supportive treatment in order to help the individual to return to a homeostatic level that allows for comfortable functioning and further progression. The catastrophic crises, however, include the unexpected, the overwhelming and disruptive events, the sudden or even gradual situations that slowly build up to a breaking point, the frightening and disorganizing situations which affect the individual as well as the family. Examples of such catastrophic crises include severe physical illness, acute malignancy, cardiac or stroke attacks, automobile accidents, Alzheimer's disease, and deaths. In addition, there are severe psychological illnesses such as schizophrenia, manic-depressive disorder, severe depression, and anxiety-panic attacks. These catastrophic crises may require professional interventions of various kinds, including individual or family psychotherapy, pharmacotherapy, or hospital based treatment.

Recent comprehensive statistical reports of Americans aged 85 or older revealed that as a group these "old old," "oldest old," or "extreme aged" are growing more rapidly than any younger segment of the population (Collins, 1985). Furthermore, this group is less frail, less likely to be institutionalized, and more independent than previously believed. The increase in numbers of the 85 and older group is engendering new concerns that relate to their impact on the economy, the health care and maintenance system, and the family and other support structures. Nonetheless, these individuals have great powers of survival, and their study can provide information that can be useful to younger generations in general, and specifically in regard to the institution of preventive measures to promote healthier processes of aging. In some ways these older adults can be linked to the invulnerables and lower risk individuals who are now attracting scientific study. What "self-righting," survival, and positive equilibrium maintenance factors do they possess that permit them to thrive despite the negative picture society has had of them? Confronted by the data, it is necessary to reexamine prior biases and preconceived notions, and to obtain additional data to extend and test newer hypotheses. Accordingly, the U.S. National Institute on Aging is inviting proposals to study people aged 85 and older.

The mental health field must begin to share with a wider audience its clinical findings arising from individual psychoanalytic psychotherapy with the "self-righting" group and those in the "younger old" as well as the "old old" categories. The author has had successful clinical experiences and can attest to the feasibility and positive outcomes of such intensive treatments with patients in age groups from the fifties to the nineties. Not all in these chronological, sociological, and psychological groupings are amenable to such treatment, but this is also true of people in their twenties, thirties, and forties.

Contrary to popular belief, increasing numbers of older people are actually adapting well. According to the 1980 U.S. Census, 8 out of every 10 of those Americans over age 65 (80 percent) describe their health as good or excellent compared with that of their contemporaries. Two-thirds of them are living in homes that they own free and clear, and in fact only 5 percent live in nursing homes. The question of why and how these people are so well adapted is now being investigated by Dr.

Gene Cohen, Director of the National Institute of Mental Health Program on Aging, who is studying a community of healthy, affluent, independently functioning older people living outside of Washington, D.C. This research will yield valuable information and help dispel the myth that assumes erroneously that when one is old, one is sick. Sufficient baseline data are needed to reveal what is normal for different aging cohorts.

In an effort to distinguish between normality and pathology, the author, along with Dr. Stanley Greenspan edited a three-volume work published by the U.S. Government entitled, *The Course of Life*. The last chapter is called "Aging or Aged: Development or Pathology" (Pollock, 1981a). The meaning of aging, despite its inevitable presence, has not been sufficiently explored. Introspective studies of what it feels like to move on in the life course are rarely undertaken—perhaps because of inherent bias against studying older adults as a result of younger investigators finding such studies threatening, perhaps because of the preponderent interest in infancy, childhood, and adolescence which has attracted investigators to these age groups, and perhaps because of other factors.

The author's work in the psychoanalysis of individuals with manic-depressive disorders has led to the obvious, rather than radical conclusion that two or more diseases of the psychic system can be present at the same time in the same person, each requiring a different kind of intervention or treatment. Patients, who previously would never have been considered for psychoanalytic treatment, now can have their manic-depressive symptomatology controlled enough to permit them to lie on a couch, five days a week, and be analyzed. Underlying pathology that was previously undiscovered can now be examined. With the knowledge that patients can have more than one kind of depression at the same time, it is also possible to deal with one kind of depression with the judicious use of certain medications, and to use psychosocial means of treatment for the other disorders. The newer conceptualizations bring increasing opportunities to the treatment situation and widen the horizons for psychological care with all patients, but especially with the elderly.

In parallel fashion, one may have normative developmental crises as well as catastrophic crises at the same time. The understanding and treatment that is instituted requires careful diagnostic, and sensitive therapeutic handling. Aging is a developmental crisis that may be less acute than other developmental crises, hence the need for normal baseline data in assessing normality and pathology. As the individual ages or develops there are other components that concomitantly develop and age as well. All the family members are aging, new members are introduced and sometimes are met with stranger-anxiety responses, the relationships and lives of siblings may shift, and work may end with retirement. Hence, aging needs to be approached, not as a single isolated entity, but as a process composed of multiple dynamic systems, all of them moving, all of them impinging upon the individual and each other, and all of them capable of being studied as discrete entities, as specifics, as well as interacting with each other.

In addition to these developmental and catastrophic crises, chronic and physical illnesses may also be present. This adds further complexity to the situation. Emotional illnesses, affective disorders, mental disturbances, and memory dysfunctions all may occur simultaneously. Drug intoxications, paradoxical reactions, allergies, degenerative phenomena, the depletion of energy, sleep disruptions, problems with hearing, sight, skin, arthritis, and pain are also associated with aging. As many changes are ongoing at the same time, at different rates, internally and externally, in a multiplicity of contexts, these changes require adaptational mechanisms to facilitate continuity and adaptation.

The author's research has focused on the phenomenon of mourning-liberation as an adaptational process in response to loss, change, and developmental progression. This is a central component of any crisis, both normal developmental and catastrophic. This mourning-liberation process is universal, found throughout human history, and is even present in animals in simple form. Actually, when death is the trigger, religious-sociocultural rituals and practices designed to diminish internal and external disorganization are evident, which, if successfully completed, can result in a freed life ready to "invest energies" in new pursuits and creative activities (Pollock, 1961, 1962, 1966, 1968, 1970, 1971a, 1971b, 1971c, 1972a, 1972b, 1973, 1975a, 1975b, 1975c, 1975d, 1976, 1977, 1978a, 1978b, 1981a, 1981b, 1982, 1983, 1984a, 1984b, 1985a, 1985b, 1985c). The premise of this chapter is that normal aging involves a mourning for past states of the self and that with liberation, one can move forward. If this mourning-liberation process does not occur, pathological mourning responses occur and serious psychopathology can emerge.

The Mourning–Liberation Process

The constant changes in the complex, interconnected mosaic of one's life confront one with stress, strains, and the need to accommodate to repeated losses. Initial research on adults who had lost parents in childhood has revealed that the effect of the loss depended on who was lost, at what stage of the individual's development the loss occurred, and the circumstances of the loss (Pollock, 1962). The discovery that certain pathological consequences were only present in a particular combination of factors gave rise to much research on the mourning-liberation process and the relationship of this process to creativity and creative living.

In an early paper on "Mourning and Adaptation" (Pollock,

1961), the author examined the impact of the loss of a parent in childhood on adult psychological functioning. Subsequently, a comparative study was done of adults who had lost a sibling during childhood, those who had lost one or both parents in childhood or adolescence, those who had lost a spouse, and those adults who had lost a child (Pollock, 1962). Later work with older adults underscored the centrality of loss to the elderly. The consequences of such losses in older adults repeatedly demonstrated the presence of arrested, fixated, or pathological mourning processes without liberation and freedom. In some, earlier life traumas had been exacerbated by the inevitable developmental changes that are an intrinsic part of the aging process; some could not adapt to change itself. Commonly, loneliness, isolation, and helplessness and the final common pathway of symptomatology, depression, were encountered. Yet the resources of some of these people were very pronounced and once the mourning process could be facilitated, pathological symptoms lifted, and liberation ensued.

For example, after intensive work with a woman in her seventies, who was depressed and whose son and daughter were very much interested in sending her to a nursing home, the depression lifted, the woman began to play golf and to take an active interest in the outer world, she developed an art collection, and visited art museums all over the world. Now in her upper eighties, she goes on cruises, tours, has made many friends, and has been able to find herself a male companion. Although the libidinal involvement is not intense, it has certainly improved to the point where she enjoys orgastic experiences in the ninth decade of life. This woman had to mourn for what was no longer present, confront some of her fantasies, understand that what was past was past, and that a new day and life would be possible.

In the context of this work, it has become evident that a very crucial element for successful aging is the ability to mourn for prior states of the self. When one can accept aging and its changes and mourn for the past the result can be a liberation, a freeing of energy for current living, including "planning for the future." One frequently sees this in individuals who have experienced serious physical illnesses and then have a "rebirth" with new life perspectives. They are able to feel, and to say to themselves, "Okay, this is behind me, and I can now see many things ahead of me for which I can begin to plan constructively." When this mourning-liberation process has not taken place, the pathological aspects of aging emerge with the obvious and ex-pected symptomatology. For those individuals who cannot ac-cept the normative crises of aging, impaired mourning is a central dynamic in old age psychopathology and depression. When catastrophic crises are superimposed on the normative crises, one must distinguish between these and institute appro-priate treatments. Depression itself is so global a descriptive term that imbedded within it can be both normative and cat-astrophic reactions.

In addition to clinical work of varying intensity with elderly persons, some observations about childhood and adult losses have been extended to include data on the meaning of signif-icant kinship relationships throughout the life course. An il-lustration: an 80-year-old mother does not mean the same to her 60-year-old daughter as she did 20 or 30 years earlier. Consequently, even though one uses the same kin terms, *mother* who is 80 has a different psychological meaning than *mother* who is 40, or *mother* who is 25. The same holds true for *father*. In working with adults who are older, it is possible to begin to study some of this changing, internal psychosocial meaning. Changing intrapsychic needs also shift the meanings of chil-dren, parents, spouses, and siblings as the life course moves on.

The meaning of children to their parents changes. One of the most devastating psychological traumas encountered clini-cally is that of a parent losing a child. Of all the loss experiences that the author has studied, this is the one in which there is seldom a complete mourning resolution, particularly for the mother. However, work with people in their eighties and nineties who lose a child who is in his fifties or sixties, often reveals that the loss of a child does not have the same meaning that it would have earlier in life. Further research on the changing meanings of loss, who is lost, and the consequences of loss, are most important in order to expand the knowledge of the inner life of the older adult.

Sibling relationships also change as life courses on. Though the family of origin dissolves as each of the siblings moves out and establishes his or her own family, as that family in turn matures, moves away, and establishes its own generation of familial nuclei there is a return to the initial sibling relationships and the nuclear family of origin, assuming that the sibling relationships were previously satisfactory. Those sibling relationships to which one returns may become the underlying basis for friendship with sibling surrogates in later life. The return to original sibling relationships can serve to renew positive ties to the past when change is occurring, promoting adaptation. Conversely, this may represent social regressions, or attempts to avoid mourning, loss, and feelings of emptiness. Here again new research data can help explain these observations.

The dynamics of friendship throughout aging is an area that has not been adequately addressed. There are types of change and loss, in each of these relational spheres, that are inherent in the process of aging. The normal process needs to be understood in order to better aid those whose processes run amiss. Cicero's essay "On Friendship" (Cicero, 44 BC), may shed further light on the study of the internal aspects of friendship.

Similarly, the changing meaning of the word *spouse* has not been examined. Spouses at 85 do not have the same meaning for each other as they did at 25 or 30. The social, sexual, supportive, and altruistic aspects of spouses throughout the life course are in need of further study. An example:

> A woman in her late seventies, married, husband alive and in relatively good health, presented such concerns. She felt increasingly unfulfilled in her relationship with her husband to whom she had been married for 55 years. In the course of work she made a very important discovery. The man she had married was a substitute for her mother and was not someone whom she genuinely loved. As she began to explore these feelings and talk about the lack of fulfillment in many areas of her life, tears came to her eyes and she said, "At this point of my life, I can't make changes; nor would I want to. I must adjust." It was a very painful experience for her, but adjust she did, and she was able to benefit from psychotherapy in this transitional process. As she became free of some of the emotional shackles of her earlier life, she returned to university studies as a later-life scholar, received her degree, and is now pursuing her interests in art and the theater with great verve and enthusiasm.

David Gutmann (1979) has written about the role shift that often occurs in the relationships of older couples. Females in later middle age become more active and more assertive, whereas males have a tendency to remove themselves and become less active and a bit more passive. This role shift is not pathological. It is a normal aspect of change in later life, and an important one to bear in mind. This is an illustration of the kind of normative developmental data that previously would have been seen as pathology. If conflict occurs over these developmental changes, they may become the focus of "catastrophic crises."

Political leaders and people who have worked in the arts all their lives are often productive well into the later decades. And many other individuals become quite creative in later life and pursue interests in the arts—music, literature, and the theater. There are countless examples of individuals who seem to

have a remarkable ability to reach out to life with joy and en-
thusiasm throughout a long lifespan, to cultivate flowers, in-
spire young people, write poetry, learn new languages, travel,
and so on. It will take more study to fully explain why this
happens, but in the author's research and clinical experience
it is evident that a successful mourning-liberation process plays
a significant role in facilitating these creative activities. The
painful internal detachment from ideals, goals, objectives, and
from individuals who no longer exist results in an acceptance
of the reality principle of functioning. With this accomplish-
ment, freedom to view the world and oneself in it serves as a
stimulus for regeneration. Although bereavement is a specific
subclass of the mourning adaptational process, it is not the only
or the most frequent precipitant of mourning; it is a process
that is continually ongoing throughout life. A disappointment,
a promotion that does not come through, a baseball game that
is lost by one's favorite team, a broken romance, a lost opportunity, are all examples of disappointments and losses which
must be mourned and relinquished. Most of these mourning-
liberation processes go on unnoticed, just as one accepts aging
and change without notice—unless there is a conflict. When a
major loss or catastrophic change occurs, the mourning-liberation process becomes a more consciously painful experience,
at times requiring professional intervention.

New work in the area of psychoimmunology has now come
to the fore which bears upon research in the mourning-liberation process. There are indications that this process can be
monitored by studying certain immune mechanisms and markers, such as T-cell changes (Schleifer, Keller, Meyerson, Raskin,
Davis, and Stein, 1984). Prenatal and infant research has also
provided new insights and new clues. For example, the fetus
can discriminate between strong light and weak light; among
rock, waltz, and jazz music. These adaptive mechanisms suggest
that the intrauterine adaptations to external stimuli may be the

precursors for the adaptations necessary to the success of the mourning-liberation process. The great controversy as to whether mourning-liberation is finally achieved at adolescence or can occur much earlier is becoming resolved through these findings. The physiological concomitants of the psychological adaptational process may be able to provide biological markers that will help monitor the psychological process, in and out of treatment.

If the capacity for discrimination and differentiation is present from such an early age, then it suggests people are continuously mourning something that once was, and adapting to what is present. This is an epigenetic process—if it is missed or negotiated poorly at an earlier stage of life it will be negotiated poorly at a later stage. It is in this area that psychotherapy may play a key role in getting the mourning-liberation process back onto an adaptive track.

To summarize some of these conclusions in a somewhat telegraphic form, in an etiological perspective one has to consider the following in working with the older adult:

1. Antecedent psychopathology, either manifest or latent, compensated or pathologically defended, detected, or undetected as a result of favorable life situations.
2. Situational crises, acute or chronic, that strain the ego's ability to maintain equilibrium. Age, physical health, and intactness of support systems are but a few of the variables one must keep in mind as contributing to signs and symptoms of psychic distress or illness.
3. Organic illness (neurological and other bodily systems) which can increase reactive symptoms, such as depression, and psychosocial needs. Helplessness, isolation, fears of loss of basic controls, and hopelessness are a few of the emotional anxieties observable. There can be regressions to earlier fixations, and if the reality disruptions are severe

and persistent, these regressions can become chronic and return the individual to infantile levels of functioning.

4. As Abraham (1919) observed, age in and of itself need not preclude psychoanalytic treatment. Indications for, and anticipations of, successful psychoanalytic treatment depend upon the individual's psychological construction as well as the nature of the subsequent psychic distress. In successful work with middle-aged and older adults, some in their eighties, the author has found:

   a. The capacity for, and utilization of, insight.
   b. The capacity for utilization of therapeutically induced transferences.
   c. The capacity to dream and fantasize and the ability to relate these dreams and fantasies to the therapeutic process, as well as to one's past.
   d. The mobilization of motivation to change, to examine goals and values anew, and to make new social relationships or restructure those of the past in more positive ways.
   e. The capacity for self-observation in the present as well as a retrospective view, more or less objective, of how one handled significant life relationships in the past, and how these can be changed in the present. Retrospective introspection assists in current retrospective activities, as well as in prospective planning.
   f. The mobilization of libidinal and constructive aggressive "energies" in ways that make life more creative, satisfying, and allow the individual to face the inevitable traumas ahead with less anxiety, depression, and pain.
   g. The institution of a mourning-liberation process that allows the past to appropriately become past and allows for "investment" in the present and future.
   h. In the treatment situation, the elderly easily distinguish between the facade of interest and genuine caring and

involvement on the part of the therapist. Older patients wish to be useful and respected, and to preserve their dignity. What seemingly concerns them most is fear and pain and suffering, helplessness and hopelessness, isolation and loneliness, physical and mental impairment, loss of competency and adequacy, and the need to rely upon those who may abandon them. Unlike younger patients, the elderly do not fear death. At times, they may welcome it as a relief from pain and anguish. Death may be a completion—a freedom.

This picture is not one that can apply to all older individuals, but can do so in selective instances (as is true of all patients), and therapists should not a priori be therapeutically nihilistic about what can be accomplished with psychotherapy and psychoanalysis. Elderly people may be understood in different ways, but they *can* be understood, and with that understanding they often can be helped.

In discussing the clinical report of a colleague, one assesses what the selected approach has led him to discover or investigate—his data, his arguments, his interpretations, his illustrations, his theoretical framework, and the universality or specificity of his findings. There is no one and only correct way of interpretation; a number of possible perspectives allow one to proceed in different ways. A brief clinical account does not allow for the elaboration of the many therapeutic nuances that may have been crucial in the therapeutic process.

The author will illustrate his own approach, by commenting on the case of a colleague, Dr. Norman Cohen, reported elsewhere (Cohen, 1982).

The patient was in his late forties when he first saw Dr. Cohen after his therapist of a few years had died. He seemingly denied feelings of grief or bereavement and contact with Dr. Cohen at that time was brief. The patient seemed to have reestablished a manageable equilibrium. The patient returned when he was in his middle fifties in a state of panic and anxiety. This time the external precipitating circumstances again dealt with loss; the death of his father and the threatened loss of the patient's homosexual partner. The response to loss and the uncompleted or pathological mourning-liberation process seems to be present in both episodes of the initial consultations with Dr. Cohen.

As the case description proceeds, it is learned that a baby brother was born, and died in infancy, when the patient was 6 or 7 years old. His mother was very depressed at the time and subsequently so overinvested in the patient that she was perceived to be intrusive. In research on the effects of childhood sibling loss (Pollock, 1962, 1982), this particular trauma, as well as the special relationship of the depressed mother to her surviving son, has been shown to be of cardinal pathogenic importance. The guilt, fear, choice of "love object," sexual preference, all can be related to this trauma constellation and could be seen as attempts to defend against more serious, covert pathology. With the patient's current presentation, it could be suggested that the patient could no longer defend himself against the strains of his earlier pathogenic trauma. In particular, with his diminishing ego resources he could no longer manage the later loss of three significant males—therapist, father, and lover. The possible significance of his forthcoming retirement from his work can also be seen as a "loss," one that is psychologically similar to the loss of a significant other, and one that comes at a time when the "high risk" individual's aging ego cannot deal with this trauma effectively. He may have turned to a male analyst as a possible replacement for his lost objects and to reestablish a manageable equilibrium but, without a mourning-liberation process. He had "great hopes that he would be cured" and indeed "his distress quickly disappeared" once he established a tie with Dr. Cohen.

This patient's pathology could have emerged at any time and is not specific for middle or later life. The vulnerability to the death of a significant other stemmed from his childhood experiences with loss—of the brother, and of his depressed mother. Issues such as survivor guilt, interrupted development, defenses against anxiety, narcissistic vulnerability, and mourning were either repressed or handled alloplastically. The early fear of death that he had after his brother's death is frequently seen in children where there has been a parent or sibling loss through death. Later loss events served to reopen the vulnerable wound; when healing cannot occur pathology emerges. Being an "only child" could also be seen as an additional factor in his "loneliness." This statement of the psychodynamic issues is intended to demonstrate that one's orientation can determine the clinical data collected and selected, as well as shaping one's interpretations, how one views the analytic process, and of course the ultimate outcome. The author's approach deals with the mourning-liberation process, the effect of childhood object loss on later pathology, for which vulnerability exists even before one is middle aged. Psychotherapy can help in the rehabilitation of such individuals.

The goal of psychoanalytic treatment is to make more of people available to themselves for present and future creative and satisfying life experiences. Psychoanalysis and psychotherapy is a humanizing force which allows an individual to be in touch with parts of himself or herself that have been forgotten, neglected, or pushed away and yet continue to exert important influences upon the individual. During analysis these parts become alive, old emotional allegiances are revived, passions and rages are reawakened, overgrown paths are walked upon anew. The past is mourned and self-investigation allows for freedom and liberation to occur. Life enjoyment ensues and the ability to confront the inevitable traumas of later life events is enhanced. Alienations that are draining get resolved, and intensely private experiences which may lie in the past but are still alive, gradually are "worked through" and become appropriately syntonic with one's being. Energy is released for new investments in life, in the inner as well as in the outer ambience in which one lives alone and with others.

The organism's attempts to cope with the internal and external strain of psychosocial disruption make use of a number of biological, psychological, emotional, social, cultural, and religious mechanisms. Psychiatry and psychology are on a new frontier that will be able to monitor these changes, just as the response of the body to an antibiotic in fighting infectious diseases can be monitored by watching the number of white cells decrease until they approximate a normal level. It is conceivable that in the very near future biological markers will be developed that will monitor various psychological processes as well as demonstrate how effective psychotherapeutic interventions are and what kinds of therapeutic interventions are appropriate.

With new perspectives on the diagnosis and the understanding of the basis of pathology, and by differentiating between normative and catastrophic crises, the maladaptations to aging, as well as successful adaptations to aging can be understood further. More precise treatments and interventions will be possible. Under appropriate circumstances, the possibility of combining supportive psychotherapy, insight-oriented psychotherapy, psychotherapy that is designed to condition the individual to certain types of responses, and formal behavior modification must be considered. For example, supportive-educational counseling may be useful in dealing with minor concerns over aging crises. Late life paranoia or severe depressive reactions may be helped with intensive psychotherapy and/or pharmacotherapy. The physical changes and illnesses of aging cannot be ignored, particularly when dealing with older adults. Bowel and bladder problems, sleep problems, weight problems, adequate nutrition, drug sensitivity and drug interactions, fatigue, boredom, the use of sedatives, tranquilizers, and sleep medications must all be considered and their impact assessed on the ongoing psychological portrait of the patient.

Psychotherapy is of enormous value in aiding the individual to get back on track with the course of mourning and circumvent the pathological outcome of loss. All people, including and especially older people, want to talk about themselves, and this is part of the therapy that promotes the mourning-liberation process. Reminiscences, life reviews, and nostalgic recollections serve the cathartic function of discharge and detachment, while also forming the basis of the more intimate psychotherapeutic relationship with the therapist. An illustration:

> When I asked one of my older patients about himself, he suddenly began crying. I paused. "You are the first person who has asked me to talk about myself," he said. "My kids are in different parts of the country; my grandchildren call me on Father's Day or other holidays. We see each other at weddings, funerals, and graduations. I want to talk about myself. I am alone; I feel lonely." And he began to talk; the affectively laden, cathartic reminiscences were the beginning of the liberation process.

The therapist became a "transference" figure, representing the patient's children and grandchildren, but in addition, the therapist helped him see past as past, and to fully recognize and see present and future. His dreams provided data that confirmed the ongoing changes. The psychotherapeutic relationship facilitated the mourning-liberation process. People who are in a state of acute bereavement have a need to talk, talk, and talk, which can be constructive and lead to resolutions. If aging must be met with mourning in order for liberation to ensue, then the process of intimate talking must be encouraged. The first therapeutic task is to allow the patients to talk about themselves and to be genuinely and sufficiently interested in what they say.

The process of psychotherapy with the elderly involves the establishment and working through of transferences, though these may be somewhat different from those of younger patients. As a younger analyst working with people in their sixties, seventies, and eighties, the author has frequently observed that patients develop what can be called euphemistically a "son transference." They would begin to have expectations of the therapist similar to those they would have of a son who was not fulfilling some of their special needs at this time in life. This transference may be seen as a reversal of old parental transferences; however, in many older adults this is not so. Its origins lie elsewhere. There is an expectation that one has of one's children and this gets placed upon the analyst. The fact of frequent contact over a long period of time, may be seen as a form of gratification, but this may apply to individuals of all age groups who are in analysis or intensive psychotherapy. By working with transferences, fantasies, dreams, symptomatic acts—the entire spectrum of what we see in psychoanalytic treatment—the patient develops insight, identifies with the analyst, and change occurs.

In working with older adults, one must also consider the question of liaison with family, with other physicians, with lawyers, accountants, social workers, and even guardians, because this may also be part of one's therapeutic and diagnostic responsibility. It is also necessary to come to terms occasionally with a change regarding where treatment takes place—house calls. This is true for the family practitioner, for the psychiatrist, and some day soon for the psychoanalyst as well. Social workers have always been involved in making home visits; these are often very therapeutic and allow first-hand observation which is of diagnostic value. The author has personally found this interesting, useful, and quite helpful in inclement weather when older patients are at risk of falling and injuring themselves. In addition, health care people (and they are called health care, not disease care people) should begin to think very seriously about prevention. There are many factors to consider, including the importance of exercise, physical therapy, particularly with people who may be homebound, nutrition and diet, the use of alcohol, no matter how judicious, the monitoring of medication, the permission for sexual gratification, be it auto-erotic or whatever. All these factors influence the quality of life as one ages.

Elsewhere the author has written about the spectrum of abandonment experiences (Pollock, 1984b) and has tried to describe the many situations in which this occurs—from the transitory internal feeling of abandonment to the actual permanent abandonment of a child by his parents, either through death, divorce, or a permanent leaving. These experiences can constitute catastrophic crises that may be of minor consequence or have a lifelong, serious impact on personality development. Such "abandonments" are found in immigrants, in survivors of concentration camps, in prisoners, in individuals placed in hospitals for long periods, in retirees, and in families where suicide has occurred. In other words, the abandonment experiences, coming at crucial times, and existing in overwhelming quantities, often persisting, all may result in a highly vulnerable individual, who will, in later life, have various responses and reactions to normative and/or catastrophic crises. The mourning-liberation process is a necessary adaptation to undoing these pathogenic consequences of earlier traumas. Intensive psychodynamic treatment, when indicated and in suitable individuals, can facilitate this healing process. Psychotherapeutic intervention in earlier life, closer to the time of pathogenic trauma, can help and prevent later decompensation, when life, with its inevitable crises, presents situations that can trigger more serious responses.

Also of great importance is the establishment of a trusting relationship with the person who is the caregiver, because older people, like children, are especially sensitive to being patronized. It is also necessary, in considering the role of psychotherapy, to consider in broad terms, countertransference. There is the need to consider: Why am I working with this patient? Why am I involved with this age group? What attitudes do I have? What is the benefit to me? Is this autopsychotherapy as well as work with my patient? One sees these "countertransference" reactions in younger colleagues and students who may either perpetuate existing myths, or, for personal reasons, have the need to defend against emerging behaviors, attitudes, and feelings of their older patients.

Plato put it well when he had Socrates state, "I consider that the old have gone before us along a road which we must all travel in our turn and it is good we should ask them the nature of that road, whether it be rough and difficult, or easy and smooth" (*The Republic*). By working with older adults we will learn about that road, and in doing so it will be smoother for us and we will make it smoother for them.

Conclusions

In clinical work with men and women of various backgrounds beyond the age of 50, the author has attempted to distill some of his thinking and current findings regarding aging and the aged, encompassing both normal aging as well as some pathological entities. The normal crises of aging have been differentiated from the unexpected crises that disrupt the equilibrium of the individual and that of various members of the family. However, the distinction may not be as precise as the conceptualization. What is a normative crisis for one person can be catastrophic for another. If a person's childhood and early life was filled with personal illness, chronic disability, the death of, or abandonment by, a parent, or serious life-threatening disasters, such an individual is often highly vulnerable to changes and to the stress of normal developmental crises. On the other hand, one increasingly finds individuals who, despite such serious earlier crises, seemingly are not at risk and might even be impervious to serious disruptions. If one sees change sensitivity or change resistance, especially in the later years, when change in, or threat of, alteration of the status quo results in major anxieties, depressions, regressions, somatizations, or paranoid reactions, one must consider the possibility of psychological disturbance that warrants therapeutic intervention. Psychoanalytic–psychodynamic psychotherapy is very useful and may be the treatment of choice in some of these disorders. This is especially relevant to aiding the crucial work of the mourning-liberation process in aging.

References

Abraham, K. (1919), The applicability of psychoanalytic treatment to patients at an advanced age. In: *Selected Papers of Karl Abraham*. London: Hogarth Press, 1927, pp. 312–317.

American Association of Retired Persons and Administration on Aging, U.S. Department of Health and Human Services (1984), *A Profile of Older Americans: 1984*. Washington, DC: American Association of Retired Persons.

Cohen, N. A. (1982), On loneliness and the aging process. *Internat. J. Psycho-Anal.*, 63:149–156.

Cicero (44 B.C.), On friendship. In: *Cicero: On Old Age and On Friendship*, trans. F. O. Copley. Ann Arbor: University of Michigan Press, 1971, pp. 43-90.

———— (n.d.), Cato the Elder on old age. In: *Cicero: Selected Works*, trans. M. Grant, Harmondsworth, U.K.: Penguin Books, 1982, pp. 211-247.

Collins, G. (1985), First portrait of the very old: Not so frail. *New York Times*, January 3, 1985, pp. 1 & 13.

Gutmann, D. L. (1979), The clinical psychology of later life: Developmental paradigms. Paper presented at the West Virginia Gerontology Conference on the Transitions of Aging, May 23–26.

Moeller, T. P. (1985), Aging: A century of change. *Progress*, March–April, 36:11–15.

Plato, *The Republic*, Quoted in *The New York Times* (1985), January 3, p. 153.

Pollock, G. H. (1961), Mourning and adaptation. *Internat. J. Psycho-Anal.*, 42:341–361.

———— (1962), Childhood parent and sibling loss in adult patients: A comparative study. *Arch. Gen. Psychiat.*, 7:295–305.

———— (1966), Mourning and childhood loss: Their possible significance in the Josef Breuer–Bertha Pappenheim relationship. *Bull. Assn. Psychoanal. Med.*, 5/4:51–54.

———— (1968), The possible significance of childhood object loss in the Josef Breuer–Bertha Pappenheim (Anna O.)–Sigmund Freud relationship. *J. Amer. Psychoanal. Assn.*, 16:711–739.

———— (1970), Anniversary reactions, trauma and mourning. *Psychoanal. Quart.*, 29:347–371.

———— (1971a), On time and anniversaries. In: *The Unconscious Today*, ed. M. Kanzer. New York: International Universities Press, pp. 233–257.

———— (1971b), Temporal anniversary manifestations: Hour, day, holiday. *Psychoanal. Quart.*, 40:123–131.

———— (1971c), On time, death and immortality. *Psychoanal. Quart.*, 40:435–446.

———— (1972a), On mourning and anniversaries: The relationship of culturally constituted defensive systems to intra-psychic adaptive processes. *Israel Ann. Psychiat. & Rel. Discip.*, 10/1:9–40.

———— (1972b), Bertha Pappenheim's pathological mourning: Possible effects of childhood sibling loss. *J. Amer. Psychoanal. Assn.*, 20:476–493.

———— (1973), Bertha Pappenheim: Addenda to her case history. *J. Amer. Psychoanal. Assn.*, 21:328–332.

———— (1975a), Mourning: Psychoanalytic theory. In: *International Encyclopedia of Psychiatry, Psychology, Psychoanalysis, and Neurology*, ed. B. B. Wolman. New York: Aesculapius Publishers, 1977, pp. 368–371.

———— (1975b), On mourning, immortality and utopia. *J. Amer. Psychoanal. Assn.*, 23:334–362.

———— (1975c), On anniversary suicide and mourning. In: *Depression and the Human Existence*, ed. T. Benedek & E. J. Anthony. Boston: Little, Brown, pp. 369–393.

———— (1975d), Mourning and memorialization through music. *The Annual of Psychoanalysis*, III:423–435. New York: International Universities Press.

———— (1976), Manifestations of abnormal mourning: Homicide and suicide following the death of another. *The Annual of Psychoanalysis*, IV:225–249. New York: International Universities Press.

———— (1977), The mourning process and creative organizational change. *J. Amer. Psychoanal. Assn.*, 25:3–34.

———— (1978a), On siblings, childhood sibling loss, and creativity. *The Annual of Psychoanalysis*, VI:443–481. New York: International Universities Press.

———— (1978b), Process and affect: Mourning and grief. *Internat. J. Psycho-Anal.*, 59:255–276.

——— (1981a), Aging or aged: Development or pathology. In: *The Course of Life: Psychoanalytic Contributions Toward Understanding Personality Development. Vol. III: Adulthood and the Aging Process*, ed. S. I. Greenspan & G. H. Pollock. Washington, DC: National Institute of Mental Health, pp. 549–585.

——— (1981b), Reminiscences and insight. *The Psychoanalytic Study of the Child*, 36:279–287. New Haven, CT: Yale University Press.

——— (1982), The mourning-liberation process and creativity: The case of Käthe Kollwitz. *The Annual of Psychoanalysis*, X:333–354. New York: International Universities Press.

——— (1983), The mourning-liberation process and creativity: The case of Käthe Kollwitz. In: *Art Therapy: Still Growing*, ed. A. Di Maria, E. S. Kramer and E. A. Roth. Proceedings of the Thirteenth Annual Conference of the American Art Therapy Association, October 20–24, 1982, pp. 9–17.

——— (1984a), Anna O.: Insight, hindsight, and foresight. In: *Anna O.: Fourteen Contemporary Reinterpretations*, ed. M. Rosenbaum & M. Muroff. New York: The Free Press, pp. 26–33.

——— (1984b), Preliminary notes on abandonment, loss, and vulnerability. Paper presented December 20, 1984 at the Vulnerable Child Discussion Group meeting of the American Psychoanalytic Association, New York City.

——— (1985a), Abandoning parent and abusing caretakers. In: *Parental Influences: In Health and Disease*, ed. E. J. Anthony & G. H. Pollock. Boston: Little, Brown, pp. 349-400.

——— (1985b), Mourning mothers, depressed grandmothers, guilty siblings, and identifying survivors. In: *Parental Influences: In Health and Disease*, ed. E. J. Anthony & G. H. Pollock. Boston: Little, Brown, pp. 235-258.

——— (1985c), The psychoanalytic psychotherapeutic treatment of older adults with special reference to the mourning-liberation process. In: *Current Psychiatric Therapies*, Vol. 23, ed. J. H. Masserman. New York: Grune & Stratton, pp. 87-98.

Schleifer, S. J., Keller, S. E., Meyerson, A. T., Raskin, M. J., Davis, K. L., & Stein, M. (1984), Lymphocyte functions in major depressive disorders. *Arch. Gen. Psych.*, 41:484–486.

2

THE AGED IN PSYCHOTHERAPY: PSYCHODYNAMIC CONTRIBUTIONS TO THE TREATMENT PROCESS

JEROME M. GRUNES, M.D.

The author's theory of psychotherapy with aged persons rests on the science of psychoanalysis and incorporates the more recent developments in ego and self psychology. The aim of this chapter is to establish certain principles which do justice to both the theoretical aspects of psychoanalysis and the relationship of this body of knowledge to the clinical data derived from work with geriatric patients. Although it is premature to attempt a definitive manual on how to do psychotherapy with the aged, certain broad principles will be stated which may be of help to those who are working with, or are becoming interested in working with, this population.

In the first truly analytic work, Breuer and Freud's (1893-1895) *Studies on Hysteria,* Freud made use of several cases of older women, as well as younger ones, to demonstrate the significance of repressed infantile sexuality in the etiology of hysteria. It is not surprising that older women were included in his sample, for hysteria is a most persistent malady and remains relatively unchanged in its manifestations throughout life. In general, however, patients who were in middle or later life were excluded from Freud's clinical sample, and hence his theory

31

remained uninformed by clinical work with older patients. The one voice of protest to this exclusion was that of Karl Abraham (1919), who postulated that the age of the neurosis, rather than the age of the patient, should be the crucial issue in deciding on the utility of psychoanalytic treatment. Later, Carl Jung, after his defection from the psychoanalytic movement, took the position that older individuals could benefit from treatment. Perhaps unfortunately, this position was usually seen by other analysts as part of his flight from the theory of libido and his need to desexualize his concept of the human psyche (Jung, 1936).

Despite the development in the late 1920s of the structural model, and in the 1940s of ego psychology, adherents of psychoanalysis continued to see the aged as unsuitable for psychoanalytic treatment. The aged were considered rigid in their character structure, difficult to change, lacking in the necessary availability of new love objects, and as possessing a reduced drive in object or selfobject hunger. In younger patients, the therapist may become a new love object with the stimulation of genital and pregenital drives. It will therefore come as no surprise that case reports of psychoanalysis and intensive psychotherapy with the aged were rare in the literature. Occasionally, such studies could be found, but more often than not, the reporter expressed surprise at the flexibility of the ego which permitted change long after the so-called "elasticity of the personality" had ended.

A basic premise of this chapter is that the aged are as amenable to psychotherapy and even psychoanalysis as those in any other age group and that the results are in general favorable. Therapists need to apply psychoanalytic and intensive psychotherapeutic techniques systematically to the aged, both as therapy and also to clarify the psychodynamic, developmental aspects of the later stages of the life cycle. Psychoanalytic psychotherapy and psychoanalysis remain the best therapeutic techniques that have so far been devised for treating older people, and are also an excellent method for elucidating developmental data. Otto Fenichel (1949), has written of the indications for psychoanalytic treatment as follows: "Psychoanalytic treatment, working by undoing pathogenic conflicts, is indicated whenever neurotic difficulties represent the outcome of a neurotic conflict; . . . in neuroses the warded-off impulses are striving for an expression in connection with a longing for objects—they produce transferences" (p. 573). These transference neuroses are amenable to psychoanalytic psychotherapy. Each psychoanalysis is a voyage of discovery for both participants. It is more than a learned technique and more than application of heretofore "proven" theory. Why, therefore, are not more older patients in psychoanalysis or intensive psychotherapy? Besides the official strictures of analyzability, often accepted as shibboleths, there are other deterrents.

Prejudice against treatment often exists in both patients and therapists. The older patient still, too frequently, views the therapist as an intrusive voyeur, interested in exposing the patient's pathology. To enter therapy may mean acknowledging one's helplessness and accepting the stigma that often accompanies such narcissistic slights. The therapist, who may be struggling with his own aging, may view the patient as hopeless, too old, and without sufficient resilience to make use of the insights that psychoanalysis can provide. Hopeless therapists make for hopeless patients, and thus, it is not difficult to understand that the aged have tended to be on the fringes of psychotherapeutic and psychoanalytic services.

Treatment of the aged in psychoanalysis and psychotherapy is in the process of change. Due in part to the increase of the aged population, and their higher levels of education, elderly patients are insisting on psychotherapy more frequently these days. Referrals, which in the past were initiated by family members, have given way to self-referrals. The older person, aware of his discomfort, wants help and is willing, and at times eager, to embark on psychotherapy, including psychoanalysis. Therapists are also seeing older patients who were previously treated in their earlier years and now want to return to therapy. Perhaps as Neugarten (1979), has suggested, psychoanalysis will eventually become part of the "age-neutral" phenomenon in which chronological age will not be an issue in the selection of patients for treatment. Age in this connection may not be a significant variable. The author has treated and supervised the therapy of several patients over 100 years of age. Some in the field might call such people *terminating* individuals, a sanitized word for dying, but as the following case example illustrates, they were not dying.

> An irascible curmudgeon who would fracture your wrist when he shook your hand, became extremely anxious as his 100th birthday approached. He refused to be photographed or interviewed by the newspapers. He had long outlived his family members and, having never married was truly alone. He felt that his longevity was due to his own prescription of oxygen, hydrogen, and "sunogen." The magical number of 100 frightened him and led to his feeling helpless, eventually becoming so anxious that he took to his bed. Psychotherapy relieved both the panic and the feeling he was "ready for the scrap heap." He chose the therapist as his heir, and in the retelling of his life and imparting his wisdom to a younger man, he perpetuated himself. The following year at 101, he permitted a party to be given in his honor and made the newspapers. He died at 104 without the anxiety that had marked his 100th year.

The following incident briefly illustrates the patient's continuing impulsivity and character structure.

> This patient liked to watch baseball games, or rather hear them because his vision was very poor, and when a younger man of 76 went to turn down the sound of the television because it

was too loud and disturbing the other residents, Mr. M. became angry and struck this man. He had been a boxer, and he broke several of his victim's ribs and fractured some of his own wrist-bones. When called into the Director's office and asked by the Director how he could do a thing like that, Mr. M. replied: "So what if I killed him, what would they do to me, give me 99 years?" The concept of adaptive paranoia (Gutmann, 1980) was based in part on this particular patient. This is an especially interesting history because it points out the survival into old age of many of the passions and energies and intrigues which exist in an individual's earlier character structure.

The overt therapeutic process begins when the patient arrives at the therapist's door. If he is with other family members, one should usher the patient into the consulting room alone, making it clear that therapist and patient will be involved in a joint venture into which the other family members cannot intrude. As a corollary, all communication with others about the patient must be by agreement with the patient. If someone other than the patient has made the initial contact, one should ask that the patient call for an appointment himself. It is essential that the collaborative effort be spelled out as early as possible in order to establish a working relationship. Psychotherapy is more apt to go awry when the basic working relationship has not been established, than by transference or countertransference problems, important as these are in the course of treatment. Some elements of the working relationship include clarification of the patient's conscious expectations, mobilization of hope, and a clear description and understanding of what the therapist and patient will do together.

The therapist's initial comments deserve mention. It is useful to explain to the patient the need to gather as much information as possible from him before coming to conclusions about how useful treatment will be. This explanation will help limit the patient's previously mentioned fears that the therapist is an intrusive voyeur. History taking is a valuable procedure as it is nonjudgmental and permits one to listen to what the patient says (and does not say) with closely hovering attention. It is also a demonstration of technique, one of many that are employed in treatment. Such demonstrations are those we hope the patient can eventually use himself, in his role of participant–observer as well as experiencer. In this regard, the therapist's early interpretations, whether of defenses, resistances, or transferences, are more apt to be useful as demonstrations of what the treatment will be like rather than touching important intrapsychic material, no matter how perceptive they may seem to the therapist.

In addition to prejudicial hopelessness, a second deterrent to therapists treating the aged exists. Heinz Kohut (1971), has stressed in his work the prime role of empathy in the treatment of patients. He has also stated, however, that "the reliability of our empathy, a major instrument of psychoanalytic observation, declines the more dissimilar the observed is to the observer . . ." (p. 37). How then can one help individuals whose life experiences, backgrounds, and attitudes are at great variance with those of the therapist? It is quite true that patients at different ages and with different pathologies present special problems of empathy; for example, children, borderlines, psychotic patients, and the aged. The child analyst who is, in age, distant from his patients, must be able to recall his own earlier experiences at both a preverbal and verbal level as he is confronted with his patients' impulses, primitive defenses, and conflicts. Countertransference is a living experience for such practitioners. The analytic work with children demands that the analyst exist not only in the present, but in his own past as well, in order to understand and communicate his understandings, in the form of interpretations, to his patient. Analysts who work with adolescents have the task of trying to experience the ephemeral moods which are so much a part of the teenager's life. Analysts of adult patients must in part be able to do the same sort of work.

Patients suffering from borderline and psychotic states place different demands on the therapist. He can deny the patient's intensely perceived internal reality, the commonest ploy of the inexperienced therapist, or, accept the unknowability of the patient's illness and attempt to remain at an optimal distance from the observed conflicts. If too close to the patient's state, the therapist may threaten to provoke in the patient the very emotional responses that precipitated the illness; if too distant, he may extinguish the patient's hope that his borderline or psychotic states are truly human experiences. A sensitive analyst, such as Frieda Fromm-Reichmann (1950), was able to perceive in herself certain similarities to the fragmented self that the patient displayed. Cognitive processes are a necessary balance to the dangers of merging with the sick patient. The relationship between empathy and cognition is of great significance since it appears that without cognition in therapy, empathy may lead to symbiosis. The task is indeed difficult and frequently requires consultation with others for the work to prosper.

When one comes to older people who present themselves for treatment, one is confronted with other problems. The therapist usually has not had the experiences of the aged. Under these circumstances, one might ask what are the parallel countertransference experiences for the therapist of the aged in comparison to, for example, the child analyst. The therapist must struggle with reexperiencing his own early relationships both to his parents and to his grandparents. On a more subtle plane, the therapeutic process may provoke the therapist's unconscious attitudes derived from his internalization of his parents attitudes to his grandparents. One sees embodied in this formulation an aspect of the three-generational impact as it impinges upon the therapist, often at an unconscious level. A further living countertransference experience derives from the often negative stereotypes and prejudices which the therapist may have adopted from society's attitude to aging.

The male aged, because of their apparent vulnerability, can easily lead the susceptible male therapist into conflict over oedipal triumph since the male patient is often in a more helpless position vis-à-vis the therapist. The male therapist dealing with a woman, must contend with the fact that the female is no longer a desirable sexual object for him. This may provoke, among other things, a profound sense of loss of the libidinally desired maternal object. While roles for therapist of child, grandchild, or lover represent ready-made counterattitudes, they are of little enduring value in the collaborative work of therapy.

The evident problems in establishing adequate empathic rapport leads to a somewhat novel proposition. It has been the author's experience over many years of treating elderly patients that empathy is not the sole domain of the therapist. The patient, too, attempts to establish empathy for the therapist, a process one may call *reverse empathy*. This important aspect of treatment, while largely unrecognized or examined, appears to be an aspect of narcissistic transference—the response of the patient attempting to bridge the empathic gap between himself and the therapist. It is as if part of the *grandiose self* (Kohut's term) seeks to establish a connection with the other (in this case, the therapist), based on the history of the patient's self, so that both patient and therapist can become mutual selfobjects. This phenomenon requires no special effort on the part of the therapist other than to allow its unimpeded emergence. For example, interest in, and a need to know significant details of, the therapist's life may be viewed as manifestations of reverse empathy. Thus, reverse empathy is not subject to interpretation in the beginning phase of treatment. It is not part of the transference neurosis wherein one might suspect seduction or competition, for example, but more properly may be deemed an aspect of the defense transference (representing the patient's wish to place the therapist in a knowable and predictable mode). It is a positive attempt by the patient to strengthen the self-object relationship and may be used to aid the formation of a working alliance. The therapist may foster this response early on in the knowledge that it will be worked through and interpreted in the middle and end phases of treatment.

The regularity of the process of reverse empathy when one is aware of it, even in severe pathology, requires an explanation. It seems to be of special importance in treating older patients. Perhaps it is overlooked because the major event of analysis is said to be the transference—the distortions from the past which color the present objects and presentations of self. The need to unravel those distortions in time, place, and person is the central work of treatment, as we usually conceive of it. However, in the author's experience reverse empathy is not only a phenomenon of treatment of the aged, but is also a precondition for successfully starting or continuing psychotherapy or psychoanalysis.

Some further aspects of the transference phenomena in aged patients are of note. The significance and the vicissitudes of object love were among Freud's most enduring contributions to the understanding of the human psyche. More recently, Heinz Kohut (1971) has elucidated certain aspects of narcissistic development as well. Freud focused on conflicts involving drives and defenses, while Kohut has emphasized early, pre-verbal structure formation, deficits, and the tendency to fragmentation of the self system. The two lines of development, narcissistic and object love, can be seen in the transferences of the aged. In periods of transition, when resolutions of old conflicts need to be accomplished and when the self system cannot accommodate to new demands, transferences in the therapeutic situation reactivate the significant objects and relationships of the past with their libidinal and aggressive components. The reemergence and the need for resolution is age specific, related to identification and the organization of the self system. Otto Fenichel (1939), in "Problems of Psychoanalytic Technique," states succinctly an aspect of this hypothesis. "Perhaps we have not stressed sufficiently that in analysis, transference actually has as its contents not only the repetition of old relationships in general, but of those especially, in which the functioning that will later be taken over by the ego and then superego are exercised by persons in the external world" (p. 441).

Aged individuals are particularly susceptible to narcissistic injuries—a susceptibility which is related to the losses so often associated with the aging process. The regulatory functions of the aged have both internal and external foci. This is especially true in the "old-old," to use Neugarten's (1979) classification. When external losses occur, therefore, it is as if part of the self is lost. For all older patients, in spite of internalization of ego and superego tendencies, there remains a trend to maintain externally the contents of these structures, including their drives, impulses, and conflicts, in the form of projective identification. It is as if whole aspects of the self need to be disavowed because of the aging process. The aging patient cannot own his lost or damaged parts. Such disavowal is necessary for growth to proceed. In other words, whole aspects of the self require what Gutmann, Grunes, and Griffin (1980) have called a "projective ecology" (p. 125) in order that the personality may function smoothly. It is a combination of narcissism and object love that permits the disavowal of the contents of the self and the projection onto others who are our own love objects. This state of affairs is significant to later life pathology when the objects change and refuse to accept the projected contents or are entirely lost due to prolonged illness or death. Therapy and the working through of such losses are possible when we understand the other as not merely an object of love, but as a selfobject. The spouse who has died, for example, is not only an object of love, a separate other, but also a symbolic *part* of the psychological structure of the remaining partner. This process is quite clear in married couples whose relationship complementarity is obvious, but it can be seen in more subtle ways in other relationships. As Gutmann (1969, 1975) has demonstrated in his cross-cultural studies, the phenomenon of projective ecology has psychobiological roots. This theoretical construction has implications for therapeutic work with the aged. Aging has been characterized by some as a continuing process of loss. This hypothesis suggests that the integration of the personality was obtained at an earlier age and that it becomes undermined by persistent and inevitable losses. Much of the pathology, therefore, perceived as incomplete mourning and depression is seen as the usual affective state of the aging. The developmental goal would thus be to accept and acquiesce to loss. This view is challenged by observations of normal aged patients and by clinical work with older people. It is a truism to say that the aged are a heterogeneous population and that late-blooming psychopathology is very broad, but it happens to be so. While one does not exclude loss or incomplete mourning as significant problems for the aged, the therapeutic perspective may be broadened to include the internal life of the individual and those aspects of the self which have been projected and have significant self and object qualities.

Treatment of patients who struggle with loss of the sense of self, require a specialized technique. As Butler (1963) has indicated in his work on reminiscence in therapy, the task of the therapist is to make the patient's past viable. The therapist's role is to experience the patient not only in the present, but also in his past. This requires a somewhat regressive state in the therapist, for he must not be bound solely to the external reality of the patient. The therapist must follow the patient into his past and view him as he wishes to be seen. He must respond appropriately to the patient's memories, so that the patient can reexperience his past in the presence of a benign person whose interest and involvement in his old memories can revivify them. The therapist's regressive capacity aids reconstruction and restitution. The patient then can reintroject these memories and use the therapist as well, as a helpful and benign transitional object (Grunes, 1981).

The externalization of past decathected memories and their reinternalization as active processes by the patient, and the regressive state of the therapist and his work of reconstruction and restitution, represent a process of therapy which is helpful to the aged. In the absence of external buttresses for the sense of self over time, the therapist becomes a replacement for, or an external carrier of, the patient's historical self. As one ages one may lose touch with core aspects of one's self-identity and past. This is especially true in cognitive decline or if the individual is overwhelmed by concrete losses, bodily deficiency, or deformity. Under these circumstances, more of the core self is invested in the actual and immediate and less of the self is invested in the abstract memories which have lost their strength as buttresses for the patient's self-concept. The psychotherapist therefore acts as a stimulator of the patient's early identifying relationships which he brings alive through his empathic mirroring.

Conclusion

The author has attempted to describe obstacles posed by the relative youth and inexperience of the therapist. In the past, such phenomena may have been subsumed under the broad umbrella of transference or countertransference. The author has examined the working relationship which has to be erected to span the space between patient and therapist before a useful and interpretable transference develops. Both the patient and the therapist are coarchitects in the bridge that must be constructed between an older, troubled patient and a younger therapist who wishes to understand and be of help to the patient.

The analyzability and amenability to psychotherapy of aged persons approximates that of people in other age groupings. Certain aspects of treatment, including "reverse empathy," can be observed and utilized in treating the aged, and the rigid distinction between internalization and externalization is less complete for older individuals. This leads to a modification of technique in working with the aged, especially with the "old old" or impaired aged.

Psychoanalysis and intensive psychotherapy are both methods of treatment and techniques for learning about human psychology regardless of age. Such therapy is a mutual experience in which patient and therapist collaborate to discover new insights about themselves and about each other. Both parties require courage and stamina, but when done well, it is a mutually rewarding, exciting experience.

References

Abraham, K. (1919), The applicability of psychoanalytic treatment to patients at an advanced age. In: *Selected Papers on Psychoanalysis*. London: Hogarth Press, 1927, pp. 312–316.

Breuer, J., & Freud, S. (1893-1895), Studies on Hysteria. *Standard Edition*, 2. London: Hogarth Press, 1955.

Butler, R. (1963), The life-review: An interpretation of reminiscence in the aged. *Psychiatry*, 26:65–76.

Fenichel, O. (1939), "Problems of psychoanalytic technique." *Psychoanal. Quart.*, 8:438-470.

——— (1949), *The Psychoanalytic Theory of Neurosis*. New York: W. W. Norton.

Freud, S. (1900), The Interpretation of Dreams. *Standard Edition*, 4 & 5. London: Hogarth Press, 1955.

Fromm-Reichmann, F. (1950), *Principles of Intensive Psychotherapy*. Chicago: The University of Chicago Press.

Grunes, J. (1981), Reminiscences, regression and empathy. In: *The Course of Life: Psychoanalytic Contributions Toward Understanding Personality Development. Vol. III: Adulthood and the Aging Process*, ed. S. I. Greenspan & G.

H. Pollock. Washington, DC: National Institute of Mental Health, pp. 545–548.

Gutmann, D. (1969), The country of old men: Cross-cultural studies in the psychology of later life, Vol. 5. *Occasional Papers in Gerontology.* Ann Arbor: Institute of Gerontology, University of Michigan. Wayne State University, April 5.

———— (1975), Parenthood: A key to the comparative psychology of the life cycle. In: *Life-span Developmental Psychology: Normative Life Crisis,* ed. N. Datan & L. Ginsberg. New York: Academic Press, pp. 167-184.

———— (1980), Psychoanalysis and aging: A developmental view. In: *The Course of Life: Psychoanalytic Contributions toward Understanding Personality Development. Vol. III: Adulthood and the Aging Process,* ed. S. I. Greenspan & G. H. Pollock. Washington, DC: National Institute of Mental Health, pp. 489-517.

———— Grunes, J., & Griffin, B., (1980), The clinical psychology of later life. In: *The Transitions of Aging,* ed. N. Datan & N. Lohmann. New York: Academic Press, pp. 119–131.

Jung, C. (1936), Aims of psychotherapy. In: *Modern Man in Search of a Soul.* London: Kegan, Paul, Trench, & Trubner, pp. 55-73.

Kohut, H. (1971), *The Analysis of the Self.* New York: International Universities Press.

Neugarten, B. (1979), Time, age and the life cycle. *Amer. J. Psychiat.,* 136:887–894.

3

REFLECTIONS ON PSYCHOTHERAPY
WITH THE ELDERLY

Martin A. Berezin, M.D.

The aim of this chapter is to describe certain principles of psychotherapy with the elderly. The author will try to retain the perspective of a discussant, and will use as major reference points in this task the ideas, propositions, and concepts of Drs. Lazarus, Grunes, Pollock, and Kahana, as described in this book, as well as his own clinical experience of the past many years.

An operational definition of therapy provides a suitable starting point for this chapter. All therapy is designed to achieve one aim—the relief of pain. This definition refers to both physical and psychic pain. The "pain" in psychiatric conditions takes various forms and varies in degree from simple tension to psychotic breakdown. Psychiatrists generally refer to pain symptomatically with such terms as *anxiety, depression, guilt,* and so on.

An old friend, *Roget's Thesaurus* (1977), can provide some help in enlarging on what may constitute psychic or emotional pain. The list is, not unexpectedly, a very long one. The various terms referring to emotional pain are not all of equal value, neither in descriptive nor etiologic terms, but here is the list, as lengthy as it is incomplete.

Discontent, sadness, unpleasantness, dullness, discomfort,

45

hopelessness, anxiety, fear, shame, guilt, depression, hostility, self-pity, resentment, self-contempt, disquietude, agony, torture, desolate, heart-broken, distress, sorrow, dreary, joyless, wearisome, disgust, humiliation, embarrassment, dismay, oppressed, exasperation, harrowing.

Some of these terms are no doubt more familiar than others. The English language surpasses most other languages in providing a vocabulary that enables shading and nuances of meaning. One reason, among others, for presenting the above list of types of human pain is to appreciate that there are many modes of therapy, mostly aimed at symptomatic relief of the kind of symptoms listed by Roget. Moreover, it appears that there are more modalities of therapy than there are symptoms and disorders, a fact highlighted by the publishing of a recent book, entitled, *The Psychotherapy Handbook: The A to Z Guide to More Than 250 Different Therapies in Use Today* (Herink, 1980). This is a seriously written book, it is not a joke. Readers will be pleased to know that psychodynamic psychotherapy and psychoanalysis are 2 of the 250 psychotherapies listed in this work.

One can also find a variety of psychotherapies and psychotherapists in the Yellow Pages of phone books. This author recently received a brochure that advertised "Psychoanalytically Oriented Dance Therapy," which begs the question of whether one can dance on a couch. A multitude of activities are now espoused as therapy: jogging as therapy, art as therapy, music as therapy, sports as therapy, bingo as therapy, and cocktails as therapy. Are there no longer any usual human experiences that are not therapy? One day while walking in Manhattan (never in Boston!) the author was accosted by a sleazy looking man and given a card advising him that if he would proceed to a certain listed address he would find there "sex as therapy." Even prostitutes can be therapists—as they have been throughout recorded history.

Pain may be felt at any age. Sometimes the pain, especially

in the elderly, is felt more by family and friends than the patient. This is especially clear in states that the author has previously termed "partial grief" (Berezin, 1970). In this situation, the pain may not even be experienced by the identified patient at all, rather it is experienced by family members and other close caregivers. Unlike the situation in death, or a final loss with its expected grief, partial grief besets family members who are confronted with the irreversible decline and loss of function and capacity in an elderly family member. In this instance, grief cannot be worked through totally, because the final stage has not yet arrived, resulting in feelings of guilt, anxiety, depression, and most importantly helplessness in the caregivers.

From the experience of pain comes the need or wish for change. The theme of this book—"The Scope for Change in Later Life"—draws attention to those modalities of psychotherapy useful in producing change in later life. *Change* may refer to various aspects of therapeutic endeavor. Obviously, while the concept of change avoids the notion of a value judgment concerning that change, it is used here to imply an improvement or desirable development, and not a worsening of a condition. Improvement and the degree of improvement, continues to be exceedingly difficult to quantify accurately, drug outcome studies notwithstanding. Change is easier to note.

In overview, there are many kinds of pain, and many kinds of therapy directed to changing that pain. These range from drug therapy to environmental manipulation; and from supportive psychotherapy to insight oriented psychotherapy. There are indications and limits to each. The choice of modality of therapy within a spectrum that ranges from supportive to psychoanalytic is determined by a number of factors. These include, of course, the clinical picture and the diagnosis itself, which may result in a positive choice or, by its very condition, may rule out other choices. As an illustration, one would not elect psychoanalysis for someone who is psychotic or someone not sufficiently psychologically minded to be able to deal with or benefit from such a process. Or one would not recommend psychoanalysis when a simple environmental manipulation will produce the desired ends. In addition, it is generally wisest to choose the least intrusive approach that is effective. Practical considerations such as availability of a particular type of therapist, geographical location, or an impoverished financial position make only certain modalities possible. However, there are some influential factors that are much less rationally based.

The stereotypical notion that explorative insight psychotherapy is contraindicated for the old person derives from several sources. The earlier studies of elderly people, which included therapeutic efforts of all sorts, involved those housed in institutions and nursing homes, since they were the easiest group with whom contact could be made. Unfortunately, this group, for the most part, came from the very sick 5 percent of the elderly population requiring custodial care. That a pessimism toward therapy of older people should emerge from managing such sick and demented patients is understandable. Another determinant for pessimism, even for the more healthy and vigorous older people, derives from ageism. As do most cultures, our own culture betrays a prejudice against the old. This prejudice is anchored in a youth-oriented, action-oriented, achievement-oriented culture which leads to an attitude of neglect and disregard toward the elderly.

Each modality of treatment has its merits. What happens with drugs is usually only symptomatic relief, but relief is a desirable change. Certainly, no objection to the use of drugs can be raised when they work and when it is clear that symptom relief is the essential aim. Drugs are available in the management of agitation, insomnia, and depression in the aged. Unfortunately, there is a prevalent tendency to overuse psychopharmacology (Salzman, 1981). The overuse of such drugs is attested to in *The Tranquilizing of America* (Hughes and

Brewin, 1979), in which there is documented evidence of the prescribing and the consumption of billions of such drugs annually.

This citation is not intended to undervalue the role of psychopharmacology, nor overvalue the role of psychoanalysis and psychotherapy. As Freud (1933) wrote: "And here I should like to add that I do not think our [psychoanalysis] cures can compete with those of Lourdes. There are so many more people who believe in the Miracles of the Blessed Virgin than in the existence of the unconscious. . . . Analysis as a psycho-therapeutic procedure does not stand in opposition to other methods used in this specialized branch of medicine; it does not diminish their value nor exclude them. There is no theoretical inconsistency in a doctor who likes to call himself a psychotherapist using analysis on his patients alongside of any other method of treatment according to the peculiarities of the case and the favourable or unfavourable external circumstances." (p. 152).

The supportive therapies may also lead to therapeutic change and relieve symptoms of pain. Perhaps the simplest form of therapy is *environmental manipulation*. The term derives from Bibring's classification of the dynamic therapies (Bibring, 1954). He refers to manipulation of emotional constellations as one principle of therapy, although he does not refer to environmental manipulation as defined here. While the clinical vignette which follows does not specifically involve aged patients, it serves as a useful illustration of the term.

> Many years ago a young newly married couple in their twenties sought help when they discovered they had become irritable and quarrelsome with each other, behavior alien to their previous experience. They were quite in love with each other and very devoted and considerate. They wondered what had precipitated this most unwelcome change. The answer was actually quite simple. A few weeks prior to the consultation, the wife's parents had moved in with the young couple. From that point on, their uneas-

iness and quarrelling began. It should be noted incidentally that husband and wife both got along quite well with the wife's parents. What had occurred, however, was that under the impact of the close presence of parents, the young couple had regressed, without conscious realization, to an earlier, classical oedipal conflictual area. The urgent recommendation of the therapist was that the wife's parents should move out as soon as tactfully possible—an environmental change. This was done and they were comfortably loving and sexual again.

Hence, when the noxious element in the environment can be identified, management may indeed be simple—sometimes but not always.

Another illustration of this device, more relevant to an aged patient, occurred with an 82-year-old woman. The patient had previously been seen in psychiatric consultation some 30 years before. At that time her husband was ill, a situation to which she responded with anxiety and depression. She was diagnosed as an obsessive–compulsive character disorder whose defensive ability was being threatened by her husband's illness. The recent visit at age 82 was precipitated by an incident with her son. Her husband had died some 10 years previously and more recently she had developed a cardiac disorder for which she was on medication. For the present she was visiting her daughter locally.

The precipitating episode with her son came about because of his remarriage which was to take place in a few weeks. She herself was Orthodox Jewish and she was deeply disturbed because her son's new wife was not Jewish. In addition, she accused him of divorcing his wife in order to marry a much younger woman, "the same age as his daughter." She wanted to prevent the marriage but felt helpless to do so for her son was determined to proceed. She told her daughter she was very upset, agitated, and depressed about the episode. She spoke often of the fact that at age 82 she was ready to die, a statement interpreted by her daughter as being suicidal in intent.

When seen in consultation again, in fact the patient was

neither depressed nor suicidal. Her son, whose impending interfaith marriage she found so negatively provocative, was 59 years old, presumably old enough to be allowed to make his own decision. He had arranged for his mother to come to the city where the wedding was to take place, and he had reserved rooms for her at a fine hotel. The patient, however, was beset with conflict. She was urged to attend the wedding by both her son and her daughter. She was reluctant to go because she felt too angry at her son and at her own helplessness to prevent, what in her eyes, was an immoral marriage. She feared if she attended she might make a public scene by verbally attacking her son and prospective in-laws. In effect, she did not want to go.

In discussing her problems the patient was in excellent contact, alert, and smiled a good deal. There was no evidence of dementia. When she spoke of her son in my presence and later also in the presence of her daughter, she expostulated, "Look what he is doing to me." This angry statement is not consistent with a depressed person. Rather, a depressed person, with guilty and self-devaluative feelings would have said the reverse; that is, "Look what I must have done to him to cause him to be this way now." Nor was she suicidal. Her statement that she was ready to die was not a suicidal threat. On the contrary, she was stating that at her age, with the concomitant loss of family and friends, she was not afraid to die, but certainly she was not suicidal. Rather, she was philosophically prepared for nature to take its inexorable course.

In addition to the problem with her son, there was the issue of where she would live. Her daughter had tried to prevail on her to live near her, but that would be 1,000 miles away from her own home of many years. She did not feel she could do this, despite depletion of support systems in her present home through loss of family and friends. She reckoned it would be better to stay where she had lived, than to move to an entirely new set of unknown surroundings.

A third element in her environmental situation was her polypharmacy. She was using not only her cardiac drugs, but other medications for anxiety and sleep.

In her case, "environmental manipulation" seemed to be the therapeutic course of choice. There was no serious concern with either depression or suicide. Given her explicit hostility to attending her son's wedding she was encouraged by her physician and family not to attend, even though there would be some degree of guilt as a result. This was regarded as part of a less costly "price tag" than if she in fact attended. In addition, the coercion to move to her daughter's city was abandoned. She was permitted and encouraged to return to her own home. To address the polypharmacy, a complete assessment of her medications was undertaken in order to adjust them for optimum benefit.

In this management, no effort to explore unconscious factors, intrapsychic conflicts, or early life determinants was made, although, as Kahana so clearly demonstrates in chapter 8, "Geriatric Psychotherapy: Beyond Crisis Management," these unconscious intrapsychic determinants must be understood by the therapist in order to arrive at accurate and appropriate interventions. In this instance, such explorations were deliberately avoided since the therapist felt that the environmental recommendations would and should work, if not perfectly, then reasonably well. This woman's current symptoms were related to external reality issues. Hence, the three elements described above were the only recommendations. An option for further treatment proved unnecessary.

There are other situations, of course, where deeper therapy is indicated, such as when the problems are characterological and long standing, and not only reactive to the environment. In an earlier report (Berezin and Fern, 1967) a fairly extensive period of explorative therapy was described in the case of a 70-year-old woman picked up by the police in a state of crisis. She was drunk at the time and had marked off a square of sidewalk as her private territory and refused to let anyone walk on it. She was brought to a mental hospital where she was diagnosed as a hysterical character disorder. She accepted explorative psychotherapy which was conducted twice a week for 15 months.

Through the psychotherapy, what emerged from beneath the manifest appearance of an old, provocative, and mysterious woman, was an intelligent, lonely woman, struggling with persistent emotional problems from her youth. She had failed to grieve her mother, father, dead fiancé, and most notably, the lost opportunity to have lived a fuller life with marriage and children. She had neither been able to separate from her parents, nor allow herself a full range of adult, heterosexual relationships. As a result of her difficulties both with separation and resolution of oedipal issues, she devoted most of her life to the intensely ambivalent care and nursing of her elderly and ill parents. The therapeutic aim was to facilitate her grieving for her lost relationships and opportunities. This ensued slowly but steadily, and she made steady progress. Dreams, early memories, and a transference that included erotic feelings toward the young, male therapist were available for clarification, interpretation and working through.

Regarding the range and value of psychotherapeutic interventions with the elderly the important contributions of Drs. Lazarus, Grunes, Pollock, and Kahana warrant further comment and questions. Dr. Lazarus raises some important ideas regarding time-limited treatment in chapter 9, "Brief Psychotherapy with the Elderly." Of major concern is that sometimes, time-limited therapy is used as a concession to cost-benefit needs and third-party payers. Elizabeth Zetzel (personal communication, 1969), once pointed out privately, from a study she did at the Massachusetts General Hospital, that patients did as well in 6–7 sessions as those who were in therapy for months or years; that is, they became symptom free or improved but were not conflict free. She remarked that given the premise that fewer sessions were better, it would appear that the best therapy would be no therapy at all! This is not to say that studies on brief, time-limited therapy should not be done, but it is necessary to recognize clearly the limitations of this type of therapy.

As reported by Dr. Lazarus, there was difficulty in providing insight therapy in a preagreement of time limitations. Freud has confessed that he made two mistakes in his therapy with the Wolf Man. One was his promise to cure his patient of constipation, in which he succeeded. The other was to set a termination date long in advance. The patient then, to protect himself from feeling deserted in the middle of an exploration, developed resistances to exploration. This latter problem must occur in varying degrees in all time-limited therapy. Patients cannot be expected to stop in the middle of an exploration, whether that exploration is psychic or surgical! The patients described in Dr. Lazarus' study entered treatment with their own unconscious agendas. They were less concerned with self-awareness than with having their self-esteem bolstered and supported.

In all fairness, it does not necessarily follow that this altered agenda would be due to resistances arising from a prearranged time-limit, for there is always the likelihood of resistances from other causes.

Essentially, resistances to therapy in the elderly are the same as those found in the young. The patient's wish to prevent any change in his adaptive-defensive position, which is what resistance is really about, occurs with equal intensity with young and old. The patient feels compelled to protect against the emergence of earlier feelings, impulses, and fantasies; that is, the unconscious must remain unconscious. The threat of regression which acts as a determinant for resistance is shared equally by young and old. If one may point to something which may be unique in the treatment of the elderly, it would be in the countertransference of the young therapist. If the therapist is uneasy or uncomfortable in treating an elderly patient, then indeed resistance may occur, for this uneasiness is transmitted to the patient. In addition, the duration of therapy should not be dictated by time constraints alone, for as one of my elderly patients said, "All I have left is my future."

Dr. Grunes's chapter, "The Aged in Psychotherapy," provides a valuable and perceptive overview of psychodynamic psychotherapy with the elderly. His historical perspective evokes additional relevant ideas. Issues of aggression and violence are not usually prevalent in dealing with problems of the elderly. Either they do not appear or else they are being ignored. This is not without precedent: Freud avoided any systematic study of aggression for over 30 years. It was not until he published his paper on "Beyond the Pleasure Principle" in 1920 that he dealt with issues of aggression as such. Certainly, aggression may appear in the elderly, but it is much "softer" and far more rare than in younger people. Aggression, as with sex, and as with the persistence throughout life of early modes of behavior, is comparative—those who were aggressive when young tend to be so when old.

To return to Dr. Grunes's chapter, this author is pleased he chose to present variables of psychoanalytic therapy, and not only because of singularity of viewpoints. Dr. Grunes's comments about "elasticity of personality" are interesting. The so-called rigidity of the elderly is a myth. Current losses and stresses may evoke all the earlier adaptive and defensive patterns used throughout life, but when rigidity of character is present in old age, it was also present at a younger age, for rigidity is not a function of age but of personality development. In fact, dynamic psychotherapy is *amenable*—Dr. Grunes's term—to the elderly, using the same criteria for its use as is the case in the younger age population.

It is true that "[h]opeless therapists make for hopeless patients" (p. 33)—or very quickly for no patients at all. Grunes's reference here is obviously to the countertransference attitude.

The principle involved here is that there can be no successful therapy without a positive transference. A hopeless or negative attitude in the therapist will quickly destroy any positive transference.

It is also necessary to raise a point of disagreement regarding techniques. Dr. Grunes states that when the patient is at the door and is with other family members, he focuses almost exclusively on the patient, a technique he bases on the belief that other members must not intrude into the patient's therapy. This author's disagreement is based upon the fact that the elderly patient is invariably in the position of the child–patient whose parents contact the psychiatrist and who are seen in order to obtain a history. A role reversal often exists for elderly patients. The children of the aged patient, except in those rare cases of self-referral, usually contact the psychiatrist about the elderly patient as parents do with children. In such cases, the "others" cannot be ignored in the beginning. Only later, if a dynamic psychotherapy is undertaken, are confidentiality and nonintrusion necessary. This role reversal is a frequent sign of regression, reflecting not so much that the children may wish to infantilize the older parent, but very often that the parent's regression is a yielding to previously defended dependency wishes. Most often such dependency needs are camouflaged by the presence of a physical disorder, which is used to justify the dependency, and which then becomes exploited in the service of secondary gain. This can be an exceedingly stubborn issue to address. (Editor's note: Dr. Breslau's chapter 6, "Exaggerated Helplessness Syndrome" elaborates this idea in detail.)

There is also a need to raise a question regarding Dr. Grunes's comments that the therapist has not usually had the experience of age—he cannot have had the same experiences as the old patient. This may be a relevant point in terms of therapists' ever-increasing desire to be able to fully understand the experience of their patients, but surely this cannot be a plea for peer therapy. After all, the conflicts of an aged person are grounded not on, or because of, his age, but on earlier infantile developmental issues and early life traumas. Those events which impinge on the old person and which may be attributable to age are reacted to by earlier modes of defense and adaptation; regression to earlier life-styles is predetermined idiosyncratically in each individual by those same earlier modes.

In addition, the transference of the elderly patient develops as it does with younger people, for transference is unconscious and is not reality oriented. Thus, when psychiatric residents are fearful that an old person would see a young 29–30-year-old person as a child or even a grandchild, they learn to their astonishment that an 80-year-old patient may well see a 30-year-old therapist as a father or mother figure. Chronological age in therapy is not as significant a factor as is so commonly assumed. During therapy, the ages of both the therapist and patient become blurred and at times invisible.

One last comment: The wish for the patient to know details about the therapist's life is a universal expression of universal curiosity. New phrases, such as Dr. Grunes's phrase, "reverse empathy" are not particularly useful in this regard. In this author's experience, older patients do not necessarily require more therapist self-disclosure than younger patients. What happens frequently, though, is that the younger therapist, out of his countertransference, finds himself being more "personal" with his older patients who may represent parental countertransferential figures. The rationale for therapist self-disclosure must hence be clear to the therapist, and not be used globally with all his older patients.

Turning to Dr. Pollock's chapter, "The Mourning Liberation Process" it appears that a fundamental consensus amongst all the contributors is evident in regards to the general aims and goals of dynamic therapy. As he says, "The goal of psychoanalytic treatment is to make more of people available to themselves for present and future creative and satisfying life experiences." (p. 21) This is true for individuals who are middle-aged, older aged, or in the younger group of analysands. In order to facilitate this, the therapist needs to acknowledge that older patients wish to be useful and to preserve their dignity. In addition it is worthwhile to add here that they also want to be approved and loved. This connects to Dr. Grunes's ideas about the therapist's positive attitudes to the patients being an absolute prerequisite for the therapy to have an opportunity to be effective.

Dr. Pollock places heavy emphasis on the mourning-liberation process. His belief that successful aging requires the ability to mourn what no longer exists for the individual, needs clarification. Mourning occurs with loss, but which losses are at issue? For example, retirement is a common loss. Does this mean that the retiree must mourn the loss of his job, his occupation? Or should the issue of retirement be examined with other variables in mind. While indeed there may be a loss of the job and also a diminution of economic income, there are other issues, as well. There are those who need a job for reasons of self-esteem, as a credential to wear, as a badge to demonstrate worthwhileness. Such people, and there are many, have never had a firm sense of self-respect or self-esteem. The loss of a job for such people does not necessarily result in mourning. Rather it may result in a regression to an earlier period of self-doubt which now reappears nakedly. It would be better and more healthy if such people could regret a retirement and adapt, but not necessarily only with mourning.

Real grief and repeated grief and mourning is a mathematical certainty as one ages, for the older a person gets, the more of his loved ones, friends, and associates he loses. In addition, there are somatic losses in all people who age, such as loss of visual acuity, of hearing, and muscle tone. There are joint pains and wrinkled skin and pot bellies. Such issues may be settled by conflict resolution in addition to, or along with mourning.

A final note would be one of agreement with Dr. Pollock regarding the myth of older people fearing death (p. 19). That old people fear death is a projection imputed to them by a younger age group. Clinical experience does not demonstrate that older people have anxiety about dying. Again this issue is a longitudinal one; those who fear death when young do so when old.

In his usual scholarly way, in chapter 8, "Geriatric Psychotherapy: Beyond Crisis Management," Dr. Kahana has touched upon the bases all of the contributors have touched upon. His apt phrasing and conceptualizations can be captured in one simple phrase of his: "Thus he [the therapist] may attempt to convert . . . irrational mistrust into self-protective vigilance" (p. 246).

He lists a number of precipitants in the vulnerable 5 percent of the aged such as "limited physical reserves, debilitating chronic illnesses, brain damage, constriction of activities, the drastic impact of personal losses, depletion of self-esteem, and precarious dependence on family and community resources" (p. 246) and points out that in such patients a precipitating stress may be minimal, at times appearing to be so trivial as to be overlooked. A colleague, Sid Levin (personal communication, 1970), once presented a case of a depressed woman of 70 who required psychiatric hospitalization. She had lived a quiet life as a widow and was a former schoolteacher. She had no children. Her sudden depression was mysterious at first, until the following was discovered. She had been accustomed each day to visiting her corner market—not an impersonal supermarket but an old-fashioned Mom and Pop market. Each day she bought what she needed and had a casual, polite conversation with the proprietor. Then he died. It turned out that this man was the only human contact this woman shared and his death left her bereft of all personal relationships. This casual connection to a casual person says something significant about our patient's intrapsychic world and her external isolation, but it could have been easily missed.

Dr. Kahana deals with therapeutic interactions in detail which range through supportive to analytic measures. He makes reference to Bibring's clarifications about the principles of therapy (Bibring, 1954), such as suggestion, abreaction, manipulation, clarification, and insight. Dr. Kahana has undertaken to describe an area of geriatric care which is not usually the province of the psychoanalyst or psychotherapist, that is the emergency patient, the patient in crisis. He contributes to such states an enlightened application of psychoanalytic thinking which enables the elderly to profit from psychotherapeutic management.

An additional, small but significant item with respect to treatment of the elderly needs to be considered. A recurrent theme in this book is the affirmation of the availability and feasibility of various modalities of treatment for the elderly, and that there exists, in the end, little difference between treatment of the young and the old. In both, the therapist deals with the unconscious, resistances, conflicts, transference, and countertransference issues and pertinent unresolved issues from an early age such as self-esteem, oedipal, and sibling rivalry struggles. However, there are some differences which should not be overlooked, as illustrated in the case of the 70-year-old woman referred to earlier who underwent one-and-a-half years of intensive explorative therapy. She demonstrated a very significant difference. This patient, at age 70, discovered that for years she had longed to have children. Her therapist was concerned that this discovery might be too traumatic to bear, for after all, at age 70, it was now impossible for her to have the children she had longed for. She was observed carefully for fear she might have a severe depression, but fortunately she was able to grieve her sense of loss and learn to regret the reality. Through this she maintained her emotional balance. In such a situation a young woman might have been able to have the children she yearned for, but obviously not this patient. The therapist would do well to remain cognizant of this kind of distinguishing factor.

Any discussion of therapy for the elderly would be incomplete if it ignored the current state of affairs with respect to third-party payers, which has a direct and significant influence on choice of therapy and choice of therapists. There are many different types of therapy and there are many new types of therapists from many different disciplines that are now vended by law for Blue Cross/Blue Shield and other third-party payers. These third-party payers are not concerned with theory, training, or qualifications. They are interested only in the cost of treatment which often is quite different from the value of the treatment.

An additional item of concern is related to philosophy and ethics. Gerontology is a powerful stimulus for philosophic and economic thinking. Cost-benefit and cost-effectiveness studies as guides for the allocation of health care are gaining in influence. At a recent symposium in Boston, reference was made to a cost-benefit study on the care of the elderly. The bureaucracy of our current administration discovered, and it should come as no surprise, that the most money is spent in care during the last year of life. That is not surprising considering that in this period the patient is most ill and requires the most aid. Whoever did the study remarked, not with tongue in cheek but in all seriousness, that if this last year of life could be eliminated then a lot of money could be saved.

A recent article by Avorn (1984) addresses itself to these questions. He states, that a great risk in the current debates and deliberations about the economics of health care is the misguided economic conclusion that old age is not economically viable. Perhaps we should abandon civilization completely, since it seems to be not very cost-effective?

In conclusion, rather than summarizing a paper that has already been a kind of overview, or summary, it makes most sense to end by quoting Plato. This author has quoted Plato previously (Berezin, 1972), a reflection of how well Plato addressed, 2,000 years ago, many of the issues discussed today.

> Socrates questions the aged Cephalus: "Is life harder toward the end, or what report do you give of it?"
>
> "I will tell you, Socrates," he said, "what my own feeling is. Men of my age flock together; we are birds of a feather, as the old proverb says; and at our meetings the tale of my acquaintance commonly is—I cannot eat. I cannot drink; the pleasures of youth and love are fled away; there was a good time once, but now that is gone, and life is no longer life. Some complain of the slights which are put upon them by . . . [relatives], and they will tell you sadly of how many evils their old age is the cause. But to me, Socrates, these complainers seem to blame that which is not really in fault. For if old age were the cause, I too being old, and every other old man, would have felt as they do. But this is not my own experience, nor that of the aged poet Sophocles, when in answer to my question, How does love suit with age, Sophocles—are you still the same man you were? Peace, he replied; most gladly have I escaped the thing of which you speak; I feel as if I had escaped from a mad and furious master. His words have often occurred to my mind since, and they seem as good to me now as the time when he uttered them. For certainly old age has a great sense of calm and freedom; when the passions relax their hold, then, as Sophocles says, we are freed from the grasp not of one mad master only, but of many. The truth is, Socrates, that these regrets, and also the complaints about . . . [relatives], are to be attributed to the same cause, which is not old age, but men's characters and tempers; for he who is of a calm and

happy nature will hardly feel the pressure of age, but to him who is of an opposite disposition youth and age are equally a burden" (Plato pp. 5–6).

References

Avorn, J. (1984), Benefit and cost analysis in geriatric care: Turning age discrimination into health policy. *New Eng. J. Med.*, 310:1294–1301.
Berezin, M. A. (1970), Partial grief in family members and others who care for the elderly patient. *J. Geriat. Psychiat.*, 4:53–64.
——— (1972), Psychodynamic considerations of aging and the aged: An overview. *Amer. J. Psychiat.*, 128:1483–1491.
——— Fern, D. J. (1967), Persistence of early emotional problems in a seventy-year-old woman. *J. Geriat. Psychiat.*, 1:45–60.
Bibring, E. (1954), Psychoanalysis and the dynamic psychotherapies. *J. Amer. Psychoanal. Assn.*, 2:745–770.
Freud, S. (1920), Beyond the Pleasure Principle. *Standard Edition*, 18:7–64. London: Hogarth Press, 1964.
——— (1933), New Introductory Lectures on Psychoanalysis and Other Works. *Standard Edition*, 22:136–158. London: Hogarth Press, 1964.
Herink, R. (1980), *The Psychotherapy Handbook: The A to Z Guide to More than 250 Different Therapies in Use Today.* New York: New American Library.
Hughes, R., & Brewin, R. (1979), *The Tranquilizing of America.* New York: Warner Books.
Plato (n.d.), *The Republic,* trans. B. Jowett. New York: Random House/Modern Library, 1955.
Roget's International Thesaurus (1977), 4th ed. New York: Thomas Y. Crowell.
Salzman, C. (1981), Psychotropic drug use and polypharmacy in a general hospital. *Gen. Hosp. Psychiat.*, 3:1–9.

Part II
MANIFESTATIONS OF PSYCHOPATHOLOGY

4

PSYCHODYNAMICS OF PARANOID PHENOMENA IN THE AGED

Adrian Verwoerdt, M.D.

In paranoid phenomena in the elderly, paranoia may be the central feature or an associated symptom. Although paranoid behavior in the aged has a reported prevalence of as much as 10–20 percent (Eisdorfer, 1980), there is little agreement about definition, etiology, and nosology. About one-third of late life paranoia is not associated with schizophrenia or organicity. (Fish, 1960; Kay and Roth, 1961; Bridge and Wyatt, 1980). Table 4-1 summarizes a classification of these paranoid phenomena.

Some years ago, after a conversation about depression in late life, one of the "grand old men" in the field of aging remarked, "old age is a depression." Indeed, one might wonder why all older people are not depressed. Why is it that, although faced with so much adversity and loss, many old people manage to come through with gratitude and with what Erikson called "integrity" (Erikson, 1959)? Conversely, why is it that in the lives of some old people, there is a movement, not toward integrity, but toward despair; not toward gratitude, but toward envy, jealousy, and vindictiveness, and in the extreme, paranoid psychosis?

Paranoid decompensation may be conceptualized as a pro-

67

gression along a pathway of three stages, from depression to
hypochondriasis to psychosis.

Figure 4-1 shows the representations of the external object
world and the "self" which is made up of the bodily self and
the core inner self. The horizontal arrows represent the ex-
changes between the outer object world and the self. The shell
which circles the inner self, that is, the bodily self, represents
a bridge between the inner self and the external object world
and contains the mechanisms for interaction with that external

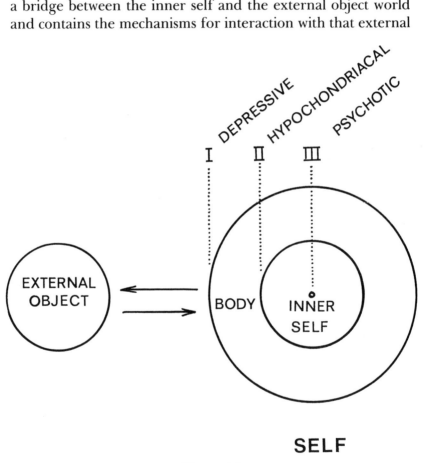

Figure 4-1

object world. This simple diagrammatic representation may help to conceptualize three stages of psychopathology—the depressive, the hypochondriacal, and the paranoid or psychotic.

In the depressive stage, interaction with the external object world is maintained and the object is experienced as being essentially good. In the second or hypochondriacal stage, a regression has occurred, and the main psychological emphasis is placed on the body. While object relations are maintained, they are more tenuous, although the object is considered to be, potentially, a good one. In the third stage, additional regression and withdrawal occur deeper into the psychic core. Under the influence of this withdrawal, contact with the external object world is ruptured resulting in psychosis or paranoia. In this final stage, the external object is experienced as threatening and bad. These three stages must be seen as interactive. For example, depressive symptoms as they deepen may lead to regression and the emergence of hypochondriacal symptoms which may then move on to psychotic paranoid phenomena. Similarly, as will be seen below, psychotic patients, as they become more other-related, will develop hypochondriacal or depressive symptoms. While these phenomena are interrelated, for clarity they will be discussed under three main headings as indicated in Table 4-1—paranoid decompensation of depression, paranoid decompensation of hypochondriasis, and paranoid psychosis.

Paranoid Decompensation of Depression

Melanie Klein (1957) describes the psychodynamics of the paranoid and depressive positions. The depressive position may be briefly stated as, "I am bad; you are good." Significantly, this position permits object relationships to remain intact. In the paranoid position, however, the reverse is true: "You are bad;

TABLE 4-1

Classification of Paranoid Phenomena

   I. Paranoid Decompensation of Depression
  II. Paranoid Decompensation of Hypochondriasis
III. Psychosis

     A. Primary Paranoia
       1. Acute Persecutory Anxiety
       2. Pathological Jealousy
       3. Paranoia with Self-aggrandizement
       4. Paraphrenia
       5. Shared Paranoid Disorder (Folie à Deux)

     B. Secondary Paranoia
       1. Late Life Paranoid Schizophrenia
       2. Organic Delusional Syndrome
       3. Paranoia in Terminal Illness

I am good," a stance which sets the stage for a rupture in contact with others. Envy and vindictiveness are an intermediate stage between the depressive and paranoid positions in the sense of, "I am bad; you are good—but I'll see to it that you are just as bad as I am. I'll make you bad." This stance, however, produces a vicious circle of ever-increasing impoverishment, and paranoid decompensation.

In many instances, the early phases of paranoid decompensation are related to the vicissitudes of depression. Of particular interest here are those depressions in which bitterness, envy, jealousy, and vindictiveness become increasingly prominent. Such states of mind are the very opposite of gratitude. In her book, *Envy and Gratitude and Other Works*, Klein (1957) states that the basis of gratitude is the full gratification experienced with the first love object. The more often gratification is experienced as life goes on, the more gratitude develops as an enduring state of mind. Internalized good objects are strengthened through the repetition of good memories and the remembrance of previous gratifications resulting in a sense of

inalienable ownership of one's past. The attainment of a position of gratitude is a powerful antidote to the feelings of envy,
vindictiveness, and jealousy. If gratitude is not attained, it then
may be harder to deal with grief and to overcome depression.

Recovery from depression is influenced by numerous psychodynamic factors. Some of these include ego strength, developmental issues, traumatic life events, and the interaction
among all of these. Inasmuch as neuroses and personality disorders are thought to originate in early life, a pattern of repeated maladjustment and failure increasingly takes its toll as
the individual is confronted with the tasks of adulthood. With
aging, it becomes more and more difficult to replace a lost
object. *Multiple losses* may occur simultaneously or one after the
other, leaving the individual in perpetual grief or depression.
Moreover, there may be a *loss of aspiration.* After painful disappointments, one may not wish to expose oneself again to
risks. Hence, an older person may not recover from grief and
depression, not only because of the relative scarcity of substitute
objects, but also because of the reluctance to reach out for new
objects, if they are available. Finally, *time perspective is altered.*
The patient despairs because time and hope dwindle, and he
may be embittered by the failure of providence to allot him
"the good life." With time running out, those who have always
been "on good behavior" may now feel entitled to rewards. He
who missed opportunities may reach for his rewards with a
vengeance, as if, in finally doing what he wants, he will get back
at the authority who has kept him so long in line. The patient's
resentment is then revealed through envy, jealousy, or irritation
at those others who did indulge, without qualms, in "the good
life."

With the passage of time there may be a decrease in the
amount of energy available, both physical and mental. On the
psychological level, this may manifest itself as *diminished ego
strength.* Thus, for example, due to an age-related, reduced

psychic energy, the ego may be less able to carry out some of its essential functions such as repression. Weakened defensive barriers may permit the breakthrough of narcissistic impulses as well as aggressive-hostile impulses, passive-dependent impulses, and oedipal wishes. Failure of repression does not immediately lead to envious or paranoid tendencies. As the following example demonstrates, however, loss of the ego's resilience and strength may diminish the individual's ability to recover from depression and promote a vulnerability to paranoid responses.

A 65-year-old accountant and father of seven children had had shortness of breath of three years duration. His doctor had told him that the cause of his symptoms was a rare form of congenital heart defect, and that "ordinarily such cases don't live beyond age 40." Soon after this diagnosis, the patient developed periodic hyperactivity which was managed by various psychotropic medications. However, he kept working until he was retired at age 65. Following this, he refused to take any more medications. He became increasingly hostile, and his cardiologist was concerned that his agitation would lead to cardiac decompensation. When he was hospitalized, the patient threatened to sue the medical staff, thereby projecting the blame for his troubles onto others. He continued refusing his medications, stated that he needed to get out of the hospital so that he could open a restaurant, that every day in the hospital cost him a thousand dollars, and that he was going to divorce his wife so as to be free. He announced plans to fly to the West Coast to attend the basketball championship games and to spend some time in San Francisco. "Since I've always wanted to go to Hawaii, I might as well spend a few weeks there." This man had finally found himself about 20 years overdue and had become, so to speak, a geriatric desperado. He had no time for grief and mourning. His flight into health and his paranoid, angry protest represented a belated attempt to add zest and color to what he considered a dutiful, staid life.

In an unremitting depression, the patient becomes progressively impoverished. There is still a sense that life in general can be good, but that fortune has smiled on others, not on him. Considering his misfortune, the patient finds it almost impossible not to feel envy toward the lucky ones. Part of this envy is the wish to spoil others' good fortune or to take it away from them.

Another dynamic of paranoid decompensation in depression is the projection of depressive guilt. Such guilt may be conceptualized as arising from an archaic primitive superego. This term refers to the pregenital precursors of the mature superego. In its primitive form, such a superego produces unduly strict, rigid, and aggressive norms and punishments within the individual. A component of this level of early psychological stages of development may be seen in the child's primitive concept of justice which involves the "talion" principle—"an eye for an eye, a tooth for a tooth." In other words, the primitive superego of a developing child lives by this principle, producing harsh self-criticisms. While normal development modifies and softens these self-judgments, they may resurface powerfully under the regressive impact of depression. The psyche, in order to protect itself, may utilize the defensive mechanism of projection and attribute the critical judgments to others in the environment. The harsh self-criticisms which originate from within are projected and then experienced as coming from others. This mechanism of projection may cause many such patients to live in perpetual, watchful anxiety, lest their persecutors should strike.

In summary, if guilt is experienced by an immature ego not yet capable of bearing it, that guilt is felt as persecution and the object that evokes such guilt is turned into a persecutor. By externalizing his own unacceptable thoughts and feelings through the defensive mechanism of projection, the individual may not only disown these feelings, but attach them to an outside danger from which he theoretically may then be able to flee. While this may sometimes work, in the presence of an archaic superego, it is not successful. One cannot flee from oneself.

Just as guilt may be projected, so may envy. The figure on which strong envy has been projected becomes particularly persecutory. Thus, due to the attribution of the patient's vindictive destructive impulses toward the other, the patient then begins to feel persecuted by this "bad object" which he has created through his own projection. The persecutory anxiety so created, can be so strong that the working through of the depressive position is impaired, and in some cases, particularly of a psychotic type, defenses may be so impenetrable that it may seem impossible to analyze them (Klein, 1957).

The following example further demonstrates the manifestations of the paranoid defense as it is expressed in the therapeutic situation.

A woman in her late sixties had suffered depression since her midforties, with her misery being steadfastly inflicted on her family. She undermined every effort by her family and her therapist to divert her or to cheer her up, by saying ahead of time, "I don't care." The few times she did cheer up were those occasions when other people had misfortunes. She blamed her family for her own emptiness and lack of grace. She was particularly critical of her son, constantly trying to write him off as an affront to motherhood and a lost cause. These criticisms warded off an underlying feeling that she herself had been a total failure as a mother. As it happened, her son had finished his professional studies, turned out to be rather mature and filial, and had landed a prestigious job. All this the therapist brought to the patient's attention—the simple fact that this reflected well on her, that she deserved some credit, and that here was some cause for gratitude. At the point of this intervention, the patient fell silent for the rest of the session, looking angry and upset. When she came back to the next session, her question was: "How could you upset me so much with your criticism?"

Her angry paranoid response illustrates the intense negative reaction which this kind of patient can demonstrate when exposed to an intervention that does not accurately mirror her own inner convictions. It should be noted, however, that the absence of a solid therapeutic alliance does not necessarily mean that there is *no* therapeutic alliance at all. The degree of alliance possible may depend on the extent to which the patient has shifted from the depressive toward the paranoid position—that is from other-relatedness to other-rejection. The more enmeshed the patient is in the paranoid position, the more impaired the therapeutic alliance. Much of this formulation also holds true in the discussion of hypochondriasis to follow.

Paranoid Decompensation of Hypochondriasis

Not infrequently, patients with a past history of involutional depression become hypochondriacal. Regression is an important element in the psychodynamics of hypochondriasis. This manifests as a regressive withdrawal of interest from external objects—the world out there—onto the self, specifically the bodily self. The disengagement resulting from chronic depression sets the stage for increased preoccupation with the one object that remains available, one's own body. Another important regressive aspect is the flight into the sick role. The perception of physical disability may provide a psychological alibi which removes responsibility for failure in the areas of intimacy and generativity, alleviates a sense of shortcoming, and thus restores self-esteem. Such a flight into the sick role is also a flight from responsibility. The underlying theme may be stated as, "I am not responsible, neither are you, but my body is." This fixing of blame and responsibility is intermediate between the depressive and paranoid positions. Since the hypochondriacal scenario leaves space for the goodness of the object or significant other, object relations may remain intact at least for a while. However, as time goes on, the patient alienates others with his complaints. He now experiences further losses of affection and approval. When his feelings of being neglected increase, and his anger rises, vindictiveness toward, and devaluation of, others sets in.

Effective management of a hypochondriacal situation will prevent paranoid decompensation. The therapist must recognize that the hypochondriac needs his complaints in order to maintain self-esteem in object relations. This recognition should not be communicated to the patient, nor should the patient's psychodynamics be interpreted to him. It is wise to treat the symptoms without expecting that they will disappear. This is not therapeutic hypocrisy, but involves communication on two levels. On the superficial level, the patient and therapist are engaged in a traditional contract—to do something about the complaint. However, on a deeper level, there is a tacit understanding that the patient needs his symptoms in order to cope. If the patient asks for a diagnosis, it is prudent to circumvent the question and respond with a statement like this: "Obviously you have trouble. I am not certain about the real cause, but I am glad to do whatever I can to help you." Such a statement seems noncommittal, but is actually a statement of the physician's commitment.

The therapist must provide a stable object relationship by being available to the patient at specific times. He must accept the fact of the patient's regression, thereby creating for the patient a "no-lose proposition." The physical symptoms are used to establish a personal relationship between doctor and patient. Finally, while commiserating with the patient about his plight, it is essential to encourage him to carry on in spite of symptoms.

The basic theoretical concept of the body as a bridge between the outer world and the inner self may be elaborated at this point. Returning to the earlier diagram, the concept of the body as a bridge helps elucidate the therapeutic value of a hypochondriacal development in the treatment of autistic and psychotic conditions, as well as the consequences of regression and withdrawal from the object world. The following case illustrates the nature of progressive decompensation moving through the three stages of depression, hypochondriasis, and paranoia.

A 65-year-old divorced woman had become an overwhelming problem to all the community agencies with which she had contact, because she was perennially dissatisfied with any place, person, or program arranged to meet her needs.

At the age of 40 she had been admitted to a mental hospital because she had been accusing her husband of being "immoral and unfaithful," and she expressed suicidal threats. Her diagnosis was involutional depression with paranoid features. During her stay in the hospital, the depressive symptoms cleared, only to be replaced by hypochondriasis. A few months later she was discharged with the new diagnosis of neurasthenia. Three years later, at the age of 43, she divorced her husband. Thereafter she did not have any contact with him or with her two sons. The patient's depressive symptoms never returned, and were permanently replaced, first by hypochondriasis and then by paranoia. Her conversation revolved ceaselessly around herself, her ailments, doctors, medicine, and diet. In the 10 years from age 55 to 65, the patient lived in 30 different boarding homes, and in one two-year timespan she moved 15 times. After a few years of this ceaseless movement and alienation of others, the patient became more hostile and suspicious. She began to write letters to heads of agencies and directors of departments explaining her plight, asking for help, and making assorted accusations.

By the time the patient reached her late fifties, her accusations acquired a decidedly paranoid delusional quality. For example: "I heard the cleaning woman beating up some old people in the room next to mine." By her early sixties, grandiose thoughts and behavior were superimposed on her symptomatology; for example, she would call the police department to deliver her medicine to her from the drugstore. By age 65, her litigious correspondence had reached ever higher and higher echelons, eventually including letters to the U.S. President.

Patients who have become very disengaged, withdrawn, or isolated, experience the external world as empty. What remains is the world of the self—the concrete, physical body and the intangible, invisible, mental content and representations. The bodily self more directly touches the outside world. In fact, the mind or inner self perceives the body as a peripheral zone that extends toward the physical world, of which it becomes a part. In this sense, the body is a bridge extending from the intimate center of the self toward the external object world. Using the analogy of a bridge, one could think of traffic in two directions: toward external objects and toward the self. If, in the course of a traffic pattern from external objects toward the self, the units of energy remain at the halfway station of the body, they will be invested at this point. This hypercathexis or overinvestment of psychic energy in the body, results in hypochondriasis. If, however, this movement proceeds on its inward course, the last contact with the real world, the body, is abandoned, and the psychic energy is now mostly used to cathect the inner domain of the self, its thoughts, images, fantasies, and memories. This pathological immersion in the inner self signifies autism, a rupture with the real world. Conversely, when a very withdrawn patient begins to turn his attention toward the real world, the first object encountered is his own body. The presence of physical complaints sets the stage for contact and interaction between the patient and another person. The following is a case example of a withdrawn schizophrenic patient which illustrates this process.

A 69-year-old schizophrenic woman was hospitalized because her weight was down to 90 pounds. She was 5 feet 10 inches tall. She stated that the food was poison; she was mute; she shielded her eyes with her hands to avoid eye contact and did not allow staff to come closer than arm's length. Her contact with the world took place by way of "earphones" which also served to transmit the "voices" to her. Her treatment included: (1) Mellaril; (2) an attitude of nonintrusive friendliness at arm's-length distance; (3) ignoring delusional statements; (4) focusing on certain physical symptoms, especially abdominal pain, in an attempt to encourage hypochondriasis and awareness of somatic symptoms. She was seen by members of the treatment team in regular, brief visits during which the focus was exclusively on gastrointestinal symptoms such as abdominal pain, bowel movements, appetite, food, and weight. A medical member of the treatment team made periodic physical checks when the patient complained of abdominal distress; the dietician would see the patient about her appetite, dietary preferences, and need to gain weight, and the nurse focused on the patient's eating behavior during mealtimes.

The first sign of improvement was steady weight gain. She then began to make eye contact, allow staff closer, and began to smile more. At this point, the patient's auditory hallucinations were almost gone. The patient rationalized this by saying, "my earphones are messed up."

Psychosis

In depression and hypochondriasis, the depressive position prevails, with object relations and reality testing remaining essentially intact. Psychosis, in contrast, is characterized by loss of contact with reality and the predominance of the paranoid position.

Paranoid disorders of a psychotic degree may be acute or chronic and although knowledge about their etiology, especially the chronic types, remains incomplete, some of the etiological psychodynamic factors can be observed and traced. One factor which distinguishes the more severe paranoid disorders from the less severe, is the extent to which the defense mechanism of projection is used. As noted earlier, projection is an unconscious mechanism which allows unacceptable feelings, impulses or self-awarenesses to be attributed to another, despite the evidence of reality. The content of this defensive projection may be (1) the attribution of feelings or impulses to another; (2) projection of the cause of a feeling or condition such that the other is seen to be that cause; (3) projection of the very condition itself.

Paranoid conditions may be divided into two main categories: primary paranoia and secondary paranoia.

Primary Paranoia

The basic elements of primary paranoia include persecutory delusions or pathological jealousy. These elements are persistent and do not occur in the context of schizophrenia, affective disorder, or organic mental disorder. The following subcategories will be discussed below: acute persecutory anxiety, pathological jealousy, paranoia with self-aggrandizement, paraphrenia, and shared paranoid disorder *(folie à deux)*.

Acute Persecutory Anxiety. Acute persecutory anxiety is characterized by the sudden onset of paranoid behavior. It may take the form of transient suspiciousness or frank psychosis. Precipitants include a variety of stresses such as sensory deprivation or overload, or relocation. Acute persecutory anxiety may occur in psychotic depression during which the patient may project the cause of his sense of impending doom onto others, for example, by saying to the staff, "you are trying to kill me."

The following case example demonstrates how severe persecutory anxiety may develop when a depressed patient projects her own vindictive, destructive impulses onto the staff.

A 72-year-old woman, hospitalized with a history of recurrent depression, became increasingly vituperative, finding innumerable clever ways of hurting the feelings of the ward staff. She complained excessively, but was recalcitrant in cooperating with corrective intervention. She showed total lack of appreciation for anything done on her behalf, and blamed others for her plight. She was not only verbally abusive, but unpredictably combative, striking fear into the hearts of those around her. During more quiet moments she would say, "nobody cares for me." She showed a striking negative therapeutic reaction, trying to prove the staff wrong, and provoking almost intolerable countertransference in them. An example of such negative countertransference was the strong tendency to act in collusion with the patient's idea that nobody cared for her, and to actually stop taking care of her and abandon her.

She went through the motions of apparently "being dead," lying mute and motionless on the bed and refusing medications, food, and liquids. In response to her own projective defense and her insistence upon viewing the staff as assaultive to her, she developed a severe persecutory anxiety, stating that people were surreptitiously entering her room, stealing her things, and poisoning her food. Amidst the panic, her rage was also evident, making her unreachable by the staff. During this stage, it was necessary to administer forced medication (IM Navane) against the patient's will. The decision to force medications clearly is not an easy one. The problem with vindictive and paranoid patients is that such an intrusive procedure only exacerbates their hostility and suspiciousness. Essentially, one has to weigh the benefits of the pharmacological effects against such disadvantages.

There are a number of important elements in the management of apparent vindictive behavior. The therapist must recognize that the vindictive behavior is a clinical manifestation of regression to an early ambivalent phase of development. The orally aggressive patient "bites the hand that feeds him." In anal–sadistic regression, the features are oppositional behavior, and "making a mess" out of things. Expression of these primitive impulses may be very taxing on the caretaker receiving this abuse. Insight into these psychological origins may make it easier to deal with the therapist's inevitable reactions and countertransference feelings.

The therapist must address himself to the underlying problems with an attitude of detached concern, avoiding overinvolvement on the one hand and rejection of a patient through distancing, on the other. The patient may have feelings of exacerbated helplessness, shameful loss of dignity, bitterness about having been betrayed, or fear of being let down. It is often necessary to use a special form of tact by meeting needs in an indirect manner, not formally, but tacitly and casually.

The initial focus of therapy is to help the patient accept what is offered to him while not dealing directly with his hostile behavior. This "collaborative phase" reaches its goal when the patient has a sense of certainty that the therapist is a reliable good object and that the patient's own ill-will cannot destroy the good object. Finally, one may try to deal with the regressive disagreeable behavior by making certain demands on the patients, such as limit setting. Thus, one could ask the patient to give up a certain type of oppositional behavior, for example, refusing to walk to the dining room, and to become more cooperative. Confrontation helps to strengthen the self-observing aspects of the patient's ego functioning, while setting limits encourages the further development of the therapeutic alliance.

Paranoid features in depression must be distinguished from the overt expression of anger which can be a sign of improvement in depression. Such outwardly directed anger is not the same as the hostility associated with paranoid phenomena. Paranoid phenomena are chiefly characterized by projection and the presence of ideas of reference, hostility, and a tendency toward grandiosity (Swanson, Bohnert, and Smith, 1970; Brink, 1980). In contrast, the overt expression of anger which hitherto had been kept repressed, often is a sign of emerging self-assertiveness which is adaptive, inasmuch as it facilitates interpersonal relations and communication.

Pathological Jealousy. Jealousy is related to envy, but unlike envy, which occurs in a one-to-one relationship, jealousy involves a relationship between at least two other people—he who may be lost and he who is taking away the lost object. Jealousy is an emotion caused by a sense that something of value, which the person feels belongs to him, is being taken away and given to a rival. When the "something of value" is the love and approval of a spouse, the pathological jealousy becomes conjugal jealousy. Sometimes, what appears to present as conjugal jealousy on the surface, turns out, on closer scrutiny, to have significant elements of paranoid envy. Both these elements are present in the example to follow.

>A 70-year-old man suspected that his wife, during her periodic travels, was unfaithful. He demanded that she stay close to him at all times. When she rebelled, he escalated the level of his accusations, stating, "she stole a million dollars from me." He had come to envy his wife's robust health; she could go on cruises while he was homebound. The patient had always been frail and sickly and he compensated for this by relentless hard work and being a show-off. He had, for example, a collection of 70 different colorful caps and a "very interesting gun collection." The depth of his envy and vindictiveness came through in the idea that his wife had stolen a million dollars from him, that is, everything he had. By this time, he was more openly displaying his gun collection, making his wife wonder if he was threatening her or just showing off.
>
>This patient's breakdown resulted from his continued use of the defense of overcompensation for his frailty and underlying insecurity. The maintenance of this high-energy defense, a fight response, meant that he was living above his psychological means, in a psychologically obsolete life-style. He became particularly vulnerable because of chronic obstructive pulmonary disease. His

wife's independence and occasional travels increased his sense of loss of control. When the defensive overcompensation broke down, it was replaced by an even more maladaptive defense; that is, projecting the cause of his insecurity onto his wife. The patient was eventually involuntarily hospitalized. His placement on a locked ward signified to him total loss of control and dignity, for which he continued to blame his wife. In keeping with this stance, he refused medication. It was decided, however, not to force medication because this may have been interpreted by him as an ultimate loss of control and probably would have outweighed any pharmacologic benefits. Neither was the patient confronted with his pathological jealousy and paranoid thoughts.

The natural tendency of a therapist may be to try to talk such patients out of their delusions, but this often only results in the therapist being included in the delusional system. However, if one indicates agreement with the patient's train of thought, one may end up becoming a pawn in his paranoid scheme. The correct therapeutic position is to side step a suspicious line of thinking, neither agreeing nor disagreeing. Such a response is not unlike that mentioned for hypochondriasis, where one would circumvent giving the patient a specific diagnosis.

An important element in this patient's management was to increase his sense of dignity and control. One method of achieving this was by expediting transfer to an open ward and expressing trust in him that he was able to handle this transfer. The element of helping the patient save face highlights the central role of self-esteem regulation in the patient's pathology. The maintenance of a supportive esteem-promoting dignity and a sense of subjective control was clearly essential to treatment. At the same time, the therapist brought up the issue of "gun control," but not explicitly as a precondition for transfer to the open ward. Rather, the issue was raised coincidentally, with the implication that it would be wise to dispose of his gun collection because "some people get scared of these things." The patient readily complied with this. Generally, in paranoid men, the potential for violence is a very important issue. It is absolutely essential to reach an understanding with the patient to do away with his weapons.

Paranoia with Self-Aggrandizement. Sometimes patients not only externalize or project the undesirable part of the self, but bolster this defense with a concomitant aggrandizement of the self. Inasmuch as the latter indicates an additional auxiliary defense, the psychopathology is more severe. The therapist may also find more significant premorbid maladjustment, such as antisocial personality or alcohol abuse.

A 70-year-old man had lived independently for many years. In both his previous marriages, he was quite abusive to his wives. His independence came to an end due to the amputation of his right leg caused by peripheral vascular disease. His son invited the patient to move in with him. A few months later, the patient's left leg was also amputated below the knee, and he became wheelchair bound. Sometime after this, he became quite angry at his son and attacked him with his old crutches, saying, "you are trying to bury me." The patient became increasingly argumentative and combative, claiming that his son did not want him in the house, and that the son and others had beaten him. In addition, the patient had ideas of grandeur, stating that he had a million dollars in the bank; that he was told by Jesus Christ to preach the ten commandments; and that "President Roosevelt has sent me to give communion." It is of note that President Roosevelt ruled the country from a wheelchair, suggesting that the patient's self-aggrandizement came about by identifying with this suitably powerful figure.

In treating this patient, it was imperative to recognize that his paranoid symptoms arose in an effort to protect his fragile self-esteem and control over his environment. Therefore interventions focused on ways in which this man's sense of potency and effectiveness could be enhanced. In this regard, the psychodynamic understanding of his subjective experience facilitated an effective treatment approach.

The patient was treated with Mellaril, 25 milligrams three

times a day. In addition, an attempt was made to increase his sense of control with physical therapy, getting him artificial legs, teaching him how to walk on his artificial legs, and giving him a choice about moving in with his son or making other arrangements. In occupational therapy, the patient increased his self-esteem by winning every game of checkers that he played. The grandiose features of his psychosis disappeared first, within one week; the paranoid symptoms cleared up after one month.

While acute persecutory anxiety, pathological jealousy, and paranoia with self-aggrandizement are acute disorders, paraphrenia and folie à deux, to be discussed next, are chronic.

Paraphrenia. The literature has been divided about the question of whether paraphrenia is a separate entity or part of the schizophrenias (Bridge and Wyatt, 1980). As of now, the tendency is to consider paraphrenia to be separate from schizophrenia. The Diagnostic and Statistical Manual (1980) (DSM-III) solves the issue elegantly by including "paraphrenia" only in the index. If one looks through the pages indicated, there is a description of chronic paranoid disorder, but not a word about paraphrenia. Thus, it is up to the reader to decide.

The term *paraphrenia* was coined by Kraepelin (1919), and Roth in 1955 reintroduced the term, which in the meantime had fallen out of use. The syndrome of paraphrenia includes a chronic paranoid disorder starting in late life, with paranoid delusions and hallucinations but without the deterioration typical of schizophrenia (Kay and Roth, 1961; Eisdorfer, 1980). It is further characterized by (1) predominance of females; (2) preservation of personality; (3) paranoid or schizoid premorbid personality; (4) absence of dementia or primary affective disorder (Roth, 1955). Many of these patients are unmarried, childless, and isolated. Physical problems, especially deafness, add the element of helplessness to the isolation (Herbert and Jacobson, 1967), and the resulting anxiety is dealt with by projection. The internal threat is externalized and becomes "an enemy out there," often resulting in prominent intrusion fantasies. The internal threat is characterized by a sense of helplessness and vulnerability prompted by such factors as physical illness and handicaps, social isolation and sensory deprivation, and dwindling economic resources.

> A 74-year-old woman, living independently and still taking care of herself and her home, had the delusion that a nightwatchman, hiding in her attic, was spying on her and stealing her money. To protect herself, she undressed and bathed in the dark (projecting, perhaps, her reluctance to see her own deteriorating body onto an "evil eye"). The nightwatchman "kept me awake for almost 3 months trying to make me think he was a bird by tapping on the ceiling. One night he even threw a bucket of water on me." She changed the locks on her house, but discovered he would enter by lifting a part of the roof. A few months later, however, she reported that the watchman was acting nicely and she talked to him all the time. At first the watchman was an old man. Then he became a young boy interested in helping her, although "he knows I have a gun that will shoot him 25 times."
>
> One psychodynamic formulation suggests that the delusion of the watchman was overdetermined. The watchman represents the evil eye that sees ugly things; he is the projection of the concretized concept of loss (he is after her money); it is the externalization of her wish to have somebody watch over her. The figurative "watch over" then becomes a literal, spatial "above"—in the attic. The delusion of the man upstairs fails to reassure her. Neither the old man nor the young boy would be much protection and so she has her magic gun ready.

In the early stages of paraphrenia, enemies are perceived as being well outside the patient's house, beyond the perimeter of personal space. Typically they are hoodlum types on the street in front of the house, acting obnoxiously or using vulgar language. During the next phase, the undesirable elements make their way across the property line, into the garden, or onto the front porch. The third stage is that of penetration into the house. This intrusion usually involves damage, for example, to the plumbing or wiring in the basement. During the last stage, the protective symbolic equation, that is body = house, breaks down and now the enemy is felt to intrude into the patient's body space itself, resulting in tactile hallucinations. This last phase may also be described by the patient as "something coming through the wall toward me."

The treatment of paraphrenia requires antipsychotic medications—phenothiazines, haloperidol, or thiothixene. Intramuscular prolixin enanthate may be very useful. With adequate, successful therapy, one may at times observe the psychopathological phenomena disappearing in a sequence that is the reverse of that outlined above. Thus, the wall may close up again and the undesirable elements are cleared out of the house. While this process takes place, the patient becomes more and more guarded, and is reluctant to talk about the delusional material.

Folie à Deux *(Shared Paranoid Disorder)*. Few entities are more intriguing than folie à deux, the "psychosis of association" in which the same delusions are shared by two people. Among the common features found in *folie à deux* patients of all ages are isolation and poverty, a very high proportion of blood relationships, particularly sister–sister combinations, a high level of dependency, and a high rate of persecutory delusions. Persecutory delusions were found in nearly all cases in which relationships had been of an extended duration. Hostility was projected outward against a common enemy (Gralnick, 1942). The two theories most commonly presented to explain folie à deux suggest, (1) that the delusion is imposed on the weaker of the two by the stronger, or (2) that the two people simply become psychotic at the same time, one borrowing the delusion from the other. While dependency is felt to be of importance in the development of the syndrome (McNiel, Verwoerdt, and Peak, 1972), it is probably more accurate to regard the need to preserve intimacy as the most important factor leading to a unitary delusional system. This view of the etiology of folie à deux would deemphasize the role of contagion, and emphasize the adaptive function of a unitary delusion—how both partners can project interpersonal and other frustrations outward while at the same time joining forces against a common enemy. One of them may assume a dominant role, but in the case to follow, it was possible for one partner to reverse roles (McNiel, et al. 1972).

> For the four years prior to being admitted to hospital, Bessie and Inez M. had been patients in a county home where they had been confined since being judged incompetent by the courts. The verdict followed a lawsuit instituted by neighbors charging that the sisters had made "unrestrained, vile, and untrue statements" about them and that the two constituted "a public nuisance."
>
> On admission to hospital, the sisters were cooperative and friendly, but insisted that their niece and nephew had taken advantage of them and were after their property. They also alluded to certain "whiskey people" who had been antagonizing them over the years by throwing stones at them, and on one occasion, placing dynamite in the basement.
>
> The sisters had boarded up their windows and put up a fence. Both of them had the delusional ideas about the neighbors, but observers noted that Inez encouraged Bessie in the delusion. The sisters further insisted that Inez was 45 years old and Bessie in her fifties, although their actual ages at this time were 72 and 77 respectively.
>
> The admitting physician felt that the sisters were quite well oriented, although they suffered from occasional memory lapses and had no insight. There was evidence that Inez had suffered a cerebrovascular accident about two years prior to admission,

with minimal residual impairment. The admitting diagnosis for both sisters was chronic brain syndrome due to arteriosclerotic cerebrovascular disease. The physician noted that both patients gave the same history.

The sisters were the youngest of six children and had lived in the family homestead for most of their lives. Both of their parents had died in 1927, approximately six months apart. The patients' oldest sister was the "foundation of the family" and the main outside interpersonal contact of the patients. When she died in 1949, Bessie and Inez were said to "go to pieces." Neither of the sisters had ever held a job and neither had married, although both of them dated minimally in their youth.

Their sexual and moral standards were very high and they did not drink. Before their illness, Bessie and Inez were said to be quite independent of each other, living in separate parts of the house, buying their own food, and handling their own finances.

Almost from the time of admission to hospital, Inez was plagued by physical illnesses including hypertension, headaches, and several bouts of pneumonia. She appeared retarded, easily led, hypochondriacal, and dependent. Although she always agreed with Bessie on delusions, she was passive and cooperative. Bessie was definitely dominant and protective toward her sister. Inez died about two years after entering the hospital. Thereafter, Bessie mellowed greatly and became the favorite of the ward staff, because of her lively personality. A mental status examination at the age of 87 revealed minimal organic brain damage. While she didn't admit to any delusions or hallucinations, it was noted that her old clothes had to be shown to her frequently or she began to think that they had been stolen. She also guarded her bed area constantly and would let no other patient near it.

Paranoia as an Associated Feature

The disorders with associated or secondary paranoia include schizophrenia of late life, organic mental disorders, and paranoia occurring with terminal illness.

Schizophrenia in Late Life. In schizophrenia in late life, it may be said that mental disorganization is even more prominent than in paranoia. Inasmuch as schizophrenia represents a "carryover" from earlier years, the psychodynamics and other features are similar to those in younger age groups. An interesting question is whether aging itself can have an effect on schizophrenia. There does appear to be evidence suggesting certain general types of age-related effects on schizophrenic and paranoid conditions (Verwoerdt, 1981). Hallucinations become less frequent and less exciting in chronic paranoid schizophrenia, although in schizophrenia with late-life onset, threatening or exciting hallucinations occur often. Psychotic motor activity tends to decrease with aging. Delusions may remain unaffected by aging, become less prominent, or even disappear in the course of aging. These latter effects may be explained by the development of physical illness, which facilitates recathexis of the body. In some cases of long-standing schizophrenia, aged schizophrenics may leave the hospital after some decades, when they are usually placed in simple boarding-home settings. This is further evidence that the aging process has a pathoplastic effect on certain schizophrenics.

Organic Mental Disorders with Associated Paranoid Symptoms. Organic mental disorders with associated paranoid symptoms include organic hallucinosis and delusional syndrome as well as dementia. Transient paranoid reactions are not unusual in patients who have deafness, visual impairment, and various medical and surgical illnesses. Typical for the paranoid phenomena, secondary to cerebral decompensation, is the lack of sophistication and systematization of delusions. Such delusional ideas are very fluctuant. It is as if the patient improvises on the spot, changing his tune without regard to consistency. The paranoid delusions or hallucinations tend to clear up as the patient's overall condition improves.

The following case of organic delusional syndrome illustrates fantasies and massive projection in an organically impaired patient.

> An 87-year-old woman had paranoid delusions for two years. Organic factors included mild dementia and severe visual and auditory impairments. The patient had the delusional idea that in the apartment above her, a man was spying on her. Hence, she turned off the lights in her own apartment at night, especially in the bathroom. That way the spy could not see her. Subsequently, however, she developed the delusion that the walls of her apartment were transparent. Finally, she had the delusion that there was a woman upstairs who could read her mind, a woman who was dying. This was apparently a projection of her own self and the end of her life.

Paranoia in Terminal Illness. There may be massive projection, indicating severe decompensation, in terminal illness. For example, a patient with terminal leukemia had the delusion of spreading a terrible odor through the hospital. Another patient with end-stage renal disease expressed the idea that her husband was already dead, and that the ward nurse was dying.

Conclusion

In this chapter the author has considered paranoid decompensation in the context of a three-stage framework—depression, hypochondriasis, and psychosis. The attainment of gratitude was viewed as an antidotal element counteracting the envy, jealousy, and vindictiveness associated with paranoid decompensation. Paranoid phenomena are universal in the psychopathology of all ages, but interestingly enough, are especially prominent in late life. Of all the psychogenic disorders listed in DSM-III, paranoia is the only one with age of onset given at middle age or late life. An interesting question is whether paranoia or paranoid decompensation is an age-specific phenomenon. The clinical observations and the line of reasoning here presented suggest that this may well be the case.

References

American Psychiatric Association (1980), *Diagnostic and Statistical Manual of Mental Disorders,* 3rd ed. Washington, DC: American Psychiatric Association.

Bridge, T. P., & Wyatt, R. Z. (1980), Paraphrenia: Paranoid states of late life. I. European research. *J. Amer. Geriat. Soc.,* 28:193–200.

Brink, T. L. (1980), Geriatric paranoia: Case report illustrating behavioral management. *J. Amer. Geriat. Soc.,* 28:519–522.

——— Capri, D., DeNeeve, V., Janakes, C., Oliveira, C. (1979), Hypochondriasis and paranoia: Similar delusional systems in an institutionalized geriatric population. *J. Nerv. & Ment. Disease,* 167:224–228.

Eisdorfer, C. (1980), Paranoia and schizophrenic disorders in late life. In: *Handbook of Geriatric Psychiatry,* ed. E. W. Busse & D. G. Blazer. New York: Van Nostrand Reinhold, pp. 329–337.

Erikson, E. H. (1959), Identity and the Life Cycle. *Psychological Issues,* Monogr. 1. New York: International Universities Press.

Fish, F. (1960), Senile schizophrenia. *J. Ment. Scien.,* 106:938–946.

Gralnick, A. (1942), Folie à deux—The psychosis of association. *Psychiat. Quart.,* 16:230–263.

Herbert, M. E., & Jacobson, S. (1967), Late paraphrenia. *Amer. J. Psychiat.,* 113:461–469.

Kay, D. W. K. (1963), Late paraphrenia and its bearing on the aetiology of schizophrenia. *Act. Psychiat. Scand.,* 39:159.

——— Roth, M. (1961), Environmental and hereditary factors in the schizophrenia of old age (late paraphrenia) and their bearing on the general problem of causation in schizophrenia. *J. Ment. Scien.,* 107:649–686.

Klein, M. (1957), Envy and gratitude. In: *Envy and Gratitude and Other Works,* 1946–1963. ed. R. E. Money-Kyrle. London: The Hogarth Press and The Institute of Psychoanalysis, pp. 176–235.

Kraepelin, E. (1919), *Dementia Praecox and Paraphrenia.* reprint. New York: Krieger, 1971.

McNiel, J. N., Verwoerdt, A., & Peak, D. (1972), Folie à deux in the aged. Review and case report of role reversal. *J. Amer. Geriat. Soc.,* 20:316–323.

Roth, M. (1955), The natural history of mental disorder in old age. *J. Ment. Scien.,* 101:281–301.

Swanson, D. W., Bohnert, P. J., & Smith, J. A. (1970), *The Paranoid.* Boston: Little, Brown.

Verwoerdt, A. (1981), *Clinical Geropsychiatry,* 2nd ed. Baltimore: Williams & Wilkins, pp. 79–97.

5

THE IMPACT OF MASSIVE PSYCHIC TRAUMA AND THE CAPACITY TO GRIEVE EFFECTIVELY: LATER LIFE SEQUELAE

HENRY KRYSTAL, M.D.

The words of Koheleth, the son of David, King in Jerusalem:
    For in much wisdom is much grief:
    And he that increaseth knowledge
    increaseth sorrow.

Ecclesiastes 1:18

Introduction

This chapter will focus on the process of integration and healing in posttraumatic states, particularly in elderly people who are survivors of massive psychic trauma. This can be best understood by first reviewing the relevant clinical observations that have stimulated theoretical advances in the understanding of psychic traumatization. The development and functions of affect, affect tolerance, and the relationship of affect to psychic trauma and its sequelae, will also be elaborated. Finally, the process and limits of mourning, healing, integration, and therapeutic interventions will be discussed.

Review

The striking constellation of sequelae observed in survivors of the Nazi Holocaust, have demanded revisions to Freud's classical psychoanalytic concepts of psychic trauma (Krystal, 1968c). These clinical observations include: problems of persistent unmanageable aggression, affect lameness, submissiveness, and certain characterological observations: "Many of the male survivors tend to be permanently inhibited in their ability for sexual initiative and potency in a manner reminding us of the ethological concept of the 'defeated' male" (Krystal, 1968b, p. 3). Many survivors were observed to be grossly inhibited in their intellectual function, memory, and interest, reflecting possibly an overcompliance with the Nazi attempt to reduce the Jews to the status of dumb slaves. There seemed to be a general collapse of the personality with a broadly based loss of ability to trust others, enjoy life, or initiate action. Expression of affect was often totally blocked with the exception of anger or demands. In addition, an exceedingly high proportion of survivors, between 30 and 75 percent, manifested some form of psychosomatic disorder (Krystal, 1971).

The difficulties in understanding psychic trauma and its aftereffects in terms of the economic view of metapsychology—that the sheer intensity of stimuli cause traumatization—were not totally surprising. Freud had such difficulties as well, moving him to postulate the death instinct theory to explain his observations of repetitive dreams in posttraumatic states; an observation he could not explain solely in terms of discharge phenomena. Although Freud tried to patch up the quantitative view of trauma in "Beyond the Pleasure Principle" (1920) it was his inability to explain some of the posttraumatic phenomena, such as the repetition compulsion, in terms of the hydraulic conceptualization of the pleasure principle that lead him to search for the " 'daemonic' force at work" (Freud, 1920, p. 35). However, what Freud tried to retain at that time, namely the quantitative view of trauma and the stimulus barrier, was not tenable because it resulted in the misleading conclusion that trauma was caused by the intensity of stimuli. In contrast, Krystal (1970) has suggested that it is the meaning of an experience that posed the challenge and generated the affective response, not the intensity alone. Krystal (1970) revised the concept of the "stimulus barrier" from a passive barrier against impinging excitation that could be overwhelmed by a sufficiently large stimulus, to the totality of the apparatus involved in information processing, perception, registration, and evaluation. In other words, "the stimulus barrier is conceptualized actively as the total of the ego's protection against traumatization. Indeed, the effectiveness of the stimulus barrier is also influenced by the intersystemic tensions; problems of guilt and instinctual impulses may be considered predispositions to traumatization" (Krystal, 1970, pp. 1–2).

Psychic trauma needed to be understood in terms of the psychic reality of the individual—how he experienced and interpreted the experience. Thus, all the memories and the nature of self-, object-, and world-representations would be involved in the shaping of the impact of a potentially traumatic life experience. This led Krystal to the conclusion that much of the pathological consequences of massive psychic trauma in Holocaust survivors reflected their confrontation with death and the "destruction of 'basic trust' or, feeling of security and belief in the general benevolence and causality of the world" (Krystal, 1971, p. 24).

Coupled with the meaning of the trauma, the role of affects and affect tolerance needed to be explored as well, in order to understand the role of a stimulus barrier. It seemed that Stern's observations (1951a, 1951b, 1953, 1968a, 1968b) about traumatic experiences, pointed to an effect of emotional overwhelming both in the adult and in the infant. Stern described the "catatonoid reaction" which was a massive shutdown in af-

fective responses in overwhelming states (1951a and b); and
Niederland (1961) and Lifton (1968) described patterns of
blocking and inhibition of emotions and other functions in traumatic states.

Further developments followed, including a significant
book on psychic trauma edited by Furst (1967). In that volume,
Anna Freud, clearly stated that the term *psychic trauma* was in
danger of becoming useless.

> Like everyone else I have tended to use the term "trauma"
> rather loosely up to now, but I shall find it easier to avoid
> this in the future. Whenever I am tempted to call an event
> in a child's or adult's life "traumatic" I shall ask myself some
> further questions. Do I mean that the event was upsetting;
> that it was significant for altering the course of further de-
> velopment; that it was pathogenic? Or do I really mean
> traumatic in the sense of the word, i.e., putting ego functions
> and ego mediation out of action [A. Freud, 1967, p. 242].

Furst (1967) thought that the traumatic neuroses could
provide an important departure for the reconsideration of the
concept of trauma by providing a model of the abrupt overwhelming experience, followed by a "regression to archaic in-
stinctive levels of function . . ." (p. 20). He felt that the outcome
of trauma could be judged by the relative degree of success in
mastering the traumatic stimulus, but that the "relationship of
trauma to pathology is obligatory; it is implicit in the traumatic
event itself. Whether or not the pathology persists will depend
on posttraumatic developments. The traumatic neuroses appear to substantiate Freud's view that while individuals differ
in their degree of susceptibility to trauma, a limit exists in every
case beyond which even the most efficacious stimulus barrier
will fail" (Furst, 1967, p. 20).

The contributions of these researchers provided the setting
for a reconsideration of the traumatic process. However, two

additional elements needed to be examined, (1) a study of the development and function of affects, including a genetic view of affects and the signal function of affects; (2) a more thorough exploration of affect tolerance.

The Genetic View of Affects

Quite remarkably, the understanding of the epigenesis of emotions, the developmental lines of affect, and the role of regressive phenomena, has not been clarified until quite recently. Schur (1955) has been the initiator and the most important explorer of this area. Other important contributors include Engel (1962a, 1962b), Krystal (1962), and Schmale (1964). The author has reviewed in detail the history of these developments elsewhere (Krystal, 1974, 1977), and will restrict the present discussion to an outline of those constructs which have an immediate bearing on the problems of trauma.

The infantile affective responses may best be understood as affect precursors, representing general and unmodulated physiological mass reactions. The two most conspicuous infantile patterns are the state of quiescence or well-being, and, the distress pattern. A third pattern, the cataleptic response disappears in the human after two months (Papousek and Papousek, 1975). Cataleptic responses are found throughout the animal kingdom and consist of "freezing" patterns of immobility accompanied by widespread inhibition. It is important to keep this response in mind, in reference to the "freezing" patterns that are encountered in the adult catastrophic patterns.

Emotions normally follow a developmental line that matures though differentiation, verbalization and desomatization. Accordingly, the two patterns of affect precursors evolve into specific emotions. Out of the state of well-being evolve the "welfare affects", which are generally experienced as pleasurable. From the pattern of distress evolves those emotions which are experienced as painful, the "emergency affects" (Rado, 1969).

In the process of maturation, emotions become more differentiated, and through verbalization they can be recognized more precisely. This developmental process can evolve and mature, providing more and more information about the nature of specific affects. Conversely, the process can regress, with loss of the capacity for differentiation and desomatization, and the result that affects manifest themselves in a physiological, physical, and nonspecific way. These often psychosomatic and undifferentiated manifestations of affect have no cognitive elements and offer little useful information about what is being experienced by the individual. For example an "attack" of asthma yields little information about the underlying affective states, although one can observe the physiological correlates of emotions quite in excess.

The infant's response to distress takes a global form, characterized by its total body involvement and by automatic responses. Painful affects are at first undifferentiated. Then a variety of developments, including neurological maturation, body image formation, the establishment of nuclei of self-representation, and object representations facilitate the separate recognition of pain as a distinct entity. There can be no adult-type pain experience until the central and peripheral nervous system is adequately matured, and until a self-representation is formed in which the body image is the core of the self experience. However, the child's autonomic nervous system is so labile that affect can be transformed into pain instantaneously, as happens when anxiety is experienced as colic. Thus, another example of regression in regard to affect function is seen in those conditions in which pain, again, becomes part of affect responses. Painful affects in traumatized adults, such as anxiety, depression, and aggression are also prone to dedifferentiation and resomatization and then can be experienced as physical pain. This phenomenon is quite common in posttraumatic states, and the history of trauma should be suspected in pain-prone personalities.

Other affects can be similarly converted into painful physical symptoms. This regressive process takes its origins from the infant's affective responses which are somatic. The infant is not protected from the overwhelming physiological experience of painful affect, afforded by the later acquisition of verbalization and desomatization. These physiological (prepsychological) distress states mobilize so much pain and painful affects that they can be considered the forerunners of mortal dread—not a fear of dying, but an enormous and overwhelming anxiety. In individuals who were traumatized in infancy and childhood, this mortal dread is linked with feelings of helplessness, immobility, and suffocation. It begins a series of unconscious pathogenic reactions which represent the trauma syndrome. Extraordinary traumatization, for example the infant experiencing a hostile rejection, morbidly reinforces the commonly occurring biotraumata resulting from normally occurring frustrations and separations, and the reaction to danger becomes permanently excessive (Stern, 1968a, 1968b). The adult's mortal dread, with feelings of impending annihilation, mobilization, and suffocation was interpreted by Stern as the reexperiencing of the infant's panic and total stress reaction resulting from the absence of the indispensable mother. The traumatic event sets in place a regressive nidus in which painful or overwhelming affects can be dedifferentiated and gain more primitive expression.

Affects Utilized as Signals

While signal anxiety is the classic alerting affect, mobilized by all painful states, in fact, all affects function as signals. When low intensities of affect are experienced, the painful affects mobilize defenses to ward off flooding of the ego functions. To be useful as signals, affects must have undergone a process of development and maturation, of differentiation from common precursors to specific affects, as well as verbalization and desomatization. Undifferentiated affect precursors, such as Valenstein's "primal affects" (1962) or Engel's "primary affects of displeasure" (1962b), are not utilizable as signals since they are mostly somatic, vague, uncontrollable, and their cognitive aspects are primitive in form and content.

Much of this process of differentiation, verbalization, and desomatization takes place very early in infancy, and continues a slow, gradual development through later life. The process reaches its highest speed in infancy and continues at a brisk pace in latency when parents and teachers are actively engaged in helping children to name and differentiate emotions and to use them as information rather than as direct action. ("Talk, don't yell—don't hit your sister—you are jealous that she has an ice cream still and you finished yours!") In adolescence, the process is revived in connection with the mourning, which has to do with the need to give up the attachment to the infantile self and object-representations, and particularly, the expectation of future gratification from them. If it is done successfully, then a self-representation consolidation is accomplished which E. H. Erikson (1959) (somewhat imprecisely) called "ego identity." But, affect differentiation, verbalization, and desomatization fluctuate throughout life. Sometimes there are regressions. At other times, even in old age, one may move ahead and develop the state of one's affects to a point that they are even more useful as signals.

Certain responses such as the early distress–anger response is apparent from birth. Next, the social smile becomes an early, recognizable affective state. These developments take place in the context of the mother–child relationship. The good, competent parent takes pride in discerning the early differentiation within the infant's vocalizations, and in being able to recognize the nature of the infant's need and instantly fulfill it. In so doing, the process of differentiation is encouraged. Since signals (vocalization) corresponding to specific needs get quicker and more accurate responses from caring parents, the child is further rewarded for specialization in vocalization and eventually for accurate verbalization. This development is greatly enhanced by the acquisition of language in childhood. Helping children to recognize and name their emotions is part of ordinary parenting. Child therapists have always recognized the need to help children in treatment to recognize their feelings and to verbalize them.

Previously, Krystal (1970, 1974, 1977) has stressed that when the emotions become normally differentiated, verbalized, and desomatized, and when an individual develops the capacity for some reflective self-awareness, then he makes the observation: "I am experiencing a feeling." However, in the ordinary practice of medicine, not all patients have this capacity. It is quite common for adults to be unable to name their feelings, or to distinguish one from another. The affects remain undifferentiated. Some people cannot tell whether they are tired, bored, depressed, angry, or hungry when they are "out of sorts." One patient, whose parents were both Holocaust survivors, reported that *upset* was the only word that she ever heard used in her parents' home.

Individuals who have particular difficulty with their emotions—in that their affects are not differentiated and are not useful as signals—are likely to be found in one of three groups: as psychosomatic patients, as substance addicted, or as those with a history of severe trauma. These three conditions may be viewed either as an arrest or a regression in affect development (Krystal, 1974, 1977). In other words, when affects are undifferentiated, they are not useful as information to the individual. Under these circumstances people tend either to become very stoical, ignoring all mental and physical danger signals, or, they become very frightened of being overwhelmed by them. The stoics are predisposed to develop a stiff posture, expressionless faces, and psychosomatic diseases. Those who fear the physical aspects of their emotions try to block them with whatever works—often drugs. Posttraumatic patients as demonstrated by Holocaust survivors, especially concentration camp survivors, have a very high rate of psychosomatic diseases and serious problems with their emotions, reflecting this process of affect regression.

Affect Tolerance

In addition to clarifying the epigenetic development of affects, it is necessary to elaborate the role of affect tolerance. How well one can manage and respond to a particular affective state will influence dramatically the individual's experience of the affect and his reactions, and hence the consequences of the affective stimulus.

Zetzel's classic papers have established the necessity to tolerate anxiety (1949) and depression (1965) for emotional growth. Physicians frequently confuse pain threshold with pain tolerance. Pain threshold is an inborn tendency, not significantly changed in the course of life. Pain tolerance, like the tolerance of affects, is an acquired function, albeit, as Jaffe (1969) pointed out, there may be some constitutional factors. People who have a good tolerance for pain may have a poor affect tolerance, since the latter has to do with the way they experience, interpret, and react to having the emotions.

Affect tolerance involves a variety of resources of the ego which make possible the conscious experience of affective emotions. The capacity to handle emotions adaptively, depends on the intensity and duration of the affects, and these in turn, may depend on the nature of all three psychic structures. Variations in aggressive drive impose a special burden by virtue of generating feelings of guilt which interfere with affective tolerance. Individuals differ greatly in their capacity to tolerate affects. Low tolerance to painful affect increases dysphoria and may perpetuate the intolerance. In many instances, helping patients to improve their affect tolerance is a necessary preliminary phase of psychotherapy. This requires special emphasis on the nature of the patient's affects and how they are handled and experienced by the patient (Krystal and Raskin, 1970; Krystal, 1975).

In contrast, individuals who can experience an emotion with tolerance, generally feel secure that a state of affective arousal is justified by their life experience, that it makes sense, and that having accomplished its purpose, or run its course, it will stop. Traumatization in childhood, however, may result in a lifelong dread of affect and a warding off of affectivity. While the difficulty is more frequent with painful feelings, some individuals develop a fear of all emotions, even of being in love or being sexually excited, viewing these emotions as dangerously irrational, uncontrollable, and inescapable.

Several factors are important in developing affect tolerance. These include the availability of diverse object-investments and possibilities for self-gratification, such that an individual is not exclusively bound to the source of painful affect arousal, without getting respite. Patterns of affect tolerance depend heavily on the internalizations of early love-objects. At the center of this process is the competent mother who allows the child to have emotions to the intensity which he can handle, but who intercedes prior to the child being overwhelmed. When the mother does intercede, she often depends on the child's distractability. The adult, similarly, may try to distract himself from the painful affect, but depending on prior childhood–maternal experiences and internalizations, the burden of his affects may dominate consciousness, and for their duration may exclude the possibility of effective distraction. For example, in the presence of excessive superego pressures, not sufficiently modulated in early life, the patient may feel that his painful state is fully warranted and should be perpetuated. Conversely, if the individual has internalized a benign parental superego that retains the provision that no matter what the offense, the individual always retains the right to live and to obtain gratification of his basic needs, perpetuation of painful affects will diminish.

The level of mastery the individual has come to expect or demand of himself also will greatly influence his experience of painful affects (Zetzel, 1965). Demanding complete affect mastery may result in the anticipation of affective stimulation as being highly stressful and therefore rigidly avoided. In order to recapture the childhood distractability and pleasure-seeking avoidance of pain, an individual may seek to restore the child's organic imperfection of his brain. Thus, the customs of people of all ages and places include the use of alcohol and other drugs to numb the emotions temporarily (Krystal, Moore, and Dorsey, 1967). The use of drugs, or other means of blocking emotions becomes a problem only if all feelings have to be blocked; a situation which predisposes to drug dependence. However, in many instances, the use of drugs or other temporary distractions actually extends one's ability to handle the feelings over the long term, and thereby represents an asset.

Throughout infancy and childhood, the parent–child relationship serves as the cornerstone for the development of affect tolerance. For example, the parent's emotional availability to the child during the phases of separation and individuation, especially the rapprochement phase, encourages affect tolerance, promoting with each ebb and flow a greater capacity to tolerate anxiety related to separation. Provision of this leads to the child's increasing capacity to diversify his object relations and enrich his ability to obtain gratification from alternative sources.

During the latency period, parents do countless things to enhance the child's affect tolerance. For example, parents teach and encourage the child to assume functions of time-orientation, in which the child learns that he or she can tolerate pain and painful affects for a short time and then for increasingly longer stretches of time, and for different objectives. The child's ego ideal is appealed to in a variety of "I can take it" activities. In addition, the good parent continues to function as a temporary stimulus barrier in the sense of trauma prevention (Krystal, 1978a). The affects are not allowed to exceed, for too long, the child's ability to maintain his poise. When it happens that the child does lose control, the parent steps in, offers support, and may even later help the child deny that he had ever lost control.

The modes by which parents promote the development of affect tolerance goes beyond their serving as objects of identification. They also have unconscious expectations as to the capability of their child to tolerate painful affects. These expectations are communicated to the child by what they allow him to handle. The parents who step in every time the child's emotion reaches minimum distress, may leave the child with a fear of affect, a lack of self-confidence, and an inordinate dependence. On the other hand, affect intolerance can be exacerbated by the parents shaming the child for expressing emotions, leading to negation of affect and resomatization.

The process of developing affect tolerance continues to be a major concern in adolescence. This centers around the operations of adolescence, the major portion of which hinges on effective grieving, related to the removal of oedipal ties to one's parents, and the giving up of one's idealized childhood self-image (Katan, 1951). This is accomplished piecemeal over a long period of time and is coincidental with the acceptance of disappointments and diminishing idealized expectations of one's parents and one's self. In order to be able to grieve effectively, one has to be able to bear depression and manage one's grief. Furthermore, the mourner must be able to make grief tolerable by being able to distract himself or herself, and then return to the grieving periodically without massive avoidance or denial. From this point of view, the achievements of affect tolerance, particularly during adolescence, become essential to the ability to "keep in touch" with reality. Every perception of reality which requires giving up something valued or accepting something undesirable, necessitates the experiencing and bearing of a number of painful emotions. The process of developing affect tolerance is subject to regressions and advances. For example, in old age one may very well develop better than ever affect tolerance through attaining wisdom and "catching on" to what emotions are all about. Sometimes this happens with the help of a therapist, counselor, or religious leader, and sometimes as a result of resources intrinsic to the individual.

Adult Catastrophic Psychic Trauma

Having reviewed in brief the development and functions of affect and affect tolerance, it becomes possible to explore some relevant questions regarding catastrophic psychic trauma. It is important to distinguish between trauma and the two other kinds of emergencies related to intense emotions. This distinction is important in light of the prevalent overuse of the word *trauma* to mean every harmful affective experience (A. Freud, 1967). The first is the panic resulting from the dread of the cognitive element in the affect—the fear of the magical powers of one's wishes. This fear is most commonly related to the dread of one's aggression. The second emergency is related to affect tolerance. Here the danger is one of becoming overwhelmed with one's own emotion resulting in a flooding that disorganizes the executive functions of the ego. Instead of being able to use the affect for information, one becomes terrified by the physiological or expressive element of the emotion, setting up a vicious cycle that perpetuates the problem (Krystal, 1982a). However, neither of these two patterns of psychiatric emergency can be considered to be true psychic trauma. The author proposes that the term *catastrophic psychic trauma* be used for a specific reaction pattern, as described below.

When one comes to the conclusion that one is facing inescapable, unmodifiable peril, the affective pattern changes from anxiety, the activating signal of preventable danger, to the "catatonoid reaction" (Stern, 1951a and b). This emotional shift may be considered the initiation of the traumatic state (Krystal, 1978a). It actually involves a surrender pattern which is universal throughout the animal kingdom (Richter, 1957; Seligman, 1975). With the surrender to what is perceived as inevitable, inescapable, immediate danger, the "catatonoid reaction" emerges as a new affective process (Stern, 1951a and b).

This reaction consists of a paralysis of initiative, followed by varying degrees of immobilization leading to automatic obedience. At the same time there is a numbing process by which all affective and pain responses are blocked, a phenomenon Minkowski (1946) called "affective anesthesia." Lifton extended this idea to "psychic closing off" (1968). Lifton's broader conception is useful because a further aspect of the traumatic process is one in which there is a progressive constriction of cognitive processes. Perception, conscious registration, including memory formation, recall, and problem solving are all impaired (Krystal, 1978a). Finally, just a mere vestige of self-observing functions is preserved (Petty, personal communication, 1975). This process may culminate in psychogenic death (Krystal, 1978a, 1982a). Alternately, it is possible for this process to stay at the point where a degree of "psychic closing off" has been accomplished which permits a certain automatonlike behavior. This can be a state necessary for survival in situations of subjugation such as prison and concentration camps (Krystal, 1968a). The picture of humans in a state of robotlike, automaton behavior is observable not just in these extreme situations. A number of long-term, institutional situations produce apathy, boredom, and withdrawal and finally produce a characteristic dullness. In the days when people stayed for years in state hospitals, it was a psychiatric commonplace that regardless of the admission diagnosis, after 20 or more years, all the inmates looked and acted alike.

In order to understand the realities of massive psychic trauma, it is necessary to distinguish between those sequelae which are direct continuations of the traumatic state, and those which are secondary. Studies of the survivors of Nazi persecution showed that there were a multitude of aftereffects resulting from various ways in which the individuals were affected by the abuse, genocide, uprooting, and loss of their homes and homeland. The clinical presentations are complex and the multitude of aftereffects has tended to cloud the picture, accounting for delay in the recognition of the traumatic process and its sequelae.

Massive trauma shatters the illusion of omnipotence, diminishing radically the usefulness of those unconscious fantasies derived from the beneficent experiences in early life that represent a kind of essential backdrop of secure feelings, or "basic trust" (Erikson, 1950). Without this basic trust, normal functioning is not possible. This trust derives in part from the earliest experiences, which may have been nonverbal or even nonsymbolic. The result is that the insecurity arising from the shattering of one's denial of existential vulnerability may not be manifest particularly in anxious ideas which require verbalization or symbolization. What is seen instead is a hypervigilance, a physical hyperactivity, and nightmares (Niederland, 1961; Krystal, 1968a, 1968b; Krystal and Niederland, 1968). In general, these are poorly responsive to psychotherapy reflecting perhaps the importance of the preverbal and presymbolic components of this lost "basic trust," and the consequent inability to engage in an expressive psychotherapy.

Furthermore, Stern (1951b) believed that the helpless surrender in the catatonoid state also represents a "primal depression." Follow-up studies of survivors show a continuation of depressive affect as well as depressive life-styles in a predominant number of survivors (Krystal and Niederland, 1968; Krystal, 1971). This observation has ethological correlations. Seligman's (1975) review of animal studies shows a continuation in both traumatized adults and untraumatized offspring of patterns of submission, helplessness, and what may be called the equivalent of depressive and masochistic patterns in animals who had previously been subjected to severe abuse in situations of total helplessness.

Lifton has elaborated on the consequences of confrontation with death and the related themes of identification with death and with the dead (1968, 1979a, 1979b). As cogent and relevant to the understanding of posttraumatic states as these themes may be, they also are a consequence of dealing with the implication of the event—rather than the direct posttraumatic continuation of a traumatic response. Those aftereffects that are a continuation of the traumatic patterns delineate most clearly the trauma picture. Hence, this clinical picture will be described in detail, following discussion of the traumatic process as a state of stress.

Coping and Mourning

Observations, such as those by Rees and Lutkins (1967) which showed that bereaved people had a mortality rate seven times higher than that of controls, have been part of an immense literature documenting the relationship between life events and health consequences. Many studies have provided an abundance of evidence that even the normative events and misfortunes of ordinary life result in harmful aftereffects (Rahe, Meyer, Smith, Kjaer and Holmes, 1964; Gunderson and Rahe, 1974; Holmes and Rahe, 1967). If that is so, then after catastrophic trauma, lasting physical aftereffects and damages to one's homeostasis are predictable. It comes as no surprise that follow-up studies of concentration camp survivors reveal very high rates of mortality and morbidity (Eitinger, 1980).

Of course, these observations provide only the link between life events and aftereffects such as illness. The causal mechanisms need their own clarification. In order to put the extreme traumatic state in its proper context, it is best to review how ordinary stress is managed.

Caplan (1981) has cogently reviewed the issue of the multiphasic mastery of stress. Initial reactions to stress center on minimizing the evoked emotional and physiological activity. Phase I is an attempt to minimize the changes in the situation and to restore the prestress state, or to escape from the untoward developments of the stressful situation. In Phase II, if the old skills are inadequate, the subject attempts to acquire new skills to deal with the disturbance. Phase III consists of responses focused on establishing intrapsychic defenses against the dysphoric emotional arousal. Finally, in Phase IV, one sees efforts to come to terms with the event and its sequalae by intrapsychic readjustment.

Even in Phase I, where there is an adaptive response to a stressful situation, a subjective dysphoric state exists. This is associated with a deterioration of mental and intellectual function. Regularly occurring phenomena include disorders of attention, scanning, information collection, access to relevant memories that associate significant meaning to perception, judgment, planning, the capacity to implement plans, and the capacity to implement feedback. In other words, the individual's usual orderly process of externally oriented instrumental ego functioning is upset. This happens precisely when it is most important for him to be operating at his maximum effectiveness so he can best grapple with his problems (Caplan, 1981). This observation is of the highest relevance to the understanding of the traumatic process.

In catastrophic trauma states, there is a progressive constriction of all of the above listed mental functions (Krystal, 1978a). A number of factors, such as the availability of group support will determine the speed and extensiveness of the deterioration of ego function. Every stress finds each individual in a psychosocial context and the harmful effects of the stress are minimized by the cognitive guidance and emotional support that a person receives from his support group. This group may compensate for the stress-induced temporary reduction in problem-solving capacity. However, the key factor for an individual is his subjective evaluation of his capacity to deal with his situation. This includes his capacity to bear the distress. When an unsupported individual concludes that the situation is both unbearable and unmodifiable, the deterioration in ego function accelerates.

Stress conditions necessitate functioning under extreme hyperarousal. The ability to tolerate affects, critical in Phase II coping, involves a whole multitude of possible reactions to having an emotion as described earlier, and obviously has special application under stress (Krystal, 1975). The "emergency affects" are characterized by their dysphoric nature and a high degree of arousal. Hyperstimulation at first improves performance, but after a point, depending on individual variables, there is a deterioration in performance. Individuals who have not been overwhelmed before have a lower physiological arousal and a better tolerance of states of high activation (Krystal,

1982a). Highlighting the activating aspect of emotions and the discovery of the central noradrenergic pathways that operate in the regulation of anxiety suggests that persistently high states of physiological arousal may correlate directly with a persistence in posttraumatic stress disorders (Van der Kolk, Boyd, Krystal, and Greenberg, 1984). Individuals with a history of psychic trauma show a physiological hyperreactivity which is part of their hypervigilance and tendency to startle, as well as a tendency for early deterioration of performance. A tendency to panic is also present, reflecting the anticipation of the return of the traumatic state. Conversely, familiarity and comfort with a situation assures longer effective performance. For this reason there are certain preparations and drills which increase affect tolerance, in anticipation of a potential disaster, such as an airplane emergency landing or fire. The traumatized older individual may be especially vulnerable to this physiological hyperarousal.

In Phase III, during attempts to restore an effective state of control and comfort, one may use denial, isolation, and other defenses against affect, such as displacement, reversal, or blocking of an affect of a temporary nature. Finally, Phase IV may be viewed as that period dealing with the aftereffects of the disaster—those aspects of the disaster that have modified one's life, undeniably diminishing one's basic sense of trust and omnipotence. To review, the reaction to stress and its aftereffects involves cognitive, physiological, and affective components.

Caplan's model is most useful in dealing with an acutely present stress—coping. Horowitz has provided a model for dealing with the aftereffects of the untoward event, and/or with those situations that leave a person and his environment substantially changed—mourning (Horowitz, 1976). According to Horowitz, the traumatic event will result first in a shock state and then an outcry—an emergency response—such as an acute affective response of weeping, moaning, screaming, or fainting.

The conscious registration of knowledge is handled by a partial denial of the implication of the situation. The tranquil state afforded by denial is disturbed by the intrusive nature of the new perception which keeps disrupting the denial and results in a renewal of affective activation. The cognitive and affective response goes on for a short time and is terminated by denial. There is a period of rest. Soon, the ideas again intrude upon consciousness, repeating the whole cycle. This working through process goes on in waves until the work of mourning is completed and intrapsychic mastery is obtained.

These "waves," developing from what Horowitz pointed out as the intrusion into denial of thoughts about the traumatic situation, are not merely a restatement of the unhappy fact. Rather, each time the idea comes back to mind, it involves a working through of related themes having to do with the cognitive mastery and acceptance of the reality of the stress. Krupnick and Horowitz have listed these themes as follows: "1) Rage at the Source (of the serious life event), 2) Sadness Over Loss, 3) Discomfort Over (discovered personal) Vulnerability, 4) Discomfort Over (reactive) Aggressive Impulses, 5) Fear of Loss of Control Over Aggressive Impulses, 6) Guilt Over Responsibility (for inciting the event or failing to control it), 7) Fear of Similarity to the Victim, 8) Rage at Those Exempted (from a loss or injury), 9) Fear of Repetition (of the event), and 10) Survivor Guilt." (1981, p. 428). Krystal has also described the very same process (1971, pp. 15–22), the major point being that the challenge to mastery of the trauma arises from the meaning and affects one has to contend with, not the quantitative amount of stimulation as suggested by Freud.

The concept of the work of mourning is useful in considering all situations in which one deals with stress, or one has to accept any bad developments. People in disaster or stress situations also describe it as a "work of worrying" (K. T. Erikson, 1976). The process of mourning is, in fact, the process of gaining intrapsychic mastery of the loss. All stress situations involve losses. Some losses are more real and palpable, but a loss is always present, even if it is only the transient loss of one's illusion of invulnerability. The sequelae of traumatic situations frequently relate to the inability to gain this intrapsychic mastery, as for example, Shatan has described in regard to Vietnam war veterans (1973).

Not surprisingly, much of the current understanding of reactions to severe stress has arisen from studying soldiers during and after wartime. Again, the tripartite reaction to severe stress manifests itself with cognitive, affective, and physiological responses. In their report on war stress in soldiers, Bartemeier, Kubie, K. Menninger, Romano, and Whitehorn (1946), reviewed the process of becoming a psychological war casuality. The manifestations of incipient failure to maintain mastery and keep the stress within tolerable limits were first registered by irritability, "hypersensitiveness" progressing to disturbances in sleep, startle reactions, and hyperreactivity to minor stimuli with increasing involuntary self-protective motor responses. Next, there was a tendency to withdrawal into a brooding attempt to "flatten" one's emotions by whatever means available. This included drugs, isolation, a general loss of interest in comrades, food, letters from home, and even in one's welfare. At the same time, there was increasing confusion, disorganization, impaired judgment, and indecision. Observable problems related to the physiological components of emotion such as tremors, vomiting, and diarrhea, could also be observed. If no help was given at this time, the confusion, irritability, and physical instability would grow to the point of recklessness and wild and incoherent behavior. Some soldiers showed either catatonoid withdrawal or excitement which could lead to psychogenic death—sudden death caused by the heart stopping in diastole, purely from psychological reasons. However, frequently at this point, some outburst of rage, or at least other activity usually became manifest. The behavior was often maladaptive and sometimes self-destructive (Bartmeier et al., 1946, pp. 374–377).

In Koranyi's (1977) review of the "psychobiological correlates of battlefield psychiatry," he similarly found that "pushed beyond endurance," one manifests "affective chaos and cognitive distortion," as well as a "reflection of disarranged physiology." These can be identified by "hypokinetic withdrawal," or "disorganization with agitation," and "vacant, helpless, poor judgemental behaviour" or a "frozen state" (1977, p. 15).

The process by which an individual is overwhelmed and his (or her) emotional and physical resources are depleted, reveals a fundamental similarity or vulnerability between people. This also helps to counteract the tendency to think in terms of a mind–body split, by highlighting the fact that in the after-effects of traumatic experience, it is impossible to separate the psychological aftereffects from the physiological ones.

Under extreme stress situations, the affect may become unbearable. The aim of long-range adjustment is best served by maintaining the affect at a level which is not overwhelming; not only because of the dangers of disorganization, but also because otherwise one may trigger the catastrophic response of the catatonoid reaction. Lieberman (1977) has pointed out that these considerations are equally relevant in the process of aging. He suggests the need to regulate a pace that promotes affect tolerance in which the blows of reality can be assimilated and accommodation can be achieved. The crucial observation made from this review is that all stressful situations evoke certain coping responses, which are very similar, and in their essential functions are identical to mourning. The objective is to master and ideally to integrate the perception of the new situation, which always entails a new view of one's self. If the impact of the developments in one's life is such that one evaluates the new situation to be overwhelming, unbearable, unmodifiable, and unavoidable, then one may respond with the surrender pattern which initiates the catatonoid reaction and the traumatic state.

The Catastrophic Traumatic State and its Aftereffects

In those situations in which the individual's subjective evaluation of the traumatic situation leads to a catatonoid reaction, the traumatic state is initiated. Ten specific and direct aftereffects of catastrophic trauma may arise, reflecting the basic continuation of the traumatic response beyond the period of the emergency. Relevant clinical issues will now be elaborated.

1. The Recognition of and Submission to Unavoidable Danger

This development breaks down a person's core feeling of safety and invulnerability, and hence may have long-lasting consequences on psychic structure. A person's sense of security depends on a set of beliefs in his own powers, augmented by various external security resources, such as family, community, and elements of faith and religion. These include a set of illusions which promote both the denial of death and the denial of a variety of dangers, concealing the actual lack of security from calamity with which one exists. This illusion permits normal functioning. In the wake of its breakdown, some individuals cannot return to their previous personality type, and instead assume submissive "slavelike" personalities, incapable of assertive behavior (Krystal, 1968a, 1971, 1978a), or display chronic anxiety including paranoid states.

Studies of disasters, such as the Buffalo Creek flood, showed that the destruction of the community and loss of supports resulted in serious and long-lasting handicaps to the community's members (K. T. Erikson, 1976). The breakdown of ordinary, familiar supports and assumptions of security may be seen as a common element in all misfortunes and disasters. The apathetic, stuporous state of people in a disaster situation, sometimes referred to as the "disaster syndrome" (Wolfenstein, 1957), may be the common sign of the loss of one's self-reliance and executive functions, and the surrender pattern which accompanies it. The continuation of the breakdown of either the feeling of security, or of the ability to utilize community supports for one's function, seriously interferes with the resumption of normal life patterns, and impairs the maintenance of one's own sense of identity and integrity.

2. The Surrender Pattern

In the situation in which surrender to an actual external enemy has taken place, two patterns may be produced—shame and passivity. On the conscious level there may be problems with shame—either directly experienced or defended against in one of a number of ways. At the same time, one may be unable to assert oneself, which actually represents a continuation of the surrender behavior. Anguish and shame because of the inability to act assertively may also be present. This difficulty may also result, especially in the case of men, in an inability to function as a parent. The surrender to authority persists, long after the external authority disappears.

3. Catatonoid Reaction as a "Primal Depression."

Niederland has repeatedly stressed the problem survivors have with chronic recurrent depression (1961, 1968, 1981). He emphasizes that the reactions covered "the whole spectrum from masochistic character changes to psychotic depression" (1968, p. 313). Most of these depressions are not diagnosed as such, but manifest themselves in a life-style of despair, and commonly in physical symptoms of chronic tiredness, weakness, and a lack of resistance to all forms of illnesses. Depression is part of the posttraumatic picture and is not limited to the survivors of genocide. Hence it is not associated only, or chiefly, with guilt of survivorship (Krystal, 1978c).

In this context, it is relevant to reconsider Stern's (1951b) view that the catatonoid reaction also represents a primal depression. In other words, the posttraumatic depression may be viewed as the direct continuation of this aspect of the traumatic state, and not a secondary phenomenon related to guilt. Depression is an inevitable consequence of the helplessness and hopelessness of the surrender. In the state of total helplessness, pain stops and a feeling of tragic sadness is experienced. No living creature is quite the same again after having experienced its own mortality and helplessness. The reconstruction of one's feeling of security, or even faith, is never again complete. It is as if the encounter has now provided a black background upon which the rest of one's life will be painted. Never again can one diminish the dark hues in one's emotional palette. Thus, the depressive attitude in posttraumatic states represents to an important extent, the loss of the illusion of security and invulnerability, and the reaction to that loss.

A second issue is that of changes in the hedonic regulation of the organism. It is unclear whether this represents a direct continuation of the immediate posttraumatic state, or whether this reflects a kind of psychological scar formation that develops over a painful wound. Krystal believes that the hedonic quality of affects is a separately derived aspect of emotions (1981b). It has a separate anatomical and endocrine derivation (Snyder, 1980), and the hedonic quality of affects may be shifted or modified. As a result, the clinical picture of "libidinization of anxiety" may be considered such a shift, in that an affect which is usually painful becomes a source of gratification. In order to understand this phenomenon, it is necessary to consider pleasure as distinct from gratification, and pain as distinct from suffering. Furthermore, it is necessary to consider that affects, gratification, pleasure, pain, or distress may be either conscious or unconscious, or somewhere along a spectrum regarding the degree of consciousness. Additionally, one must consider that gratification may relate to excitatory or gratificatory pursuits. One may get gratification in excitatory activities like foreplay or gambling, or in gratificatory activities such as eating or orgasm. In those who survive massive adult catastrophic trauma, or infantile trauma, residual anhedonia is very common. When no pleasure is possible, one may learn to obtain gratification from pain, sometimes resulting in an attachment to painful feelings. The shift in the hedonic component of emotion may result in an "addiction" to gratification derived from consciously painful experiences (Krystal, 1981b). The burgeoning work on hedonic regulation may provide a theoretical and clinical framework to help understand the wide spectrum of masochistic and depressive phenomena in posttraumatic states. These depressive phenomena are very common and often subclinical. In posttraumatic states, people simply experience themselves and life as tragic, and the pain is accepted as an inescapable component of reality.

4. Affective Blocking

In his early observations of survivors of concentration camps, Minkowski (1946) described an affective anesthesia, the earliest reported aftereffect of the Holocaust. The same observation has since been made by others (Niederland, 1961; Lifton, 1968). Since part of the catastrophic trauma response is the blocking of the conscious registration of pain and painful affects, one may assume that one is dealing with the continuation of that numbness. The possible association between this affective blocking and alexithymia will be addressed later.

5. Continuation of "Emergency Regimes"

In a manner exactly corresponding to the depressive problems, there is a tendency to continue prior hypervigilance (Niederland, 1961, 1981; Krystal and Niederland, 1968). This may include physical anxiety responses such as startle patterns, increased muscular tension, and all those components of anxiety which are sometimes referred to as sympathetic nervous system overactivity. Once the feeling of security has been destroyed, the fear of recurrence is one of the regular aftereffects of disaster (Wolfenstein, 1957), and of individual stress (Horowitz, 1976; Krupnick and Horowitz, 1981). What survivors of disaster usually refer to in terms of the fearful expectation of the return of the traumatizing situation, for example, "I am afraid the Nazis are coming back," actually refers to an expectation of the return of the traumatic state and in particular, the return of the unbearable affective reactions. Many clinical syndromes of chronic anxiety and/or panic states need to be understood from this point of view (Krystal, 1974, 1975). In older people who experience loss and who have experienced severe infantile or adult catastrophic psychic trauma, the reaction to loss encounters them in a state of "doomsday expectation." They have lived their lives in the dread expectation that the traumatic state will return. When something bad happens, the anxiety tends to snowball and a panic state, including psychotic states, may ensue.

It is particularly important for the caretakers to keep such possibilities in mind in regard to the sequelae of infantile psychic trauma states, of which the patients have no recollection, and sometimes not even the slightest suspicion (Krystal and Raskin, 1970; Krystal, 1978a). With such patients, a therapeutic intervention of crucial importance is to address these fears. Frequently patients do not understand the nature of these apprehensions and may think that they suffer an inordinate fear of death. What they actually fear is that their mental and emotional pain will get worse and worse and go on forever. This is the closest an adult can come to imagining the return of infantile traumatic states. The descriptions of hell with eternal and ever worse torture also refer to the same fears. These fears are disabling, particularly in regard to affect tolerance. Since the emotions are experienced as heralds of the return of the disaster which almost destroyed them, the dread is transferred to all affects.

Due to the regressive phenomena of dedifferentiation and resomatization of affects, timelessness, as well as the return of the infantile traumatic views of the world and of the self, much slow work may be required to reconstruct for an individual even the present contents of such fears. It is often an enormous relief for such people to discover that someone understands the fears they have been experiencing and is able to talk about them.

The occurrence of such fears, which frequently dominate these patients' lives, may be accompanied by either somatization or frank psychosomatic diseases reflecting the dedifferentiation and resomatization of the affects, or significant addictive problems reflecting the impaired affect tolerance. When found together with alexithymia, anhedonia, attachment to painful feelings, and impairment in the capacity for self-soothing, they are indications of severe infantile trauma, even when no history is available (Krystal, 1981a). Reconstruction may not be possible, and the therapeutic intervention may be limited to the recognition that a terrible disaster took place during the patient's early life. The challenge may consist chiefly of managing and living with its aftereffects (Krystal, 1981a).

The chronic anxiety states may manifest themselves entirely in physical symptoms, particularly in the presence of alexithymia, or in terms of a cognitive set of chronic worry, rumination, and preoccupation with insecurity. Thus a survivor of the Nazi persecution might comment, when being shown the home of a new acquaintance: "Oh this would make a very good hiding place!" (E. Tanay, personal communication). Repetitive anxiety and persecutory dreams are part of this problem, as may be certain waking confusional states (Niederland, 1961, 1981). From a therapeutic perspective, the physical symptoms of anxiety may be poorly modulated by the traditional techniques of exploring the cognitive elements of the affects in psychotherapy. The therapist may need to address directly the hyperactivity states by various relaxation and retraining techniques (Krystal, 1982d).

6. Alexithymia

Many observations about the very high frequency of psychosomatic diseases in survivors of Nazi persecution have been made (Bastiaans, 1957; Niederland, 1961; Krystal and Niederland, 1968). Similarly, follow-up studies of war veterans and prisoners of war after World War II indicated an impressively consistent high rate of psychosomatic diseases in all posttraumatic studies (Cohen and Cooper, 1954; Brill and Beebe, 1955; Archibald, Long, Miller, and Tuddenham, 1962; Archibald and Tuddenham, 1965). In particular, those who were adolescents during the persecution showed a much higher rate of psychosomatic disease than the rest of the survivor population (Krystal, 1971), suggesting that the regressive potential of youth may be a condition that increases vulnerability to this posttraumatic aftereffect. This observation has a pertinence to war veterans, many of whom were still adolescents when traumatized.

The work of Marty and deM'Uzan (1963); Marty, deM'Uzan, and David (1963); Nemiah and Sifneos (1970a), and McDougall (1974) has demonstrated that prominent in psychosomatic diseases is a disturbance in cognition which they have called "operative thinking" or alexithymia (Sifneos, 1967). Both survivors and addiction prone individuals demonstrate this (Krystal, 1962, 1974, 1978a). Common findings were that the emotions of these patients were not fully differentiated. Hence they were unable to discriminate between various specific affects or to name them specifically. In addition, the patients could not verbalize the cognitive component of the affects, nor describe where they felt them. The outcome was that the affects were not useful as signals but rather were experienced as burdensome and distressing nuisances. In the face of these regressive disturbances or defects, some individuals tended to develop a stoicism, rigidity of posture and expression, and either ignored or tried to ignore all signs of physical and emotional distress. Consequences of this include a propensity to develop psychosomatic disease. Other people affected by the alexithymic inability to use affects as signals, develop a dread of the physiological component of emotions and try to cope by use of drugs, predisposing to drug abuse.

Alexithymia commonly coincides with the clinical diagnosis of psychosomatic diseases or substance abuse and dependence (Krystal, 1974, 1978a, 1978b, 1978c, 1981a, 1982a). In both groups, posttraumatic situations are common suggesting a correlation between alexithymia and a history of severe trauma. This can be war related, or, as studies of alcoholism and drug dependence reveal, can be related to infantile psychic trauma of a severe degree (Krystal, 1982b, 1982c). The infantile traumatic state results from the nature of affects in infancy being undifferentiated and mostly somatic, overwhelming the immature individual. Under these circumstances, it is readily understandable that all affects are dreaded and blocked in every way possible. Such an experience results in an arrest of the genetic development of affect, in contrast to the aftereffects of adult trauma which are a regression in affective development.

Alexithymia represents the most severe and frequent block that prevents individuals from utilizing psychoanalytic psychotherapy (Krystal, 1971, 1982a). The differentiation between patients whose alexithymia represents a regression, as opposed to those whose alexithymia represents an arrest in development has therapeutic implications. Although it is not yet possible to distinguish between these two groups, this distinction will be essential because it is likely that those patients who have alexithymia based upon a regression in affective development, may be initially prepared through a modified psychotherapy, so that the rehabilitation will become more practical (Krystal, 1979, 1982a). Otherwise, these patients are not able to utilize their emotions in the psychotherapeutic process. They experience only the physiological components of the emotions and in a way that is not useful to them. In this instance there is a danger that psychotherapy may evoke more unmanageable affect, exacerbating psychosomatic disorders, and hence may be contraindicated (Sifneos, 1967, 1973). A major consideration in the future capability to treat and rehabilitate posttraumatic states will depend upon the ability to diagnose and treat alexithymia, thereby promoting effective psychotherapeutic intervention in regard to all the other aftereffects of the traumatic states.

7. Continuation of Cognitive Constriction

The traumatic constriction of all of the cognitive functions, including memory, judgment, problem solving, discrimination, and perception may manifest itself in one of two basic patterns. The first is a continuation of a general dullness, obtuseness, and lowering of performance in familial and occupational spheres. Frequently, posttraumatic survivors limit themselves to very unambitious low-grade work. For instance, people who have been in jails or state hospitals for a long time are generally portrayed as having this burned-out stance. The second pattern is a tendency to "freeze" suddenly when under any pressure. This may happen at odd and unpredictable times, and be manifest as blundering or dumb behavior. The blunderer's behavior reveals a combination of poor judgment and poor decision making, with physical incoordination. Excessive anxiety and physical tension add to the impairment resulting from the cognitive difficulty.

8. *Pseudophobia*

Pseudophobia is related to the general tendency to create traumatic screens. Traumatic screens are memories behind which are hidden the memory traces of a traumatic event. A memory relating to a traumatic event may both represent and conceal the risk of the recollection of an event. The difficulties resemble classical phobias, in the sense that there is an irrational fear of a certain object which may become disabling. However, the pseudophobias differ from classical phobias in that there is no repressed unconscious wish or symbolic expression involved. Instead, the pseudophobia represents a working over of the fear of the return of the psychic trauma state. In these states, the patients frequently complain that they are afraid of some specific thing, feared in the real past, such as uniformed men or the sound of explosions. Some individuals may also be afraid of their own dreams which represent ongoing, unremitting "reruns" of the traumatic past. Sleeping pills are taken often in order to suppress dreaming rather than to regulate sleep. The chronic intense anxiety may be represented in phobialike syndromes. Unlike the true phobias, which have behind them a structure of fantasies and conflicts which make up the neurosis, here the phobic objects are traumatic screens. They are a private "shorthand" representation of the dreaded and expected return of the traumatic state. Realistic danger situations may become even more terrifying if in addition the fear of the return of the infantile trauma is aroused. For example, the childhood fear of abandonment, referring to specific traumatic situations, may exacerbate the older person's fear of loss and isolation. The unverbalizable dread of the return of the infantile trauma state turns the fear of loss into something horrific and overwhelming.

9. *"Dead to the World" Reactions*

The "dead to the world" reactions are the most devastating aftereffects of psychic trauma and have been best described by

Murray (1967). He defined this either as a cessation of one's affect—experiencing part of one's self as almost dead, or, as a cessation of the orientation to conscious life—experiencing part of one's external world as being dead. In addition, one's social world or spiritual world may be experienced as being dead. Being dead to one's inner world means reaching a situation of cessation, the goal being to stand for no life at all. Murray also pointed out that some people stop at the point of near cessation; being as good as dead. An illustration of such a character is given by Wallant (1962) in *The Pawnbroker*.

The tragic depletion of one's life resources, a picture of life in death, has been referred to in the Holocaust literature by many authors, under many names including "a break in the lifeline" (Venzlaff, 1963). The idea of the traumatic state as a primal depression seems relevant as these states of chronic surrender, self-diminution, and cessation have much to do with the causation and conceptions of suicide (Shneidman, 1976a). The idea of "cessation" is common to the catastrophic adult traumatic state as well as to suicide patients (Shneidman, 1976b). Studies of suicide notes also reveal that, in order to give themselves up to death, suicidal patients undergo a constriction of their cognitive functions similar to that described earlier in this chapter.

This leads to the question of the aftereffects of the confrontation with death. As already mentioned, Lifton (1968, 1979a, 1979b) has elaborated on the aftereffects of confrontation with death, as an identification with death and dying. It is virtually impossible to separate the aftereffects of the continuing cognitive constriction, from those of the identification with the dead. This is why the idea of the "dead to the world" identity and behavior has such great poignancy for us. A special related issue has to do with the confrontation and immersion with death which may result in a variety of fantasies and ideals of identification with death and with the dead. This sometimes results in the survivors seeing themselves as walking dead or "dead to the world" (Murray, 1967; Krystal, 1978a). The elderly sometimes demonstrate a similarly disabling development in which they view themselves as identified with old age and nothing else (Baum and Baxley, 1983).

A common manifestation of the residue of survivorship of mass destruction is a sense of the meaning of one's life being limited only to being a memorial to those who perished. Where the lost relatives and others have fallen victim to an external enemy, these reactions become even more driven as they are reinforced by the need to deal with the residual chronic aggression. Once established, the "monument" or "witness against evil" pattern in survivors' lives becomes reinforced additionally as it provides a means to "work off" some survivor guilt (Krystal, 1981a).

10. The Problem of Aggression

The anger, which so often has to be suppressed in the traumatic situation, only goes underground and returns as a most permanent challenge to the future adjustment of the individual. The appearance of it can be marked as soon as safety is reestablished. For instance, E. Sterba (1949), working with adolescent Holocaust survivors, found that as soon as they were brought to this country and placed in foster homes, they gave vent to constant complaints and unbridled aggressive behavior. As long as she was able to follow up these patients (Sterba, 1968), she found them struggling to manage their smoldering rage. A. Freud and S. Dann (1951) similarly described survivor children as aggressive and difficult to handle.

Arising from his psychotherapeutic work with survivors, Hoppe (1962, 1968, 1969) felt that survivors showed either depressive or aggressive problems. His patients, who developed "reactive aggression" and "hate addiction" (1962), were "protected from unconsciously relating to their torturers as parental figures by a firm ego-ideal, and by shame, pride, and the idea of having a mission. The aggressive survivor permanently externalizes a part of his superego and is fighting against representatives of the externalized negative conscience. The aggression creates new guilt feelings, especially if the survivor's hate addiction turns against his own family members" (Hoppe, 1971, p. 179). In survivor families in which the handling of aggression was particularly problematic, it used to be common for the parents to experience, and even call, a child their "Hitler." In general, it may be said that any family or group which has suffered severe abuse, is prone to have problems in managing aggression and is prone to scapegoating.

The dichotomy of the depressive or aggressive survivor takes on an additional dimension in the work of Danieli (1981a), who described the "adaptational styles" of survivor families. She contrasted the depressive families of "victims" where the victim identity was prevalent and shared by the family, with those families of "fighters." The latter were characterized by a need for mastery, and neither depression nor guilt (or shame) could be tolerated. "Unlike victims . . . they encouraged aggression against and defiance of outsiders" (1981a, p. 10). The role of activity which distinguishes these two family styles helps to reemphasize the difference that total helplessness makes. Any type of activity possible during the traumatic situation tends to minimize the severity of the aftereffects. However, activity in the face of overwhelming stresses exacts its own price. The activities of the heroic and otherwise actively resistant survivors show a similar drivenness to continue active and heroic behavior and ward off any bereavement, shame, or guilt. The inability to bear these painful affects may spawn a need to create a mythology, portraying the cataclysm as a Heroic Era. A myth is created, since what cannot be faced from the past is converted to a personal version of history in order to expiate the guilt of the survivors and remember the victims.

Integration or Hate Addition

Based upon work with Holocaust survivors (Krystal, 1981a), it appears that the survivor of severe trauma makes a fundamental choice between integration or "hate addiction." This kind of a choice becomes especially clear in old age in the course of one's life review, and in psychoanalysis and psychoanalytic psychotherapy in general. In these travails, the authorship of all of one's memories and object-representations is laid bare. The question posed is whether self-healing can proceed, or whether the internal wars continue to be waged, projected, and externalized. Integration can be further blocked by the use of self-righteous blame to ward off depressive, deadened, and deflated states (Horowitz, 1981). Rage is generally much more activating than depressive affects, hence it is often preferred (see Krystal [1983] for a discussion of the activating aspects of emotions).

In order to be able to relinquish both the projective defenses and the anger which serves to deny the tragic prior submission to the aggressor, one has to be able to grieve effectively. Both the giving up of illusions, ideas, or fantasies either past or future, and the conscious self-acceptance of undesirable traits or memories, can only be achieved through a process of mourning. This requires adequate affect tolerance, with sufficient emotional reserves to permit the addition of painful modifications of the self-representation. If these and related requirements cannot be met, when grief develops it quickly becomes associated with anger, fear, guilt, and a fall in self-respect. In other words, it becomes depression. Once this pattern develops, the patient may be going through reactions similar to mourning many times, but his attitude toward himself and his past never changes. Frequently he angrily refuses to accept the painful information and fails to make the necessary changes in his self- and object-representations. Painful memories are disavowed and not integrated, resulting in these recurrent patterns.

This process becomes increasingly difficult, as mourning puts the mourner in touch with the intrapsychic representations of his abhorred opponents. Recognizing the intrapsychic existence of the hated object can threaten the sanity of the survivor (Krystal, 1981a). While Freud (1917) put forth the view, held to this day by most analysts, that the "introjection" is done after the loss of the object and represents part of the mourning process, work with survivors indicates that one's introjections are always being formed. The lack of recognition of the self-sameness of these object-representations puts them in a class similar to that of repressed mental material. In the sense that upon object loss the survivor is confronted with the continuing existence of such mental representations, mourning represents a return of the repressed.

For these and other reasons, the outcome of mourning in posttraumatic states depends upon a multitude of factors, related to the experience of affects, especially the intensity of one's aggression. In turn, the question of the choice between integration and hate addiction is most of all determined by one's capacity to mourn effectively. Dealing with the memories of trauma repeatedly evokes the painful affects of shame, guilt, helplessness, and sorrow. When affect-tolerance is poor, these affects may have to be warded off and replaced by rage. The primary gain in the continuing rage is a narcissistic one, refusing to acknowledge the possibility that the catastrophic events were and are beyond one's control. In addition, there may be diverse secondary gains.

General Considerations

The review of the work with psychic trauma has a number of implications for therapy and prevention. A most important overview observation is that people are fragile and perishable. This is true not only in the ultimate physical sense, but it is also in the emotional sense. They are easily damaged when forced into a situation beyond their capacity to cope. Situations in which individuals are deprived of their usual supports and thrown into circumstances of overwhelming danger, and in which they are coerced into breaking their taboos (Krystal, 1968a), especially those related to aggression, will produce lasting, if not irreversible damage. Distinguishing infantile psychic trauma from the adult catastrophic state helps to explain that while there are certain similar aftereffects in both, such as alexithymia, anhedonia, and a diminution of affect tolerance, there are also great differences. There is, for instance, no recollection of the infantile psychic trauma, whereas the adult psychic trauma is frequently connected to problems of the direct continuation of elements of the traumatic state, as well as problems of guilt, survivorship, and identification with the aggressor.

Unfortunately, despite our increased knowledge of the consequences of massive psychic trauma, there is little we can do to prevent it, human nature and politics being what they are. The idea of primary prevention of psychic trauma would entail such things as never putting people in any kind of a prison camp and never uprooting them or interning them in refugee camps. Certainly, people should be free of oppression and deprivation of their dignity and personal rights. Although these subjects are beyond the scope of this chapter, secondary prevention of psychic trauma is well within the scope of current knowledge. This includes modulating or preventing overwhelming affects and demoralization arising from disasters.

The emotional needs of victims of catastrophe must be a

priority of the highest order. People require emotional support and preventive intervention as soon as possible after a disaster or overwhelming experience (Krystal, 1982d). There is much evidence that what has been learned from dealing with wartime experiences will have a great impact on the handling of disasters and the postdisaster experience with survivor populations. The Buffalo Creek disaster referred to earlier, is one such example, where knowledge gained from studying survivors of concentration camps, was useful in aiding victims of a natural disaster.

It is interesting to note, for instance, that in 1975, Horowitz and Solomon predicted that Vietnam veterans would present in the future with their war-caused psychological disturbances. Shatan (1972, 1973) and Lifton (1973) demonstrated that Vietnam veterans had problems of delayed posttraumatic states, and at the same time identified a number of unique problems resulting from the isolation and specific stresses of Vietnam. Shatan (1973) pointed out that the emotional harm to Vietnam veterans in some cases occurred not in battle, but from training in emotional desensitization and counterguerilla tactics which discouraged grief and intimacy, inducing dehumanization and obliteration of normal affective modes. Thus, current knowledge about trauma and trauma prevention may be applied to the planning of the handling of personnel. If the opportunity is missed to do preventive work in handling soldiers, then the "repair" work will need to be done later. Shatan reported on forms of intervention with Vietnam veterans after the war, demonstrating that group treatment may be helpful in the integration and resocialization of war veterans (Shatan, 1973). Additional innovative therapeutic techniques will be needed, as well.

Establishing the details and dynamics of the traumatic processes in which humans are damaged, is important in that it provides information useful for primary prevention. A basic step in this is the ability to recognize and identify the relevant aftereffects. When an emotional and mental checkup is performed on survivors of a potentially harmful situation, the examiner must know what he is searching for. A case in point is a paper by Mende and Ploeger (1966), describing a mining disaster which took place in 1963 in Germany. The study included a careful description of the interviews with the 11 miners who had been isolated for 10 days in a completely dark cavity without any communication or food. The authors, performing very well in terms of the "state of the art" skills of descriptive psychiatry and mental status examination, failed to ask themselves what it meant that some miners reported having hallucinations while isolated, that there were suicide attempts in the group, and that a group process developed with leadership and heroism displayed. In other words, the eyes of the examiners were trained too specifically on familiar symptomatology and identified disease entities which they expected would give them an immediate indication of damage. They were not prepared to explore the coping reactions and their sequelae. If they could have understood the elements of the stress responses, they would have been attuned to searching for specific aftereffects.

The studies of mass disasters have always provided clues to the basic patterns of human damage. The implications are clearly demonstrated in the brilliant "Essay on Disaster" by Wolfenstein (1957), as well as such works as those of Farber (1967), Glass (1970), and Chamberlin (1980). An understanding of the principles of the traumatic process is essential in order to provide a framework within which such studies can be made (Krystal, 1978a). The work of Horowitz (1976), Caplan (1981), as well as other approaches to stress responses, for instance, that of Coelho, Hamburg, and Adams (1974), expose and explain the various coping mechanisms, drawing attention to the results of coping failures and/or the lasting aftereffects of this failure.

The descriptions and the understanding of the sequelae are but prologues for approaches to therapy, and ultimately, prevention. However, the study of aftereffects of trauma is hampered by obstacles from within both the investigators and the survivors. Survivors may be reluctant to volunteer information or even to view themselves in terms of the victimization. Part of the problem in this regard may be the frequency with which trauma is experienced as fateful—that is the way things were supposed to be and the victims accept it as such. Therefore, the whole trauma is dealt with as "fate" and covered with a cloak of silence. In fact, this conspiracy of silence has repeatedly been emphasized in relation to posttraumatic states (Krystal and Niederland, 1968). Forced silence and secrecy becomes a problem in postdisaster states, both public and private, such as child abuse (Lister, 1982). A common observation in dealing with traumatized individuals, for example, veterans, is that they may have a voluminous chart, but nowhere in that chart can be found an account of what actually happened to them in combat, or other traumatic states. In the restitution files of Holocaust survivors, especially in the early years of claim-related examinations, it was common to find an entry: "The claimant reports having been in X concentration camp for 18 months." Frequently, there was no evidence that any further information was obtained, and on occasion, the giving of such information was actively discouraged. Because the material is likely to evoke intense emotional responses on the part of the therapist as well as the patient, if the patient is in psychotherapy, and it is necessary for the treatment and the patient can take it, a special effort has to be made to discover what happened—and particularly, the nature of the intrapsychic experience. Under these circumstances, the therapist frequently has to help the patient to put his feelings, reactions, and the meanings attributed to the event into words for the first time ever. While it is necessary to help some patients to verbalize their ideas and affects, this does not mean that one should automatically rush into doing so. In fact, when the patient is reluctant to delve into his or her traumatic past, the well-intentioned help giver should scrutinize his motivations and ask himself whether it is absolutely necessary to the progress of the case to uncover the material in question. If the patient is not in psychoanalytic (i.e., "uncovering") psychotherapy, one should be mindful that we can do harm, not only by what we say, but also by what we listen to. The careless encouraging of confessional "abreactions" may instead flood the patient with guilt, shame, anxiety, and may precipitate a serious depression or even psychotic state. The following is an illustration of this point:

> A Holocaust survivor presented himself with a problem of memory. He complained that he could no longer perform his work and was laid off because he was forgetful and could not concentrate. In beginning to review his history, it was discovered that there was a period of about 10 months about which there were inconsistencies in the chart and the patient was evasive. Instead of pursuing the matter with the patient, the therapist contacted certain individuals who knew the patient's background, and were in a position to know how he had spent this period. From them he discovered that the patient, in all likelihood, spent those months in a unit which was being taken to various sites of mass graves and was digging them up and burning the corpses, and covering up the evidence of the mass murders. In this manner he was forced to dig up whole Jewish communities and then burn the remains and destroy all the traces. When he next met with his patient, the therapist changed his tack. Instead of "uncovering," he explained to the patient that sometimes it is better not to remember everything. Thinking that the problem was actually that the patient's concentration and memory were disturbed by intrusive references of his horrible past, he addressed himself to the affective disturbances; that is, "anxious depression," as well as current problems in the patient's life, helping him to bring his affective state back to manageable intensity.

Not only is it potentially disturbing for a patient to be confronted with a repressed and forgotten part of his past, but even the idea that one was damaged by the persecution may be very disturbing to Holocaust survivors who experience it as evidence of the Nazis having succeeded in their destructive designs.

If one determines to support the patient instead of uncovering the old wounds, one has to get to know the individual well in order to discover what interventions might be helpful and acceptable to him (or her). No preconceived program is possible, but the attention and care for the individual's needs and feelings, and respect for their sensibilities, may bring to mind a menu of helpful approaches from which the patient may pick those that are suitable and helpful to him or her.

From the perspective of the investigators, dealing with victims of disaster and abuse is a most difficult task because the surviving victim often becomes the object of projection of a multitude of disavowed sins. Much of the therapist's aggression may turn to the victim rather than to the perpetrator of the disaster (Krystal, 1971). The ambivalence toward the damaged population, be they survivors, veterans, or disaster victims, is frequently manifested by a capricious and inconsistent administration of restitution and rehabilitation programs. As an illustration, a study of 367 consecutive cases of survivors of the Nazi Holocaust, revealed there was no correlation between pension or restitution discussions and diagnosis of degree of damage or extent of suffering of the survivors. The recognized percentage of disability correlated most accurately with the locus of the German restitution office that handled the case, and not with any other factor in the survivor's history (Krystal, 1971). What this meant was that regardless of the detailed instructions spelled out in the German restitution laws, and the precedents set by the German courts, the officials in each of the restitution offices had set up their policies and procedures according to their own views, feelings, and prejudices. To counteract such forces in public policy, hard facts about human damage and rehabilitation are required.

The work on traumatization also needs to be expanded in experimental areas, such as responses to stressful stimuli and the nature of stress response patterns (Horowitz and Becker, 1971). Special situations need to be studied for the extraordinary methods of coping revealed. These could include studies of shipwreck situations (Henderson and Bostock, 1977); death row experiences (Hussain and Tozman, 1978); and victims of terrorism and hostage situations (Hillman, 1981). In general, the exploration of the process of response and aftereffect of man-made and natural disasters provides a continuing and ample source of study in this area. In addition, the difficulties and opportunities involved in the process of rehabilitation and management of the victims of psychic trauma need to be explored. These challenges will multiply when whole communities need to be rehabilitated posttraumatically (K. T. Erickson, 1976).

Specific Considerations

In dealing with severely damaged individuals, helpers must renounce therapeutic zeal and think of approaches which help to make life bearable. Frequently the patient's symptoms cannot be removed or essentially modified. Rather, the patient needs help to live with them (Krystal, 1968b). The common defense of avoidance of personal relationships will impede or block therapy: "One common problem in the survivors of the Holocaust is a profound fear of getting to love someone. Having lost most, if not all, of their early love objects, they now fear that to love anyone is to lose them and go through the pain all over again" (Krystal, 1968c, p. 248).

Dewind's (1971) careful studies of his own work as well as that of other psychoanalysts and psychotherapists, demonstrated again that there are a number of special problems in the treatment of survivors of major traumas. There are complicated links between the extraordinary traumatic situation, such as in the survivors of the Nazi persecution, and the "ordinary" childhood trauma. The memories of the catastrophic adult trauma become associatively linked with the infantile psychic trauma states. In the psychotherapeutic work these connections have to be worked out and the interlacing of the intrapsychic conflict and traumatic situation must be worked with in a gradual and careful way.

Acceptance of painful views of one's self, the giving up of unattainable wishes, and the acquiescence to one's entire past depends upon the ability to grieve effectively (Wetmore, 1963). In psychotherapy, and in old age, we have the opportunity to achieve wisdom and self-healing through the process of integration of one's self into a stable and coherent whole. The most severe and harmful aftereffect of psychic trauma consists of creating the tendency to intrapsychic splitting, through which conscious recognition of part of one's selfhood is denied. Large parts of one's own memories, both cognitive and affective, are handled through various mechanisms of repression, denial, externalization, projection, and projective identification. In contrast, the more mature or healthy states include a more comprehensive self-representation and the conscious recognition of the authorship of one's object-representations. Approaching this ideal is accomplished by lovingly accepting one's life, one's past, and everything that took place in it. In the review of one's life, whenever memories that are not integrated are broached, the individual experiences pain in the physical or emotional sphere, be it shame, guilt, anger, depression, or anxiety. In the posttraumatic states of Holocaust survivors, it is particularly clear that if integration is not achieved, then hate-addiction may ensue (Krystal, 1981b).

In those exceptional cases when posttraumatic self-healing

is attempted, in therapy, the central question is whether the subject and the therapist are able to bear the mourning process. As reviewed throughout this chapter, certain conditions must first be met. There is the question of whether the affects are available as signals, that is, in the mature form. In individuals with alexithymia, the trend to physiological responses in place of affective ones, impedes the work of mourning and prevents self-integration. On the other hand, if the affects are in a reasonably differentiated, verbalized, and nonsomatized form, then the question of affect tolerance and reflective self-awareness becomes very important. For it is only if one can prevent getting caught up in the vicious cycles of maladaptive responses to affect that one can go on with the utilization of one's affects for information processing.

If affects are differentiated, utilizable as signals, and tolerable to the mourner, then one can proceed with the work of mourning, which consists largely of modifying one's self- and object-representations. The essence of grieving does not lie in its physiological components, such as crying or screaming, but rather in the nature of the modifications of self-representations that are possible. Thus, the problem with object loss in childhood is not that children cannot mourn, in the sense of weeping and signaling their sorrows, but rather that the mental representations of the lost objects retain the characteristics they had at the time of the loss. Object-representations are elaborated in accordance with the type of cognition and fantasies predominant at that particular stage of development. When one repeats, unthinkingly, Freud's metaphor that objects are introjected after they are lost, some confusion may arise. In fact, object-representations are not introjected from the outside to the inside at any time. They are created by the subject in his or her own mind from inception. However, whenever one is not able to consciously deal with the ambivalence and resulting guilt about object loss, the lost object is idealized. The simultaneous guilt and self-disparagement make it appear as if all the "good-ness" was transferred to the object-representation and drained from the self-representation where it was replaced with "bad-ness." In fact, these phenomena are but an exaggeration of the infantile way of dealing with ambivalence by splitting of the object-representation and self-representations, idealizing and vilifying the split-off parts.

One's self-representation may be experienced as impov-erished and one has to plead with the adored lost object for the "return of the magical power of love." Hence, the greater the ambivalence with which the original relationship was held, the less the mourner's capacity will be to own his own aggression, and the less the capacity for effective grieving will be. This increases the likelihood of an arrest in one of the stages of the grieving process which was reviewed earlier. In effect, much of clinical depression can be understood as incomplete and miscarried mourning just as Freud felt in 1917. Successful mourning can be measured by the degree of self-integration that ensues. In effect, with every object loss one has to review, rebuild, and recreate a whole new world-representation into which the new self- and object-representations will fit.

In posttraumatic cases, especially in Holocaust survivors, it is only the exceptional person who may be able to tolerate the depression and bear the pain of consciously dealing with all of the traumatic losses. Since all the painful memories have to be worked over in slow, laborious fashion, the work of achiev-ing self-integration becomes a very painful, practically super-human task. The grieving is done under constant protest, in an atmosphere of great anger in which much of the time the painful memories are reexperienced and recapitulated within ambivalent transferences. This is the reason that therapists tend to limit the depth of psychotherapy with war veterans and Hol-ocaust survivors. Even dealing with them on a supportive level can be quite difficult and strenuous.

Hoppe (1969) studied the special reactions of psychiatrists involved with survivors of the Nazi persecution. He pointed out that because of the special difficulties encountered in dealing with the traumatized individuals and their life story, the psychiatrists (whom he called "experts" here because they were "pension examiners" at the time) tended to react in one of the following patterns. The psychiatrists' reactions in turn stimulated symptomatic responses in the survivor. These were the corresponding "sets" of behavior patterns:

1. Expert: Complete denial.
   Survivor: Increase of symptoms and defense mechanisms.
2. Expert: Reaction-formation, rationalization and isolation.
   Survivor: Conformity, followed by confusion and distrust.
3. Expert: Over-identification.
   Survivor: Dependence, followed by identity resistance. An overly sympathetic attitude on the part of the examiner may mobilize dependency yearnings in the survivors, which may threaten the survivor's ability to maintain his integration of self, and hence he may resist the therapist.
4. Expert: Controlled identification.
   Survivor: Decrease of defense mechanisms and distrust.
                              [Hoppe, 1969, p. 189]

In this attempt to qualify the repertoire of responses on the part of the therapist and the survivor, Hoppe was very clearly aware of the impact upon the therapist of dealing with very painful material, particularly the kind that tends to revive sadomasochistic conflicts within the therapist. Major transference–countertransference reverberations can obviously ensue. Eissler (1967) keenly highlighted the dilemma of intense emotional reactions toward the defeated and humiliated survivor.

He felt that along with other emotions one also had to be prepared to face these difficulties:

> The archaic contempt, scorn or spite for the sufferer is rather complex. It is connected with the whole problem of sadomasochism and the reaction to various shades of narcissism. The awe and respect that strongly narcissistic personalities evoke are well known.
>
> The persecuted one, however, has presented a configuration of exactly the opposite character: he has been utterly depleted of any narcissistic cathexis. During his persecution nothing belonged to him any longer—not even his own body. No decision was left to him; he was reduced to sheer nothingness. . . .
>
> I am compelled to draw the conclusion that among the many causes for hostility toward victims of persecution, regression to the pagan feeling of contempt for those who are suffering physically must be included. And it may well be the most insidious and most potent cause of all [p. 1358].

Eissler was highlighting one type of countertransference that was particularly difficult to handle because it ran contrary to the therapist's ideal views of himself and his reactions to a patient. In fact, a multitude of difficult countertransferences are encountered (Krystal, 1967).

These difficulties experienced by the therapist may be due to several factors including: (1) the survivor's present condition—in other words, what the patient had become; (2) reactions to certain "stimulating" character defenses—extreme passivity, obsequiousness, defiance; and, (3) transference reactions on the part of the survivor who may be experiencing the therapist as a Nazi or a capo. One need not elaborate on what a painful experience such an exposure may be. The author has himself considered the question in supervision with a therapist who was considering treating a survivor in psychotherapy: "Do you think you could bear being experienced as a murdering Nazi sadist day after day?" Thus, all these very difficult situations may interfere with the usual performance of the therapist. However, beside the survivor himself as an individual, being a challenge, there are problems in dealing with what he "stands for"; the kinds of images and associations he evokes in his audience (therapist). As Eissler (1967) pointed out, disgust may be experienced directly. The general problem of shame and our specific reactions, such as pity, suspicion, or blame are examples of difficult and nontherapeutic responses.

One gains the impression from the literature on Vietnam veterans that the unconscious wish of the general population to undo the common pain of the Vietnam experience, promotes the wish that the veterans would disappear. The very existence of some survivors may be offensive to the potential caregivers. Danieli (1981c) studied in great detail therapists' countertransference problems and a variety of other difficulties arising in dealing with survivors of the Nazi Holocaust and their children (1981d). Basically, all these considerations have to be considered as a special kind of challenge, preparing the psychotherapist for dealing with a special population. The difficulties in trying to treat such patients with the methods and conceptual tools developed for neurotic patients are obvious. When dealing with individuals who have lived in a crazy environment, and whose reality was beyond the scope of the ordinary life and expectable environment, the therapist must be prepared to deal with extraordinary feelings and responses on his own part.

Conclusion

In this survey of the field of psychic traumatization, it is evident that special difficulty exists in the diagnosis and the treatment of victims of psychic trauma. This accounts for a delay in understanding the traumatization process. Nonetheless, there is overwhelming evidence that individuals are severely damaged when their physical safety is threatened, when their autonomy is violated and they are subjected to oppression and humiliation, be it within the family setting, or in situations of extraordinary external stress. The post-Vietnam war experience demonstrates that it is harmful and destructive to place an individual in a situation in which his aggressive impulses are encouraged to run in an unbridled manner and in which fundamental affective experiences are overwhelmingly disrupted.

Studies of trauma are incomplete and incorrect as well, if the fate of the oppressor is not examined, as well as the fate of the victim—the slaveholders as well as the slaves. Conversely, harmful aftereffects of having been in a situation in which heroism was necessary are as relevant to dealing with victims of massive psychic trauma as having to live with the memories and consequences of cowardice. Both may preclude self-integration. People must come to see that in being the oppressor, the aggressor, or the activator of disasters or holocausts, they are engaged in an activity that is going to be harmful to their emotional and mental health. They will have to pay an unending emotional price just as will the victim of the conquest.

The psychoanalytic approach to problems of aggression and man-made disasters, including war, has always been basically pessimistic, stemming from the philosophical and psychodynamic perceptions of the idea of aggression. Freud's early conception of a death instinct provided a pessimistic view in regard to mankind ever being able to prevent the periodic outbreak of cruelty, inhumanity, and war. Despite different dynamic formulations put forward since that time, no new findings or theories diminish this pessimism. For this reason, in the foreseeable future, the field of trauma exploration will have to address itself basically to secondary prevention, therapy, and rehabilitation rather than the ultimate prevention of traumatization.

Among the lessons to be learned is that massive traumatization has dynamics and a history of its own. The therapy and the dynamics of neuroses may not be applicable to these kinds of psychic traumatization. The separation of the infantile psychic trauma state from the adult catastrophic type provides one framework in which these events may be studied. A multitude of other views is necessary to provide a full understanding of how individuals develop, cope, and how they can be harmed. In this way, the variety of factors that interfere with people's harmonious maturation and function can be addressed. Forces that represent abuse tend to modify the hedonic regulation of an organism and may produce an attachment to painful feelings. The very function of the pleasure and distress registering centers and their regulation activities may be significantly altered (Krystal, 1978a, 1981b).

In dealing with victims of massive trauma, therapists must be prepared, not only to make various modifications in psychotherapy, but also to keep available to their patients a variety of retraining methods. Chronic muscle tension and hypervigilant emergency states may need to be approached through a combination of various relaxation techniques, biofeedback, hypnosis, or relaxation training, as well as drug therapies. Some individuals are irreparably damaged and therefore will have to be given special protective environments in which they be allowed to function to the best of their residual capacity.

The problem of anhedonia, however, remains a major challenge. How people can be helped to cultivate or restore their capacity to experience pleasure, joy, or happiness demands the profession's attention.

Similarly, alexithymia, which constitutes a significant barrier to psychotherapy, needs more exploration. It is possible that some alexithymic patients may be capable of receiving help so that they can be prepared to benefit later from individual or group psychotherapy, for which they now have a serious limitation. Other special problems such as posttraumatic limitations in the capacity for self-care may require special attention (Krystal, 1981b). Certainly both prevention and rehabilitation training require special continuing research, and new techniques need to be developed. At the same time, the continuation of studies and dissemination of knowledge in regard to the patterns of human damage cannot help but contribute to minimization of psychic trauma and human damage in the future.

References

Allerton, C. W. (1964), Mass casualty care and human behavior. *Med. Ann., Dist. Columbia*, 33:206–208.

Archibald, H. C., Long, D. M., Miller, C., & Tuddenham, K. D. (1962), Gross stress reaction in combat—A 15-year follow-up. *Amer. J. Psychiat.*, 119:317–322.

———— Tuddenham, R. D. (1965), Persistent stress reaction after combat. *Arch. Gen. Psych.*, 12:475–481.

Bartemeier, L. H., Kubie, L. S., Menninger, K. A., Romano, J., & Whitehorn, J. E. (1946), Combat exhaustion. *J. Nerv. & Ment. Dis.*, 104:358–389.

Bastiaans, J. (1957), *Psychosomatische Gerolgen von onderdrukking en verzet*. Amsterdam: Noordhollandische Vitgerers Maetschappii.

Baum, S. K., & Baxley, R. L. (1983), Age identification in the elderly. *Gerontol.*, 23:532–536.

Beebe, G. W., & Appel, J. W. (1958), Variations in psychological tolerance to ground combat in World War II. Washington, DC: National Academy of Sciences, National Research Council.

Bergmann, M. V. (1982a), Thoughts on superego pathology of survivors and their children. In: *Generations of the Holocaust*, ed. M. S. Bergmann & M. E. Jucovy. New York: Basic Books, pp. 287–310.

Breuer, J. & Freud, S. (1893-1895), Studies on Hysteria. *Standard Edition*, 2. London: Hogarth Press, 1955.

Brill, N. W., & Beebe, G. W. (1955), A follow-up study of war neuroses. Washington, DC: Veterans Administration Medical Monograph.

Caplan, G. (1981), Mastery of stress: Psychosocial aspects. *Amer. J. Psychiat.*, 138:413–420.

Chamberlin, B. C. (1980), The psychological aftermath of disaster. *J. Clin. Psychiat.*, 41:238–244.

Coelho, G. V., Hamburg, D. A., & Adams, J. E., Eds. (1974), *Coping and Adaptation*. New York: Basic Books.

Cohen, B. M., & Cooper, M. A. (1954), A follow-up study of World War II prisoners of war. Washington, DC: U.S. Government Printing Office.

Danieli, Y. (1981a), Differing adaptational styles in families of survivors of the Nazi Holocaust. *Children Today*, 10:6–10.

—— (1981b), Families of survivors of Nazi Holocaust: Some short and long term effects. In: *Stress and Anxiety* (Psychological Stress and Adjustment in Time of War and Peace), ed. C. D. Spielberger, I. G. Sarason, & N. Milgram. New York: McGraw-Hill/Hemisphere Publishing, pp. 405–421.

—— (1981c), Countertransference in the treatment and study of Nazi Holocaust survivors and their children. *Victimology*, 5:355–367.

—— (1981d), Therapists' difficulties in treating survivors of the Nazi Holocaust and their children. Unpublished doctoral dissertation. New York University.

Dewind, E. (1971), Psychotherapy after traumatization caused by persecution. In: *Psychic Traumatization*, ed. H. Krystal & W. G. Niederland. Boston: Little, Brown, pp. 93–114.

Dimsdale, J. (1980), *Survivors, Victims, and Perpetrators*. Washington & New York: Hemisphere Publishing.

Eissler, K. R. (1967), Perverted psychiatry? *Amer. J. Psychiat.*, 123:1352–1358.

Eitinger, L. (1980), The concentration camp syndrome and its late sequelae. In: *Survivors, Victims and Perpetrators*, ed. J. Dimsdale. Washington & New York: Hemisphere Publishing, pp. 127–162.

Engel, G. L. (1962a), Anxiety and depression-withdrawal, the primary affects of unpleasure. *Internat. J. Psycho-Anal.*, 43:89–98.

—— (1962b), *Psychological development in health and disease*. Philadelphia & London: W. B. Saunders.

Erikson, E. H. (1950), *Childhood and Society*. New York: W. W. Norton.

—— (1959), Ego development and historical change. In: Identity and the Life Cycle. *Psychological Issues*, Monogr. 1. New York: International Universities Press, pp. 18–49.

Erikson, K. T. (1976), *Everything in its Path—Destruction of Community in the Buffalo Creek Flood*. New York: Simon & Schuster.

Farber, I. J. (1967), Psychological aspects of mass disaster. *Nat. Med. Assn.*, 59:340–345.

Freud, A. (1967), Comments on psychic trauma. In: *Psychic Trauma*, ed. S. Furst. New York: Basic Books, pp. 235–246.

—— Dann, S. (1951), An experiment in group upbringing. *Psychoanalytic Study of the Child*, 6:217–268. ed. R. S. Eissler, A. Freud, M. Martmann, & E. Kris. New York: International Universities Press.

Freud, S. (1883a), Sketches for the "Preliminary communication." *Standard Edition*, 1:146–154. London: Hogarth Press, 1966.

—— (1917), Mourning and melancholia. *Standard Edition*, 14:237–258. London: Hogarth Press, 1957.

—— (1920), Beyond the pleasure principle. *Standard Edition*, 17:3–64. London: Hogarth Press, 1955.

—— (1926), Inhibition, Symptoms and Anxiety. *Standard Edition*, 20:75–175. London: Hogarth Press, 1959.

Frost, R. (1916), Birches. In: *The Norton Anthology of Poetry*, rev. ed., ed. A. W. Ollison, H. Barrows, C. R. Blake, A. J. Cerr, A. M. Eastman, & H. M. English. New York: W. W. Norton & Co., 1975.

Furst, S. (1967), Psychic trauma: A survey. In: *Psychic Trauma*, ed. S. Furst. New York: Basic Books, pp. 3-50.

Glass, A. J. (1970), The psychological aspects of emergency situations. In: *The Psychological Aspects of Stress*, ed. S. H. Abrams. Springfield, IL: Charles C Thomas, pp. 62–69.

Gracey, D. R., & De Remee, R. A. (1981), The University of Vienna Medical School. *Mayo Clin. Proc.*, 56:634–638.

Greenspan, S. T. (1981), *Psychopathology and Adaptation in Infancy and Early Childhood: Principles of Clinical Depression and Preventive Intervention*. Clinical Infant Reports-Report No. 1. New York: International Universities Press.

Gunderson, E. K., & Rahe, R. H. (1974), *Stress and Illness*. Springfield, IL: Charles C Thomas.

Henderson, S., & Bostock, T. (1977), Coping behavior after shipwreck. *Brit. J. Psychiat.*, 131:15–20.

Hillman, R. G. (1981), The psychology of being held hostage. *Amer. J. Psychiat.*, 38:1183–1197.

Holmes, T. H., & Rahe, R. H. (1967), The social readjustment rating scale. *J. Psychosom. Res.*, 11:213–218.

Hoppe, K. D. (1962), Persecution, depression and aggression. *Bull. Menninger Clin.*, 26:195–203.

——— (1965), Persecution and conscience. *Psychoanal. Rev.*, 52:106–116.

——— (1968), Psychotherapy with concentration camp survivors. In: *Massive Psychic Trauma*, ed., H. Krystal. New York: International Universities Press, pp. 204–219.

——— (1969), Reactions of psychiatrists to examination of survivors of Nazi persecution. *Psychoanal. Forum*, 3:182–211.

——— (1971), The aftermath of Nazi persecution reflected in recent psychiatric literature. In: *Psychic Traumatization: International Psychiatry Clinics*, 8:169–240, ed. H. Krystal & W. G. Niederland. Boston: Little, Brown.

Horowitz, M. J. (1976), *Stress Response Syndromes*. New York: Jason Aronson.

——— (1981), Self-righteous rage and the attribution of blame. *Arch. Gen. Psychiat.*, 38:1233–1238.

——— Becker, S. S. (1971), Response to stressful stimuli. *Arch. Gen. Psychiat.*, 25:419–428.

——— Solomon, G. (1975), A prediction of delayed stress response syndromes in Vietnam veterans. *J. Soc. Issues*, 31:67–80.

Hussain, A. H., & Tozman, S. (1978), Psychiatry and death row. *J. Clin. Psychiat.*, 39:183–188.

Jaffe, W. G. (1969), A critical review of the status of envy concept. *Internat. J. Psycho-Anal.*, 50:533–547.

Johnson, D. A. (1970), An experimental evaluation of behavioral inaction under stress. *IRAD Technical Report #D23-70-215, McDonnell Douglas Corp. Rept. #g1008.*

Katan, A. (1951), The role of displacement in agoraphobia. *Internat. J. Psycho-Anal.*, 32:41–50.

Klein, H. (1968), Problems in the psychotherapeutic treatment of Israeli survivors of the Holocaust. In: *Massive Psychic Trauma*, ed. H. Krystal. New York: International Universities Press, pp. 233–248.

Klein, M. (1946), Notes on some schizoid mechanisms. *Internat. J. Psycho-Anal.*, 27:99–110.

Koranyi, E. R. (1977), Psychobiological correlates of battlefield psychiatry. *Psychiat. J. Univ. Ottawa*, 2:3–19.

Krupnick, J. L., & Horowitz, M. J. (1981), Stress response syndromes: Recurrent themes. *Arch. Gen. Psychiat.*, 38:428–435.

Krystal, H. (1962), The opiate withdrawal syndrome as a state of stress. *Psychiat. Quart.*, 36 suppl. pp. 54–65.

——— (1967), Reactions of psychiatrists to examination of survivors of Nazi persecution. *Psychoanal. Forum*, 3:205–207.

——— (1968a), Study of juvenile survivors of concentration camps. Paper presented to discussion group of "Children of Disaster." American Psychoanalytic Association, New York. Dec. 10, 1968.

——— (1968b), Patterns of psychological damage. In: *Massive Psychic Trauma*, ed. H. Krystal. New York: International Universities Press, pp. 1-7.

——— (1968c), Psychotherapy with survivors of Nazi persecution. In: *Massive Psychic Trauma*, ed. H. Krystal. New York: International Universities Press, pp. 204–276.

——— (1970), Trauma and the stimulus barrier. Paper presented at the American Psychoanalytic Association Meeting, San Francisco, May 8, 1970 and to the Michigan Psychoanalytic Society, October 10, 1969, mimeographed.

——— (1971), Trauma: Considerations of its intensity and chronicity. In: *Psychic Traumatization*, ed., H. Krystal & W. G. Niederland. International Psychiatry Clinics, Boston: Little, Brown, pp. 11-28.

——— (1974), The genetic view of affects and affect regression. In: *The Annual of Psychoanalysis*, 2:98–126. New York: International Universities Press.

——— (1975), Affect tolerance. In: *The Annual of Psychoanalysis*, 3:179–219. New York: International Universities Press.

——— (1977), Aspects of affects. *Bull. Menninger Clin.*, 41/1:1–26.

——— (1978a), Trauma and affects. In: *The Psychoanalytic Study of the Child*, ed. A. J. Solnit, R. S. Eissler, A. Freud, M. Kris, & P. B. Neubauer. New Haven, CT: Yale University Press, 33:81–116.

——— (1978b), Self-representation and the capacity for self-care. In: *The Annual of Psychoanalysis*, 6:209–246. New York: International Universities Press.

——— (1978c), Psychic trauma and psychogenic death. In: *Psychiatric Problems in Medical Practice*, ed. G. U. Balis, L. Wurmser, E. McDaniel, & R. G. Grenell. Boston: Butterworth Publisher, pp. 79–97.

—— (1979), Alexithymia and psychotherapy. *Amer. J. Psychother.*, 33:17–31.

—— (1981a), Integration and self-healing in posttraumatic states. *J. Geriat. Psychiat.*, 14/2:165–189.

—— (1981b), The hedonic element in affectivity. In: *The Annual of Psychoanalysis*, 9:93–114. New York: International Universities Press.

—— (1982a), Alexithymia and the effectiveness of psychoanalytic treatment. *Internat. J. Psychoanal. Psychother.*, 9:353-388; 1982-1983.

—— (1982b), Character disorders. In: *Encyclopedic Handbook of Alcoholism*, ed. E. M. Pattison & E. Kaufman. New York: Gardner Press, pp. 607–617.

—— (1982c), Adolescence and the tendencies to develop substance dependence. *Psychoanal. Inquiry*, 2/4:581–617.

—— (1982d), Early preventive psychotherapy after disasters. *Psychosomatic Medicine: Theoretical, Clinical and Transcultural Aspects*, ed. A. J. Krakowski & C. P. Kimball. New York: Plenum Press, pp. 737–744.

—— (1983), The activating aspects of emotions. *Psychoanalysis and Contemporary Thought*, 5:605-642.

—— Moore, R. A., & Dorsey, J. M. (1967), Alcoholism and the force of education. *Personnel & Guidance J.*, October:134–139.

—— Niederland, W. G. (1968), Clinical observations of the Survivor Syndrome. In: *Massive Psychic Trauma*, ed. H. Krystal. New York: International Universities Press, pp. 327–348.

—— Petty, T. A. (1968), Rehabilitation in trauma following illness, physical injury and massive personality damage. In: *Massive Psychic Trauma*, ed. H. Krystal. New York: International Universities Press, pp. 277–326.

—— Raskin, H. (1970), *Drug Dependence*. Detroit: Wayne State University Press.

Levy, D. M. (1945), Psychic trauma of operations in children—And a note on combat neurosis. *Amer. J. Dis. Children*, 69:7–25.

Lieberman, M. A. (1977), Adaptive processes in later life. In: *Life-space Developmental Psychology*, ed., N. Datan & H. W. Reese. New York: Academic Press, pp. 135–159.

Lifton, R. J. (1968), *Death in Life: Survivors of Hiroshima*. New York: Random House.

—— (1973), *Home from the War*. New York: Simon & Schuster.

—— (1979a), *The Life of the Self. Toward a New Psychology*. New York: Simon & Schuster.

—— (1979b), *The Broken Connection. On Death and the Continuity of Life*. New York: Simon & Schuster.

Lindemann, E. (1944), Symptomatology and management of acute grief. *Amer. J. Psychiat.*, 101:141–148.

Lister, E. D. (1982), Forced silence: A neglected dimension of trauma. *Amer. J. Psychiat.*, 139:872–876.

McDougall, J. (1974), The psychosoma and the psychoanalytic process. *Inc.*

Rev. Psycho-Anal., 1:437–459.

Marty, P., & deM'Uzan, M. (1963), Le Pensée Opératoire. *Rev. Franç. Psychoan.*, 27 suppl.:345–456.

—— David, C. (1963), *L'Investigation psychosomatique.* Paris: Presses Universitaires.

Mende, W., & Ploeger, A. (1966), Das Verhalten und Erleben von Bergeunten in der Extrembelastung des Eingeschlossenseins. *Nervenarzt,* 37:209–219.

Minkowski, E. (1946), L'anesthésie affective. *Ann. Medico-psychologiques,* 104:8–13.

Murray, H. A. (1967), Dead to the world: Passions of Herman Melville. In: *Essays in Self Destruction,* ed., E. S. Shneidman. New York: Science House, pp. 7-29.

Nemiah, J. C., & Sifneos, P. E. (1970a), Affect and fantasy in patients with psychosomatic disorders. In: *Modern Trends in Psychosomatic Medicine,* Vol. 2, ed. O. W. Hill. London: Butterworth, pp. 26–34.

Niederland, W. G. (1961), The problem of the survivor. *J. Hillside Hosp.,* 10:233–247.

—— (1968), Clinical observations on the "survivor syndrome." *Internat. J. Psycho-Anal.,* 49:313–315.

—— (1981), The survivor syndrome: Further observation and dimensions. *J. Amer. Psychoan. Assn.,* 29:413–426.

Papousek, H., & Papousek, M. (1975), Cognitive aspects of preverbal secret interaction between human infants and adults. In: *Parent–Infant Interaction,* ed. R. Porter & M. O'Connor. Ciba Foundation Symposium 33. New York: Association of Scientific Publishers.

Rado, S. (1969), The emotions. In: *Adaptational Psychodynamics,* ed. J. Jameson & H. Klein, New York: Science House, pp. 21-30.

Rahe, R. H., Meyer, M., Smith, M., Kjaer, G., & Holmes, T. H. (1964), Social stress and illness onset. *J. Psychosom. Res.,* 8:35–44.

Rees, W. D., & Lutkins, S. G. (1967), Mortality of bereavement. *Brit. Med. J.,* 4:13–16.

Richter, C. P. (1957), On the phenomenon of sudden death in animals and man. *Psychosom. Med.,* 19:191–198.

Schmale, Jr., A. H. (1964), A genetic view of affects with special reference to the genesis of helplessness and hopelessness. In: *The Psychoanalytic Study of the Child,* 27:411–436, ed. R. S. Eissler, A. Freud, M. Martmann, & E. Kris. New Haven, CT: Yale University Press.

Schur, M. (1955), Comments on the metapsychology of somatization. In: *The Psychoanalytic Study of the Child,* 10:119–164, ed. R. S. Eissler, A. Freud, M. Martmann, & E. Kris. New York: International Universities Press.

Seligman, M. E. P. (1975), *Helplessness: On Depression, Development and Death.* San Francisco: W. H. Freeman Co.

Shatan, C. F. (1972), The post Vietnam syndrome. *New York Times,* May 6, 1972.

—— (1973), The grief of soldiers: Vietnam combat veteran's self-help movement. *Amer. J. Orthopsychiat.*, 43:640–653.

Shneidman, E. S. (1976a), A psychologic theory of suicide. *Psychiat. Ann.*, 6:76–89.

—— (1976b), Suicide notes reconsidered. *Psychiat. Ann.*, 6:90–91.

Sifneos, P. E. (1967), Clinical observations on some patients suffering from a variety of psychosomatic diseases. *Proc. 7th Europ. Conf. on Psychosomatic Res.*, Basel: Karger.

—— (1973), The prevalence of "alexithymic" characteristics in psychosomatic patients. *Psychother. Psychosom.*, 22:257–262.

Snyder, S. H. (1980), Brain peptides as neurotransmitters. *Science*, 209:976–983.

Sterba, E. (1949), Emotional problems in displaced children. *J. Casework*, 30:175–181.

—— (1968), The effect of persecutions on adolescents. In: *Massive Psychic Trauma*, ed. H. Krystal. New York: International Universities Press, pp. 51–59 & pp. 259–263.

Stern, M. M. (1951a), Pavor nocturnus. *Internat. J. Psycho-Anal.*, 32:302–309.

—— (1951b), Anxiety, trauma and shock. *Psychoanal. Quart.*, 20:179–203.

—— (1953), Trauma and symptom formation. *Internat. J. Psycho-Anal.*, 34:202–218.

—— (1968a), Fear of death and neurosis. *J. Amer. Psychoanal. Assn.*, 63:3–31.

—— (1968b), Fear of death and trauma. *Internat. J. Psycho-Anal.*, 49:458–461.

Tanay, E. (1968), Initiation of psychotherapy with survivors of Nazi persecution. In: *Massive Psychic Trauma*, ed. H. Krystal. New York: International Universities Press, pp. 219–233.

Terr, L. C. (1979), Children of Chowchilla. In: *The Psychoanalytic Study of the Child*, 34:552–623, ed. A. J. Solnit, R. S. Eissler, A. Freud, M. Kris, & P. B. Neubauer. New Haven, CT: Yale University Press.

—— (1981a), Psychic trauma in children. *Amer. J. Psychiat.*, 138:14–19.

—— (1981b), "Forbidden Games": Posttraumatic child's play. *J. Amer. Acad. Child Psychiat.*, 20:741–760.

Tyhurst, J. S. (1951), Individual reactions to community disasters. *Amer. J. Psychiat.*, 107:764–769.

Valenstein, A. F. (1962), The psycho-analytic situation: Affects, emotional reliving, and insight in the psycho-analytic process. *Internat. J. Psycho-Anal.*, 43:315–324.

Van der Kolk, B., Boyd, H., Krystal, J. H., & Greenberg, M. (1984), Post-traumatic stress disorders as a biologically based disorder: Implications of the animal model of inescapable shock. In: *Post Traumatic Stress Disorder: Psychological and Biological Sequelae*, ed. B. A. Van der Kolk. Washington, DC: American Psychiatric Press, pp. 123–134.

Venzlaff, U. (1963), Über Defeutzustaende nach Schweren Haftzetten, insbesondere nack K-Z Haft. In: *Erlebnisgrund und Dynamik seelicher verfolgrupschaden in Psychische Spaetscheden nach politscher varfolgung*. Basel: Karger, pp. 111-124.

Walker, J. I., & Cavenar, Jr., J. O. (1982), Vietnam veterans: Their problems
    continue. *J. Nerv. & Ment. Dis.*, 70:174–180.
Wallant, E. C. (1962), *The Pawnbroker*. New York: MacFadden.
Wetmore, R. J. (1963), The role of grief in psychoanalysis. *Internat. J. Psycho-
    Anal.*, 44:97–103.
Wolfenstein, M. (1957), *Disaster: A Psychological Essay*. reprint. New York:
    Arno Press, 1977.
Zetzel, E. R. (1949), Anxiety and the capacity to bear it. *Internat. J. Psycho-
    Anal.*, 30:1–12.
———— (1965), On the incapacity to bear depression. In: *Capacity for Emotional
    Growth*, ed. E. R. Zetzel. New York: International Universities Press, 1970,
    pp. 82-114.

6

EXAGGERATED HELPLESSNESS SYNDROME

Lawrence Breslau, M.D.

Definition

"Exaggerated helplessness" refers to behavior and attitudes on the part of an elderly person which highlight, in intensified form, his state of passivity, and which are intended to convey to the caretaker an inability to cope with a feared loss of care and self-esteem. Such behavior targets the caretaker and is calculated to stimulate and intensify concerns known to already exist in the caretaker. The behavior is learned by the elderly patient through earlier experiences in which he has monitored, perhaps unconsciously, the reactions of his caretakers to his increasing disability. The patient may, for instance, state or imply: "I can't eat, walk, see, sleep; I'm neglected, I cannot hold my urine, I cannot breathe. I wish to die, I can't remember, I can't be alone." Such expressions of anguish cause certain vulnerable caretakers to actively seek solutions *for* the patient, and to feel responsible for doing so, even though such responses may be detrimental to the elderly patient.

The vulnerable caretaker becomes responsive to the patient because of needs that are equally strong, although submissive in nature. In some instances the vulnerable caretaker has been particularly wounded narcissistically earlier in life by the parent and tries to undo that painful rejection by serving the needs of the parent as they arise over the long term. When this persistent need competes with other needs and ambitions of the caretaker, such as marital, parental, and occupational roles, he is placed in conflict. At times the caretaker may achieve a sense of right-eousness as, for example, the only child who "truly" loves mother, and will chastise other siblings for being disloyal. At other times the same caretaker may feel emptiness in this in-dentured role and that life has passed him by as a result of commitment to a fruitless pursuit.

Aside from these complex psychological forces which re-verberate throughout the family, external forces such as cul-tural and religious proscriptions relevant to the parent–child or husband–wife relationship influence the responsiveness of the caretaker. When reminded, for instance, of the wife's mar-ital obligation to her husband "in sickness" it may be hard for the caretaking wife to distinguish between fulfilling obligations on the one hand and responding to manipulations on the other.

When expressions of helplessness find their mark in the patient's caretaker and the two participants become intensively united in a mutual system, one may consider this the Exagger-ated Helplessness Syndrome (EHS). The clinical pertinence of this development is that it reduces the patient's capacity to overcome the psychic conflict related to his disability. It is there-fore responsible for the development or prolongation of a chronic maladjustment, usually depressive in mood. It encour-ages the patient to seek psychological solutions through the caretaker's support when only intrapsychic adjustment will be effective.

Theory

External solutions, sought in a supportive caretaking re-lationship, are precarious solutions. They inevitably prove to be only partial, since the reality of disability intrudes repeatedly and disrupts the fragile balance established by the exaggerated helplessness bond. At those times, one may observe the recurrence of depressive, paranoid, confusional, regressive, or behavioral symptoms. Consequently, instead of synthesizing a fully contemporary self-image that includes the new disability, the patient, with the "help" of the caretaker, clings to his former self-image and attempts to convince himself that nothing has really changed. Thus, patients over the long term seek an internal intrapsychic solution in an external relationship that cannot provide it.

As a disability progresses, the patient is narcissistically assaulted. Inevitable loss of self-esteem and subsequent depression ensue, leading then to the development of a new adaptive relationship between patient and caretaker. In another paper (Breslau, 1984), the author attempted to demonstrate that the mechanism of externalization provides, in many cases, a way for elderly patients to repair the damage to self-image which has been caused by disability.

Externalization is a member of a family of mechanisms involving "the subjective allocation of inner phenomena to the outer world" (Novick and Kelly, 1979). As opposed to projection, which denotes the allocation of *drive* or impulse to the outer world, externalization denotes the allocation of aspects of *self* to the outer world. The author has suggested that the restabilization of self-esteem depends on the use of externalization which allows the patient to join with the caretaker and share the perceived qualities of the caretaker as though they were his own. The end result of the externalization is that the weakened self-image of the patient is strengthened even though the integrity of his own self-image is dependent on the continuation of this caretaker–patient relationship and the deemphasis of the boundaries between individuals. While externalization is "a defense of the narcissistic pre-object period of ego development" (Brodey, 1965), and as such, is a primitive mechanism, from the viewpoint of what it accomplishes in stabilizing the self-image of the disabled elderly it may be highly adaptive and age appropriate. These externalizations develop slowly as disability becomes apparent to the patient. For some, the loss of confidence in memory brings about a painful loss of self-esteem. It is reparative for the patient to experience the caretaker's memory as part of his own, inseparable from himself. Similarly, the loss of influence over others, for instance, may be humiliating to the aged patient, but his impression that the caretaker's influence over others belongs to his own self-image is at least a temporary solution. These relationships become more or less stable depending upon many factors; internal, such as personality factors, and external, such as the financial resources and time of the caretaker.

Since this interdependence becomes a preemptory need for the aged, both in terms of actual care needs, as well as in aiding the cohesion of the personality and self-esteem, any threat to the system is conceived as a potential catastrophe. Moreover, any weakening of the healing externalization will threaten the aged patient once more with the experience of functional failure, helplessness, and loss of self. It is not remarkable, then, that the elderly often react to the potential loss of a caretaker by energetic attempts, however regressed, to maintain the relationship.

EHS and Chronic Secondary Dysphoria

Exaggerated helplessness may play a role in situations in which elderly individuals need to intensify the desperate bond to their caretaker and is common as a feature of chronic depression, secondary to illness. Such depressions provide an excellent model of the role exaggerated helplessness plays in chronic illness.

Akiskal (1983) has described the features of "chronic secondary dysphoria" which are "superimposed on long-standing, non-affective psychiatric disorder, incapacitating medical disease or both." He states that when incapacitating psychiatric and chronic medical disorders coexist in the same patient they are particularly "potent in producing refractory dysphoric reactions." Using his model as a basis one can describe "chronic secondary dysphoria of the elderly" as follows:

1. The most common preexisting disorders are likely to be central nervous system (CNS) disorders; either the cognitive disorder of primary degenerative dementia, multiinfarct dementia, or cerebral infraction with noncognitive disability.
2. The onset is usually not associated with symptoms that satisfy the criteria for major depression (though it may be) but is commonly associated with symptoms considered part of an adjustment disorder, the physical disability being the precipitating stress. At first, the dysphoria is often not viewed as a separate entity.
3. Family history for major affective disorder is absent and REM latency is not reduced (Kupfer, Foster, Coble, McPartland, and Ulrich, 1978; Akiskal, Lemmi, Yerevanian, King, and Belluomini, 1982). Such findings are consistent with an illness that is largely the result of maladaptation to a powerful external stressor.
4. The dysphoric mood is intermittent, concomittant with the occurrence of events that highlight the patient's disability.
5. Exaggerated helplessness syndrome is commonly associated.

The depression itself attests to the patient's failure to adjust to the disabilities of aging. Rather than attempt a reality solution or to work through the loss of function and its meaning, the patient attempts to demonstrate not only his physical helplessness but helplessness in finding a psychological solution to disability. In this sense, exaggerated helplessness is a metaphor drawn from the experience of physical disability. The following example will illustrate these concepts.

> An elderly woman became increasingly unable to live independently because of problems in cognition. She developed intermittent panic attacks, withdrawal from social activities, and chronic secondary dysphoria.
>
> The patient's neurologist referred her for psychiatric care, but after one visit the patient complained that she would be unable to endure further visits. The patient's family quickly acquiesced to this. Similarly, when the patient rejected psychiatric care her neurologist quickly offered to hospitalize her for these same symptoms. Thus, both the family and the patient's physician encouraged the development of exaggerated helplessness by suggesting to the patient, by their behavior, that the responsibility for finding a psychological solution was not hers. This encouraged the patient to mention repeatedly her sense of personal worthlessness, depression, and a wish to die, as a new means of dealing with her plight. These statements tended to fix the responsibility with the family and the doctor and made further work on her frightening cognitive failure impossible. The impediment to therapeutic progress was perhaps the most disturbing aspect of the newly evolved patient–family–physician interaction. Since the frightened patient felt safer clinging to a caretaker rather than finding a reality solution, her depression was not worked through. Rather, it became fixed and chronic, and, in keeping with the description of chronic secondary dysphoria in the elderly, came to clinical prominence whenever her disabled state was highlighted. Such elderly patients thus alternate between the discouragement of being unable to overcome a major disability and the feeling of abandonment by the caretaker.

In summary, the elderly patient defends against the unintegratable assault of disability by a union with his caretaker. When this union is threatened, the elderly patient attempts to preserve it by exaggerating the helpless state. The impact of this exaggeration is to make the caretaker feel responsible for the patient's state. This inevitably leads to a painful relationship that preempts the patient's problem-solving behavior. Consequently, instead of finding a psychologically useful solution, the patient develops chronic secondary dysphoria. Such dilemmas are typical of a large number of chronically depressed elderly whose failure to improve represents a major problem in health care.

Clinical Illustrations

The following account describes exaggerated helplessness syndrome as it may emerge as one aspect of an anxiety state. It is presented to demonstrate that active psychiatric treatment, focused specifically on this syndrome, may avert a chronic dysphoric state.

> The patient was an 84-year-old widow who lived alone in an apartment building for senior citizens and whose history included great pride in her own past independence. She did well until one evening when she called one of two nieces who assisted her, to say that she was developing sinus trouble. She attributed her apparent difficulty in breathing to insect spraying done that day in her building. Soon, shortness of breath ensued with increasing anxiety, air hunger, fear of being alone, decreased oral intake, and insomnia. Day by day her nieces increased their availability to the patient and the patient's physician examined her repeatedly, each time from a slightly different perspective. The doctor was eager to find a noxious element such as thyroid disease, toxic medications, congestive heart failure, chronic lung disease, transient ischemic attack, or panic disorder to explain her symptoms. During the six weeks that these symptoms persisted, the patient could contribute little to an understanding of her situation and

it was thus left to her nieces to make sense of her formless and nameless fears. When both doctor and nieces were sufficiently discouraged, a psychogeriatric consultation was arranged. The consultant was able to demonstrate that the patient's cognitive function was far worse than anyone knew—the nieces, doctor, and even the patient herself. He suspected that this finding explained the patient's extreme anxiety and her unwillingness to examine the possible causes of her problem. With deteriorating intellectual function, it appeared unlikely that the patient could continue to live independently in her highly cherished apartment. Rather than see these forbidding issues, she chose the vehicle of exaggerated helplessness to shift the focus of her problem and her anxiety to those around her. Thus began an interaction during an acute problem that threatened to give birth to an ingrained exaggerated helplessness syndrome and chronic depression.

At the time of admission to the hospital, two elements suggested exaggerated helplessness syndrome. First, the patient's two nieces seemed preoccupied with the danger that their aunt might feel abandoned by them, and second, the doctor was engaged in a kind of overly frenetic attempt to solve the problem of the patient's anxiety. It appeared that the patient believed it was up to those taking care of her to solve her problems. Those in the care system believed this also. The patient manifested her exaggerated helplessness by avoidance of any active examination of the problem. Staff members seem exquisitely sensitive to this behavior and often perceive it as a "taking advantage" of them. It often results in feelings of irritability amongst the staff. When staff members were open about these emotional reactions to the patient, they were frequently able to obtain important information not otherwise available.

Further evaluation needed to be directed toward understanding the underlying problem which was confronting the patient and the resulting pattern of exaggerated helplessness needed to be interpreted to the family as a pathological attempt to deal with this underlying problem. In addition, the physician and nieces needed to be guided toward an appropriate therapeutic role. The nieces needed help in understanding what, in themselves, caused them to be fearful that their aunt would feel abandoned and why they felt so much was up to them and so little up to the patient.

The treatment plan in the hospital was executed by a variety of individuals all participating in the management plan—social worker, primary nurse, medical doctor, psychiatrist, and the patient's two nieces. A team of these individuals, led by the psychiatrist, worked together to block the patient's attempt to diffuse her helplessness and to encourage her to articulate her own observations of her anxiety and the possible connections to her current life.

It was conjectured from the beginning that the patient's anxiety was related to a significant cognitive deficit which the patient would not acknowledge. Deficits in the demented range were registered on the "put the numbers on the clock" test. When the patient was asked to write her name and address, she did so in a scribble that could not be read, but she expected others to consider it an acceptable performance. She was unable to calculate serial 3s backward from 20. In addition when asked about her memory, she denied a problem and emphasized her ability to remember "way, way back."

The psychiatrist saw the patient individually, three times per week. He also spoke three times weekly with the patient's primary nurse and three times weekly with the patient's social worker, as well as meeting once a week with the patient's two nieces. The patient first described her problem as "the fear of dying." When her diffuse and multiple complaints were pointed out to her, she could recognize that "I am angry at myself and my body." These steps were accompanied by elements of depression and the complaint "if only I could cry." She identified further that her anxiety had to do with "nighttime, being alone, worrying about dying, decreased vision, and the preliminaries to dying." She told her body to "behave" but her heartbeat still pounded and she felt a loss of control over her body and was "mad." She said she feared going to sleep and not waking up and feared "not being my own boss." She began to see that people might get "disgusted with me," which was a potential reality problem as well as a projection of her own devaluation of herself: "I am just a zombie," she said.

Once the patient began to raise concerns about managing by herself in her apartment, arrangements were made for the nieces to take the patient on leave so she could spend increasing amounts of time there. This was preparation for discharge, but more important, it was a stimulus to the patient to think through her focal dilemma—the need to remain in her own home for many complex psychological reasons and the decreasing likelihood of this being possible owing to her cognitive decline. This had originally proved to be such an overwhelming challenge to the patient that she felt helpless, could not call problem solving into operation, and ultimately used her helplessness to alarm and mobilize her family.

The patient was finally discharged to her home after a 27-day hospital stay. Her reduced anxiety was abundantly confirmed by her ability to aggressively and competently make arrangements for supplementary help at home.

An important feature of this case is its demonstration that the presence of cognitive impairment does not preempt the orderly psychotherapeutic work required to master it. This is especially true when one treats patients who suffer from the initial cognitive impairments associated with primary degenerative dementia and whose preponderant mental capacity is intact.

The next case illustrates how interpersonal pathology between patient and caretaker, predating exaggerated helplessness syndrome, may stymie therapeutic efforts.

A 72-year-old widow with mild dementia and insulin dependent diabetes refused to allow professionals into her home to supervise her diet and insulin administration. She thus acted out symbolically, in projective fashion, her defiant refusal to allow the new realities of her cognitive disability to enter her life. This typified attitudes of self-righteousness and grandiosity with which she lived her life. She had insisted that her youngest daughter remain close and at this time in her life insisted that her daughter be available to support her attempt to ignore her cognitive defects.

Because she was quite unable to manage her insulin herself, yet refused all help, she was hospitalized as an involuntary patient in an acute psychiatric division. The daughter's participation in this was gained only after several counseling sessions during which she came to understand her mother's inability to make decisions for herself. The patient thus created a situation about which she could convincingly say "my daughter did it to me." Upon admission her efforts were strenuously directed, once again, toward proving that she could reverse the involuntary admission and/or what the involuntary admission stood for—the things that she could not control. She defiantly overturned her food trays on the floor and exhibitionistically banged her head on the wall, demonstrating a ruthlessly suicidal intent.

Staff were helpless to control either. This both obscured the nature of her own problem, the cognitive disability, and at the same time augmented her control over her daughter. Even though the patient settled down during the first three days of her admission, she persisted in targeting her daughter as letting her down, not caring, and forcing her into an intolerably humiliating and helpless position.

Although the daughter was seen by several counselors, who attempted to explore with her, her vulnerability to her mother's attempts to control her, and even though she learned the realistic things one could say to her mother and indeed needed to say as therapy for her and her mother, she remained emotionally unconvinced. In complementary fashion, the patient could never give up her own grandiose position that through her daughter she could avoid the painful reality of impaired cognition.

The crucial feeling and interaction between patient and caretaker, here demonstrated, clearly involves the deepest emotions of both. Merely to say the correct thing is not enough, as long as this covers a conscious lack of conviction, or unconscious wish to sabotage. Consequently, in order for the caretaker to be gen-

uinely useful as a therapeutic instrument or psychotherapist surrogate for the patient, he must truly work through his own
inhibiting conflicts and develop freedom from the patient's need
to control. This suggests that the caretaker must be treated with
some intensity, and in many cases must be willing to be identified
as a patient.

As opposed to the nieces described in the previous example,
the daughter of this patient had passively allowed her mother
to direct her life over the years. This made her especially vulnerable to her mother's current need to control her. Exploration
of the immediate situation was bound to be insufficient to correct
this lifelong pattern.

In this case the caretaker had already been in therapy for
more than two years. It was unsuccessful, in that it had failed to
help her to live more independently from her mother. Even
though she had begun to feel that much of the effort she had
spent in taking care of her mother was wasted, she always returned to her overconcern and an exaggerated sense of duty.

Serious obstacles exist in arranging psychotherapy for caretakers who are embroiled in exaggerated helplessness syndrome.
They may be just as resistant to intervention as the patient and
especially fearful of looking at the situation in depth. Moreover,
when psychotherapy is agreed to and arranged, unless the work
can be integrated into the overall effort and unless it is guided
by the same set of hypotheses, it may work at cross-purposes with
what has already been undertaken in the treatment of the patient.

The third case illustrates one way in which long-term care may
be structured to facilitate management of exaggerated helplessness syndrome.

Mrs. S. was an 80-year-old widow of many years, the mother
of two daughters whom she had pridefully raised, mainly in the
absence of her husband. Her closest relationship was with her
younger daughter H., with whom she retained daily contact by
phone and visits. The patient had become increasingly dependent on H. during recent years as her mild memory impairment

and faltering gait progressively worsened. On two occasions the patient had been admitted as an emergency patient to the acute hospital complaining of abdominal pain. No specific medical cause was diagnosed. An evaluation by a psychiatric consultant, at the time of the second admission, had clarified the fact that the brief absence of her daughter had immediately preceded one episode and the threat of the daughter's absence preceded a second. A third acute situation required psychiatric hospitalization because of an acute confusional state with paranoid delusions. It was also precipitated by a threat of H.'s absence. Although institutional placement had been discussed earlier, only this time did it become an acceptable alternative to H. who agreed to work toward such a plan with her mother.

The psychiatric casework and nursing effort was initiated by the psychiatric hospital staff and continued in a nursing home setting. While still in the hospital, the patient's lingering confusional state allowed her to alternately express contradictory attitudes without a sense of conflict. At times she could rationally recite the benefits of nursing home placement and the reasonableness of such a plan for her. Alternately, she fiercely reproached her daughter for instigating the plan for placement. This alternation continued through the first week of the placement and much of the early stay passed peacefully without other evidence of distress. An important change came when H. called to announce that a family celebration would occur during the weekend and that the patient would not be able to participate. Within two hours after this call, the patient once again developed acute abdominal pain and was transferred to the acute ward of a nearby hospital, this time by a physician unaware of the previous episodes.

On return to the nursing home setting within 48 hours, the patient was radically changed and demonstrated progressive mental adaptations to her new perceptions of the reality of placement. Initially she was withdrawn, depressed, and forgetful and remained in her room. After three days, she began to come to nursing with physical complaints that seemed inconsequential. She complained of pains in her throat and demanded that nurses and doctors examine it. When her demands for examination were not met, she became infuriated and bitterly expressed her wish that "it should happen to you." This, in time, became translated into "I wish you could become stuck in a place like this. How would you like it?" At the same time a variety of exaggerated helplessness behavior appeared. She relayed her physical complaints to H. and begged to have something done. She complained that she was mistreated and that it was criminal for her daughter to have arranged the placement. She vowed never to accept her role as a patient in the nursing home and said she wished she were dead. She rang her call bell incessantly with exaggerated complaints, and was described as saddened and depressed.

The patient's behavior was a compelling provocation for her daughter, who had already felt uncertain of the need for, or the moral purity of, placing her mother. Since it was felt that the daughter's vulnerability would delay or even completely abort the adjustment process of her mother, the therapeutic team saw the daughter frequently. The therapist pointed out to her that her mother was having difficulty accepting what she needed and was attempting to manipulate H., hoping ultimately to leave the nursing home. They counseled her at the family meeting to firmly advise her mother of the lack of other alternatives to the placement.

The team in the long-term care setting was composed of the social worker, the patient's primary nurse, and the psychiatrist. Specific time was reserved for working with the patient's family on a weekly basis. This time was used to help the family understand their therapeutic role. The nurses needed to clarify the management plan repeatedly and to monitor the family's behavior in the immediate clinical situation. For example, H. needed to be corrected when she tried to conceal her vacation plans from her mother and when she reacted to her mother's urgent telephone calls by rushing in to check her condition. The social worker maintained regular contact with the family and focused particularly on the many ways in which H. subtly undermined the treatment objectives. The psychiatrist helped conceptualize the problem, developed a management plan and contributed his expertise on complex issues having to do with timing, authority, psychological interpretation, psychotropic medications, and connected medical problems.

With this arrangement of therapeutic forces, Mrs. S. was able to progress toward reduction of exaggerated helplessness behavior. Eventually, Mrs. S. articulated how painful it was to relinquish ties to her two daughters: "That's all I ever had." By then, the exaggerated helplessness behavior had been reduced and the patient began to participate increasingly in programs that the nursing home provided.

Management and Treatment

Exaggerated helplessness syndrome presents in a variety of ways to individual physicians, neurologists, psychiatrists, hospital emergency rooms, assessment units, and nursing homes. Presenting complaints tend to be medical and obscure the quixotic family situation. Since it is usually not identified as a complex maladjustment of patient and family to disability and then managed as such, definitive intervention is usually lacking. Physicians may rule biological diseases in or out, but because of lack of expertise and necessary team members aboard (i.e., psychiatrists and social workers), they cannot begin to see the problem in necessary depth. Acute hospitals are not able to go beyond the limits of their traditional care, even though with the addition of social workers they aspire to care for the "whole patient." It is possible that specialized care programs for the elderly, with the interdisciplinary team of psychiatrist, internist, social worker, and nurse may ultimately be able to handle these problems, if backed up by psychogeriatric inpatient services and long-term care institutions that are staffed and programmed to deliver sophisticated care.

Patient and family come for help during a crisis when the supportive network of the family can no longer patch together or maintain the personality integration of the patient. Presenting symptoms may be more prominent in the family caretaker or more prominent in the patient. Family members complain that they can "no longer go on like this," frequently meaning they feel paralyzed by the disabled parent's control over them, feeling on the one hand angry and on the other solicitous and responsive, unable to extricate themselves from this conflict. Moreover, the caretaker may be unaware of, or unwilling to disclose, the existence of the underlying distress. In either case, the feelings of the caretaker must be carefully reviewed and laid out gently in their parts—the frustration, resentment, and sense of paralysis as well as the reasons why the caretaker has felt responsible for solving the psychological problems of the patient. When there are other internal family conflicts and splits, they must be explored so that a family consensus exists, from which to carry forward a consistent management plan. No therapeutic work proceeds without this consensus.

On the patient's side, the underlying disability must be assessed, as well as reasons why the patient has been unable to confront it. In addition, one must clarify the methods the patient uses to embroil the caretaker in his problem and how this fits with the caretaker's vulnerability. As with many other forms of psychological treatment, clarification of the nature of the problem is as much treatment as it is assessment. Here too, once the situation is clarified in depth many natural forces may come to the fore in the healing process. The work must be brought together at the propitious moment by the physician, in a statement indicating that the principal objective is to help the *patient* deal better with the upset that his disability has caused.

Because patients and families are expected to accept views initially foreign to them, confrontation may need to be more aggressive than in traditional psychiatric settings. Moreover, improvements must occur relatively quickly because of limitations of professional time and patient resources.

Many features, however, serve the purposes of the treatment: the family distress in their quest for relief; the offer of help and support from a team of geriatricians who are willing to see the problem through to a reasonable conclusion; a professional care system that provides continuity, from office evaluation to acute hospital to long-term care; the availability of the acute hospital for those situations that become too chaotic for ambulatory care; and finally, an understanding of the situation that is convincing to the family and is conveyed to them in a supportive way.

A major obstacle is that the therapeutic team must ask the family to change certain beliefs related to their responsibility to parents and the role they should play. These beliefs die hard, but the benefits can be a new relationship with disabled parents or spouses compatible with their true physical and psychological needs. McEwan deals with these issues in greater detail in chapter 10, "The Whole Grandfather: An Intergenerational Approach to Family Therapy."

References

Akiskal, H. S. (1983), Dysthymic disorder: Psychopathology of proposed chronic depressive subtypes, *Psychiatry*, 140:1.

———— Lemmi, H., Yerevanian, B., King, D., & Belluomini, J. (1982), The utility of the REM latency test in psychiatric diagnosis: A study of 81 depressed outpatients. *Psychiat. Res.*, 7:101–110.

Breslau, L. (1984), Ties to Family and the need for geriatric care, *J. Geriat. Psychiat.*, 18:189–201.

Brodey, W. M. (1965), On the dynamics of narcissism, externalization and early ego development. *The Psychoanalytic Study of the Child*, 21:165–194. New York: International Universities Press.

Kupfer, D. J., Foster, G. F., Coble, P., McPartland, R. J., & Ulrich, R. F. (1978), The application of EEG sleep for the differential diagnosis of affective disorders. *Psychiatry*, 35:69.

Novick, T., & Kelly, K. (1979), Projection and externalization. *The Psychoanalytic Study of the Child*, 25:69–95. New York: International Universities Press.

Skodal, A. E., & Spitzer, R. L. (1983), Depression in the elderly: Clinical criteria. In: *Depression and Aging*, ed. L. Breslau & M. Haug. New York: Springer, pp. 20–29.

7

CHARACTER DISORDERS IN THE ELDERLY: AN OVERVIEW

Joel Sadavoy, M.D.

Introduction

The general psychiatric literature has burgeoned with papers on character disorders and character pathology over the last 20 years. By comparison, very little has appeared in the geriatric psychiatry literature on this subject. However, if sought after, this disorder is often identified and represents a significant proportion of the psychopathology found in the geriatric population. Because these patients are so difficult, they are easily and frequently avoided. Not only does this further worsen the pathology, it prevents the treating staff from understanding, relating to, and ultimately helping this very vulnerable and distressed group of patients.

Clinicians will readily recognize the behavioral syndrome of the characterologically disordered patients. These are the patients who are unreasonably demanding and overly sensitive to criticism or disappointment. Their personal relationships are unstable and they cause others to feel burdened. Their emotional reactions are intense, impulsive, and labile, especially with respect to rage and depression. Crisis and stress are often badly handled and may lead to severe breakdown, suicidal impulsivity, or other forms of self-destructiveness. While severe symptoms may appear intermittently, the core pathology has been present throughout life and does not diminish with aging, although its manifestations may change.

The clinical material which forms the background of this chapter is based on the author's experience in treating and supervising the treatment of character disordered elderly patients in outpatient private practice, nonpsychiatric chronic institutions, and an active care geriatric psychiatric unit. In each of these formats, as will be evident from the cases, therapy has been based on an integrated psychoanalytic theoretical approach.

Definition of Character Disorder

Character disorder is a life-long maladaptive style of behavior which reflects a number of specific psychological vulnerabilities stemming from early-life environmental or interpersonal deprivations and failures.

The problem of defining this patient group clearly is illustrated by the diagnostic confusion surrounding the syndrome. Broadly stated, these patients fall into a heterogeneous group of behaviorally and therapeutically difficult individuals who do not fit well into the traditional diagnostic groups of neurotic, psychotic, or organic (Silver, 1983). A partial list of diagnostic labels would include: borderline (Stern, 1938; Knight, 1953; Grinker, Werble, and Drye, 1968; Kernberg, 1975; Gunderson and Singer, 1981); narcissistic (Kohut, 1977; Kohut and Wolfe, 1978); special (Main, 1957; Burnham, 1966); manipulative (Mackenzie, 1978); hateful (Groves, 1978); pseudoneurotic schizophrenic (Hoch and Polatin, 1949); ambulatory schizophrenic (Zilboorg, 1941); as if (Deutsch, 1942); schizoid (Guntrip, 1971); psychotic character (Frosch, 1964); and Freud's term—*a common scoundrel* (Michels, 1977). Perhaps the most useful term is Michels's (1977) *difficult* or Silver's (1983) *char-*

acterologically difficult. The term *difficult* is clinically descriptive and avoids the pitfalls of the current diagnostic debates, but has the disadvantage of being a general rather than a specific label.

These labels each reflect a variation on a common theme, but, following Silver (1985), four main groupings may be created: (1) schizophrenic spectrum disorders (Zilboorg, 1941; Deutsch, 1942; Hoch and Polatin, 1949; Knight, 1953; Schmideberg, 1959; Frosch, 1964;; (2) affective spectrum disorders (Klein, 1975; Masterson, 1981; Soloff and Millward, 1983); (3) organic dysfunction (Andrulonis, Glueck, Stroebel, and Vogel, 1982); (4) character pathology (Goldfarb and Sheps, 1954; Kernberg, 1975; Masterson, 1981). Other authors have subclassified these patients differently on the basis of clinical severity (Grinker, et al., 1968); character structure (Kernberg, 1975; Giovacchini, 1979); and descriptive symptoms (Groves, 1978). Despite the obvious specific distinguishing characteristics in each of these diagnostic subgroups, the author has been impressed by the similarities of the descriptions of the behavioral manifestations, and by how the essential clinical picture remains strikingly similar from one author's description of the syndrome to another's.

The largely descriptive diagnostic labels are associated with a variety of explanatory psychodynamic theories. A complete definition of character disorder must include both the descriptive and the psychodynamic, each of which will be discussed in more detail.

Psychodynamics of the Characterologically Difficult Patient

The variety of theoretical explanations which has been proposed for the symptomatic behavior of the characterologically disturbed patient attests to the difficulty which therapists and theorists have had in understanding the underlying meaning of these symptoms. However, the essential and basic premise in the psychodynamic formulation of character pathology is that the disordered individual is vulnerable to breakdown under stress because of early life failures of intrapsychic development. This may have had a variety of causes; for example, premature overwhelming stresses secondary to neglect, abandonment, unavoidable separations, or death of parents; failure of the maternal object to create an appropriate facilitating environment for formation of a cohesive self; failure of the interpersonal environment, particularly the maternal environment, to provide appropriate good enough external objects for incorporation into the psychic structure of the individual; early failures in the structure of the environment because of war, disease, hunger, and so on leading to physical and emotional traumata. These failures of the early life systems of the individual predispose him to developing a pathological defensive character style, and the need for primitive defensive behavior.

The link between early life developmental problems and later pathology has not always been clear. However, as general theories of behavior and development have evolved, more helpful models for describing and understanding the inner world of such patients have emerged. Silver (1985) has summarized the evolution in psychoanalytic theory which has provided a more sound theoretical base for understanding the clinical manifestations of characterologically disordered patients. Specifically, he cites the move away from drive theory (classical Freudian) to object relations theory, and from psychosexual developmental theory to general personality developmental theories. More recent, and with respect to these patients, more relevant models include object relations theories (Fairbairn, 1954); Guntrip's (1971) concept of the schizoid; Kernberg's (1975) masterful synthesis of object relations, drive theory, and genetic theory; Mahler, Pine, and Bergman's (1975) developmental theories; Erickson's (1959) life cycle concepts; and Kohut's (1977) self psychology principles. It is now possible to better understand that an individual is composed of a variety of experiences and perceptions of others. In the course of development, he has abstracted these perceptions of others and himself from the environment, filtered them through his unique psychological processing mechanisms, and internalized and forged them into a more or less coherent self, replete with unconscious processes, strengths, and vulnerabilities. This perspective clarifies the relationship between the inner, psychological realities of the individual and the outer concrete existential realities of his life. Obviously these are highly complex models, and it is beyond the scope of this chapter to review them in detail. Suffice it to say that these theories give an essential structure to the bewildering array of symptoms of the difficult patient. Without a model for understanding the motivations of the character disordered individual, therapists may be easily confused and overwhelmed. The inappropriate responses and reactions of the therapists that result make things worse, causing exasperation and defeat.

While each of the major psychodynamic theories offers relevant perspectives, no one of them is all-inclusive. At the risk of eliciting an accusation of "eclecticism," the following five basic issues are proposed as central to character pathology:

1. The fear or experience of abandonment or empty aloneness.
2. Real or fantasied narcissistic injury to self-esteem and failure of the self-selfobject relationships. Selfobject is a self psychology term (Kohut, 1977) which refers to an important external relationship which, put simply, bolsters the individual's sense of power, importance, and value through its mirroring and idealized responses.
3. Impaired affect tolerance (see Krystal, chapter 5, "The Impact of Massive Psychic Trauma and the Capacity to Grieve Effectively").

4. Constitutional failures in the development of modulators of rage leading to overreliance on the defense of splitting, a complex concept rooted in object-relations theory. It refers to the internal, unconscious need of the patient to keep good and bad aspects of the self and others separate. This reflects a failure in integration of early good and bad representations of the self and others into whole and constant representations. The external manifestation of this inner phenomenon is seen in the "split" loyalties of caregivers and others who come under the influence of the patient's projections. Splitting is a central primitive defense of this patient population. By maintaining an internal separation of good and bad elements (part-objects) the patient protects against being overwhelmed by bad internal part-objects. When threatened, the individual may defensively externalize or project the bad onto an available other whom he may then either attack or flee from. If projection involves the good part-object, an idealized relationship may result. This defense of projection and the subsequent reaction of the individual to the "distorted other" is termed *projective identification*.

5. The fear and experience of loss of self-cohesion (the inner sense of wholeness) secondary to stress which causes actual or fantasied ego fragmentation; that is, loss of ego boundaries as occurs, for example, in minipsychotic states.

The reader is referred to the work of Frosch (1964), Kernberg (1975), Volkan (1976), Adler and Buie (1979), and Adler (1981), for a more detailed discussion of the theoretical basis of these principles.

Description of the Symptoms of Character Pathology

Table 7-1 lists a variety of behavioral features associated with the characterologically difficult patient. Not every patient

TABLE 7-1
Behavioral Features of the Characterologically Disturbed Individual

Interpersonal	Affective	Self-Destructive	Cognitive & Perceptual	Somatic	Functional
Blurred ego boundaries	Impaired intensity and range of emotion	Drugs	Impaired relationship to reality	Hypochondriasis	Variable school performance
Demanding	Rage, depression, and panic	Alcohol	Minipsychoses		Variable job performance
Guilt or hate induction	Sense of emptiness	Suicide	Flooding		Impairments in creativity
Demeaning	Intolerance of affect	Self-mutilation	Body image distortion		
Ambivalent	Pseudoequanimity		Depersonalization		
Inconsistent and unstable relationships					
"Special relationships"					
Rejection sensitive					
"The Bargain"					
"The Appeal"					
Help rejection					
Withdrawal					

will exhibit all of these features and the severity of expression of pathology will vary greatly, not only from patient to patient, but also in a given individual from time to time. The list, while not exhaustive, organizes the often bewildering array of symptoms. The description of the behaviors which follows will help to place these features into a clinical context.

Interpersonal Symptoms

A central and most troubling feature of the "difficult patient" is his unstable interpersonal relationships. One cause of this instability is the inability of the patient to recognize others as "separate" individuals who have their own struggles and needs. The others are made to feel like impersonal objects controlled at the whim of the haughty, grandiose patient who reacts with rage, panic, or depression if disappointed. The most difficult and demanding patients demonstrate little or not gratitude in return for the efforts of the "other." This reaction may provoke either a guilty sense of inadequacy in others for having failed to do enough, or anger and withdrawal in the face of the patient's insatiable needs.

Ambivalence, inconsistency, and unpredictability are hallmarks of the style of interpersonal relatedness of this group of patients. Friends, family, and therapists often do not know where they stand with the patient or how to avoid inducing the patient's negative reaction. With some idealized "special others," the patient will develop a seemingly unique relationship, giving these "others" a warm sense of being united closely with the patient, while the rest of the world continues to be vilified, demeaned, and rejected. In his paper "The Ailment," Main (1957) describes the havoc caused on a ward, as staff try to deal with the patient's alternating idealization and devaluation of the staff. Failure to provide a consistent, integrated approach results in casualties amongst both the staff and the patients.

A special feature of this difficulty occurs on wards and within institutional settings, wherein the patient seems to have the ability to externalize his own contradictory feelings and create opposing groups. One group (perhaps only a group of one) feels that it has "cornered the market" on understanding of and true caring for the difficult individual. The other camp, often devalued and attacked by the patient, views the efforts and sacrifice of the first as inappropriate and naive. Several other authors have clearly described this situation arising in a "split" staff dealing with a "special patient" (Main, 1957; Burnham, 1966; Ploye, 1977; Book, Sadavoy, and Silver, 1979; Sadavoy, Silver, Book, and Hamilton, 1981; Sadavoy and Dorian, 1983). Burnham (1966) described two mechanisms unconsciously used by the patient to control the institutional staff—the bargain and the appeal. When appealing, the patient cries poignantly for special help from the caregiver, implying, in the bargain, that a response will lead to his cure. Unfortunately, the bargain is never fulfilled since the patient is never satisfied and often ends up rejecting the help which was offered. Ultimately, both parties to the bargain suffer, the staff because of the frustration and guilt induced in them, and the patient because he feels abandoned, disappointed, and rejected.

While aggressive demandingness characterizes some patients, others, equally disturbed, display more passive, withdrawn pictures presenting either an icy cold aloofness or a depressive, hopeless, inconsolable picture.

Affective Symptoms

The affective states of the characterologically difficult patient tend to be intense, but restricted in range. The major emotional reactions are variants of rage, empty depression, and panic. Occasionally, a false picture of calmness, or pseudo-equanimity, belies the inner turmoil. In fact, most such patients do not tolerate any feelings well and may panic at any sense of emotional change, even a usually pleasant one. One consequence of their affective intolerance is the use of impulsive activity, acting out, to relieve emotional tension. This ranges in severity from relatively mild (although infuriating) negativistic resistance to more severe forms of impulsive behavior such as drug and alcohol abuse, self-mutilation, and overt suicide attempts.

Cognitive and Perceptual Symptoms

Under the influence of intense affect, the patient's reality testing may suffer, leading to cognitive and perceptual disturbances such as paranoid delusions or hallucinations (minipsychoses), which are generally short-lived but may be dramatic. For example, an 83-year-old woman saw images of frightening faces flash in the window. Less severe manifestations include feelings of unreality, depersonalization, or distorted self-perceptions of ugliness and deformity, which fluctuate with the patient's variable mood states. At the greatest level of agitation, in the most vulnerable individuals, "flooding" states of uncontrolled panic and unfocused motor activity may be released (Volkan, 1976).

Somatic Symptoms

The primitive, unmatured character structure of the difficult patient leads to bodily or somatic expression of emotional states. Fleeting or more prolonged hypochondriacal symptoms often result. This feature is common in the elderly and will be discussed more fully later on.

The Impact of Aging

Having reviewed the phenomenology and dynamics of character pathology, it is now possible to examine the special impact of aging on the psychic apparatus of these individuals with the resultant specific behavioral manifestations as they present in old age.

In a previous paper, Sadavoy and Dorian (1983) noted "the substantial numbers and variations of these (characterological) disorders" (p. 224), with special reference to the institutionalized aged. While for the author, there is no doubt about the truth of this statement, both for the institutionalized and non-institutionalized elderly population, the reader should be careful to keep a critical eye on these "facts." This chapter represents an initial attempt to define the problems and their treatment, but much research remains to be done, both to confirm "the numbers and variations of these disorders in the elderly" and to develop further effective programs of management. In this regard, a further word of caution may be raised. As will be evident later in the chapter, the elderly, even those who possess well-integrated, mature personalities, are vulnerable to a degree of transient regression under the stresses of aging. To make a valid diagnosis of character pathology in the elderly, therefore, one must be able to identify pathological behavioral reactions and relationships throughout life.

Old age imposes inevitable assaults which exacerbate character pathology. These assaults, listed below, while not necessarily unique to old age, are obviously more important in the last phases of life. Moreover, they tend to occur in a converging pattern, one crisis impacting on the next. While the individual may be able to bear a single event, the interplay of numerous factors is often too overwhelming. A partial list of such factors, which represent crisis or strain in the aging individual, and which will precipitate the symptoms of breakdown in the vulnerable, characterologically difficult patient includes:

1. Severe and frequent interpersonal losses, especially of close, sustaining relationships.

2. Physical disability with functional decline.
3. Loss of external manifestations of the self; for example, beauty, muscle power and bulk, and physical stature.
4. Loss of role; occupational, parental, societal.
5. Loss of defensive outlets and options previously available to deal with intolerable affective states.
6. An increased reliance on caretaking relationships which mobilize a variety of responses in the difficult patient, including magical fantasies, dependency conflicts, abandonment anxiety, rage reactions, and fear of engulfment.
7. Confrontations with the realities of mortality and death which were previously only fantasized.
8. Conflicts over the wish to live versus the wish for death.

It should be noted that these eight age-related stressors unfortunately dovetail with the five basic vulnerabilities of the character disordered individual—dread of abandonment, narcissistic conflict, affect intolerance, absence of rage modifying structures, and fragmentation of ego capacities. As a result, the person who has demonstrated the symptoms of character pathology under stress, will find himself, as he ages, assaulted by the very things he has most feared throughout his life.

Interpersonal Loss

Death of important others is very hard for the character disordered patient to contend with, because of an impaired ability to grieve. The capacity to grieve is an essential human function, since it permits an adaptation to loss, especially death, and allows emotional healing to occur so that life can go on. The work of grieving requires a period of some withdrawal from emotional life, during which the survivor encounters, repeatedly, the still vibrant images and memories of the deceased. When the lost relationship was relatively conflict free, this encounter creates sorrow, but does not generate undue rage, panic, or depression. The individual comes to terms with the loss, gives up a large part of his emotional investment in the relationship, and puts his energies back into daily life and ultimately into new relationships. In the course of his grief he will also tend to reexperience aspects of other losses, but if these have been adequately mourned, they will not be too hurtful.

Why then is grieving impaired in the character disordered individual? The answer is twofold: first, the relationship to the deceased is conflicted and ambivalent in death as it was in life. The survivor experiences panic at being left empty and alone. Frequently he feels rage, stemming from a primitive conception that the deceased "willfully" abandoned him. Each time the images and memories of the deceased are recalled, they stimulate overwhelming affect. No peace is achieved and reinvestment in normal life is greatly delayed. The second cause of impaired mourning is the fact that reexperiencing of previous losses reactivates those previously unresolved conflicts adding fuel to the emotional chaos. In other words, new losses in old age reactivate old unresolved conflicts with earlier lost objects which were never adequately mourned. This often leads to a late life breakdown of the capacity to effectively mourn new losses.

Elsewhere in this book (see chapter 1, The Mourning-Liberation Process), Pollock has described the liberating function of the mourning process in allowing personal growth to continue throughout life. Because the passage of time, per se, does not much modify the specific intrapsychic vulnerabilities of the character disordered person in this group, grief and mourning in old age is often aberrant—excessive, prolonged, and chaotic—and hence may mobilize the full picture of pathological breakdown. Such patients are often referred a few months after a death for treatment of apparent "depression." It is essential to realize that the patient's reaction is an aberrant expression of grief which will take much longer to resolve, be more dramatic in its expression, and lead to greater morbidity than would a similar process in a person with a less vulnerable psychic structure.

A 75-year-old woman was referred because of symptoms of withdrawal, periods of shouting, nightmares, sleeplessness, and rage. She had been widowed approximately one year prior to the referral. Her marriage had been full of conflict. She described her husband as an emotionally brutal man, who was at times also capable of kindness. During her therapy the patient fluctuated between deep regret at his loss, and raging accusations at his previous unfairness, rejection, and brutality. She could not put him to rest, but maintained a raging battle with him. Each time she thought of him, she became furious and then deeply depressed and suicidal. From the onset of treatment, it became evident that her impaired and intense grief process was fueled by severe emotional and economic deprivation during her childhood. She had never had a toy of any kind and claimed never to have heard a kind word. Although not physically abused, she portrayed a lifelong picture of emptiness and loneliness. Her intense and vivid memories of her parents were infected by conflicted feelings of hatred and longing—hatred of their unempathic coldness and longing for the fantasied goodness she imagined had been withheld. Despite their long-ago deaths, she had never mourned their losses either, continuing an unmodified battle with them as though they were still alive. Her husband's death reactivated her internal conflict with the unmourned lost parental objects, which reverberated with the current conflict with her husband, leading to a prolonged pathological mourning. In passing it may be noted that therapy with this difficult but bright and verbal woman has been successful over a three-year period in modifying her struggle with her inner object world. She has become appropriately assertive and separated successfully for the first time from her symbiotically tied adult son.

Physical Disability

The physical changes of aging also require a mourning-adaptation response; that is, changes in bodily function and appearance require the capacity to accept the unchangeable, grieve for it, and give it up. Additionally, however, as Berezin points out in chapter 3 "Reflections on Psychotherapy with the Elderly," there is a need to work through the unconscious conflicts which may be specifically attached to a given aspect of the physical self.

This process is somewhat more involved than simple mourning because physical losses have a real and ever present impact on the person's life; for example, the inability to walk after a stroke. Equally important is the impact of the symbolic loss, which is different for each person. A given attribute or capacity may be highly invested unconsciously, and represent an important element in the maintenance of the person's sense of self-esteem. Moreover, not only does a physical loss represent loss per se, it may also be experienced as a symbolic attack by the "bad" (weak, vulnerable, or depriving) part of the self on the good (vital and gratifying). In other words, not only must the individual mourn and give up the real function or attribute, he must, in the process, have the capacity to work through the symbolic elements. In the following vignette, the lost attribute of physical beauty had a severe narcissistic impact on a vulnerable woman. The loss represented a failure of her capacity to continue to generate admiration, so essential to the maintenance of her sense of self. In general, the more primitive the psychic structure, the greater is the individual's reliance on external reinforcement for the maintenance of the self.

A woman in her seventies was referred for psychiatric consultation following an acute decompensation. Her history revealed that she had relied heavily on her good looks and appearance throughout her life to sustain her sense of "self-worth." One day while entertaining a friend, she glanced casually in a mirror, and as if for the first time, truly saw herself as old. This crystalizing experience had a catastrophic effect. She collapsed crying, agitated, and fearful, necessitating urgent psychiatric treatment.

For the elderly, this kind of confrontation is frequent and unavoidable. It occurs, for example, when patients are admitted to a geriatric facility and suddenly find that they are undeniably a part of a group of old peers who mirror their own illness and decline, from whom they can no longer distance themselves through denial. Less dramatic forms of narcissistic trauma occur repeatedly. Examples include the former executive who was no longer recognized by his younger successors; the sculptor whose arthritis had crippled his creativity; the self-sufficient dominant mother who began to be patronized and advised by her previously admiring children; the self-reliant, dignified businessman humiliated by his growing inability to control his bladder function; the former socialite who became withdrawn as she lost the capacity to get in and out of a taxi without help; the aristocratic matriarch who attempted suicide because she feared the humiliation of having to remove her impossible-to-fit dentures in public. In each of these capsules of patients who were seen in therapy, the actual assaults, while objectively seemingly trivial, attacked the vulnerable narcissistic core of these patients, who became seriously emotionally impaired as a result. Even the healthiest individual would cringe at this unpleasantness, but the vulnerable individual collapses.

Loss of Defensive Outlets

A serious, but little recognized change of old age is the blocking of channels for acting out or sublimating unconscious conflict. For example, in the young, characterologically disordered person, abandonment fears may be compensated for by a variety of actions—flight, sexual promiscuity, drug abuse, or frenetic social activity. In the aged, physical, social, and economic realities prevent these mechanisms from operating. Willing and able partners are scarce; social circles are narrowed by illness and death of peers; the self-reliance necessary to run in search of replacements for disappointing, abandoning objects is often halted by physical deficiencies. This is especially true of the hospitalized or institutionalized elderly who are "trapped" with their caretakers for better or worse. Anxiety and inner tension may build unbearably if the patient has no avenue for acting out.

Reliance on Caretakers

All aged persons, at one point or another become increasingly and unavoidably reliant on others. At a superficial level it is easy to relate to aspects of the humiliation which may be experienced as the result of forced intimacy and reliance on others. The deeper meaning of this change for some characterologically disturbed individuals is more dramatic. On an unconscious level, intense relationships mobilize two sides of a basic psychological dilemma. On the one hand, dyadic relationships stimulate intense and at times overwhelming regressive wishes to be held and emotionally fed. While craving this closeness, however, the patient may fear the full extent of his primitive wishes for closeness, as these wishes lead to fears of loss of the self, either through merging with the caregivers or through engulfment by the object.

Associated with fears of loss of the self through engulfment, is the patient's fear of loss of the loved object. As noted earlier, real relationships are inevitably disappointing and the vulnerable and primitive individual is easily moved to feelings of rage at this disappointment and abandonment by the caretaker. However, because the "other" may be either symbolically or actually essential to the person's survival, the patient fears his primitive rage reactions, since rage threatens to magically destroy the very object he needs so much. Intense relationships, therefore, produce great anxiety in the character disordered individual either because of fear of engulfment and merging, or because of fear of destroying the needed object through primitive rage in response to abandonment. When the individual is free to act on these anxieties, one sees repeated scenarios of relationships forming rapidly and building intensely, only to end in breakup. When, for reasons of necessity, the dyad cannot break up to relieve the anxieties (as is often true for the elderly), the more primitive person in the relationship regresses and manifests more of the various symptoms of character pathology. One example of such a phenomenon is seen in Breslau's syndrome of "exaggerated helplessness" (Breslau, chapter 6, "Exaggerated Helplessness Syndrome").

If unrecognized and unmodified, intense relationships produce increasingly aberrant symptoms in the patient. Main's (1957) descriptions of the effect of these relationships is instructive.

In the elderly, the crucial element in this model of the inescapable relationship, is the frequency with which caretaker and patient are bound together in a closed system with no possibility of separation. Not only are they bonded by the patient's fantasied fears of separation and empty aloneness, they are bonded by the patient's real and inescapable dependency needs. In the younger patient, there is a fantasied and unconscious life-sustaining reliance on the caretaker–lover–therapist. In the old patient this fantasy is much more likely to be a reality. Separation might truly be lethal for the patient. As the following vignette illustrates, these enmeshment factors are often most intense in the institutional setting.

Mrs. A. was an 89-year-old woman living in a home for the

aged which provided medical, psychiatric, nursing, and social work services. In the three months following admission, she had a litany of complaints—the food was no good, she had no intellectual peers, the nurses were inadequate, she didn't get quick enough attention, she was constantly unhappy or depressed, and her doctor was "forcing" medication on her. She rejected help and at the same time was demanding of it. She directed haughty, demeaning, insulting comments at the nurses, although one or two were always her current favorites. She emphasized to all who would listen, her excellent memory and previous social status. Her moods were unpredictable and nurses did not know if they would be favored or rejected when approaching her. In addition to fluctuating rages which alternated with intense depressive feelings and expressions of hopelessness, she regularly threatened suicide. She twice attempted suicide, in fact, once with a razor blade which she kept hidden in her room.

Her full and complex history reinforced the image of her self-proclaimed "specialness." Prior to World War II, she was a member of Viennese high society who had conversations about psychoanalysis with her friends, Freud and Jung. She married a "brilliant" doctor, gave birth to an "exceptional" son, and lived a sparkling life-style—all somewhat idealized in her recounting. Then came the Holocaust. She was the only survivor of her family. Her life and identity were totally wiped out.

Clearly, the determinants of this lady's aberrant and at times chaotic behavior in the institution were complex and very easily misunderstood by the caretakers. They became intensely involved with her, at first trying to placate her by responding to her unceasing demands, only later to become increasingly angry and rejecting of her as their efforts were constantly rebuffed. They feared her suicide, but felt impotent to deal with her. Moreover, because of her true physical needs—diabetes, osteoarthritis, mild cataracts, and partially resolved left-sided weakness secondary to CVA—they were trapped with her in a state of mutual suffering.

Explorations in subsequent psychotherapy, revealed a woman alone in the world, struggling internally with massive unresolved losses from the war. Her prewar experiences indicated a reliance on external idealized relationships to bolster and maintain her self-esteem. As long as the environment supplied this structure, as it largely did in her adult years in Vienna, she could function reasonably well.

Whatever the primary determinants of her character structure—early life experiences and/or the transmuting effects of the concentration camp and Holocaust—her behavior demonstrated interpersonal, affective, and self-destructive features of character pathology which produced serious negative effects on the caretaking staff. While enraged at her unremitting expressions of entitlement, they had a guilty awareness of her underlying vulnerability. Her demands were not simply a need for narcissistic satisfactions; they also reflected her terror at her vulnerability, her intense inner aloneness, and her battle with all the disappointing and destructive figures of her life which she carried within her. The mutual entrapment of patient and staff led to unwitting enactment of these conflicts. Since neither side could disengage, the affective intensity grew, leading to breakdown in the patient and disruption and distress in the staff.

With weekly psychotherapy and environmental changes, this patient's depressive symptoms improved, as did her relations with the staff. Intermittently, however, as her physical state declined stepwise, her symptoms flared, requiring renewed therapeutic efforts.

One must stress here that a useful understanding of the patient's behavior can only come about if caretakers look beyond the manifest and superficial. If behavior is taken at face value and only described with such terms as *adjustment reaction, loneliness,* or *manipulation,* the patient's behavior will inevitably be viewed simply as troublesome. The more depth of understanding available, the greater will be the specificity and effectiveness of the treatment response.

Conflict Over Death

Characterologically disordered patients struggle with conflicts over personal death. They frequently fantasize death as a source of relief from suffering, as well as representing the outcome of inner attacks of malevolent, internally-split bad objects. Primitive reunion fantasies with unmourned, idealized lost objects may predominate, or simply an ill-defined concept of peace and relief from overwhelming affective states of intolerable anxiety may fuel wishes for death. With the onset of physical decline in old age, death becomes a more immediate reality. The potential pain, helplessness, and infirmity which the patient imagines as a prelude to death often provokes intense fear and anxiety in the vulnerable person. Paradoxically, however, actual death may still retain its appeal and the suicidal ideation prevalent in younger character disordered patients remains in old age. Having said this, it is still necessary to recognize that little is known about death anxiety in old age and even less about the nature of suicidal impulses and death fantasies in the aged character disordered individual. Yalom (1980) has written cogently about death anxiety. He points to the presence of certain universal primitive defenses against death anxiety; specifically, psychological attempts to erect magical protective barriers against death. These barriers may take the form of a grandiose, counterphobic denial of death, or a search for a magical protector.

Meerloo (1955) suggests that all the aged fear death. "In all dreams of the old-aged, we find attempts to secure a secret, magic pact for immortality" (p. 88). He attributes various symptoms of old age—phobic symptoms, senile paranoia, and fear of insomnia—to death anxiety. The work of Jacques (1969) may help to sharpen the perspective on the problems of facing death for the vulnerable individual. While writing about death as part of the midlife crisis, Jacques identifies the need for "self-mourning", that is, the mourning of one's eventual death. As previously described, the psychological complexity of this process presents a major barrier to the emotionally impaired individual who will often be unable to reach this stage of maturity.

Behavioral Pathology of the Characterologically Disordered Elderly

The old patient with character pathology who comes under stress may demonstrate any of the symptoms seen in younger patients. However, the aging process imposes factors which highlight some features and inhibit others.

The younger patient may present a picture of interpersonal chaos and frenetic activity aimed at reducing feelings of aloneness and tension. Object hunger—the intense need for contact with others—may be expressed, for example, as promiscuity. Relational or occupational disappointments frequently lead the individual to desperately seek out more fulfilling replacements. In the better integrated individual, a driven immersion in work, projects, or political and social movements, may mask or structure a stressful circumstance and prevent breakdown. Other forms of dramatic acting out behavior express the individual's inner pain, rage, or depression; for example, suicide threats and attempts, abuse of street drugs or alcohol, and repeated psychiatric crises.

As noted earlier, in contrast to younger people, the elderly individual, although equally disturbed, has a more restricted range of behavioral expression, both in terms of the pathology itself, and the efforts of reducing emotional distress. Dramatic forms of acting out involving sexuality, mobility, immersion in work and activity, and even suicidal options are much more limited. The elderly, for example, attempt suicide much less frequently than young adults, although they are more often successful in completing the suicide. Various forms of physical and social disability limit the ability to seek out others to bolster self-esteem and satisfy their intense relational needs. Narcissistic exhibitionism and other forms of eliciting admiration are lost as the youth-oriented culture not only ignores the old person but may be actively revulsed by the visible signs of age or frailty.

Three major pathways of symptom expression predominate in the old:

1. Aberrant interactional patterns with family members, friends, and caretakers, primarily demonstrated through clinging, depressive panic, or angry entitlement. The nature of these relationships in old age exacerbates narcissistic defenses.

2. Heavy focus on somatic hypochondriacal concerns, as the body is used as a form of primitive communication of all needs, with consequent overreliance on the health care system.

3. Depressive withdrawal as a prevalent manifestation of psychopathology and expression of hopelessness and defeat in the face of the crises of old age. In each of the three major areas there is evidence of the core psychopathology of the individual, expressed through a variety of defensive or behavioral modes. The picture is further complicated by the frequency of the additional realistic stresses found in old age—the intensity of institutional life, primitive anxieties associated with severe illness and hospitalization, and organic impairment which further compromises ego functioning.

Before going on to describe in more detail the three major manifestations of geriatric character pathology, two dramatic accompaniments of these three major features are noteworthy—suicide and panic-flooding.

As avenues of action are more restricted, the older individual, already vulnerable to the impact of losses (Sadavoy and Dorian, 1983) will become desperate in the face of mounting narcissistic assaults. In those who have been prone to action earlier in life, active suicidal attempts become an option. Such individuals may use suicide attempts as desperate messages of hopelessness which, as in the young, will escalate if not heeded, until the message no longer can be ignored.

> An 82-year-old man had a lifelong history of behavioral difficulties, psychopathy, and aberrant interpersonal relationships. His children had "given up on him" and felt that they were no longer able to respond to his unremitting demands and self-centered narcissistic stance. Following his move to a home for

the aged, and functioning at a relatively independent level, the patient continued his lifelong acting out patterns, albeit in greatly modified form. He focused much of his energy on trying to find a remedy for his self-diagnosed urinary tract problems, which he believed produced incontinence (objectively minimal), and spent a good deal of his time doing what he "did best" which was selling raffle tickets. This behavior, while presenting various complications in his management in the home, was for a long time viewed tolerantly and with some amusement by the staff who were able to admire him as a "feisty old man." His spirited uncooperativeness, however, became a serious challenge to his caretakers as his decreasing cognitive capacities outstripped his demands for independence. Moreover, his indiscriminate use of physicians in the community conflicted with the institution's medical services offered to him, frequently leading to inappropriate self-medication and a suspicion of intermittent drug toxicity. As some of his frustrations grew, he began to express wishes to die and threatened suicide. For a period of time, the staff, although concerned, did not recognize the extent of his growing desperation, since he continued to mask it with concerted attempts to leave the nursing home in order to sell his tickets or find a doctor who would listen to him. With the passage of time, depressive periods of withdrawal began to be interspersed with his more active periods of what may be seen as acting out. Ultimately, his increasing, and to an extent unheeded messages of desperation finally led to a serious suicide attempt, and he had to be transferred to an inpatient psychiatric unit for a period of more intensive psychiatric treatment.

Emotional flooding is a reaction which develops in the more primitively developed or regressed patients. This symptom presents as the rather sudden breakdown of the patient's previously more controlled attempt to maintain self-cohesion and mastery through manipulation, pleading, bargaining and so on. A sudden increase in internal or external stress can lead to the outburst of chaotic emotionality. The patient becomes acutely expressive, crying, shaking, wailing, and screaming. If mobile, he may engage in aimless, agitated pacing and appear alarmingly out of touch with his environment. Unlike more controlled episodes of affective expression, the presence of another individual is not calming and may even exacerbate such situations. Words do not get through and anyone present experiences the patient's desperate panic. With time, such states generally abate spontaneously, but require a watchful, patient, and unintrusive presence to keep the patient safe. As the affect diminishes, the patient may then be approached verbally. On rare occasions, urgent mediation may be required.

The three major features of the behavioral expression of character pathology in the aged will now be examined in more detail.

Pathological Interpersonal Relationships

As previously noted, character pathology expresses itself most dramatically in situations of intense interpersonal conflict. To summarize briefly: The primitive patient needs unlimited mobility in his relationships for his defensive maneuvers to be most effective. The back and forth movement in the expression of intensity or distance in the relationship helps the patient modulate his feelings so that he is not overwhelmed by fears of merging and engulfment, or by the anxiety of his primitively fantasized destructive rage. It is this ambivalence in relationships which accounts for much of the interpersonal chaos seen in the earlier life of such patients, such as a series of intense, unsuccessful liaisons, or, symbiotic, enmeshed relationships full of rage, frequent separations, and passionate reconciliations. The more restricted the relationship or escape routes, the greater the intensity of the emotional buildup within the relationship. In the older patient, as dependency needs, both real and fantasied, become more intense and the escape routes become more restricted, marital relationships, parent–child relationships, and patient–caretaker relationships of the characterologically disturbed individual become emotional traps. The patient cannot run to reduce tension and the spouse, child, or nurse feels enmeshed and trapped by the realistic needs of the patient.

In discussing the younger characterologically disordered patient, Silver (1985) has emphasized the need for caution in undertaking too ambitious a therapeutic program. "In some cases, minimal or no intervention at all should be the treatment of choice. Friedman warns that without close attention during the assessment process, a novice therapist may undertake treatment . . . without any awareness of the extreme fragility of the patient's self structure." (p. 362) Silver continues, " 'the engaging and distancing thermostat,' indicates the degree to which a patient must resort to protecting his inner cohesiveness by controlling the closeness or distance of relationships." (p. 365) Intensive, long-term therapy may be contraindicated in some patients because of their incapacity to tolerate the intensity of the forced therapeutic relationship.

As stated already, such evaluations in the dependent elderly often become academic. Whatever the vulnerability of the patient, whether caretakers are trained or not, whether one ideally should maintain intermittent contact rather than intense involvement, all of these factors may be overridden by the unavoidable reality of the patient's need to have someone do for him, what in reality, he cannot do for himself.

> A 42-year-old man described his early life with his aging mother. She was a primitive woman with no capacity to understand the feelings of a child. She freely expressed her wishes, that he (her son) disappear or die; she was jealous of his friendships, and accused him viciously of imagined wrongdoing. When his father died, his mother accused him, in her panic, of having killed him.

Throughout the son's adolescence and early manhood, he openly raged at her and she at him. As he matured, he established, with great effort, a degree of separation from her, which calmed them both. As she aged into her late seventies and eighties, however, she began to have to turn to him for help. The content of her accusations shifted to his selfishness and lack of concern for her bodily needs. No longer, however, could he ignore her and control the battling through separation and distance. Because of her real physical needs, once again they were thrown into passionate and unavoidable conflict. When the mother became ill and was hospitalized, the son panicked and came into treatment where he gradually came to a better understanding of the intensity of the merging bond which he and she had together. As he became less fearful of her illnesses, secondary to a reduction in his rage and his own fears of abandonment, the fights diminished and he was once again able to establish appropriate distance. While this aided his adjustment, it did little for her, except to reduce the frequency of her affective storms.

This vignette illustrates two important principles. First of all it demonstrates a shift in the pattern of the expression of emotion in the frail elderly to bodily concerns. Second, it demonstrates the need for children to free themselves from the conscious and unconscious need to continually rescue the enmeshing parent, thereby protecting themselves from their own fear of the parent's death and their subsequent abandonment.

Narcissistic Symptoms

In keeping with the thoughts of others (Berezin, 1977; Breslau, 1980; Lazarus, 1980), it is the author's observation that narcissistic defenses are more readily mobilized by the stresses of old age. Some aspects of aging predispose all individuals to using these forms of defensive operations. In the first instance, as Berezin (1965) notes, the greatest blow to the individual as he ages is often to his self-image and to the vehicles for the maintenance of self-esteem. Accomplishments, power, ability, and beauty increasingly become aspects of memory rather than current displays of the self. The individual is then thrown back onto a variety of inner resources. The more solid the foundations for self-cohesion laid in early life, the greater the individual's tolerance of dysphoric affect and inner experience. The more positive the internalized object world, the less will be the individual's need to support self-cohesion and self-esteem through inappropriate narcissistic defensive behavior. In the characterologically impaired patient, however, there has often been a lifelong reliance on these narcissistic mechanisms, and at times, on even more primitive defenses indicative of still greater degrees of fragility of the self. Hence, the first major precipitant to the overuse of narcissistic defenses in the aged is the late life narcissistic assaults which derive from actual failures of the self.

In addition to the narcissistic assaults derived from actual failures of the self are the traumata generated by environmental circumstance and the nature of interpersonal relationships in this phase of life. The old person is often thrown into repeated situations of inferiority—reliance on a sales clerk to help pay for a purchase, a bus driver to aid with that first step, a visiting nurse to help get into the bath, and on and on. An incident poignantly highlighted this phenomenon to the author when he encountered an aging, respected colleague in a pharmacy. This dignified and talented physician was attempting to purchase some medication for himself, something he had done frequently in the past. On this occasion, however, the pharmacist rather abruptly and rudely questioned his credentials, implying this man was not in fact a physician. In response, the physician became flustered, agitated, and helpless as he fumbled through his wallet to find some appropriate identification, which he eventually did. This assault, although humiliating, was encompassed by virtue of this man's fundamental sense of intactness. The characterologically vulnerable patient, however, may find such encounters intolerable and become increasingly aggressive and rejecting toward any form of relationship which may increase his sense of vulnerability. This, of course, may extend toward all forms of help. Institutional life brings such experiences with greater frequency, intensity, and threat. Needed help may then be rejected because the narcissistic blow of acknowledging one's needfulness is too great.

> A young psychiatric resident was asked to see an 81-year-old woman in consultation. Previously, the patient had reluctantly seen a psychiatrist of great stature at another institution, but had permitted this only because she was able to convince herself that he was a personal friend. She had known him socially some years in the past. When the resident took over the case, she rejected him immediately. While she could tolerate the humiliation of seeing a psychiatrist who was famous, she could not tolerate the humiliation of seeing a resident whom she regarded as inferior to her and a mirror of how vulnerable and truly needy she had become.

Another similar example, in a more extreme form, is seen in the following vignette of the experience of yet another resident in geriatric psychiatry.

> The resident had undertaken to treat a very difficult, highly narcissistic 89-year-old woman recently institutionalized in a home for the aged. The initial referral was made because of "a past history of a suicide attempt" and because "since admission she is angry, noncooperative, and verbally and physically abusive toward staff." She described to the therapist a mood of constant sadness and said that she would kill herself except she did not have the means anymore—"they have taken it all away from me." Her relationships with staff were full of constant confrontation. She belittled and demeaned them at every opportunity, pointing

out their every misstep and lack of status or full nursing registration. She emphasized her own previous grandness, social status, independence, knowledge, and memory. Currently, she felt
that no one understood her needs or treated her in the special
way she deserved.

In weekly psychotherapy, the resident at first felt rejected
and demeaned by the patient. Gradually, however, he gained
acceptance because the patient perceived him as a person of high
status in the institution. Her initial haughtiness, bitterness, and
rage diminished as the therapist responded to her with am empathic understanding of her need for specialness. Simultaneously, he also helped the nursing staff appreciate this feature of
her care. The resident's accurate, empathic mirroring gradually
facilitated the development of a sustaining narcissistic transference in which the patient felt valued and acknowledged. The
patient developed a more stable adaptation as her narcissistic
needs were recognized and more appropriately met.

Somatic Preoccupations

Younger patients, under various circumstances may become preoccupied with bodily concerns. Although various body
and self-image distortions, self-mutilating behaviors, and other
less dramatic somatic foci, such as headaches, or anxiety symptoms such as tachycardia or light-headedness may be prevalent,
and at times, powerful expressions of inner feeling states, they
are for the most part not as ubiquitous as in the older patient.
Moreover, except in the most entrenched states, the somatic
focus in younger patients is often less intense and more amenable to confrontation, clarification, interpretation, and the redirection of anxieties to a more appropriate focus. One factor
which facilitates this process is, with some exceptions, that there
is generally little that is objectively physically disordered in the
younger patient. However, in the older patient, the body's
frailty creates a fertile environment for somatization. Bodily
concerns cannot be dismissed as only "fantasy." They must be

attended to by physicians and caretakers, and it is extremely difficult to sort out fact from anxiety and distortion.

Illness is a compelling force in relationships. For the old patient whose relationships may be already strained by years of pathological interpersonal stress, illness may become the best method of extracting needed emotional supplies of caring, time, and attention from the caretakers. It would be an error, however, to see this process merely as a manipulation. In addition to whatever secondary gain may be achieved, the patient is essentially responding to conscious and unconscious fears of weakness and pain—either actual or potential. Illness or decline may reawaken or stimulate the previously controlled internalized bad object world, creating for the patient an experience of being assaulted and in mortal danger. The attributes of the mobilized bad object world may be attached to the illness which then becomes overwhelmingly potent and destructive, although in fact, the illness at the moment may be benign. In addition, or instead, the bad object may be projected into the environment creating a paranoid interaction. The concept of a split inner world has been introduced earlier. This complex theory derives from the apparent, early developmental process whereby the infant internalizes aspects of others (especially mother) from the outer world. These aspects may be either "good and rewarding" or "bad, depriving, and assaultive." In the course of normal development, these aspects (part-objects) merge into a cohesive unified self. In pathological development, however, the bad and good remain split. The result is that later assaultive stresses, for example, a physical illness, may be imbued with the "projected" and split-off, bad part of the self. The illness itself, then becomes the feared and hated enemy.

Gitelson (1948) has pointed out that older people tend to become more and more sensitive to their bodily function. "The tendency is for the organism to try to cope with vague general anxiety by attaching it to specific vulnerable organs. Constipation, aching joints, or paresthesias are matters which can be legitimately looked upon as being of interest and concern to relatives or to the doctor. Under these circumstances, one must consider that the patient's own body may be the only vehicle remaining to him to express the intensity of his inner emotional pain and anxiety" (p. 11).

Depressive Withdrawal

This feature of character pathology is evident at all ages. Three major dynamics seem operative: the first has already been examined; that is, the loss of avenues of acting out, which drives affective expression inward. In the place of acting out, one finds forms of expression more reflective of the empty, giving-up hopelessness of the patient's inner experience. In some respects the withdrawal may be conceptualized as a defensive stance which delimits the experience of intense anxiety. As Easser (1974) has pointed out, the primitive patient may resort to empathic inhibition in an attempt to prevent the breakthrough of the full extent of his emptiness and of his need for a caring but unavailable other. The author (Sadavoy, Silver, and Book, 1979), has previously described how such patients, when intensely despairing, experience others as hurtful. Under such circumstances, any attempt to establish a caring bond with the patient reevokes the maternal bonds which, for the infant, were depriving and painful. The caretaker becomes imbued at these moments, through projective identification, with the affectively charged characteristics of the depriving, maternal object. When, for some aging individuals, the avenues of protest and paranoid projection narrow, the only remaining recourse is to give up the "protest" and retreat into despair. This kind of withdrawal may resemble syndrome depression and is often the precipitant for psychiatric referral. Careful examination, however, will often reveal the psychological and relational source of the feelings and their roots in rejection-sensitivity. If the experience of abandonment is prolonged or intense, a true, albeit somewhat atypical depression may supervene requiring not only a psychotherapeutic response to the patient's experience of abandonment, but also more vigorous antidepressant therapy such as medication or ECT.

Two other crucial factors of aging which alter the expression of pathology in the aged in the direction of withdrawal and hopeless depression are the forced dependency relationships of the old on the young, and societal attitudes about how the old should be cared for. With aging there is a gradual, often subtle shift in the attitudes of family and caretakers toward the old individual. As frailty becomes more apparent, others begin to feel the right to take liberties with the personal space of the older individual, both physically and emotionally. One sees this inherent in certain therapeutic biases. For example, psychotherapists have been told that old people like to touch and be touched, that they may be spoken to more familiarly, and that one ought to "sit closer." As noted above, this intrusion may increase feelings of panic in a vulnerable individual, already highly ambivalent about close relationships. One of the great dangers in such well-meaning but paternalistic attitudes is the subsequent predisposition of caretakers to identify regressed or anxious behavior as a normal outcome of aging, instead of attending to the patient's protests or acting out as expressions of psychopathology, needing specific treatment and understanding. At the other extreme are patronizing comments such as "she has always been difficult." Unlike younger patients, therefore, there is a social climate which permits or encourages regressive, external control of aberrant behavior in the aged.

One outcome of severe behavioral pathology which appears quite frequently in the elderly, is institutionalization. Old age may finally allow those enmeshed with the characterologically disturbed patient "a legitimate route to disengagement." As

Breslau's cases illustrate, this mechanism may not take hold until a desperate situation arises. Only then can the ambivalent relationship between child and parent or caretaker and patient be altered so that the caretaker, for example, may enact his latent wish to extrude the difficult patient, passing on the problem to a new caretaker. Unlike the younger patient, whose hospitalization may be temporary, institutionalization is a permanent solution for the geriatric patient, an enactment of the very abandonment scenario so feared by the patient all his life. Moreover, in contrast to younger patients, institutionalization may be accomplished even over the patient's protest because of the "justification" of physical infirmity or an inability to live alone or get along without help. Indeed, the very behavioral characteristics which are an expression of fear and emptiness in the old patient, drive away potential help (for example, community resources and companions) and further increase the likelihood of institutional placement.

As a result of the rejection and abandonment inherent in the dynamics of forced dependency and institutionalization, the character-disordered individual may first respond with agitated protest and rage. If the inexorable process continues, however, many such individuals succumb to bitter, helpless withdrawal. This picture is most often seen on chronic units of hospitals and nursing homes.

Treatment

The treatment process for the elderly character disordered patient is complex. As stated earlier in the chapter, the patient's characterological difficulties are exacerbated most dramatically when relationships become intense and intrusive. One of the important forums for the full display of behavioral pathology in the elderly, therefore, is the institutional setting. Here one sees all the major precipitants of regressive symptoms— abandonment, aloneness, loss of identity and sense of self-worth, absent outlets for action and control, intense intrusive relationships (staff and patients), noxious mirroring of aging by the other old patients, proximity to true illness and death, and frequently, inappropriate, unsophisticated staff responses to patient behavior. Because of the interplay of these forces within the institution, and the frequency and intensity of behavioral pathology in this vulnerable patient population, the author will focus on treatment issues as they apply to the institutionalized individual. Many of these principles of treatment are relevant in the ambulatory setting as well.

The goals of treatment are: (1) containing and limiting pathological behavior; (2) establishing a working alliance between patient, staff, and family; (3) developing a cohesive team approach to the patient; (4) reducing the patient's reliance on primitive pathological behavior by reducing inner tension levels, altering interpersonal stresses, and where possible changing or modifying defense mechanisms. Each of these four areas will be briefly reviewed followed by a detailed case illustration.

Containing and Limiting Pathological Behavior

Containment and limiting of pathological behavior requires a coordinated staff approach. Bolstered by a carefully constructed formulation, which provides a conceptual model for understanding the patient's behavior, the staff are in a position to implement the treatment plan. Often this begins with a written statement (for both staff and patient) of the expectations of the patient with special emphasis on the tolerable limits of behavior. These are discussed in detail with the patient and, if appropriate, the patient's family. The plan must take into account the needs of the patient for some sense of control and self-regulation as distinct from the essential requirement that the patient's behavior become tolerable to the staff. Specific items are addressed; for example, the limits of verbal or physical acting out, the requirements of participation in therapeutic milieu programs, visiting hours, medications, and so on. The plan is laid out in writing to reduce confusion, both for the patient and for the staff, about the terms or intent of the treatment plan. Additionally, and, most importantly, this limits the potential of character disordered patients to try to defensively control the environment through a process of splitting the staff. If all staff members are clear about the treatment plan and adhere to it, the patient will get a single, unified, clear message which will not only be more effective, but also reduce the patient's anxiety by containing and restricting the sense of his internal chaos being enacted in his environment.

The Establishment of a Working Alliance

Greenson (1972) defined the working alliance as "the relatively non-neurotic rational relationship between patient and analyst which makes it possible for the patient to work purposefully in the analytic situation" (p. 46). Although he was applying this definition to a relatively healthy patient population, the concept is useful in any treatment endeavor. The key issue is that the patient and therapist define and work toward a mutual goal, on behalf of the patient. While various complications in the relationship may arise, both participants are anchored by the mutual goal. Establishing such a healthy alliance is no mean feat with this patient group. Healthier patients can, relatively easily, discover a therapist's sincerity, hopefulness, strength, consistency, and caring. The patient with a character disorder puts defensive barriers in the way of this process. Only by careful therapeutic approaches can these defenses be modified. Some of the crucial elements are accurate empathic mirroring, appropriate titration of therapeutic intensity, consistency, reliability, firm and fair limit-setting, and the ability to encounter the patient's attacks and neither be driven away, destroyed, nor become retaliatory.

The establishment of a working alliance with the institutionalized elderly patient is further confounded by the need to create an alliance, not only between two individuals, but among the patient, the patient's family, and the whole therapeutic team.

Ideally families should be involved from the outset of treatment. The degree of involvement will depend on the degree of enmeshment within the system. In some situations, children have fled or been driven away, and one must be cautious before intruding on this homeostasis. However, often the distance is more apparent than real and attempts to reactivate appropriate family relations should be initiated. At first family members are often reluctant to get reinvolved in a relationship with a patient that has generally been painful for years. However, family involvement may be a crucial element for the success of the therapeutic process. Often it will occur whether it is planned for or not, and it is therefore preferable that it happen under better controlled, thought-out circumstances. In the family forum, the therapist is in a position to aid the family in developing a perspective on the patient which focuses less on the current pathology and more on the long-standing system of strain, tension, and ambivalence within the family. Rather than institutionalization being solely a mechanism for relief of stress in the system, it can be a powerful agent for change, beginning a process of reconciliation and correction of lifelong pathological and distorted relationships (see McEwan, chapter 10, "The Whole Grandfather: An Intergenerational Approach to Family Therapy").

Development of Cohesive Staff Team Approaches

In the case to follow, treatment was carried out by a skilled, cohesive therapeutic team. In most institutions, such teams are unavailable and must be forged on an ad hoc basis. This is a difficult task, but often possible if the core therapists (generally a psychiatrist and social worker) are able to take the time to form the team. In essence this is a dual process, involving first reestablishing goodwill toward the patient, who generally has been extremely difficult prior to the onset of the treatment process, and second, of educating the team about the nature and psychodynamics of the patient's problems and effective therapeutic strategies. Often, staff are initially very skeptical of psychiatric treatment. In particular they express worry that the treatment plan is too complex, that they do not have enough time to carry it out, or simply that the consultant–therapist is expecting too much of them. These fears are indeed valid unless the therapist is prepared to remain intensively involved at the outset of the treatment. At that time, not only must the patient and family be seen, but the staff must be involved in regular, educational sessions which reevaluate and regularly modify the treatment plan, to realistically adapt to the patient's difficulties and the level of staff effectiveness.

It is at the level of staff cooperation and skills that treatment frequently falters. Historically, custodians of the elderly have not been of high status, and hence staff in geriatric institutions are of widely varying levels of training and sophistication. While often dedicated and sometimes saintly in their tolerance, such helpers are frequently untrained and relatively unsophisticated. They may have great difficulty conceptualizing psychological models and not vilifying the patient only as bad and requiring discipline. However, even in the less well-endowed institutions, simplified and concrete versions of treatment plans and approaches to difficult patients have been successful. To an extent, however, the goals and methods must be adjusted to the skills of the staff. This is the limiting factor in any inpatient or institutional management program for this patient population.

Basic staff education and team building can be accomplished in approximately six hours of once-a-week, hourly meetings, during which staff should be encouraged to describe encounters with the patient in detail and receive carefully expressed, empathic, and constructive suggestions. They must be helped to maintain a nonpunitive stance toward limit setting and tolerate, without submitting to, the patient's demanding or otherwise attacking behavior. In very severe cases, where the patient's behavior has reverberated throughout the institution, as it often does, for example, through threats of litigation or calls to administration, the administrator of the facility should be informed of the treatment plans and his support enlisted (Sadavoy and Dorian, 1983).

In the old patient, as in the young, the contract must lay out the realistic expectations. The capacities of the staff, who become the "family" for many isolated older patients, must be realistically defined for the patient; that is, how fast they can respond, what are the real differences between day and night shifts; the type of interventions which they will use; and the limits of their tolerance. This aspect of a contract helps to establish separateness between the patient and the staff, reducing the ambivalent wish of the patient to merge with caretakers, and allowing the staff to maintain an appropriate distance from the engulfing problems of the patient.

Because of the multiplicity of "real" (as opposed to fantasized) problems of the old patient, one should try to include in the contract a specific discussion, albeit simple and brief, of the patient's physical, social, and economic difficulties and a definition of the staff's duties and obligations with regard to them. In light of the rejection-sensitivity and lack of object constancy (i.e., the ability to hold a comforting consistent image of another in mind even in the absence of that person) of these patients, they may often be best helped, in this early contract stage of therapy, by knowing about the comings and goings of the staff. The daily changes of shifts, for example, especially from day to evening staff can be evocative of anxiety and even panic. Vacations of key staff produce similar anxiety in the patient and may also evoke guilt in the staff members. Sometimes sustaining, concrete reminders of the staff person, for example a note about the next time they will meet, will help to reduce the abandonment anxiety and emptiness.

Reduce the Patient's Reliance on Primitive Pathological Behavior

It is an axiom of treatment with this patient population that uncritical therapeutic zeal and unrealistic goals will lead not only to failure, but probably to exacerbation of symptoms. One must also guard against becoming overwhelmed by the bewildering array of pathology and the natural tendency, under such circumstances, to try to control the patient's behavior mechanistically, with medication, avoidance of the patient, or in other ways not respond to the core problems. Some therapists may see attempts to address and change characterologically based behavior as grandiose. In commenting on this, one therapist has said, "once a crank always a crank." Such therapeutic nihilism offers little either to the suffering patient or to the equally suffering staff.

Beyond structure and contracts in limit setting, how can one deal with the deeper level of pain, emptiness, and panic of the patient? Here, a more sophisticated approach is necessary. The three steps already mentioned are effective and can be implemented by the staff without going any further. These approaches have a behavioral and learning thrust which induces change in behavior and may then reciprocally reduce anxiety. Some of the triggers for feeling and action, however, require psychotherapeutic approaches. This task should be left to a more experienced therapist. Regular sessions may be established at a frequency tolerable to the patient, wherein the patient, perhaps for the first time, begins to express feelings in words rather than converting them to defensive behaviors. In this process, cause and effect between vaguely understood but overwhelming feeling states and triggering events in the environment are established.

It is important to remember that such patients frequently demonstrate an intolerance of affect of any kind, living in fear of being overwhelmed by their feelings. They cannot clearly distinguish different types and intensities of emotion. Moreover, they lack a language to describe what they feel. The therapist's task is to provide order and structure for the patient's inner chaotic, emotional experience. This process is a painstaking one. It involves labeling feelings (for example, you are angry, sad, depressed, blue, anxious, fearful, panicky, happy, excited, frustrated), to separate and distinguish the colors and hues of the patient's feeling states. These feelings are then connected with causal events, not from the distant past, but immediately present in the environment. For example, "you were angry last night because the nurse did not come immediately." "You are very frightened because you imagined no one would look after you when I am away on vacation this week."

Unlike outpatient therapy, inpatient work permits careful observation of the feeling states and affective triggers and allows the therapist the opportunity to intervene rapidly and more accurately. The labeling and confrontation process helps the patient experience more order and control over his feeling states, and hence, over time, to be less reactive. There is no implication that basic intrapsychic structural change has occurred, only that control is established.

All of this work is most productive when it fosters not only a sense of internal mastery, but also an alliance with the therapist which helps gratify some of the patient's narcissistic needs. Although not specifically referring to this patient group, Goldfarb and Sheps (1954) have described this aspect of the therapeutic process. They stressed the need of the institutionalized patient to identify with the powerful parental qualities of the therapist and to experience a sense of dominance, triumph, or victory over the therapist. There are dangers here of course, not the least of which is that the perceived triumph over a therapist can make a characterologically disturbed patient fearful of his aggressive power and lead to escalation of anxiety. A more appropriate model is to help the patient experience a sense of value, acceptance, and unity with the therapist which strengthens the patient's sense of self-cohesion, without mobilizing competitive rage.

Once a therapeutic relationship and early working alliance forms, and, if the patient has begun to tolerate his feeling states, a further stage of therapy may be undertaken—that of mourning. Pollock and Berezin, in separate chapters have both commented on the centrality of this process to growth in later life. Clinically, the patient's task is to "face" verbally and in imagination, the major areas of loss in his life. Many elderly patients are unable to undertake this process because the burden of loss is too great, and the resources for substitution for the losses and reintegration of life activity too restricted. Generally, no attempts can or should be made to work through a broadly based mourning process. Rather, specific, immediate issues may be addressed; for example, physical changes, or illness, or death of a spouse or sibling.

On occasion, with the most well integrated of this vulnerable group, and where consistent and long-term psychotherapy is available, the patient may be able to go on to deal with earlier life experiences and take steps in the direction of some true characterological change. Sometimes, object constancy may evolve, with some merging of the inner, split-object world, leading to a reduction of anxiety and rage reactions, and a greater capacity to trust and be soothed. Such changes, however, are not the norm and in most cases this level of therapeutic ambition is not only unreachable, it is contraindicated. For not only are therapists confronted with fragile psychic structures, but the difficult therapeutic work necessary to induce change is occurring at a time of life which is fraught with crisis. Almost inevitably during the course of psychotherapy, renewed crises will arise beyond the control of either therapist or patient and unrelated to the therapeutic process. Further object loss, narcissistic trauma, or physical decline often intrude and may inhibit further progress or induce regression. If therapy has had a chance to take effect, however, these events may not be calamitous (Sadavoy and Dorian, 1983).

Finally, what is the role of medication? In the elderly, it is an axiom that medication should be kept to a minimum. In the character disordered patient, crises are generally interpersonally or situationally related and should, first, be dealt with as such as much as possible. In cases of severe agitation, medication may be necessary, but it should be used for specific target symptoms, and generally should not be used indefinitely. Where psychotic (generally paranoid) features are prominent and cannot be altered using all the other means described, small doses of major tranquilizers are helpful. The same is true of severe nighttime agitation, although this is generally better managed by contact, reassurance, and personal relationship. Intermittent, severe agitated anxiety or panic states may be best managed using a short-acting minor tranquilizer on a PRN basis. Staff, however, must be cautious not to deal with their own anxieties by medicating the patient. If true depressive symptoms appear, then antidepressant treatment including ECT may be useful and essential. In general, however, with adequate staff, accurate diagnosis and formulation, and careful treatment intervention, medications can and should be kept to a minimum. Although a full and comprehensive treatment approach is often necessary, especially for the severest problems, it may be modified for less demanding situations. For example, contracts may be focused and presented verbally, or staff contacts be somewhat less formalized. It is, of course, a practical impossibility to approach each patient with the complete treatment program.

The case example to follow will help to illustrate the goals of treatment of the character disordered patient, and the principles and methods of treatment used to achieve these goals. It also highlights some of the complexities of the interaction of physical and emotional factors in the treatment process. The case will describe some of the early life contributors to the patient's late life psychopathology. The relevant characterological features will be described and a formulation of the case connecting the physical and psychological elements will be offered. The treatment plan, which is based upon the formulation will be described including contract and limit setting, involvement of family, the use of psychotherapy and aspects of the working through process.

> Mrs. A. was a 72-year-old separated woman initially referred by her physician while she was living in a senior citizen's apartment building. Prior to referral, the patient had become a constant source of irritation and anger to those around her, other residents and staff alike. Her behavior included withdrawal, agitation, anxiety and worry, dangerous and irresponsible smoking in her apartment, borrowing and demanding money from other residents in order to buy cigarettes, and failure to fulfill basic obligations to the community life of the institution as she had originally agreed.
>
> Five years prior to her referral, the patient had a colostomy following bowel resection for rectal cancer. Thereafter she became increasingly emotionally dysfunctional. She moved in briefly with one of her two daughters, but shortly thereafter was angrily extruded from the house because of the intense family conflicts which she apparently created. She then moved into a senior citizens' apartment complex.
>
> In this institution her aberrant behavior appeared to stem

primarily, from her intense self-consciousness and sensitivity about her colostomy. She feared that it would make noise or smell. She frequently and consistently complained to her attending doctor that she had diarrhea, and as a result she was given codeine and Lomotil for bowel control, this, despite the fact that her symptoms had never been objectively confirmed. While never popular and never integrated into the social system around her, the patient maintained a kind of stable instability until she learned that one of her acquaintances had developed bowel cancer. It was this knowledge which apparently led to an exacerbation of her chronic emotional disability. She became gradually more agitated and reclusive, increasing her careless smoking to the point that there was a significant danger of fire. The result was that she became completely intolerable to the institution and was forced to leave.

A brief, unsuccessful period of outpatient psychiatric treatment ensued and an initial, ultimately inaccurate diagnosis of depression was entertained. A trial of antidepressant therapy was entirely unsuccessful. Because the patient was not motivated for treatment, could not at that stage engage in any alliance in therapy, and resorted to lying and avoidance to handle any stress, it became clear that her symptoms could only be managed by hospitalization. She was admitted to an active care geriatric psychiatry unit.

At the time of admission, there was no evidence of cognitive dysfunction, psychosis, or major affective disorder.

Her medications on admission included Lomotil, codeine, and very small, likely homeopathic doses of doxepin. The patient had no formal past psychiatric history, nor was there a family history of psychiatric disorder. However, the patient's past history is important for understanding the development of her symptoms, and will be presented briefly.

The patient was born in a large Canadian city in 1907, fourth in a family of five. She described an "idealized" happy childhood in a large family where her mother always kept her house open for any friend or family in need. Indeed, there were two orphaned cousins living with them. Initially the patient described her mother as warm and caring. Later, however, a contrasting picture emerged as she remembered a punitive relationship with her obsessional mother who rigidly required compliance, neatness, order, and cleanliness from all her children.

Mrs. A. completed high school, describing herself as an average student. Although she claimed many friends throughout high school and said that she still had contact with them currently, there was never any evidence of a significant friendship from that or any other part of her life.

The patient's father was a cabinetmaker who died at the age of 93. With her characteristic inability to describe deep emotional relationships, the patient said that her father was quiet, busy, and a good man. She seemed unable to elaborate further. The patient's two older siblings, a brother and sister had died many years ago. Her surviving brother and sister were married and aging. Here, too, there was no evidence of a significant relationship with either of the surviving siblings.

At the age of 21 the patient married and lived unhappily with a man whom she said "ran around with other women for many years." They had two daughters, with whom she claimed to be close. Once again, a marked inconsistency was observed between her own perception and the obvious fact that there was severe tension and angry relations between mother and daughters. This was attested to by the fact that her elder daughter was unable to tolerate her mother's presence in her home, as well as consistent expressions, from both daughters to the treatment team, of intense and long-standing anger and resentment toward the patient.

Since 1945, when Mrs. A. divorced her husband, she showed no interest in any long-term relationships. Although she socialized occasionally, she had no relationships of any kind with men and no sex life following her divorce.

Throughout her life then, Mrs. A. was unable to maintain any long-standing, warm, and caring relationships. The extent of this disability is highlighted by the descriptions, given by her and her children of her earlier relationships. Her marriage was stormy, full of argument and recrimination which carried on beyond the separation and divorce. The patient continued to hold a vicious, unforgiving view of her husband after he left and would rail against him to her still young children. Her children described her lifelong emotional instability, cruelties, and distortions. For example, she would persistently lie to them about her husband's uncaring and unsupportive attitudes. Whatever kernel of truth there may have been in her descriptions, she exaggerated dramatically. Frequently, long before she had any hint of physical illness, she would call her husband and tell him she was dying of cancer and that he must come in and look after her and the children. The full extent of her inability to understand and care for others was evident in how she not only told her husband that she was dying, although she knew quite well that this was untrue, but she also told her little children the same thing, with apparently no awareness of the terror that this aroused in them.

In summary, this patient's history demonstrates many of the factors which are characteristic of the characterologically disordered patient. She had a rigid, unsatisfying, and probably fearful relationship with her mother, an inability to maintain close relationships throughout her life, and a capacity to express vicious and at times cruel emotionality. Under the impact of physical crisis, her behavior regressed to primitive levels, and under the further stress prior to admission she became impulsive, dishonest, and unable to use the supportive environment offered to her.

Once she was admitted to hospital, the patient's initial behavior on the ward recapitulated the descriptions of her behavior throughout the years following her colostomy. She was unable to sit still for any length of time, constantly agitating to go out to buy herself cigarettes, newspapers, candy, and so on. She tried to borrow money from other patients and staff, especially to buy cigarettes, continuing the pattern she had established in her apartment building and which had led to much rejection and ostracism.

While apparently polite and cooperative, she, in truth, would not listen to any direct advice or attempts to educate her about her colostomy care. She would smile and apparently comply on the surface, but then continued to manage her colostomy in the same pathological way. The extent of her disability and self-de-structiveness was evident in the fact that there were various for-eign objects, such as open safety pins and pieces of Kleenex found stuffed into the mouth of her already excoriated, raw stoma which she treated roughly and aggressively. The level of her regression was demonstrated during her bag changes when she would rock back and forth and moan. Any movement of her bowels, she would call diarrhea and immediately run to change her bag. Her greatest fear was that her colostomy would reveal itself and humiliate her by noise and smell. As a result she with-drew from all others and refused to have any social contact or eat meals with the rest of the patients. She handled all of her feelings by denying any unpleasant affect, particularly anger or depression, and would not respond to any outreach or attempts to understand her.

The early deprivations which underlay Mrs. A.'s charac-terological pathology were never fully revealed. As with many such patients, young or old, early memories are often repressed and disavowed. From the available data, she struggled from her earliest years to "reach" a cold, forbidding mother, who could only relate instrumentally. In particular, the patient had a life-long anxiety about her bodily functions, as they related to clean-liness and her mother's rigid perfectionism. Her colostomy constantly threatened her with "dirt," provoking unconscious terror of retaliation from the internalized, intolerant part-object representation of her mother. This view of the mother was introjected by the patient, forming a central component of her view of herself and her world. As a result, the colostomy came to unconsciously represent a malevolent enemy—her critical mother—which she viciously attacked in fear and rage, recap-itulating the early mother–child interaction. The news of an acquaintance's cancer was experienced as further evidence that she could not escape destruction, and drove her anxiety to intolerable levels.

The first task of therapy following admission, was to try to establish a rudimentary working alliance to allow her to experience the support and caring which was available to her. This was a difficult process, since the patient viewed an intrusion into her personal emotional space as dangerous. To accomplish this, the therapy team had to contain her defensive activity and impulsivity. Hence, therapeutic limits were set and privileges were restricted to the ward. For example, each time she left the ward, she was brought back firmly and gently. Any request for cigarettes, candy, newspapers, and the like was carefully discussed. Although apparently minor issues, these controlling maneuvers were the surface evidence of her underlying anxiety. The therapeutic task which the team had set itself was to help her convert this inappropriate and ultimately self-destructive and isolating activity into a verbal expression of affect with her therapist and nurses. These restrictions also gave the staff a chance to watch how she truly dealt with her colostomy rather than having to rely on her own inaccurate descriptions. In keeping with the formulation which hypothesized her desperate struggle with her implacable colostomy–mother, the nurses took over complete management of her colostomy care since the team believed that she could not deal with this conflict unaided. All medications, specifically Lomotil and codeine, with which she had been self-medicating were withdrawn, despite her objections. A geriatrician, a member of the team, was closely involved in the daily evaluation of the patient's physical management and the state of her colostomy care.

Intensive individual psychotherapy was undertaken four times a week with a psychiatric resident. Although the resident was supervised by an experienced staff psychiatrist, treatment was arduous. The patient, for a long time could only focus on the details of her physical state, her privileges, and her denial of "any problems." The resident meanwhile persisted, maintaining consistency and a determination not to be driven away. The details of the sessions were discussed in team meetings so that psychotherapy could be coordinated with environmental interventions. It is worthy of note that throughout her treatment her therapist made no direct psychological interpretation to her of the symbolic meaning of her behavior. Rather than trying to make her intellectually aware of the roots of her behavior, therapy focused more on her need for true, empathic understanding and support. In that context much effort was spent to label her feelings, confront her with their existence, and link them to immediate, concrete, interpersonal, or physical events.

As the containment process continued, the patient gradually began to shift. She started to give up her constant denial of affect and began to confront the therapist and nurses directly with her anger. Her long-standing feeling of aloneness and wish for help was revealed, as was her resentment of her daughters for not helping her. Most importantly, she was able to expose her fears of living alone and supporting herself. As she softened she revealed a wider range of affect which she tolerated without recourse to somatic preoccupation, anxious avoidance, or regressive withdrawal to moaning and rocking. Slowly, the nurses turned back to her the care of her colostomy, titrating this move with her capacity to tolerate the attendant anxiety without distortions and overreactions. With time, her off-ward privileges were also restored, and she handled them appropriately most of the time.

The whole process took approximately six months to complete. During this period, concomitant family work occurred with the daughters. The main goal was to help the daughters establish appropriate distance without having to resort to angry rejection or to experience undue guilt or responsibility. They were helped to understand both the manifest and latent content of the conflict in their family system and were encouraged to relinquish their angry conflict with their mother. As they understood that the staff and institution would accept the functional responsibility for Mrs. A., their guilt and fears of being overwhelmed by her ceased.

Although Mrs. A. began her treatment, inchoate, agitated, emotionally unaware, and distrustful, she ended softer and more accepting, of herself, her family, and the institution. In turn, her need for a supportive structured environment became clear and arrangements were made for her transfer to a standard care ward in an affiliated home for the aged.

On the basis of her history, the staff of the home was quite apprehensive about accepting her. It is significant that she became very popular with them almost immediately. So successful was her integration into the home, from the hospital, and so strong was her connection with the hospital and her treatment, that she helped create a new position of patient-liaison between the hospital and the home, became an executive of the resident council of the home, and was one of the patients consulted on aspects of design for the new geriatric hospital then under construction.

In summary, this case illustrates the potential to induce important changes in aged characterologically disturbed individuals. The goals of her therapy were to develop specific staff understanding and responses; limit future regressive potentials by facilitating working through (to the limits of the patient's capacities); contain pathological behavior and limit regression; reduce her reliance on primitive defense mechanisms; and establish patient–family–staff homeostasis.

The technique required an interdisciplinary approach using a coherent psychodynamic formulation to guide interventions. These included contractual limit-setting, therapeutic encirclement (Sadavoy, Silver and Book, 1979), intensive individual psychotherapy, family therapy, and environmental manipulation. While the patient's capacity for insight and understanding limited the degree of working through possible, Mrs. A. was able to establish a strong working alliance and begin to internalize some of the good objects offered through therapy. This process helped to counter the assaultive effects of her physical illness and lessened the unconscious retaliatory anxieties she struggled with at the beginning.

Conclusion

This chapter represents an attempt to utilize the theoretical and descriptive information already available from work with young, characterologically difficult patients to examine the late-life manifestations of this disorder. After a definition of the character disordered patient and an overview of the psycho-dynamics and phenomenology, the author summarizes eight factors which cause crisis or strain in the life of the aging individual: interpersonal loss; physical disability; loss of external manifestations of the self; loss of role; loss of defensive outlets; forced reliance on caretakers; confrontation with death; and conflict over the wish to live versus the wish to die.

These eight age-specific stressors lead to the emphasis of three specific aspects of the behavioral pathology of the aging character disordered individual: aberrant interactional patterns with exacerbation of narcissistic defenses; hypochondriasis; and depressive withdrawal.

The final section of the chapter outlines the approach to treatment of the institutionalized elderly character disordered patient and outlines four goals of treatment: containing and limiting pathological behavior; establishing a working alliance; developing a cohesive treatment team, and altering the patient's reliance on primitive pathological behavior. These principles and goals are demonstrated in a detailed case example.

References

Adler, G. (1981), The borderline-narcissistic personality disorder continuum. *Amer. J. Psychiat.*, 138:46–50.

——— Buie, D. H. (1979), Aloneness and borderline psychopathology. The possible relevance of child development issues. *Internat. J. Psycho-Anal.*, 60:83–96.

Andrulonis, P. A., Glueck, B. C., Stroebel, C. S., & Vogel, N. G. (1982), Borderline personality subcategories. *J. Nerv. & Ment. Dis.*, 70:670–679.

Berezin, M. (1965), *Introduction in Geriatric Psychiatry: Grief, Loss and Emotional Disorders in the Aging Process*, ed. M. A. Berezin & S. Cath. New York: International Universities Press, pp. 13–20.

——— (1977), The fate of narcissism in old age: Clinical case reports. *J. Geriat. Psychiat.*, 10:9–26.

Book, H. E., Sadavoy, J., & Silver, D. (1979), Staff countertransference to borderline patients on an inpatient unit. *Amer. J. Psychother.*, 32:521–531.

Breslau, L. (1980), The faltering therapeutic perspective toward the narcissistically wounded institutionalized aged. *J. Geriat. Psychiat.*, 13:193–206.

Burnham, D. L. (1966), The special-problem patient: Victim or agent of splitting. *Psychiatry*, 29:105–122.

Deutsch, H. (1942), Some forms of emotional disturbance and their relationship to schizophrenia. *Psychoanal. Quart.*, 11:301–321.

Easser, B. R. (1974), Empathic inhibition and psychoanalytic technique. *Psychoanal.*, 60:552–579.

Erikson, E. H. (1959), Identity and the Life Cycle. *Psychol. Issues.*, Monogr. 1. New York: International Universities Press.

Fairbairn, W. R. D. (1954), *An Object-Relations Theory of the Personality*. New York: Basic Books.

Frosch, J. (1964), The psychotic character. *Psychiat. Quart.*, 38:81–96.

Giovacchini, P. (1979), *Treatment of Primitive Mental States*. New York: Jason Aronson.

Gitelson, M. (1948), The emotional problems of elderly persons. In: *Readings in Psychotherapy with Older People*, ed. S. Steury & M. L. Blank. Washington, DC: U.S. Dept. of Health and Human Services, Public Health Service, Alcohol Drug Abuse and Mental Health Administration, National Institute of Mental Health, 1981, pp. 8–17.

Goldfarb, A. I., & Sheps, J. (1954), Psychotherapy of the aged. *Psychosom. Med.*, 16:209–219.

Greenson, R. R. (1972), *The Technique and Practice of Psychoanalysis*, Vol. 1. New York: International Universities Press, p. 46.

Grinker, R. R. Sr., Werble, B., & Drye, R. C. (1968), *The Borderline Syndrome*. New York: Basic Books.

Groves, J. E. (1978), Taking care of the hateful patient. *New Eng. J. Med.*, 298:883–887.

Gunderson, J. G., & Singer, M. T. (1981), Defining borderline patients: An overview. *Amer. J. Psychiat.*, 138:896–903.

Guntrip, H. (1971), *Psychoanalytic Theory, Therapy and the Self*. New York: Basic Books, pp. 145–173.

Hartmann, H. (1939), *Ego Psychology and the Problems of Adaptation*. New York: International Universities Press, 1958.

Hoch, P., & Polatin, P. (1949), Pseudoneurotic forms of schizophrenia. *Psychiat. Quart.*, 23:248–279.

Jacques, E. (1969), Death and mid-life crisis. In: *Death: Interpretations*, ed. H. M. Ruitenbeek. New York: Delta Books.

Kernberg, O. (1975), *Borderline Conditions and Pathological Narcissism*. New York: Jason Aronson.

Klein, D. F. (1975), Psychopharmacology of the borderline patient. In: *Borderline States in Psychiatry*, ed. J. E. Mack. New York: Grune & Stratton, pp. 75–92.

Knight, R. P. (1953), Borderline states. *Bull. Menninger Clinic*, 17:1–12.

Kohut, H. (1977), *The Restoration of the Self*. New York: International Universities Press.

————— Wolfe E. S. (1978), Disorders of the self and their treatment: An outline. *Internat. J. Psycho-Anal.*, 59:413–425.

Lazarus, L. W. (1980), Self psychology and psychotherapy with the elderly: Theory and practice. *J. Geriatric Psychiat.*, 13:69–88.

Mackenzie, T. B. (1978), The manipulative patient; An interactional approach. *Psychiatry*, 41:264–271.

Mahler, M. S., Pine, F., & Bergman, A. (1975), *The Psychological Birth of the Human Infant*. New York: Basic Books.

Main, T. F. (1957), The ailment. *Brit. J. Med. Psychol.*, 30:129–145.

Maltsberger, J. T., & Buie, D. H. (1974), Countertransference hate in the treatment of suicidal patients. *Arch. Gen. Psychiat.*, 30:625–633.

Masterson, J. R. (1981), *The Narcissistic and Borderline Disorders—An Integrated Developmental Approach*. New York: Brunner/Mazel.

Meerlo, J. A. (1955), Transference and resistance in geriatric psychotherapy. In: *Readings in Psychotherapy with Older People*, ed. S. Steury & M. L. Blank. Washington, DC: U.S. Dept. of Health and Human Services, Public Health Service, Alcohol Drug Abuse and Mental Health Administration, National Institute of Mental Health, 1981, pp. 86–93.

Michels, R. (1977), Treatment of the difficult patient in psychotherapy. *Canad. Psychiat. Assoc. J.*, 22:109.

Ploye, P. M. (1977), On some difficulties of inpatient individual psychoanalytically oriented therapy. *Psychiatry*, 40:133–145.

Sadavoy, J., & Dorian, B. (1983), Treatment of the elderly characterologically disturbed patient in the chronic care institution. *J. of Geriat. Psychiat.*, 16:223–240.

————— Silver D., & Book, H. E. (1979), Negative responses of the borderline to inpatient treatment. *Amer. J. Psychother.*, 33:404–417.

—— —— —— Hamilton J. (1981), The resident and the inpatient borderline, A supervisor's perspective. *Canad. Psychiat. Assoc. J.*, 26:155–158.

Schmideberg, M. (1959), The borderline patient. In: *American Handbook of Psychiatry*, ed. S. Arieti. New York: Basic Books, pp. 398–416.

Silver, D. (1977), The difficult patient in psychotherapy. (Editorial). *Can. Psychiat. Assn. J.*, 22:99–101.

—— (1983), Psychotherapy of the characterologically difficult patient. *Can. Psychiat. Assn. J.*, 28:513–521.

—— (1985), The psychodynamics and psychotherapeutic management of the self-destructive character disordered patient. In: *The Psychiat. Clin. of No. Amer.*, ed. A. Roy. Philadelphia: W. B. Saunders, 8:357–376.

Spitz, R. (1945), Hospitalism. In: *Psychoanalytic Study of the Child*, ed. R. S. Eissler, A. Freud, H. Hartmann & E. Kris. New York: International Universities Press, 1:53–74.

—— Wolf, K. M. (1946), Anaclitic depression. In: *Psychoanalytic Study of the Child*, ed. R. S. Eissler, A. Freud, H. Hartmann & E. Kris. New York: International Universities Press, 2:313–342.

Soloff, P. H., & Millward, J. W. (1983), Psychiatric disorders in the families of borderline patients. *Arch. Gen. Psychiat.*, 40:37–44.

Stern, A. (1938), Psychoanalytic investigation of and therapy in the borderline group of neuroses. *Psychoanal. Quart.*, 7:467–489.

Volkan, V. (1976), *Primitive Internalized Object Relations*. New York: International Universities Press.

Yalom, I. D. (1980), *Existential Psychotherapy*. New York: Basic Books.

Zilboorg, G. (1941), Ambulatory schizophrenias. *Psychiatry*, 4:149–155.

Part III
SPECIFIC PSYCHOTHERAPEUTIC MODALITIES

8

GERIATRIC PSYCHOTHERAPY: BEYOND CRISIS MANAGEMENT

RALPH J. KAHANA, M.D.

Human crises are, for the most part, grim and alarming occurrences. The term *crisis* brings to mind large-scale disasters, serious illnesses, alcoholism, drug addiction, and various forms of aggression such as suicide, battering, and rape. In geriatric psychiatry abuse of older persons has been added recently to our catalogue of catastrophes. (To lift momentarily the pall of descending gloom and discern some clarifying landmarks, one may begin with a crisis [or near crisis] that could only have happened in Boston:)

Cleveland Amory, in his book, *The Proper Bostonians*, (1947) records the following incident circa 1895. The setting is the breakfast room of a proper Boston suburban home. Old Judge John Lowell, the last of a line of three judges of that name, is seated at one end of the table behind a newspaper. His wife, a capable Boston dowager, is at the other end. The maid enters and in a low voice reports bad news. Cook has burned the cereal. There is no more in the house. Mrs. Lowell communicates this to the judge at once, concluding slowly, "There isn't going to be any oatmeal this morning, John." Amory remarks that this was no minor domestic tragedy. To the best of Mrs. Lowell's knowledge her husband had had oatmeal every single morning of his life. Moreover there were other Lowells, or Cabots, or Higginsons eating their daily oatmeal up to the writing of Amory's book in 1947 (and perhaps today). The breakfast scene continues with a brief millenium of nerve-racking silence. Finally, the newspaper is slowly lowered, the Judge's face appears, and he replies, "Frankly, my dear, I never did care for it."

(Amory wrote for the generation who had read *Gone with the Wind*—or had seen the movie, echoing its hero, Rhett Butler, whose famous exit line was, "Frankly, my dear, I don't give a damn.")

At this point the reader might well ask, "What kind of crisis is this?" and demand his or her money back. However, in this low-keyed incident, one recognizes certain characteristics of a crisis. It marks a turning point (in the continuity of Proper Boston breakfasts). It comes with a certain surprise or shock, and has individual, interpersonal, familial, social, and historical dimensions. The historical aspect alone, the breaking with tradition, is a major attribute of a geriatric crisis.

Characteristics of Psychological Crisis

Crisis usually means a full-blown emergency. Coming from the Greek word *decision*, it refers to a decisive moment, a turning point for extraordinarily better or drastically worse. In medicine, a crisis is a vitally important change in a disease leading to recovery or death. More generally, it denotes a difficult, strained, uncertain, unstable, or suspenseful time or state of affairs, marked by acute distress.

The psychological crisis, centered in mental life, threatens a mental, social, or physical collapse. It may lead to resolution and even to improved functioning, but often results in a chronic, disturbed state, worsened functioning, or even death. While a psychological crisis is usually perceived as such by the patient, it may also spread and appear in family members and other caretakers, and even in the professional therapist.

The concept of psychological crisis has been extended to encompass a variety of crisis situations, experiences predisposing to crisis, and events precipitating a crisis. In designating a crisis we may refer, somewhat loosely, to any of these. Commonly recognized situations of crisis include severe mental illness, destructive behavior, extreme states of confusion, panics, and intense physical or mental suffering.

Among predisposing circumstances we find the developmental or normative "crisis" of critical periods of the life cycle: infancy, the oedipal phase, puberty, pregnancy, parenting, midlife, aging, and dying. These are expected periods of life in which the balance of inner needs, regulative controls, and adaptive methods are destabilized. Puberty is a paradigm of these periods, featuring concomitant shifts in both somatic and psychological functioning. In puberty an excess of sexual needs and the challenge of increasing independence from parents may strain the capacity for control of behavior. Under favorable conditions this destabilization leads to maturational steps toward new age-appropriate functions, but during these periods individuals are also more exposed and vulnerable to specific stresses. The major predisposing events of normal aging include the ending of childbearing in menopausal women, grown children leaving the home, reaching the limits of achievement, retirement from employment, physical decline, illness or infirmity, personal losses of relatives and friends, and the eventual reality of dying (G. L. Bibring, 1966).

Crises may be precipitated by a wide variety of stresses acting singly or in concert. With sufficient predisposition even a minor stress can set off a major reaction, as we often see in the very frail aged. The precipitating event may be as common and apparent as bereavement, physical illness, or interpersonal tension, or it may be as idiosyncratic and obscure as failure to achieve a privately held personal ideal.

The most striking symptoms of psychological crisis are marked intensification of painful affects, such as anxiety, fear, guilt, shame, depression, and anger. This emotional pressure may lead to confusional states and poorly controlled irrational impulses to action. The individual may experience loss of integration or cohesiveness of the self, expressed as "going to pieces." The need for relief becomes imperative and regressive. Regression is often most apparent in personal relationships in the form of repetitive, childlike demands for attention and relief, magical expectations of help, confusion of the self with others, overdependence, helplessness, and low frustration tolerance. Conversely, it may be expressed as excessive and unrealistic independence, negativism, or withdrawal.

In a crisis, the patient's attempts to cope may contribute,

paradoxically, to the evident disturbance. Thus, efforts to reach out for help have an urgent and indiscriminate quality. When not in crisis, the individual normally responds smoothly and automatically to the mere signal of tension, with efforts to define the problem, remove stresses, and increase self-control. In the midst of a crisis, however, there is excessive use of defenses such as suppression of conflict, emotional discharge, and obsessional worrying, and the appearance of regressive defenses of denial, projection, and withdrawal.

Classification of Crises in the Elderly

The author has had the opportunity to assess clinical crises in about 40 patients ranging in age from the early sixties to the mid-nineties. The prevalence of particular crises reflected the population seen by the author in psychiatric office practice, with a general hospital connection and located in a largely middle-class community. The following crisis categories were seen: Crisis arising mainly from (1) normal development; (2) emotional trauma; (3) anxiety of family members; (4) acute psychosis; (5) danger of suicide; (6) general debilitation; (7) dementia; (8) organic confusion; and (9) terminal illness. The order of listing is arbitrary. Certain crises were related to age, such as those precipitated by retirement and widowhood in the youngest group and those giving rise to the need for a legal guardian in the oldest. Others, though shaped by aging, could have occurred in earlier periods of life.

Normal Development

Patients predisposed to emergencies by expected or normal development were among the most promising for psychotherapy. Most of those seen were in the period of late middle age and represented reactions to children leaving home, retirement from work, economic reversals, and widowhood. Several men and women had intense emotional responses to the breakup of their children's marriages and particularly to loss of their relationships with their children-in-law and their contact with their grandchildren. Some needed help only during the acute crisis, relying thereafter on their ego strength and on family and social support systems. Others were alerted by the emergency to undertake more extensive psychotherapy aimed at character change.

> Mrs. B., a generally well-functioning woman in her sixties, is representative of patients in this category who had therapy beyond crisis management. The strain of caring for her husband when he had a major illness had made her more painfully aware of long-standing marital discontent. A crisis of acute depression brought her into treatment. She undertook further psychotherapy with the goal of character change when she became aware that her own attitudes of excessive passivity and anxious submissiveness contributed to the marital conflict. In time she was able to assume a more active role in her marriage, becoming appropriately responsive to her husband's partial retirement and his increased dependence on her to initiate their social activities.

Emotional Trauma

A crisis arising principally from direct emotional trauma is illustrated in the following vignette.

> Mrs. C., an 80-year-old woman, was in good physical health and living with her husband. Until two months prior to being seen, she had worked as an effective saleswoman in a fashionable store. Then, without warning or sympathy, a new, young woman manager informed her that she was through—laid off from her job of 10 years. She left the store in a daze, and shortly thereafter became depressed, tremulous, and emotionally numbed. Her daughter, who accompanied her to the first interview, remarked that "mother was too civilized to hit back at that stupid woman," the manager. A few months prior to the event, the patient had been knocked down and robbed of her purse in the street, and this memory too, preoccupied her and rendered her phobic. Her recovery began after four interviews in which these traumatic experiences were recounted, thus initiating their working through. Abreaction of anger was encouraged, and sympathy and respect were offered to her.

Anxiety of Family Members

The anxiety of family members was a major component of the crisis in a significant group. In some instances the family members were the main focus of therapy because of the severity of their suffering or because they were more accessible to treatment than were the actual malfunctioning, older patients.

> Mrs. D., an active, intelligent woman, was worn out by the task of managing her husband who suffered from early onset Alzheimer's disease. She had capably taken over direction of their joint business but was exhausted by the additional job of keeping watch over him. Although his condition did not warrant admission to a hospital or nursing home, at times, caring for him was like directing and protecting a toddler who had the strength of a grown man. Mrs. D. reacted, especially, to the danger of her husband's impulsive behavior—he might suddenly insist on driving the car—the loss of the adult person she had known, and the lack of intellectual companionship.

Most spouses and children were concerned and helpful, and several cases were seen where an incipient or worsening crisis was averted by their dedicated and skillful efforts.

> A prolonged crisis was precipitated by chronic illness in an 80-year-old woman in whom osteoporosis had led to fractures, disfiguring spinal curvature, and spastic bladder requiring an indwelling catheter. Mrs. E. had become depressed in reaction to pain, disability, marked sensitivity over her appearance, increasing frailty, urinary incontinence, and episodes of confusion. She appeared frustrated and complained bitterly, with a sense of hopelessness. Throughout this distressing illness her 84-year-old husband sustained her physically and emotionally, getting her up and dressing her, providing foot care, taking her to the bathroom, and trying to reason with her and cheer her up. He gave up his part-time job so that she would not be alone, and he accompanied her and participated in her psychotherapy. Between husband and therapist it was possible to reinforce her self-esteem, tap into her sense of humor, and patiently circumvent her characterological subbornness.

In some families one could observe the revival of conflict

between the generations, precipitated by problems of the aging parent or the adult "child." The crisis of the old parent might elicit a reaction of disappointment in the children, as if the parent were still powerful and had willfully let the children down. In another instance the grownup "child," turning to the parent for help in a crisis, reawakened an old struggle between the "rebellious adolescent" and the "rigid parent."

Exacerbations of Psychosis

Exacerbations of psychosis in older persons produced among the most difficult family crises. Psychosis mobilizes disturbed responses of excessive alarm, panic, and projective blaming in the family members. In these situations a team approach is helpful, whereby multiple transferences are handled by two or more therapists.

Sometimes crisis issues extend beyond the family boundaries to involve the wider social environment. Such crises were observed in the oldest patients, ranging in age from 88 to 96. Typical of this group were conflicts around legal guardianship in patients with advanced Alzheimer's disease, and crises of patients in nursing homes which involved other residents and staff members.

Acute psychotic crises formed a very diverse group including refractory psychotic depression, paranoia, and schizoaffective illness.

> In a dramatic crisis coming near the end of life, Mrs. F., a frail 86-year-old woman, developed intense paranoia. She insisted that her husband was keeping her prisoner and that her son was stealing her property. She recovered dramatically after one minimal dose of a neuroleptic medication. However, she died of advanced heart disease within six months.

Some patients with exacerbation of chronic psychosis resist any help beyond crisis intervention.

> Mrs. G., a 72-year-old woman with a schizoaffective illness marked by depression, thought disorder, and minimal tolerance for painful affect, would cancel or postpone interviews whenever

she had temporary relief. Her condition, which was long standing, had worsened following the recent death of her 95-year-old
mother. She insisted that experiencing any sadness over this bereavement could only be useless and disruptive. Her resistance
was reminiscent of the ancient fiddler in the folk song, "The
Arkansas Traveller," who says he can't repair his leaking roof
during the rainstorm, and then afterwards, denies the need because "my roof never leaks when it doesn't rain."

Patients Who Threaten or Attempt Suicide

Among patients who threaten or attempt suicide the crisis
is apt to be prolonged, lasting weeks or months. It is important
to get a clear diagnostic picture of the kind and degree of
psychopathology, past and present, and of the seriousness of
suicidal intent. One thinks of suicidal threats or acts as cries for
help, and assumes that these patients should be treated beyond
the crisis because of the often grave problems which culminate
in such a drastic resolve. In some instances one can indeed
proceed with treatment in this manner. But in other cases the
therapist discovers that the suicidal impulse was a consequence
of long-standing resistance to solving emotional problems. The
patients were brought for treatment unmotivated, after impulsive threats, or acts. They had failed in previous attempts
at therapy. Their family members were uncooperative or disruptive. Their "recovery" takes the form of a rapid flight into
pseudohealth based upon the discharge of accumulated tension,
denial, projection, and the appeasement of inner guilt. Preexisting fixed psychopathological patterns are reestablished.

The following illustrative case belongs to the more fortun-
ate group in which favorable factors predominate. Suicide was
a serious threat—it tends to be an ominous one in older
men—but it was not yet an act. The repeated threat *was* a cry
for help. The precipitating cause, a physical illness, was slowly
improving. The psychopathology was a character neurosis
rather than a psychosis. The patient's family was available, cooperative, and emotionally healthy. Recovery was sustained,
although, because of the patient's relatively fixed character
structure, treatment did not extend beyond resolution of the
crisis.

Mr. H., a 79-year-old, retired businessman had become increasingly depressed over a three-month period following a stroke. Symptoms of depression included a small weight loss, increased need for sleep, and intensified mood disturbance in the morning. The stroke, from which he had made an almost complete physical recovery, had affected the sensations of his right hand and foot without impairing motor functions. A questionable slurring of his speech and minimal memory impairment cleared up subsequently when his depression lifted. He was seen six times during two months, and follow-up information was given by family members up to six years later. His wife was interviewed both with him and on her own.

The patient was a handsome man who looked troubled and anxious, was agitated, and spoke repetitiously. His sensorium was clear and cognition intact. The most alarming behavioral symptom was a threat to jump off the 11th floor of their apartment building. Psychiatric hospitalization was recommended but he refused and his family did not want to force the issue. In time it became clear that his dramatic threats and complaints expressed his wishes for help, relief, and affirmation rather than the intention to die. Although an antidepressant medication, prescribed by his family physician had not helped, he was started on a different one which, eventually, seemed mildly beneficial. His neurologist, who had prescribed an anticonvulsant as a preventive measure, changed to a new one which was also believed to have analgesic effects.

The therapist commended the patient's wife for her devoted support of the patient and for firmly encouraging him to be more active by taking him along to the library and to classes that she attended. The therapist observed that his complaining increased when she tried to give him direct reassurance—partly as a reaction to her own frustration. She was advised to stop telling him he was better. On the other hand, the patient responded favorably to sympathetic recognition and affirmation of his suffering with lowering of tension between them, widening the scope of their discourse, and increasing his ability to listen and reflect.

In therapy his physical symptoms were explained and depressive responses identified. His fantasies, such as the fear of becoming totally and permanently helpless, were brought out and contrasted with his real situation, and his character responses were clarified; for example, it was pointed out how he displaced, onto his environment, his angry fight against the assault of illness.

As his depression gradually lifted, with ups and downs, he began to speak about his life, expressing legitimate pride in his children. When he had achieved what the family regarded as his normal attitude of mild depression with occasional irritability, doing more and complaining less, he announced that he would not come anymore; it cost too much. Subsequently he maintained his improvement despite another serious illness and increasing frailty.

Among the frail aged, one sees the kind of person in whom the crisis is brought on by general debilitation, a combination of physical disabilities and personal losses, sometimes superimposed upon a lifelong pattern of limited adaptability. Crises due to dementia are more common in this group. A sudden physical illness in a frail older person may produce an organic confusional state with all its attendant and subsequent anxieties. Several elderly patients in this series, some quite frail, experienced crises in consequence of adverse drug reactions, for example, to levodopa, steroids, or antidepressants. When undertaking psychotherapy with debilitated or frail patients one anticipates that physical illnesses may interrupt treatment more frequently and for longer periods than in those who are more vigorous. Unless illness leads to further, lasting debilitation, one can usually resume therapy after the break without notable setback. However, frequent or long interruptions may limit treatment to the aim of basic support. It is important to keep in touch with the patient or family during a prolonged lapse, to affirm one's availability and interest. Ordinarily a telephone contact or written note is sufficient.

Terminal Illness

Several patients with terminal illness were seen.

Mr. I., a 69-year-old man had bowel cancer with metastases. His internist observed that he appeared preoccupied with his illness to the point of obsession. It was estimated that he had a 20 percent chance of survival with chemotherapy. The patient was a nice-looking, well-spoken man who appeared his age. He recounted the course of his present illness which had begun with a fever six months previously. The fever subsided and three months later the disease was discovered to have spread to his liver. It was cancer and he knew that he would die. He did not want chemotherapy. His younger sister had died of cancer a year before, after a colostomy and chemotherapy. He stated, "her suffering kicks around in my mind."

Three weeks before the psychiatric consultation he had sold his business of 40 years and had given up social activities connected with his work. Then it all hit him, producing feelings of anxiety, helplessness, and terrible insomnia. He commented, "nobody lives forever. Your time comes. I'm in my 70th year. I have to reprogram my life. I was very active and had a lot of recognition." He had sold his business, a good one, to his office manager of 30 years with the thought that he would spend his remaining time traveling to places he wanted to visit. For the past 25 years he had spent five or six weeks in Florida each winter and, more recently, had traveled once or twice a year to California where his daughter and grandchildren lived. He spoke briefly about his children and his second wife, a widow whom he had married 10 years ago.

He had disclosed his illness to his family, neighbors, and friends in his principal business club. His major frustration was that he became easily exhausted, making travel and social activities difficult and leaving him with a feeling of inadequacy. He wanted to make peace with himself and to feel more effective.

In this first session, after reviewing Mr. I.'s reactions of shock, transient denial, and grief in response to his illness, the therapist made approximately the following comments: The patient's preoccupation with his illness was evidence of his effort to cope with his painful feelings. As a man accustomed to working and doing, the main threat that he experienced now was of becoming passive and helpless. He needed to redirect his activities, for example, by resuming contact with his business associates and friends and allowing them to grieve for him. The therapist concluded by remarking on Mr. I's perfectionism as reflected in his need to cope with his illness flawlessly. It would help if he would become more realistic in his self-expectations so he would not be letting himself down.

In the second meeting, the patient spoke of a variety of concerns associated with illness and loss. His internist had prescribed an antidepressant, but the patient had stopped taking it because of a dry mouth. Fatigue was a constant distress and deprived him of the pleasure of traveling. He had felt strong grief for his first wife whom he had loved dearly. When he remarried he had made careful arrangements about what was to be left, in the event of his death, to his children and his second wife. He had not got along too well with his son but this had improved recently. He tended to avoid visits with his 93-year-old mother, living in a nursing home, because she made him feel very guilty. At the end of the session he said that he realized he was grieving the loss of his body. He appeared to have achieved some peace with himself and it was agreed that he would stop coming but could contact the therapist if he wished.

Patient and therapist never met or spoke again. The patient's internist reported that he had managed quite well until his death some months later.

This case illustrates a type of psychological crisis and its brief management. The patient seemed able to handle well the remainder of his illness and life, but the minimal follow-up does not allow us to evaluate in detail the effectiveness of the therapeutic intervention in this particular case. However, one can describe the rationale of the intervention which is based upon well-established principles.

The patient appeared to be a normal, very responsible man who had accepted his own approaching death realistically. A crisis of depression ensued when he gave up his business. He had to deal with the frustration of limited time and depleted energy and with the trauma of impending loss by his own death. He wanted to make peace with himself. One might say that he wanted to resolve his inner conflict and restore his self-esteem. Giving up his business and social contacts left him bereft of his usual, major way of coping with tension and reinforcing his self-esteem through active, constructive work and receiving the recognition this gained him from his associates. Increased isolation and, ironically, "time on his hands" intensified his preoccupation and self-criticism. Instead of being able to grieve and thus accept his limitations and impending loss, he was thrown into the vicious circle of frustration and lowered self-esteem leading to self-blame and to further lowering of self-esteem.

In the initial interview the therapist identified and clarified the patient's symptoms (his grief had become depressive; his obsessive preoccupation, painfully intensified by his isolation, was part of his effort to cope) and his immediate dynamics (he was threatened by passivity; he expected too much of himself). Grief was normal, depression was not. Isolation and passivity could be overcome by redirecting his activity (allowing his friends to grieve). His depressive self-blame was based in part on too high self-expectations and could be corrected through insight. During the second interview the patient gave evidence of the processes of grieving and of therapeutic work proceeding simultaneously. He was less self-preoccupied and spoke, with feeling, of the principal people he had lost or would be leaving. His spontaneous gain of insight was exemplified at the end when he observed that he was grieving for his body.

General Principles of Crisis Management

With better definition of psychological crises, their management has become an established part of our therapeutic armamentarium (Goldfarb, 1976; Hoff, 1978). In addition to office and institutional treatment, there are crisis clinics and teams, hot lines, and various prevention centers offering expanded access to special expertise. Psychoanalytic therapy and its applications in the dynamic psychotherapies provide a flexible method for treating crises. The dynamic psychotherapies form a continuum, being at the one end predominantly supportive and at the other end mainly exploratory (Knight, 1949, 1952). Supportive therapy serves the reestablishment of adaptive techniques that had previously functioned most effectively, while exploratory therapy attempts to mobilize and resolve pathogenic conflicts in order to achieve favorable changes in character structure. Crisis intervention almost always begins with support. Patients in crisis come for help because of their distress, or the concern of their families or of society. They seek relief, and initially at least, are not usually motivated to undertake character modification. Nor is the latter always necessary or possible.

In crisis intervention the therapist's first supportive aim is to remove or reduce the patient's external stresses and to relieve inner tensions. He assists the patient's efforts to reestablish well-integrated cohesive functioning, by providing appropriate medical, environmental, and psychological support. Medical care is directed first to urgent, dangerous conditions. Psychotropic medication may help relieve the pressure of anxiety, depression, or psychotic thinking. Environmental change may reduce stresses and provide the basics of personal care, protection, limit-setting, and reassurance. Because the first goal of crisis therapy is support, the principal psychological methods are mobilization of positive transference, abreaction, and clarification (G. L. Bibring, 1947; E. Bibring, 1954). Positive transference revives and reinforces feelings of security and encouragement stemming from early parental care. Abreaction discharges pent-up feelings. Through clarification of perceptions, motives, and cause and effect, the therapist supports rational thinking, strengthens ego boundaries, and mobilizes the patient's adaptive strengths. Thus he may attempt to convert overdependence or excessive pseudoindependence into reasonable dependence, obsessional preoccupation into planful action, and irrational mistrust into self-protective vigilance.

Crisis Management in the Frail Elderly

Older people, when they first come to psychiatrists, often present because of full-blown crises. This is particularly true of the frail aged who comprise 5 to 10 percent of those over age 65. The population of frail aged are predisposed to crisis by limited physical reserves, debilitating chronic illnesses, brain damage, constriction of activities, the drastic impact of personal losses, depletion of self-esteem, and precarious dependence on family and community resources. Because of their uncertain homeostasis, the stress precipitating their crisis may appear to be minimal or insidious. Psychiatric treatment for this group of frail elderly proves, by and large, to be restricted to basic supportive measures. Their limited adaptability, poor tolerance of painful affects, and potential for regression dictate interventions that are least disruptive of their accustomed life-styles (Kahana, 1979). Confusion, acute psychosis, or suicidal threats usually require medical intervention and hospital care, but otherwise the therapist should try to keep the patient at home and treat him or her in the office or clinic. Mobilizing the protective and reassuring presence of close relatives and friends whom the patient trusts is the first consideration. When psychotropic medication is added, one should prescribe small initial doses, monitoring carefully for side effects to which these older patients may be sensitive. Therapy is aimed at reducing stresses, relieving symptoms, strengthening reality testing, offering encouragement and hope, and utilizing the patient's personality strengths.

Treatment may end when the patient has achieved better integrated functioning, more bearable affects, clearing of confusion, minimal employment of regressive defenses, and a degree of coping. But what then? What lies beyond crisis management?

Psychotherapy Beyond Crisis Management

With the frail elderly, support through a crisis, rather than character change, is the goal of therapy. The frail aged person may achieve a lasting remission, may have episodic treatment of further crisis, or may require continued minimal supportive therapy. In contrast is that much larger group of vigorous elderly, better able to tolerate strong affect, for whom therapy goes beyond crisis management. In the latter group, crises become opportunities to begin reconstructive psychotherapy aimed at gradual character change. Clues to the suitability of this approach for a given patient are found in character structure, the degree of insightfulness, the accessibility of memories and feelings, the quality and extent of personal relationships, and the patient's capacity for interest and enjoyment.

Character Structure

Evidences of patients' leading conflicts and defenses, as expressed in their character structures, are found in various individual "meanings" of the crisis experience (Kahana and Bibring, 1964). For instance, a patient who experiences a critical illness as if it were a punishment for not being good or not taking good care of himself may be consciously aware of this

meaning and say so directly, or he may be unaware, yet unwittingly express his guilt and self-blame recognizably in words
and actions. Such a "meaning" tends to be characteristic for an
individual. In this instance the patient would tend to experience, over time, a series of different kinds of stresses, each as
a punishment. This might be typical of a guilt-prone person
with a masochistic–depressive character structure. Other examples of such "meanings" include feelings of being challenged,
controlled, abandoned, attacked, and betrayed, or left un-
touched (the absence of feeling).

In general, as in younger people, the less pathological character types such as the mildly hysterical ("dramatizing," "feeling
challenged"), the mixed hysterical and obsessional ("rational,
active, and in control"), and the less severe instances of the
masochistic–depressive ("self-sacrificing") respond more favorably. Another positive indication for psychotherapy is evidence
of previous shifts within a character style, for example, from
an attitude of rigid overcontrol to one of greater flexibility.
This includes the resilient capacity to recover from regressive
states, as a change from a condition of helpless overdependence
to an attitude of greater initiative and autonomy.

Insight

Insight begins, of course, with a basic awareness of one's
self and immediate circumstances. It is more promising for
therapy if the insight includes understanding of the precipitating causes of the crisis. It is still more promising if the patient's insight extends to knowledge of his current and past
motivations, anxieties, defenses, personal relationships, and
crucial experiences, especially as these are predisposing to the
crisis. Finally, in probing the deepest level of insight, the therapist seeks to know if the patient is open to discovering as yet
unknown or unconscious motivations. Related to insight is the
essential ability of the individual to acknowledge those pathological aspects of his character of which he had been unaware
and previously regarded as normal. The capacity for this level
of insight permits the previously ego-syntonic maladaptive char-

acteristics to become appropriately viewed as ego-alien; that is, foreign to and harmful to the self.

Memories

Memories are pathways to insight and to resolution of conflicts. The first significant, accessible memories to appear during crisis treatment are often of associated earlier crises or traumatic experiences. The therapist encourages expansion and enrichment of these and associated memories, and fuller and more discriminating expression of accompanying affects. The capacity to elaborate and to differentiate memories, affects, and motives is a criterion of the maturity and ego strength which help make character reconstruction possible.

The Patient's Personal Relationships

In addition to the history provided by the patient and others, the attitudes of accompanying family members are important evidences of the quality of the patient's personal relationships. Blaming and recrimination by family members may point to similar qualities in the aging patient, who may have a paranoid or borderline character disorder and a history of troubled and limited interpersonal relationships. When the family are thoughtfully objective, caring, and forgiving, it is often observed that the patient is a loving, realistic person with solid self-esteem, who gains satisfaction from friendships. Excessive attitudes of self-sacrifice in children may call attention to qualities of demandingness, dominance, or guilt induction in their aging parent.

Knowledge of the nature of the patient's personal relationships is further supplemented by the emerging transference. The transference, directed at the therapist, expresses unconscious attitudes displaced from important figures of the past, which tend to be repeated indiscriminately in a variety of later relationships. Here the irrational, emotionally significant elements of personality and social behavior are revealed, often with clarity and intensity. The history of having a number of gratifying personal relationships points to the capacity for experiencing a positive transference and the possibility of forming a therapeutic alliance.

The Patient's Interests

The possibility of successful reconstructive therapy is enhanced when the patient has sustained a variety of interests and maintained a balance between work and recreation. Accordingly, the therapist wants to know about the patient's interests and activities, interpersonal, cultural, intellectual and spiritual, physical, occupational, and recreational. He further wants to understand how these interests and activities have evolved from the patient's earlier life. Have they stagnated or developed? Does the patient share interests with the younger generation? Has he or she a capacity for pleasure? These questions bear upon the outcome of psychotherapy for many problems in later life, and particularly where issues of retirement from work and constriction of activities are concerned. The maintaining of interests and personal relationships is a hedge against excessive self-preoccupation and narcissistic regression.

Four Paradigms of Crisis Therapy in the Elderly

Brief Therapy of a Traumatic Reaction

The brief therapy of a traumatic reaction exemplifies crisis management in its simplest form.

Mrs. J., a 68-year-old, twice-widowed woman had undergone a gradual personality change, reaching crisis proportions, over a four-month period following a serious leg fracture. The fracture, resulting from a fall, had required an operation and six weeks of hospitalization. After discharge home she made a good physical recovery, but felt helpless and anxious with her leg in a big cast. Her youngest daughter, who had made the initial contact by telephone reported that despite removal of the cast her mother had become overdependent and demanding to the point that she had a hard time keeping her home care helpers. Mrs. J., who came alone to the first interview, confirmed and amplified this information. She said that she had always been very independent, never leaning upon her children, but rather assisting them. Now she felt that her nerves were shot and it was hard to cope.

She had grown up, worked, married, raised her family, been widowed, then remarried all in one locality. After the very upsetting loss of her second husband, she had moved to be closer to her children. Even though this was the first major move of her life, she adapted well and made new friends, until the accident limited her mobility. The neighbors living above her apartment were wonderfully helpful. They were her salvation. After giving this brief history and expressing the feeling that she was over the worst of it, she began to cry and said that the tears came too easily. She then remarked apologetically that she still had to use a cane because her foot was painful.

When asked about her past medical history she reported only good health. Her thoughts then went to one of her children who had a serious adolescent depression, a delayed reaction to the death of his father, her first husband. Her first husband had suffered two years from a terminal malignant tumor. After he died, his business partners gave her job training so that she could support her children. She remarried a dozen years later and enjoyed a wonderful second marriage until her second husband died of a myocardial infarction. He had been a widower and his children and grandchildren remained very devoted to the patient. At this point she asserted again that she was very independent, saying, "I drive and come and go as I please. I don't want to depend on the children. I help them. Suddenly I feel useless."

The therapist was impressed by three elements of this story which suggested therapeutic interventions. First, Mrs. J.'s injury, surgery, and convalescence had indeed been traumatic, and had awakened painful memories and feelings from earlier traumas—the deaths of her husbands and the illness of her son. The accessibility of associated memories was promising for abreaction of her pent-up feelings and resolution of conflicts. Second, her tendency to idealize important helpful figures in her life—her "wonderful" second husband and neighbors, her devoted stepchildren—suggested that she could gain therapeutic support by forming a positive idealizing transference. Third, she was at least partly conscious of her evident leading conflict, between dependence and independence. She had dealt with this conflict by asserting independence, until her injury, suffering, immobilization, and partial isolation made her more dependent on others. Her subsequent, defensive overassertion of independence had interfered with acceptance of help. The prominence of this conflict and her awareness of it indicated the possibility of influencing it constructively through clarification and redirection of her efforts.

Accordingly, at this point the therapist expressed his impression that Mrs. J. had remained frightened after her injury, and must have felt (unconsciously) further injured by the surgery and enforced hospitalization. He told her that she appeared to be in conflict between her strong wish to be independent and her temporary increased dependence upon others. She was trying too hard to be independent and this interfered with her acceptance of necessary help. It was her task now to make the best possible use of available assistance.

Mrs. J. listened to this clarification and then spoke briefly of her fear of taking a tranquilizer prescribed by her orthopedist, despite early morning awakening with depressive thoughts. She added, tangentially, that she planned to get back to swimming (it was summertime) and to seeing friends again. The therapist suggested (with the power of positive transference) that she take her tranquilizer when she awoke depressed, and that she try to accept help without thanking people excessively (a tendency of hers) since it put people off. He gave her an appointment for another visit. One week later, she returned and said that she had followed the therapist's advice about activity, including resumption of driving and swimming (which was actually her own self-advice). She had taken the tranquilizer upon early awakening and had found it easier to resume sleeping. However, despite this progress, she said she had experienced some "digression" (by which she meant a return of symptoms) in the form of back pain and anxiety. In contrast to her previously reported history of good health, she now told of having had back trouble, possibly a lumbar disk, and rheumatoid arthritis for nine months following the birth of her youngest child. Her accessible memories were expanding.

Then the patient reported a nightmare: "I fell on the street. There were many people around." This traumatic dream seemed to be a modified repetition of her fall. She went on to describe her accident, which had occurred at the top of four or five concrete steps outside the door of her apartment building on a windy day. The door blew open when she unlocked it, striking her so that she fell down the steps and broke her leg. She was unable to move and there was no one around. Then a man drove into the parking lot and found her and called the police. A policeman took her to her apartment, telephoned her children and the hospital, and left. Most frightening of all, she was alone between the time he finished calling and the time her children came. The dread, which led directly to her memory of the accident, underscores what was most psychologically traumatic, her helplessness and isolation at that time. The "many people around" in the dream represent her wish that she had not been left alone then. This was communicated to the patient.

At her third and final interview, she expressed concern and puzzlement because she tended to become tearful when good things came to mind. She said that her back pain had frightened her: it might be an old trouble returning. She was lonely because she could not yet resume her volunteer work at a local hospital. However, she was improving with her swimming and driving. The therapist reviewed with her the characteristic course of resolution of acute trauma as seen in her case, clarifying her intolerance of strong emotions, good or bad, and her effort to work off the impact of the traumatic experience, through repetition of the event, by remembering and dreaming.

A follow-up appointment was made but she called to cancel. Her improvement had continued.

In this example the traumatic stress of the accident and what followed intensified a long-standing, active conflict between dependence and independence, but did not lead to a major regression. As often happens, the psychological crisis was delayed until after the physical danger had passed, with healing of the fracture. Psychotherapy freed the normal process of recovery from trauma. In this process the traumatic events are abreacted, that is they are reexperienced in the form of emotion-laden memories. Traumatic dreams represent a breakthrough of feelings, whereas in memories the original terrifying and paralyzing events are faced, survived, mastered, and overcome in manageable increments. The painful emotions are discharged in affects such as fear, rage, and weeping, affording some relief. As affective pressure subsides, defenses can work more effectively and normal activities are resumed. Finally,

traumatic dreams disappear and the traumatic events are recalled less frequently.

The main therapeutic methods employed were suggestion,
which provided reassurance, encouragement to verbalize memories and feelings, and facilitation of abreaction. Adaptive intervention and clarification had a more limited role. The
intensified conflict, which retarded and complicated her recovery, was approached specifically with these last two methods.
Her efforts were redirected toward accepting help, and her
conflict was discussed in the context of making sense of her
symptoms. Since the therapist did not have to deal with deeper,
predisposing conflicts rekindled by regression and was not preparing to attempt character reconstruction, he was not concerned with uncovering the basis of her reactions in her early
developmental experiences.

The treatment of another woman, who likewise had a delayed crisis following a fracture, illustrates a further typical
development in crisis intervention.

Treatment of a Crisis Which Has Mobilized Predisposing Conflict

Mrs. K., 70 years old, had broken her leg in a fall three-and-
a-half months before the initial psychiatric interview. Her injury
required open reduction, pinning, and a cast. A month and a
half later she fell again, fracturing her wrist. She then developed
symptoms of depression, including weeping, anorexia, insomnia,
and fear of dying, leading to the psychiatric referral.

In the initial interview, Mrs. K. recounted her injuries and
depressive symptoms and then said that she tried to keep her
feelings in because she did not like to upset family members,
especially her husband. She went on to say that her mother died
when she was 10 years old. Her father lived 10 years longer and
then died of a stroke. Following her mother's death, an aunt, her
mother's single, younger sister, took care of her and then, after
Mrs. K. married, lived with her for 25 years: "I feel guilty, I
couldn't please her, I should have done more but I couldn't get
along with her. She had difficulty getting along with people in
general. She made one of my sons a favorite but was critical of
my other son and daughter." Her aunt had died 6 years previously. At the end, the aunt was bedridden for two months and

the patient kept her at her home. The patient's bronchial asthma, which she had had for many years, was worse for a year after her aunt died. As she told her story she switched back and forth between her aunt and her mother.

After talking about her children and a car accident 17 years before, she returned to speaking of her aunt. As a young adolescent she used to worry about the aunt leaving. On one occasion the aunt had actually threatened to go. The aunt was very religious and good but "she could break your heart with criticism." Once she said that the patient was not a good mother. At this point in the session the patient began to weep. Then she balanced her resentment and sadness by remarking that her aunt was only 21 years older than herself. At first, they had been like pals, but when the patient became an adult, the aunt became overcritical. She acted as if *she* should be the child and the patient the adult.

In the second hour Mrs. K. continued to express feelings of guilt in relation to her aunt, which had preoccupied her for some time. In particular, she felt very bad because she had forgotten to call in the priest on the day before her aunt died. Although this had been entirely unintentional, and the aunt had been visited regularly by the priest, she had been unable to forgive herself. Some interpretation was offered to the patient relating this excessive feeling of guilt to her mostly unconscious anger and conflict over her aunt's behavior during her last years. The aunt had been hypercritical and difficult while the patient had knocked herself out trying to please. The therapist further suggested that the patient's feelings about her aunt had been intensified by her memories and feelings related to losing her mother.

By the fourth weekly hour, the patient's mood, anxiety, and sleeplessness had improved, and one week later she reported walking for two days without her cane and eating better. She felt satisfied with her improvement. At this time a few evidences of her character neurosis appeared. For example, she had made a joke and then was worried that it might be too aggressive and hurtful to people. Also she had greeted someone by touching them with her cane and then imagined that they had been hurt or offended. She was aware that she tended to be overly good and excessively scrupulous. Despite this insight and the progress in therapy from the prevalence of symptoms to the appearance of character-related conflicts, it was agreed not to continue the therapeutic process—which would have led to efforts at character change.

In this case the patient had moved in her thoughts and feelings from her recent injuries into memories of important events in her life, particularly a key relationship with her aunt which formed part of the predisposition to the crisis. Her crisis was precipitated by illness (injury), and illnesses, deaths, and at least one prior auto accident had played an important part in her life.

The patient was a psychosomatic reactor, that is, her emotions were linked to and expressed through her bronchial asthma. Her mother's early death (from streptoccocal throat infection) had been a severe trauma for the patient, unconsciously felt to be a desertion and leaving a residue of ambivalent feelings. Her aunt, who became her surrogate mother, inherited these love–hate feelings which were reinforced later by the aunt's hypercritical behavior. The patient felt extremely guilty about her anger and overcompensated by making extraordinary efforts to please her aunt. The aunt's terminal illness became the focus of the patient's ambivalence and guilt, centering upon the last rites, which ask forgiveness for sin and for healing of the soul. Unconsciously, Mrs. K. experienced her fractures as punishment for anger and she may have brought them about in unconscious acts of self-punishment. Her depression also unconsciously represented punishment. The strain caused by her injuries had weakened her usual psychological defenses, particularly reaction formation (overcompensation) and repression, exposing her to painful, potentially disruptive feelings. The emerging defense of regression then mobilized a deeper conflict, expressed in her preoccupation with polarized thoughts about anger and punishment, and sin and salvation.

Psychotherapy assisted her symptomatic recovery by means of positive transference, the therapist's attitude of acceptance, and a modest degree of insight. After she had reestablished her precrisis equilibrium, the decision not to attempt character modification was based upon two considerations: her sustained improvement and the therapist's impression that she lacked the strong motivation necessary to face her deep-seated, regressive, ego-alien conflicts.

In the two preceding case examples the patients' character structures were not a central issue in treatment. Character or personality type is the focus of a different kind of treatment process in which the main therapeutic principle employed is adaptive intervention (or therapeutic manipulation). Adaptive intervention is based upon knowledge of the patient's personality, and makes use of the patient's characteristic emotional systems for achieving therapeutic change (G. L. Bibring, 1947; E. Bibring, 1954).

Adaptive Intervention Utilizing the Patient's Existing Character Structure

Mrs. L., a very pretty, exquisitely groomed woman in her early seventies, developed a slowly deepening depression after her husband's death (Kahana, 1978). Antidepressant medication and psychiatric hospitalization had failed to alleviate her condition. Family members who recognized her almost lifelong struggle over self-esteem, began her rehabilitation by transferring her from a busy, utilitarian psychiatry ward, to an elegant residential nursing home, a setting in keeping with her need to maintain "the feeling of superiority" (Kahana and Bibring, 1964). When first seen she was in a continuing crisis marked by suffering, agitation, sleeplessness, anorexia, hypochondriasis, self-devaluation, and paranoia. Her paranoid ideas had a narcissistic focus. She was convinced that the other residents in the nursing home were wealthier and better dressed and that they looked down upon her as inferior and as a disturber of their tranquility. The origin of her narcissistic vulnerability was a repressed attitude of excessive entitlement associated with a mildly crippling injury sustained at age 5 in an accident, which she blamed on her father.

Excessive entitlement is normal in very small children. Persistence of this attitude may stem from two opposite causes. It may be a consequence of overindulgence and lack of limit setting, the essence of "spoiling." Or it may arise from severe and "unfair" deprivation. Freud (1916) described as "The Exceptions" people who believe unconsciously that the world owes them compensation because they were deprived or injured. He cited Shakespeare's Richard the Third, the vengeful hunchback, as a classical illustration. In this case the patient's crippling, which brought her special consideration, had the effect of fixating her over-entitlement.

Mrs. L.'s lifelong physical beauty accentuated the importance of her appearance, and she became painfully self-conscious, especially when others remarked upon her disturbance of gait. At the same time, by limping slightly, in an unconsciously appealing fashion, she stimulated people to offer assistance. A severe state of anxiety and depression had set in at age 11, following partially successful reparative surgery for the injury caused by the earlier accident, and had persisted for most of her adolescence.

The patient's mother had remained, for her, an almost perfect person and this idealization was reaffirmed when mother remained sweet and uncomplaining, despite blindness, in her last years. Mrs. L.'s recovery was marked by the dramatic return of her ability to enjoy music. Her mother had had a beautiful singing voice and the patient had thereby regained the capacity to participate in her mother's perfection. As she recovered, she began to assist older, infirm fellow guests, making amends for having been such a burden, as she saw it. This led to the discovery that she had a knack for managing other people. She had a very winning manner and could persuade people to get out of bed, to go to meals, and in general, to do more for themselves. After her return home she continued as a volunteer in two nursing homes, thus helping to stabilize her own recovery.

The treatment modalities were narcissistic support from the milieu of the nursing home, psychotherapy, and an antidepressant—the same medication that had previously failed. The psychotherapy featured affirmation of her self-esteem, clarification of her motives and illness, and acceptance of her limited capacity for modification of character. Her achievements and personal attractiveness were acknowledged by the therapist, and her paranoid ideas were identified as such and interpreted as projected self-criticisms. Her reaction formations of somewhat excessive goodness and charm were simply accepted as normal aspects of her personality. The treatment helped her to repair her self-esteem by mobilizing her pattern of identifying with her idealized mother and then caring for others as mother had cared for her.

This case illustrates the need to use as full an understanding as possible of the patient's psychodynamics to achieve favorable change in supportive psychotherapy. Supportive therapy is often equated with providing a patient with certain basic conditions, such as a sympathetic listener and privacy. This implies that it is a limited modality that can be applied indiscriminately by untrained or semitrained people. In fact it is an instrument of great flexibility and specificity which includes a range of approaches and can utilize numerous combinations of therapeutic principles. Levine (1949) described 25 supportive "methods" (approaches) available to the general medical practitioner and five more for the physician with aptitude and some additional psychodynamic training. Among the former are such methods as "using an attitude of authoritative firmness," "giving of information," and "fostering of socialized living." Among his more advanced methods are "life-history discussion," and "emotional desensitization." In supportive psychotherapy the various methods and the principles of suggestion, abreaction, adaptive intervention, clarification, and interpretation are used with the *aim* of support, as contrasted with the aim of reconstruction. During treatment we often move back and forth between these aims. Support facilitates reconstruction by sustaining motivation for arduous exploration or providing a respite from painful self-confrontation.

Beyond Crisis Management: Character Change Through Insight and Maturation

Mr. M., a married man who began treatment in a severe crisis of suicidal despair, was seen from middle life into the beginning of old age (Kahana, 1983). He had been "on a roller-coaster" of depression and remission for two years following the suicide of his older brother and business partner.

At the age of 4, the patient and a younger sister had been placed in foster care after their mother's death. Subsequently he lived in an orphanage with his sister and his older brother until he was 12, when his father remarried and reconstituted their home. His brother had been his protector, leader, role model, and rival. The loss of his mother and his experiences in foster care and the orphanage left a residue of persistent feelings of insecurity, inferiority, shyness, and fear of poverty. He compensated by overworking.

There were two distinct periods of psychotherapy. In the first six years, comprising almost half of the total hours of treatment, he was seen weekly, ending with his discharge as improved. He returned to therapy after a year, following his father's death.

This time the treatment schedule was less intense, with sessions only once a month. The initial segment was psychodynamic psychotherapy of a depressed adult following a familiar and established form. The second, much longer, though less intense portion, evolved into a prolonged process of sustained support, assistance of maturation, and very gradual working through of narcissistic conflicts. Initially, therapy centered around the patient's grief for his brother, transference, and resistance, and the emergence of significant fantasies and conflicts associated with strong affects. Over the long term the therapeutic course could be charted by his responses to current stresses or positive gains, his reactions to his children's development, and his reassessment of his life.

Grief was a major issue in the first two-and-a-half years of therapy. In time the patient could recall his wish, associated with intense guilt, to have his brother out of the way. In his introjective identification with his brother (i.e., his unconscious confusion with regard to his separateness from his brother) he feared that he too would end as a suicide. With the fading of his grief, his guilt was replaced by a masochistic aspect of his character, the fear of success.

Transference issues centered at first around the establishment of trust and a working alliance. Then he spoke of envying the therapist's youth, success (his idealization), Ivy League education (imagined), ability to understand and to verbalize feelings, and eventually, even the therapist's vacations.

Resistance in treatment appeared first as his fear that confronting certain feelings might lead to a breakdown. This became modified into a concern that he might appear stupid or crazy, so that the therapist would look down on him as weak and worthless. He was particularly afraid of frightening off the therapist with his occasional, expressed thoughts of suicide.

Feelings of anger were initially directed out of the therapeutic relationship toward the psychiatrists who had failed to save his brother. Then, as his envy emerged, he recognized that he was angry at the therapist (in the transference) and feared retaliation. He came to realize that this was displaced from his envy and anger toward his brother. Eventually he connected this with his anger at his father for having been a poor provider and role model.

As he became more conscious of his anger, an element of competition with the therapist emerged, and soon the patient became aware of his strong competitive urges directed at other people as well. In contrast to his aggressive competitiveness, the patient's strong dependency needs were thrown into relief in the transference, when brief interruptions of therapy led to intensification of depression because of separation and abandonment conflicts. Gradually, the treatment process uncovered his underlying, grandiose self-expectations which contributed to his tendency to overwork. With the emergence of memories and fantasies, the sources of his guilt and shame became more understandable. These feelings were attached to his mother's death as well as his brother's, and also to persistent adolescent sexual fantasies involving his stepmother and stepsister.

As noted, the second period of treatment was precipitated by a second crisis, his father's death. This loss, like the deaths of his stepmother, mother-in-law, sister, and others during the following 16 years, mobilized memories and feelings and promoted reassessment of the meaning and impact of old relationships. These losses confronted him with his own mortality and aroused a wish to improve his life before it was too late; for example, to enjoy some leisure and undertake adult education. Major losses were not the only, or even the main, stimuli to continue working through conflicts, mastering traumata, and filling in deficits in his life. Much of the therapeutic work dealt with day-to-day matters. Periodic crises were centered on his business. For example, he would be most depressed when orders were slack, but also very anxious if business was active and he had to meet deadlines.

With the purchase of a house, a measure of his gain in self-confidence, the patient began to become rooted. His wife and he gave parties occasionally for friends and neighbors. His children's developmental experiences promoted reworking of his own formative experiences. These included their gender and sexual development, oedipal attachments, transient neurotic episodes, and adolescent adventures. This slow, extended psychotherapy was not only concerned with the working through of conflicts related to the sources of the symptoms, but also with the rediscovery of past pleasures. Ordinary parent–child experiences, such as taking his daughter sightseeing, introduced an element of pleasure into his existence. His children pulled him into cross-country skiing. From time to time he mentioned playing golf on weekends. His wife and he bought a half-interest in a country cottage near a lake where he could again sail a small boat—he had learned to sail as a child at a summer camp run by the orphanage.

As his 60th birthday approached, he began to consider the possibility of retirement in the future. Two years later he spoke thoughtfully of his eventual, normal death, with practical concern for the security of his family.

There were in all about 480 treatment hours, the time equivalent of two-and-a-half years of psychoanalysis. Extended therapy had been undertaken because of Mr. M.'s initial vulnerability, limited tolerance of therapeutic regression, and persistent need for support, based on severe traumatization in childhood. He proved to have qualities of character flexibility, insightfulness, and affect tolerance that permitted structural change. Left on his own he would have endured moderate chronic anxiety and depression, interrupted by episodes of more severe and alarming regression. In contrast, by age 65, while he still experienced envy in the transference or responded to an improvement in a guilty fashion, he recovered quickly, showing evidence of objectivity and self-awareness. He saw the repetitiveness and exaggeration in his behavior, even its humorous aspect. Although he retained the general tendencies of his masochistic-depressive character structure, he showed greater appreciation of his own accomplishments, increased acceptance of himself, more realistic ideals, more sense of responsibility as opposed to self-sacrifice and a capacity for relaxation and enjoyment. Over the long run the criteria of progress, reflecting structural changes, were indices of maturation, not simply the easing or disappearance of symptoms.

Conclusion

In this chapter, psychological crisis is defined and common crises are identified. In particular, the stressful events predisposing to crises in the aging are noted. Certain psychodynamic principles and procedures are singled out as especially useful in crisis management. Treatment of the frail aged is distinguished from that of the more vigorous majority of aging patients. Crises observed in office practice in about 40 elderly men and women were categorized as arising from the normal "developmental crises" of aging—emotional trauma, anxiety of family members, the danger of suicide, psychosis, delirium, general debilitation, and terminal illness. Four case examples illustrated paradigms of the treatment process in and beyond crisis management: brief therapy of a traumatic reaction; treatment of a traumatic reaction which has mobilized predisposing conflict; adaptive intervention making use of the patient's existing character structure; and character change through insight and maturation.

References

Amory, C. (1947), *The Proper Bostonians*. New York: Harper & Brothers.
Bibring, E. (1954), Psychoanalysis and the dynamic psychotherapies. *J. Amer. Psychoanal. Assn.*, 2:745–770.
Bibring, G. L. (1947), Psychiatry and social work. *J. Soc. Casework*, 28:203–211.
——— (1966), Old age: Its disabilities and its assets. In: *Psychoanalysis: A General Psychology*, ed. R. M. Loewenstein, L. M. Newman, M. Schur, & A. J. Solnit. New York: International Universities Press, pp. 253–271.
Freud, S. (1916), Some character-types met with in psycho-analytic work. *Standard Edition*, 14:311–331. London: Hogarth Press, 1957.
Goldfarb, A. I. (1976), The aged in crisis. In: *Psychiatric Emergencies*, ed. R. A. Glick, A. T. Meyerson, E. Robbins, & J. A. Talbott. New York: Grune & Stratton, pp. 241–257.
Hoff, L. A. (1978), *People in Crisis: Understanding and Helping*. Reading, Mass.: Addison-Wesley.
Kahana, R. J. (1978), Psychoanalysis in later life: Discussion. *J. Geriat. Psychiat.*, 11:37–49.
——— (1979), Strategies of dynamic psychotherapy with the wide range of older individual. *J. Geriat. Psychiat.*, 12:71–100.
——— (1983), A miserable old age—What can therapy do? *J. Geriat. Psychiat.*, 16:7–32.
——— Bibring, G. (1964), Personality types in medical management. In: *Psychiatry and Medical Practice in a General Hospital*, ed. N. E. Zinberg. New York: International Universities Press, pp. 108–123.
Knight, P. (1949), A critique of the present status of the psychotherapies. *Bull. N.Y. Acad. Med.*, 25:100-114.
——— (1952), An evaluation of psychotherapeutic techniques. *Bull. Menninger Clinic*, 16:113–124.
Levine, M. (1949), *Psychotherapy in Medical Practice*. New York: The Macmillan Co.

9

BRIEF PSYCHOTHERAPY WITH THE ELDERLY: A STUDY OF PROCESS AND OUTCOME

Lawrence W. Lazarus, M.D.
and
Lesley Groves, M.S.
with
David Gutmann, Ph.D.
Andrew Ripeckyj, M.D.
Rhoda Frankel, M.S.W.
Nancy Newton, Ph.D.
Jerome Grunes, M.D.
Sophia Havasy-Galloway, M.S.

Introduction

Psychotherapists, beginning in the 1930s have reported successful psychotherapeutic outcomes with elderly patients. These pioneering therapists (Martin and DeGrunchy, 1933; Grotjahn, 1940, 1955; Martin, 1944; Weinberg, 1951; Goldfarb, 1953; Meerloo, 1955, 1961) and others advocated modification of traditional psychoanalytic technique, advising therapists who work with the elderly to be warm, supportive, and active. Although these and subsequent clinical reports (Pfeiffer, 1976; Lazarus, 1980; Lazarus and Weinberg, 1980) about the elderly's responsiveness to psychotherapy have been positive, there have been few empirical studies with elderly outpatients that support

This study was supported, in part, by the Geriatric Mental Health Academic Award from the National Institute of Mental Health, Center for Studies of the Mental Health of the Aging.

this optimism. Rechtschaffen's conclusion in his excellent review of geriatric psychotherapy is, in some ways, as pertinent today as it was in 1959: "As is true for psychotherapy as a whole, systematic, controlled studies of the effectiveness of various treatments of older people are still lacking" (Rechtschaffen, 1959, p. 82). This is particularly so in the area of a time-limited psychotherapy.

Theoretical Considerations

Due to the shorter duration of therapy and the selection of specific and measureable foci for treatment time-limited, or, brief psychotherapy has been less difficult to study, than the longer-term therapies. Generally, large-scale studies of psychotherapy outcome often use global outcome measures that provide an overall assessment of outcome but do not capture the nuances of the psychotherapeutic process. In contrast to large-scale clinical trials, David Malan (1963) developed a methodology for studying in detail the process and outcome of brief, psychodynamically oriented psychotherapy with adult outpatients, based upon the premise that each patient has highly individualized problems and a unique personality. Hence individual and specific measures were emphasized, instead of global outcome measures. Malan (1976b, 1979) found that brief, dynamically oriented psychotherapy not only helped to resolve current conflicts and improve symptoms, but even brought about characterological change. According to Malan, successful outcome was positively correlated with the adult patient's capacity for insight and for establishing a good working relationship with the therapist.

Horowitz (1976) and his colleagues also concentrated their brief, dynamically oriented therapy research on adult outpatients, especially those with neuroses and stress response syndromes. In one of their recent studies of 52 bereaved patients treated with psychotherapy, (Horowitz, Marmar, Weiss, DeWitt, & Rosenbaum, 1984), patients' symptoms improved more than did their social and work functioning. Significant predictors of outcome were found when two process variables—therapeutic alliance and actions by the therapist—were considered in interaction with two patient variables: motivation for dynamic therapy and developmental level of the self-concept. They concluded that more exploratory psychotherapeutic approaches were better suited for highly motivated and/or better organized patients; more supportive therapeutic approaches were better suited for patients with lower levels of motivation and organization of the self-concept.

Although not specifically studying brief psychotherapy, Buckley, Conte, Plutchik, Wild, and Karasu (1984) found, as did Malan (1976a) and Horowitz (1976), that psychodynamic and process variables are useful as predictors of outcome. In a study of predictors of outcome of 21 medical students treated with psychodynamic therapy, Buckley, et al. found that the defense of projection, and its comparable coping style of blame, were surprisingly good predictors of a positive outcome. In addition, three process variables, as rated by the therapist—support by the therapist, identification with the therapist, and improved self-esteem—correlated most highly with positive outcome.

To date, there have been few investigations (Silberschatz and Curtis, 1982) of the process and outcome of dynamically oriented brief therapy with elderly outpatients. It would appear that brief time-limited dynamic psychotherapy would be especially appropriate for selected elderly patients because its time-limited nature takes into account the comparatively shorter duration of the older person's remaining life, and simultaneously conveys the therapist's confidence in the patient's ability to master current stress, just as the patient has in the past. Setting a time limit to therapy may also reduce the patient's fear of protracted dependency. Brief therapy quickens the pace of therapy, brings into focus the inevitable termination, and reduces the patient's financial burden.

However, a key question needed to be answered. Would elderly patients utilize brief psychotherapy, in a way similar to younger adults (Malan, 1963), or would age-related developmental challenges and tasks specific to the aging process influence the process and outcome of psychotherapy? To evaluate the efficacy and process of brief dynamic psychotherapy with the elderly, an interdisciplinary team of geriatric psychotherapists at the Illinois State Psychiatric Institute (ISPI), in collaboration with Northwestern University in Chicago, Illinois, began in 1979 to apply an individualized psychotherapy outcome methodology to a study of elderly outpatients. The research team was composed of three psychiatrists, three psychologists, and a social worker. In an earlier report of the initial patients treated (Lazarus, Groves, and Newton, 1984), the authors found that elderly patients' symptomatic improvement was achieved with comparatively little change in their major psychodynamic conflict. Three major factors within the patient–therapist relationship contributed to a positive therapy outcome and to improving patients' self-esteem and sense of mastery: (1) patients' positive feelings toward the therapist; (2) therapists' use of more supportive, rather than insight-oriented therapeutic techniques; and (3) patients' use of the defense mechanisms of externalization and projection. Patients tended to attribute the cause of their difficulties to a spouse, adult child, physician, or organization and then assertively separated themselves psychologically and/or physically from the perceived source of their problem. Improvement in these patients' symptoms and self-esteem, however, occurred with a concomitant decline in their relationship with the person or organization they blamed for their problems. In other words, the defense mechanisms of projection and externalization boosted self-esteem at an interpersonal cost. These changes were reflected on the individualized scales and the process notes of the patients' treatment.

Method

Referral and Selection of Subjects

Elderly subjects who presented for assessment to the outpatient clinic at the ISPI were considered for inclusion in the study if they were:

1. 60 years of age or older;
2. of average intelligence and showed no evidence of psychosis;

3. not taking psychotropic medication;
4. troubled with a problem that had a definable focus;
5. willing to work within the time limit of 15 sessions and to be videotaped.

Patients meeting these criteria were referred to a member of our research team who conducted an extensive videotaped diagnostic interview that was later reviewed by the entire research team. The interview focused on presenting symptoms, precipitating stresses, current psychosocial support, and relevant historical information. Because previous research by Malan (1976b) indicated that successful treatment outcome was related to capacity for insight, a trial interpretation was usually made to help assess the subject's suitability for dynamically oriented psychotherapy. Special note was made of the subject's ability to hear and respond to the interpretation. For diagnostic and evaluative purposes, the Rorschach Ink Blot, Thematic Apperception Test (TAT), and the Wechsler Adult Intelligence Scale (WAIS) were also administered.

After reviewing the diagnostic interview and the results of the psychological testing, the research team discussed the patient's suitability for brief treatment and arrived at a *Diagnostic and Statistical Manual III* (DSM-III) diagnosis (American Psychiatric Association, 1980). On the basis of these data and the case discussion, subjects judged to have a potential for serious regression or in need of psychopharmacological treatment were referred elsewhere. As the research group discussed each case and arrived at a dynamic formulation, a central theme or focus was defined. It was believed that the focal issue or conflict was sufficiently circumscribed to be dealt with in brief, time-limited treatment. If a focal issue could not be determined for a particular patient, it was judged that the patient's problems were mainly characterological and/or of long-standing nature and that more extensive, long-term therapy was needed. These patients were referred to other therapists for such treatment.

Patients accepted for the study agreed to be videotaped, and to have these videotapes reviewed by our research group. They would be assessed at the midpoint and termination of treatment, as well as six months after completion of treatment.

Each patient knew at the beginning that treatment would be limited to 10 to 15 sessions. The study was explained and informed consent was obtained before treatment began.

Construction and Nature of Outcome Scales

In an attempt to delineate the process, as well as the efficacy of brief psychotherapy, the individualized outcome scaling technique pioneered by Malan (1976a) and elaborated by Horowitz (1976) was followed.

In this study researchers similarly developed a set of individualized rating scales for each subject tailored to the unique situation and dynamics of each patient. After the initial evaluation, treatment outcome was predicted based on an understanding of the subject's psychodynamics, symptomatology, self-concept, focal issue, and the anticipated therapeutic relationship. These individualized outcome scales facilitated comparison of change across subjects as well as the assessment of discrete changes specific to each subject.

The conceptual model underlying the construction of the individualized rating scales was developed from work with a pilot sample of four subjects. The complete set of the seven scale definitions that gradually evolved was used in constructing scales for the subsequent four subjects. As the model evolved with use of the scaling technique, the first four subjects were not assessed on all seven scales. The conceptual model used to construct the complete set of seven scales is presented in Table 9-1.

All seven scales were designed as 9-point indices of change with the zero or entry point describing the subject's initial condition at the time of the diagnostic evaluation before treatment began. A score of $+1$ or $+2$ was described, reflecting moderate or excellent improvement respectively; while a score of -1 or -2 represented moderate or extreme worsening. Detailed descriptions of each scale point were discussed by the research team and constructed for each individual subject, reflecting the hypothesized positive or negative changes. The research team rated each subject at .5 increments on each scale.

TABLE 9-1

Conceptual Model Used for Construction of the Individual
Outcome Scales

---

1. *Symptom Scale*—describing in concrete, behavioral terms the subject's presenting major complaint(s) and symptomatology.

2. *Focal Issue/Affect*—describing the major troublesome affect associated with the focal issue.

3. *Focal Issue/Defense*—describing the major defense used by the subject to deal with the affect associated with the focal issue.

4. *Self Scale/Continuity and Self-Esteem*—reflecting the subject's ability to recognize important, valued aspects of the self as stable and continuous in the face of emotional lability and environmental discontinuities.

5. *Self Scale/Disavowed Aspects*—defining the aspects of self disavowed by the subject, which may be reintegrated and reworked positively by the subject into an expanded, yet still coherent sense of self.

6. *Psychodynamic Scale*—identifying the major underlying psychodynamic(s) of the focal conflict.

7. *Therapeutic Alliance*—assessing the subject's ability to utilize the therapist and the therapeutic relationship for resolution of the focal issue and for psychodynamic growth.

Treatment

After the diagnostic interview and inclusion into the study, each subject was referred to a different, experienced, dynamically oriented therapist for 15 weekly sessions of 50 minutes each. Except for the first case, the psychotherapists were not members of our research team and therefore had no knowledge of the scales or the ratings for their patients. Therapy sessions were videotaped for subsequent review by the research team after treatment was completed.

The videotaped assessment interviews done at midpoint, end of treatment, and six months posttreatment, were examined independently by the members of the research team. Using the individualized, outcome scales and without reviewing their previous ratings, each rater independently assessed each subject. The ratings were then discussed by the research group for mutual learning and for improving interrater reliability for subsequent ratings.

Rating Scale Reliability

The reliability of the individualized outcome scales was assessed in three ways.

1. The first method addressed the question of each scale's reliability, independent of the other scales. The researchers examined the probability that individual ratings would agree solely by chance, instead of rating agreement reflecting the fact that independent raters could reliably draw similar conclusions from observing the same assessment videotape, interpret the specific scale points, and reach accurate agreement on the same rating for a subject (Lawlis and Chatfield, 1974). Using the chi square as a nonparametric measure of rater agreement, the agreement in ratings was calculated for each subject, on each scale, at the three ratings times. Consistently high levels of agreement ($p < .001$ or $< .005$) were found for all scales on all subjects at the three rating times (with the exception of one scale for one subject at a single rating time).

2. The second method examined the variability of ratings on a single scale for bias that could be attributed to the raters. In other words, when looking at the raters' assessment of change in a given patient on a single scale across the three rating times (midpoint, end of treatment, and six-month follow-up), was part or all of the difference in scores due to the way in which raters interpreted the scale or judged the change, or did the difference in scores reflect actual patient change, for better or worse? For each patient on each scale, a separate one-way analysis of variance with a repeated measure factor was calculated for the four raters over the three rating times. A significant rater effect ($p < .05$) was found in only three patients on a single, different scale for each patient. Consequently, the researchers concluded that patient improvement or worsening could be attributed to treatment effects rather than rater bias and that the scales accurately reflected subject change over time.

3. The third method of assessing reliability addressed the issue of consistency within each subject's set of scales. This method determines if the subject's change is reflected equally in all scales or differs by degrees in each individual scale. The intraclass correlation coefficient (ICC) was used to assess the

consistency of the set of rating scales for each subject at the three points of evaluation (Bartko, 1966; Shrout and Fliess, 1979). The ICC results are presented in Table 9-2. The reliability estimates ranged from .10 to .98. Lower correlations (such as those for Mr. P.) were interpreted as evidence that the subject's amount of change was not consistent on all scales. In other words, the subject improved (or worsened) more in some areas than in other areas as defined by the scales. Higher correlations (such as those for Mrs. T.) indicated that the subject improved (or worsened) about equally in all scale areas. This differential rate of change in various areas of the patients' functioning was anticipated at the outset of our study, and was a major consideration in deciding to use several, individualized outcome scales rather than a single, global measure of change, that might mask specific change.

Analysis of Treatment Outcome

One-way analyses of variance with repeated measures were used to assess treatment and rater effects as measured by each individualized outcome scale on each subject. A two-way analysis of variance was used to compare the treatment response of men to that of women in two areas assessed by the scales; that of symptoms and psychodynamics.

TABLE 9-2
Consistency of Individualized Outcome Scales as Measured by
Intraclass Correlation Coefficients (ICC)

	Midpoint	*End of Treatment*	*Six-Month Follow-up*
Mr. K.	.93	.49	.19
Mr. M.	.81	.29	.89
Mr. T.	.79	.86	.47
Mr. P.	.31	.10	.35
Mrs. R.	*	.45	.89
Mrs. L.	.75	.28	.68
Mrs. T.	.85	.98	.96
Mrs. W.	.88	.88	.77

*Only two raters were used for this case; therefore no ICC was ascertained.

Findings

Eight subjects were studied; four men and four women, ranging in age from 63 to 77 years. At the time they entered the study, all subjects were married except for one widower and one divorced woman. Each subject was from a low or middle socioeconomic class, which is reflective of the geographical area served by the ISPI, a nonprofit public facility. Seven patients met the DSM-III criteria of either adjustment disorder with depressed mood or dysthymic disorder, while one subject met the criteria for a panic disorder.

Outcome as Measured by Individualized Scales

Table 9-3 shows the means and standard deviations for the eight subjects on the individualized outcome scales at the end of treatment and at six-month follow-up. Table 9-4 summarizes the significance levels of the results of the analyses of variance. By way of overview, significant positive treatment effects, as measured by the individualized outcome scales, were found for all subjects. At the end of treatment or at six-month follow-up, seven of the eight subjects showed a significant lessening of their presenting symptoms (six subjects at p < .01; one at p < .05). With regard to the psychodynamic scale, four of the subjects also made significant, positive changes (p < .01). Additionally, seven subjects achieved some resolution of their focal conflict as indicated by improvement on the focal issue-affect scale and the focal issue-defense scale.

Two scales concerning aspects of self (scales number 4 and 5 described in Table 9-1) were constructed for six and four subjects respectively. Four of the six subjects showed improvement in self-continuity and self-esteem (scale 4, p < .05 or < .01) and three of the four subjects showed an expanded, more integrated sense of self (scale 5, p < .05 or < .01). Finally, of the four subjects evaluated for therapeutic alliance, three had established a positive working relationship and two of these three subjects maintained their generally positive feelings toward their therapist and treatment after termination (p < .01). The other four subjects, who were the first four subjects studied

TABLE 9-3
Means and Standard Deviations of Ratings on Individualized Outcome Scales

Subject	1 Symptom	2 Foc Issue Affect	3 Foc Issue Defense	4 Self-Con Self-Est	5 Denied Aspects	6 Psy Dyn	7 Ther Alli
Mr. K. End†	.8 ± .4	1.0 ± .2	.9 ± .1	1.0 ± .2	*	*	*
6 mos.‡	.4 ± .4	.5 ± .4	.7 ± .5	**			
Mr. M. End	.0 ± .4	.0 ± .4	.4 ± .3	.0 ± .4	.4 ± .9	.3 ± .7	.9 ± .3
6 mos.	.9 ± .3	1.0 ± .4	-.4 ± .8	.0 ± .6	1.1 ± .8	.9 ± .3	-.4 ± .8
Mr. T. End	1.1 ± .4	.7 ± .2	1.3 ± .2	.7 ± .2	1.1 ± .3	.6 ± .3	1.6 ± .3
6 mos.	.4 ± .5	.8 ± .3	.8 ± .5	.9 ± .3	1.3 ± .3	.5 ± .7	1.0 ± .7
Mr. P. End	.5 ± .0	.5 ± .0	.4 ± .3	.4 ± .3	.3 ± .7	.6 ± .5	.0 ± .4
6 mos.	.0 ± .8	-.1 ± .3	-.5 ± .6	-.4 ± .5	-.4 ± .5	-.5 ± .4	-.5 ± .7
Mrs. R. End	1.3 ± .2	1.3 ± .3	*	*	*	1.2 ± .6	*
6 mos.	1.6 ± .3	1.2 ± .4				1.6 ± .3	
Mrs. L. End	1.4 ± .4	1.3 ± .2	1.2 ± .2	1.1 ± .4	.9 ± 1.3	1.4 ± .5	1.5 ± .4
6 mos.	.6 ± .8	1.0 ± .7	.6 ± .5	.2 ± 1.0	1.0 ± .5	.9 ± .4	1.1 ± .3
Mrs. T. End	1.8 ± .1	*	1.3 ± .2	*	*	.9 ± .3	*
6 mos.	1.8 ± .1		.8 ± .2			.7 ± .4	
Mrs. W. End	1.6 ± .1	.1 ± 1.0	.3 ± .2	.8 ± .7	*	*	*
6 mos.	1.2 ± .2	-.2 ± .7	.6 ± .5	.3 ± .7			

Scale points = + 2 = excellent improvement   − 1 = moderate worsening
             + 1 = moderate improvement   − 2 = extreme worsening
               0 = no change

*Scale not used for these subjects
**Not ascertained at this time
†End of treatment
‡Six-month follow-up

TABLE 9-4

Degree of Significance (p < .01 or p < .05) in the Assessment of Outcome

Scale	Mr. K.	Mr. M.	Mr. T.	Mr. P.	Mrs. R.	Mrs. L.	Mrs. T.	Mrs. W.
1 Symptom	.05	.01	n.s.	.01*	.01	.01	.01	.01
2 Focal Issue—Affect	.01	.01	.05	.01*	n.s.	.01	**	n.s.
3 Focal Issue—Defense	.05	.01*	.01	.01*	**	.01	.01	.01
4 Self-Continuity and Self-Esteem	.01	n.s.	.05	.05*	**	.05	**	n.s.
5 Denied, Disavowed Aspects of Self	**	.05	.01	n.s.	**	.05	**	**
6 Psychodynamic	**	n.s.	.01	.01*	.01	.01	.01	**
7 Therapeutic Alliance	**	.01*	.01	n.s.	**	.01	**	**

n.s. = nonsignificant at .01 or .05 level
* = Reflects significant change by end of treatment which was not sustained at 6-month follow-up
** = Scale not used for this subject

and were not rated on the therapeutic alliance scale were observed clinically to have maintained a very positive experience of the therapist and the treatment.

Gender Differences in Outcome and Process

The men and women in this sample responded in somewhat different ways to their treatment. Regarding outcome, the women showed greater symptomatic improvement and psychodynamic change than did the men, and their positive changes began occurring earlier in the therapy. These changes continued throughout the therapy and were still evident at six-month follow-up. Compared to the women, the men were slower to show symptomatic relief, showed less improvement overall than the women (p $<$ .05), and did not maintain the degree of symptomatic improvement as well as the women did at six-month follow-up. Whereas all three women assessed on the psychodynamic scale showed significant improvement at the end of treatment and at the six-month follow-up, only one of the three men showed significant psychodynamic change at these points.

Although the small sample size in this study makes these findings tentative and preliminary, the overall impression of outcome as measured by these scales is that brief psychotherapy with these elderly subjects had a positive effect encompassing both dynamic change, as well as symptomatic improvement. With the exception of one subject, the overall improvement was maintained six months after completion of treatment. Furthermore, the individualized psychotherapy outcome methodology appears to be a useful and sensitive method for assessing quantitative and qualitative change.

Clinical Observations of Process

Clinical observations, based on a review of therapy tapes, notes, psychological testing, and case discussions with the therapists after completion of treatment, supports the quantitative results obtained from the individualized outcome scales and helps to better clarify some of the nuances of the therapeutic process. The impact of therapy on the regulation of self-esteem and the reestablishment and maintenance of a sense of self-continuity, as well as the therapist's role in this process will be elaborated. To this end, Kohut's (1977) thoughts and writings on self psychology will be reviewed and an extensive case study will be presented to illustrate the changes made by many of the subjects during treatment and in follow-up. Additionally, the differential response of men and women to brief therapy will be examined, using Gutmann's (1964, 1977, 1980a) developmental perspective to explain the source of these gender differences. Finally, age biases of therapists and researchers, and age differences in response to brief treatment will be discussed.

Self Psychology and the Elderly

The elderly are especially vulnerable to breaches or discontinuities in their sense of self. Decreases in self-esteem may occur in response to the many assaults and losses of aging (physical, interpersonal, and social) that may be experienced as narcissistic injuries (Lazarus, 1980; Atchley, 1982). In addition, Gutmann (1980b) points out that the sense of self is not only vulnerable to disruption by losses, but also to the appearance of new or emergent capacities or potentials that have their origins in internal, developmental changes and pressures occurring naturally as the individual grows older. One of the most striking observations of this study was the way in which the patients used the therapist and the therapy sessions to restore self-esteem and self-continuity and/or to consolidate diverse, disparate, or emergent aspects of the self into a more positive, coherent sense of self. A brief review of self psychology as theorized by Kohut is helpful to explain the changes shown by patients in this study.

Kohut and Wolf (1978) believe that the self is a central, organizing structure of the personality that is made up of three major parts: (1) basic strivings for power and success; (2) goals and ideals; and (3) a set of basic abilities and skills that are used by the person to resolve tensions between the first two aspects, the ambitions and the ideals. The self evolves as a result of the interaction between the person's inherent predispositions and his experiences with his environment, specifically with those individuals within the environment who are experienced by the developing child as selfobjects. These selfobjects are not felt by the individual as separate or autonomous, but rather, are integral, psychological parts of the self, aiding in the maintenance of the individual's self-esteem and a solid, cohesive sense of self. The stability, maturity, and health of the adult self depends upon the quality of these interrelated self-selfobject interactions. Kohut and Wolf (1978) state:

> The adult self may thus exist in states of varying degrees of coherence, from cohesion to fragmentation; in states of varying degrees of vitality, from vigor to enfeeblement; in states of varying functional harmony, from order to chaos. Significant failure to achieve cohesion, vigor, or harmony, or a significant loss of these qualities after they have been tentatively established, may be said to constitute a state of self disorder [p. 414].

Disorders of the self may be primary, resulting from pervasive, early life deprivation or inadequacy of selfobjects, or secondary, as a reaction of a structurally undamaged self to the vicissitudes of life, notably the losses and narcissistic injuries that may be associated with the aging process.

For the most part, it was the secondary disturbances of the self which were seen and treated in this study. Although some patients may have had some aspects of a primary self disorder as well, they were not incapacitated and had compensated for the deficits adequately, enabling them to have functioned well for the better part of their lives.

The Impact of Brief Therapy on the Elderly Self

In treatment, most patients used the therapeutic experience to effect a reestablishment of self-continuity and positive sense of self that had been threatened or disrupted by the stresses of their current situation (typically the focal conflict) or by issues related to aging. Consciously experienced aspects of the self which were previously unacceptable to the patient were brought into treatment, acknowledged, and accepted by the therapist, and consequently consolidated by the patient into a more cohesive sense of self. Additionally, unacceptable parts of self that had been split off, denied, or repressed were made conscious through interpretation, and through the empathic understanding of the therapist, "normalized." This enabled the patient to acknowledge without dismay aspects of his self that had been previously disowned. Some patients even embraced these refound parts of themselves with zest and excitement.

It was a two-step process: First, the therapist recognized and reaffirmed the patient's consciously believed view of himself and reestablished for the patient a sense of continuity with his past. The therapeutic environment thereby became comfortable, familiar, and safe. Then, in such a safe environment, buttressed by a renewed sense of self, the patient no longer needed to defensively ward off threatening and potentially damaging aspects of the self, and could risk exploration of ostensibly negative aspects of self. The therapist's understanding and acceptance, served to destigmatize and alter the patient's preconceptions of these aspects as abhorrent or dangerous.

Transference and the Therapeutic Role

The patient transference and therapeutic relationship was crucial to effect the improvement described. Kohut and Wolf (1978) describe two types of narcissistic transference commonly found in disorders of the self. In the first, the mirror transference, the patient requires the therapist to serve as a mirroring selfobject, reflecting back to the patient an unqualified and enthusiastic acceptance and confirmation of his vigor and essential goodness. In the second, the idealizing transference, the patient experiences a need for merger with a source of idealized omnipotence, infallibility, and calmness. In the therapies of these patients, mirroring of the patient by the therapist was especially important in restoring a positive sense of self. The idealizing transference was especially useful in establishing a protective, safe environment for the patient in which he could explore egodystonic aspects of the self.

However, it must be emphasized that the different therapists in this study were not Kohutian in orientation, although they were undoubtedly cognizant of Kohut's theories and concepts. Initially, the therapists did not set out to foster the types of transference which eventually emerged. Yet, the patients seemed to enter treatment with their own unconscious agendas, in large part focused on issues of self-esteem and other aspects of the self. The more successful therapies were those in which the therapist flexibly shifted interpretive frameworks, whether intuitively or by conscious design, from a more traditional ego psychological perspective to a self psychological one.

Furthermore, psychodynamic changes were not inextricably linked with, or dependent on, *the* correct, timely interpretation. A single experience (in this case, the interpretation) did not seem to cause irreparable damage or effect repair. Rather, it was the entire therapeutic experience and the attitude and responsiveness of the therapist as a trustworthy, nonjudgmental, and empathic object over the course of treatment that seemed to be most important for the patient.

At times, the repair of the elderly subjects' self-esteem was achieved with little or no gain in insight. In general, patients reported very positive feelings toward their therapists. They responded to their therapists' respectful and empathic attitude with surprising tolerance of the therapists' errors. Instead of becoming angry or hurt when they felt misunderstood, patients simply clarified what they really meant, as if they were dealing with a well-intentioned, but naive young person. This may also reflect the patient's need to view the therapist in idealized fashion as an all-powerful confirming and permissive authority, who could be called upon for protection from external adversaries or their own internal persecutors.

Clinical Illustration

The case of Mrs. W. illustrates the changes and restoration of the self described above. In addition, it demonstrates the successful resolution of a focal conflict and the relationship of a current focal issue with an unresolved issue from early adulthood. Finally, her case also suggests the emergence of new strengths and capabilities that evolved during and after treatment, demonstrating the older person's capacity for continued growth.

> Mrs. W. was referred for treatment by a psychologist who knew Mrs. W. personally. In her initial interview, Mrs. W. a 64-year-old married woman, related symptoms of anxiety, insomnia, depression, and overwhelming fatigue related to caring for her husband who was afflicted with Alzheimer's disease. The research team anticipated that the focus of the treatment would be her anger, disappointment, and grief about the loss of her husband as he had been before the onset of his disease. It was also suspected that the latter phases of treatment would deal with her guilt about these feelings, fears of being unable to cope, and anxiety about the future. Perhaps most telling, although it was not appreciated at the outset, were her comments that she no longer felt like her old self and she was frightened by actions that were "not like me" in dealing with her husband.
>
> Mrs. W. was a middle-class wife of an accountant who had been diagnosed six years earlier as having Alzheimer's disease. He was beginning to deteriorate rapidly, becoming more confused, unpredictable, and physically difficult to manage. Although their son and daughter were both married and lived nearby, Mrs. W. cared for her husband with minimal support from either. She was furious at her children for their lack of support and tremendously ashamed of her husband's increasing impairment which, for many years, she had successfully hidden from close friends and relatives.
>
> One of two daughters from a close-knit and caring family, Mrs. W. had always been the dutiful, compliant daughter who relied on, and obeyed her parents. When she married, Mrs. W. transferred her somewhat idealized conception of her father to her husband. The marriage was described as quite satisfactory, with traditionally defined marital roles. Mrs. W. had both financial and emotional security until her husband developed Alzheimer's disease when she was forced to assume a more dominant and managerial role. With her husband's increasing disability, she became more anxious, depressed, overwhelmed, and isolated. Mrs. W. felt she could not share these feelings with her children and friends or depend on them for emotional support and assistance with her husband.
>
> Although she recognized the practical need to place her husband in a nursing home in the near future, Mrs. W. was

paralyzed by feelings of guilt stemming from an earlier experience with her father. In the last years of her father's life, he
underwent considerable physical and cognitive deterioration requiring continuous care that was provided at home, primarily by
Mrs. W.'s sister. Consequently, Mrs. W. felt unjustified in asking
for help with her own husband and unconsciously viewed her
current situation as retribution for her earlier failure for not
having assumed more of the caregiving responsibility for her
own father. Hence, despite her anger, she made excuses for her
children's avoidance of their father.

The Process and Outcome of Treatment

Initially, Mrs. W. met the DSM-III criteria for an anxiety
disorder. She was seen for 10 weekly, 50-minute sessions. Mrs.
W. initially focused on her difficulties in managing her husband
and tried to elicit advice and suggestions from the therapist.
Instead of responding directly to her demands for the "right"
answer or solution, the therapist reflected upon her fear of becoming weak and powerless, and her fear of hurting her husband
should she assume a more assertive and direct approach to his
dependency and behavioral problems.

Mrs. W. responded to the therapist's empathic understanding and acceptance by internalizing the therapist's view of her
as a competent, intelligent person who could creatively deal with
her demented husband's difficult behavior. This marked the
beginning of a process by which she repaired her damaged, dis-
continuous sense of self. Additionally, Mrs. W. formed an idealizing transference to the therapist who became an idealized
"good" daughter, one that was young, energetic, able to cope
with the patient's grief over her husband, and willing to soothe
and comfort her. Mrs. W. became more self-assured, confident,
and calmer. Her home life, although still difficult and occasionally chaotic, settled down.

Once she was able to deal more effectively with her husband,
and felt protected and safe in the therapy sessions (through association with her therapist whom she now perceived to be powerful and knowing), Mrs. W. began to explore her own reaction
to her husband's dementia. She was gratified by the therapist's
acknowledgement of her pain and disappointment, which justified the feelings of rage and unfairness she had considered
selfish and unimportant (part of the "normalization" process

described above). While searching for an answer to the question: "Why was my husband afflicted and not me?" Mrs. W. consciously experienced "survivor guilt." Feeling a need for herself to suffer, she felt and behaved as if she were totally devoted to her husband. The therapist's interpretations of this guilt allowed Mrs. W. to give up her masochistic, martyred stance and a need for others to acknowledge her self-sacrifice. Instead, she began to appreciate the value of her caregiving and to accept her husband's dementia. Consequently, she no longer felt compelled to deny and single-handedly compensate for his cognitive decline and personality changes.

With an acceptance of her husband's illness, Mrs. W. felt less ashamed, and more willing to share her problems with family members and friends. Interpretations linking the experience of her father's decline with her guilt about asking for help with her husband enabled Mrs. W. to modify the way in which she asked her children for support. Instead of couching her requests in terms of the children's responsibility for helping their father and forcing them to guess what she wanted, Mrs. W. was able to ask directly for specific help for herself.

Her children's increased responsiveness diminished her anger somewhat, but a more significant shift occurred in Mrs. W.'s perception of her anger. The therapist neither condemned nor recoiled from Mrs. W.'s anger. Support from, and alliance with, what Mrs. W. perceived to be a powerful yet empathic therapist allowed her to redefine her angry feelings. Rather than being frightening and destructive, the anger became a justified and constructive aspect of her personality that could be used creatively to protect her husband and herself and to obtain benefits for both.

Throughout treatment, Mrs. W. struggled with considerable conflict about whether or not to place her husband in a long-term care facility. She finished therapy feeling more confident and competent to cope with her husband. Although the caregiving burden was increasing because of his deterioration, the psychological stress associated with it had decreased, and she was able to maintain her husband at home for an additional six months.

At her six-month follow-up, Mrs. W. was in the midst of placing her husband in a nearby nursing home. She was able to call on her son to assist her with the arrangements. She used her brief contact with the research team's interviewer to reaffirm the positive, accepting view of herself established in therapy, and experienced the interviewer as supporting her decision to place her husband in a nursing home. Despite the crisis, she was dealing effectively with her grief and anxiety and was maintaining the gains previously made in treatment. Mrs. W. was able to surrender care of her husband to the nursing home staff without guilt, but she continued her caregiving by visiting him twice daily until his death seven months after placement.

Serendipitous contact with Mrs. W. a year later showed her to be doing well and consolidating the gains begun in treatment. She was amazed that her life could be so free, spontaneous, and enjoyable.

The Integration of Developmental Potentials

Mrs. W. brought considerable strengths to therapy, some of which may not have been consciously recognized or accepted by her. Developmental theory regarding normative changes in men and women in middle and late life are particularly relevant to a fuller understanding of Mrs. W.'s changes in therapy.

Gutmann describes a transition occurring in the postparental years that has a major impact on the psychological organization of older men and women. He states:

Men relinquish some part of their active, competitive and production-centered stance in favor of a more socioemotional, communalistic emphasis; women take on some of the managerial and "political" stances that their husbands appear to be abandoning. In effect, there takes place, in both sexes, a universal "return of the repressed," in which the psychological structures maintained by men and women during the period of active parenthood are dismantled in the postparental period [Gutmann, Griffin and Grunes, 1982, p. 247).

Thus, the aspects of self which were previously submerged in the service of active parenting, or vicariously lived out through the spouse, become accessible to both sexes. Men are more free to express "feminine" potentials, while women are able to assert themselves in the more traditionally "masculine" ways. Each sex "reestablishes, internally, a sexual bimodality that was previously partialed out externally, between self and mate" (Gutmann, 1975, p. 181).

Mrs. W.'s case illustrates the developmental shift that occurs in many women in late middle age. Her assertiveness, energy, and instrumentality could no longer be expressed vicariously through her husband because of his illness. As she assumed the dominant role in the marriage, she was both angry at him and guilty, fearing her aggression had somehow caused or contributed to his decline. Consciously, she was greatly troubled by having to assume the instrumental functions in their marriage and viewed this as stripping him of his potency. In reality, this was an inexorable consequence of his dementia. Unconsciously, she was excited by, and enjoyed, her new powers and competency, but being tied to a vulnerable spouse made their expression difficult. Because of his cognitive decline, her gain was seen by her as his loss. In therapy, she was allowed to explore these new capacities without fear of damaging anyone. Her therapist survived, even appreciated her growing self-sufficiency and assertiveness, which she had negatively viewed as a selfish stubbornness.

Gender Differences in Response to Brief Therapy

As measured by the individualized outcome scales, men and women responded differently to brief therapy regarding overall amount of improvement and the rapidity, and permanence of these changes. Additionally, men and women showed differences in their relationship with the therapist, use of defenses, and manner of resolving their focal conflicts.

The elderly women thus far studied used their therapist to reaffirm their competency and to gain permission to carry out some assertive, instrumental plan. They became free to recognize, discharge, and even enjoy the "masculine," aggressive aspects of their personalities which had been suppressed with the advent of parenting in early adulthood. Therapy for these elderly women functioned not to reveal some dormant insight, but to catalyze the release and integration of these submerged aspects of self. This developmental process, which occurs naturally in most women sometime after completion of the task of parenthood, had been blocked or inhibited before they entered therapy. Therapy for these women served to set them developmentally "back on track."

The women patients' refound assertiveness and active mastery seemed to be supported as well by their use of the defense mechanisms of externalization and projection. The women tended to externalize intrapsychic conflict, splitting off from themselves the blame or "badness" onto an easily identifiable, related person or organization, who could then be psychologically and/or physically dispensed with. In other words, the women first separated themselves psychologically from the designated "bad" person or place and then proceeded to replicate this separation by actually extruding that person or place from their lives.

> For example, Mrs. R., another woman in the study, was a partially sighted woman who had been involved with the Lighthouse for the Blind for over 20 years before becoming totally blind. She began psychotherapy soon after losing her sight. A psychiatric referral was made because of her increasing conflict with the Lighthouse staff. She accused the staff of misunderstanding and infantilizing her. Due to limited vision as a child and adolescent, Mrs. R.'s father had overprotected her, which she resented and overcame by repeatedly proving her independence from him. Although it was expected that psychotherapy would help her work through the disappointment regarding her now total blindness, and help her interact more constructively with Lighthouse staff, this did not happen. Upon completing treatment she promptly quit the Lighthouse, maintaining that it was they who were at fault and not she. She continued to externalize her conflict by blaming the Lighthouse staff. She moved into a nicer apartment and began counseling her internist's patients at a nearby hospital, indicative of an idealizing transference to her therapist and her identification with him. As an additional consequence of therapy, Mrs. R. became, both emotionally and sexually less conflict- and guilt-ridden over her long-standing relationship with her male friend.

In contrast to the women patients, the men were far less active, psychologically or physically, in trying to resolve their focal conflict. Instead they tended to remain enmeshed in the provocative interpersonal relationship or situation that precipitated their entry into psychotherapy. The therapist was used by the men as a substitute for nurturant, supportive, and calming objects currently not available either in their intrapsychic or external worlds. Consequently, the men became very dependent on the therapist and had difficulty terminating treatment. Therapy for these men seemed to stimulate the dependent, passive yearnings; feelings that may be normative for some men in their seventh or eighth decade. In contrast to the women, the psychosocial environment of the men was not conducive to satisfying or tolerating these emergent potentials, nor were they as comfortable as the women in accepting and reclaiming aspects of themselves which seemed so foreign and contrary to traditionally defined gender roles.

The therapeutic relationship for the men not only stimulated passive strivings by diminishing suppression of the needs, but the psychotherapeutic relationship was often also the only legitimate arena for their expression. The therapist became the only person who could acknowledge, accept, and appreciate their passive and dependent longings. Time-limited therapy may not have allowed them enough time to thoroughly explore, integrate, and find suitable external means of satisfying this "formerly" disavowed side of their nature.

> Mr. T., a 72-year-old married, semiretired real estate salesman with a compulsive personality entered therapy because of chronic feelings of depression, marital disharmony, self-doubt, and social inhibitions. His retirement resulted in increased time with his wife who had recently become active in the feminist movement. She was critical and impatient with his passivity and dependency. Mr. T. attributed his lifelong insecurity to the sudden death of his father when he was 10 years old, and his mother's depression and consequent emotional unavailability. He compensated for his lifelong insecurity and low self-esteem by developing his intellect, and through success in his career.
>
> In therapy, he formed a dependent, eroticized, idealized transference to his 30-year-old female therapist, wishing that she could compensate for his wife's depreciation of him. Although his self-esteem was enhanced by the therapeutic relationship, he was not able to sustain the improvement without the continued

presence of the therapist. At six-month follow-up, some of his depressive symptoms had returned and he was about to enter into therapy with a male therapist.

Age Bias in Predicting Process and Outcome of Psychotherapy

The early stages of this research were sometimes affected by a subtle age bias. Commonly, the assumptions and expectations of patient change in therapy are based on the psychological theories derived from the study of child and adult development. Consequently, many existing psychological and behavioral rating scales have been constructed for, and been standardized on, populations other than the elderly. By devising individualized measures specific for each patient, it was hoped that the measures would be more sensitive and relevant to assessing older patients.

Despite the considerable training and experience of the research team in the diagnosis and treatment of the elderly, this age bias sometimes influenced construction of scales and definition of scale points. For elderly subjects, the predicted positive or negative outcomes on the individualized scales were sometimes inaccurate or seemed irrelevant when rating the subject at the end of treatment or at six-month follow-up. Instead of the hypothesized outcome, some patients achieved a resolution of focal issues and relief of symptoms in an unexpected, but from the subject's standpoint, an equally satisfactory manner.

Although the ability of a patient to resolve conflict and to improve his or her interpersonal relationship was originally viewed by the research team as a positive outcome, a negative outcome was often scored on the individualized scales developed to reflect these changes. For example, Mrs. R. quit the Lighthouse rather than resolve her interpersonal conflicts with the staff. In the case of Mrs. W., the predicted positive outcome in therapy centered on an increased understanding and empathy for her children's negative response to their father's dementia, and their wish to distance themselves from both parents. It was hoped that interpretation of her masochistic behavior and her assumption of the role of a martyr would provide the insight necessary to improve her relationship with her children and thereby enlist more of their cooperation and support. At the end of treatment the anticipated improvement in Mrs. W.'s interpersonal relationship with her children had never materialized, but she was dealing with them in a more direct, effective, and personally satisfying fashion. Several other patients tended to use externalization and projection to blame others for their problems, thus boosting their self-esteem at the cost of further interpersonal alienation.

The process of change, and standards of measuring "improvement" or "worsening" for the elderly may require another set of norms, different from those used with younger patients, that acknowledges some of these age-specific ways of dealing with internal or external conflict.

Conclusions

The results of our preliminary study support the original supposition of this chapter, that elderly outpatients can benefit from brief, dynamically oriented psychotherapy. Individualized outcome scales showed that symptomatic improvement and resolution of the focal problems were the most consistent changes among the patients and sometimes occurred in the relative absence of insight or self-understanding. Clinical observation supported the findings of the outcome measures and provided additional insights regarding the process of therapeutic change with elderly outpatients.

One of the most striking findings was the way patients used psychotherapy to restore their self-esteem and sense of mastery, and to validate their essential normalcy. Patients often used the therapeutic relationship to reestablish a sense of self over time and/or to consolidate diverse and disparate aspects of the self into a more positive sense of self. For some patients, other aspects of the self, suppressed in earlier life or newly emergent in later life, were given conscious expression in therapy and integrated into a more cohesive sense of self.

An unexpected finding was the differential response of men and women to brief psychotherapy. As measured by outcome scales, the women showed improvement earlier, to a greater extent, and maintained improvements longer than the men. Additionally, men and women showed differences in their relationship with the therapist, use of defenses, and manner of resolving focal conflicts.

The generalizability of these results to other elderly patients seeking outpatient psychotherapy is limited by the small sample size, reliance on unvalidated individualized scales, and the particular biases of the research group. Nevertheless, it is believed that the individualized outcome methodology facilitates a study of the process, as well as the outcome, of psychotherapy and an examination of some of the nuances of the therapeutic relationship with elderly people. The research team continues to reappraise these preliminary results in light of the study of additional elderly patients.

References

American Psychiatric Association (1980), *Diagnostic and Statistical Manual of Mental Disorders*, 3rd ed. Washington, DC: American Psychiatric Association.

Atchley, R. C. (1982), The aging self. *Psychother.: Theory, Res. & Pract.*, 19:388–396.

Bartko, J. (1966), The intraclass correlation coefficient as a measure of reliability. *Psychol. Rep.*, 19:3–11.

Buckley, P., Conte, H. R., Plutchik, R., Wild, K. V., Karasu, T. B. (1984), Psychodynamic variables as predictors of psychotherapy outcome. *Amer. J. Psychiat.*, 141:6, 742–747.

Goldfarb, A. I. (1953), Recommendations for psychiatric care in a home for the aged. *J. Geront.*, 8:343-347.

———— Turner, H. (1953), Psychotherapy of aged persons. Utilization and effectiveness of brief therapy. *Amer. J. Psychiat.*, 109:916–921.

Grotjahn, M. (1940), Psychoanalytic investigation of a seventy-one-year-old man with senile dementia. *Psychoanal. Quart.*, 9:80–97.

———— (1955), Analytic psychotherapy with the elderly. *Psychoanal. Rev.*, 42:419–427.

Gutmann, D. (1964), An exploration of ego configurations in middle and later life. In: *Personality in Middle and Later Life*, ed. B. Neugarten. New York: Atherton, pp. 114-148.

———— (1975), Parenthood: A key to the comparative study of the life cycle. In: *Lifespan Developmental Psychology: Normative Life Crises*, ed. N. Datan & L. Ginsberg. New York: Academic Press, pp. 167-184.

———— (1977), The cross-cultural perspectives: Notes toward a comparative psychology of aging. In: *Handbook of the Psychology of Aging*, ed. J. E. Birren & W. Schaie. New York: Van Nostrand Reinhold, pp. 302-306.

———— (1980a), Observations on culture and mental health in later life. In:

Handbook of Mental Health and Aging, ed. J. E. Birren & R. B. Sloan. Englewood Cliffs, NJ: Prentice-Hall, pp. 429-447.

——— (1980b), Psychoanalysis and aging: A developmental view. In: *The Course of Life: Psychoanalytic Contributions Toward Understanding Personality Development. Vol. III: Adulthood and the Aging Process*, ed. S. I. Greenspan & G. H. Pollock. Washington, DC: National Institute of Mental Health. pp. 489–517.

——— Griffin, B., & Grunes, J. (1982), Developmental contributions to the late-onset affective disorders. In: *Life Span Development and Behavior*, Vol. 4., ed. P. B. Baltes & O. G. J. Brim. New York: Academic Press, p. 247.

Horowitz, M. (1976), *Stress Response Syndromes*. New York: Jason Aronson.

——— Marmar, C., Weiss, D. S., DeWitt, K. N., & Rosenbaum, R. (1984), Brief psychotherapy and bereavement reactions. *Arch. Gen. Psychiat.*, 41:438–448.

Kohut, H. (1977), *The Restoration of the Self*. New York: International Universities Press.

——— Wolf, E. (1978), The disorders of the self and their treatment: An outline. *Internat. J. Psycho-Anal.*, 59:413–425.

Lawlis, G. F., & Chatfield, D. (1974), *Multi-Variate Approaches for the Behavioral Sciences: A Brief Text*. Lubbock, TX: Texas Technical Press.

Lazarus, L. W. (1980), Self-psychology and psychotherapy with the elderly: Theory and practice. *J. Geriat. Psychiat.*, 13:69–88.

——— Weinberg, J. (1980), Treatment in the ambulatory care setting. In: *Handbook of Geriatric Psychiatry*, ed. E. W. Busse & D. G. Blazer. New York: Van Nostrand Reinhold, pp. 427-452.

——— Groves, L., & Newton, N. (1984), Brief psychotherapy with the elderly: A review and preliminary study of process and outcome. In: *Clinical Approaches to Psychotherapy with the Elderly*, ed. L. W. Lazarus. Washington, DC: American Psychiatric Press, pp. 16-35.

Malan, D. H. (1963), *A Study of Brief Psychotherapy*. New York: Plenum Press.

——— (1976a), *The Frontier of Brief Psychotherapy*. New York: Plenum Press.

——— (1976b), *Toward the Validation of Dynamic Psychotherapy*. New York: Plenum Press.

——— (1979), *Individual Psychotherapy and the Science of Psychodynamics*. London: Butterworth.

Martin, L. J., & DeGrunchy C. (1933), *Sweeping the Cobwebs*. New York: Macmillan.

Martin, L. J. (1944), *A Handbook for Old Age Counsellors*. San Francisco: Geertz Printing.

Meerloo, J. A. M. (1955), Psychotherapy with elderly people. *Geriatrics*, 10:538–587.

——— (1961), Modes of psychotherapy in the aged. *J. Amer. Geriat. Soc.*, 9:225–234.

Pfeiffer, E. (1976), Psychotherapy with elderly patients. In: *Geriatric Psychiatry*, ed. L. Bellak & T. B. Karasu. New York: Grune & Stratton, pp. 191–205.

Rechtschaffen, A. (1959), Psychotherapy with geriatric patients: A review of the literature. *J. Gerontol.*, 14:73–84.

Shrout, P., & Fleiss, J. (1979), Intraclass correlations: Uses in assessing rater reliability. *Psychol. Bull.*, 86:420–428.

Silberschatz, G., & Curtis, J. (1982), Psychodynamic psychotherapy with the elderly. Paper presented at the Conference on Psychodynamic Research

Perspectives on Development, Psychopathology and Treatment in Later Life, National Institute of Mental Health, Bethesda, Maryland.

Weinberg, J. (1951), Psychiatric techniques in the treatment of older people. In: *Growing in the Older Years*, ed. W. Donahue & C. Tibbits. Ann Arbor: University of Michigan Press, pp. 61–70.

10

THE WHOLE GRANDFATHER: AN INTERGENERATIONAL APPROACH TO FAMILY THERAPY

ETTA GINSBERG MCEWAN, M.S.W.

Introduction

"One of the problems for daughters and sons is that you come into life with an unpayable debt, the mortgage of all time," says playwright Marsha Norman, succinctly stating the complex and unique relationships between children and their parents for all time. The giving of life establishes an everlasting link with the past and the future. Creating life is so profound an experience that words alone do not describe the dyad of the giver of life and the recipient of life. This view of life and relationships makes clear the need for a therapeutic perspective, which takes into account the universal transgenerational commitments (Nagy and Spark, 1973), "the mortgage of all time." The inevitable decline that comes with aging and the specter of death may stimulate intergenerational conflict. Nagy and Spark (1973) have described five key concepts which help to clarify the underlying sources for intergenerational conflict: (1) loyalty; (2) entitlement; (3) ledger balancing; (4) justice; and (5) the legacy for posterity. These concepts form the brick and mortar for family therapists, regardless of the specific techniques employed, and are perhaps most relevant to family therapy of the aged.

This chapter, using Nagy and Spark's organizing concepts, will examine the process of intergenerational therapy. While family therapy has long been recognized as a significant treatment modality for younger people, it is only in recent years that this approach has been incorporated as a crucial and integral treatment for the aged and their families. Historically, families of older persons were interviewed only for basic information and history. The impact of family dynamics on the various members of the family was not valued as part of the presenting problem. Family treatment for this group, however, is vital in order to place the older person's life in perspective, to help him gain a sense of his achievements, to help adult children put to rest unresolved issues so that they do not contaminate the present, and to help the grandchildren view their grandparents in a more complete, positive light, by helping them to recognize the fullness of their grandparents' lives and to understand that sickness or dementia do not define grandparenthood.

Loyalty

Nagy and Spark have recognized that an operational definition of loyalty must include the motivations for the manifestation of loyalty in a system. Some of these motivations are obvious and conscious; for example, external coercion or conscious recognition of socially and morally imposed obligations. Other motivations are subtle and arise from unconscious processes within individuals, of which they are intellectually unaware. As Nagy and Spark (1973) state, these "can only be inferred from complex, indirect clues, often only after prolonged acquaintance with the person and group concerned" (p. 39).

Loyalty issues are more evident to the mental health professional working with the elderly, since these issues are often explicitly or implicitly expressed by the parent to the adult children. This conflict over loyalty is frequently seen in the intake departments of agencies serving the elderly. The majority of agency referrals come from adult children who are unable to cope any longer with an ill parent or parents, or when the adult child feels that the parent *must* become involved in some activity to keep busy. In the author's observations of these families at the time of referral, the parent is usually silent, withdrawn, and angry at the child for going outside the family for help. From the older person's perspective, the binding obligations and the invisible loyalties are brought into an arena of strangers.

Loyalty issues are further complicated when external forces impose loyalty. This situation arises, for example, when social policies have not kept pace with the needs of a growing aged population. Government and care institutions impose de facto demands on children to carry the major responsibility for their parents. Social workers frequently find themselves caught in the paradoxical situation of having to enforce government or institutional policy while trying to carry out their therapeutic mandate to assist with emotional issues. Under these circumstances, loyalty issues must be sorted out for the families; what is real, what is possible, and what they have no control over.

Ledger Balancing and Entitlement

The concept of the ledger in relationships highlights the human expectation that effort will be balanced by grateful rewards from those served. In the parent–child relationships of antiquity such expectations often led parents to believe they had the right to exploit their children, sometimes mercilessly, and the children in turn, extracted their rewards from their own children. Modern ethics and values have altered this simple formulation. "Parent–child relationships, in our age, are embedded in a mixture of scientific knowledge and anachronistic, often hypocritical and pseudoethical value formations regarding the rights of parents and the rights of children" (Nagy and Spark, 1973, p. 85).

Nagy and Spark (1973) view healthy or normal entitlement as an ethical issue. The parent should be able to earn the entitlement without believing that he will be repaid in concrete terms. Rather, the rewards will be for doing the right thing, and lead to satisfaction in caring as well as an inner sense of freedom for the parent to do as he wishes with his own life, now that his child is an adult. Ideally, a parent will know and feel that he has done his best to raise his child, and the child, in turn, will understand that his parent did his best. This ideal, reciprocal process requires a high degree of maturity in both parent and child, each of whom must possess a secure sense of self.

The conflict over the child's right to ask for more or refuse further giving was illustrated in the following situation. In a psychotherapy group of older women which the author led for over three years, the adult children joined the group for several sessions. One daughter told of how she used her mother as a baby-sitter but always rushed home with the vague and guilty knowledge that her mother didn't like it. She wished her mother could have said no, although she had never told her so. A daughter-in-law spoke of her deceased mother-in-law's demand for attendance at the Friday night supper ritual and how much better those suppers could have been if she had only felt that it was all right to miss a dinner once in a while. In the final phases of this group, if a member lapsed into wanting her children to be all things to her, she was sure to be confronted by another group member with the story of the eagle who had to carry her children over a large body of water from one mountaintop to another. As the mother eagle carried the first eaglet, she asked whether the eaglet would take care of her in her old age. He replied, "Mommy, I will." She dropped him in the ocean. As she carried the second eaglet, she asked him the same question. He responded that he would not be able to care for her in her old age as he would have his own family. She carried him safely to the other mountaintop.

Achieving a healthy and realistic sense of entitlement is an ongoing struggle for parents and children. Some aspects of expectations and giving are valid and healthy. It is these to which Norman was referring. Other aspects of entitlement reflect "neurotic" needs. The therapist has the often difficult task of helping the child distinguish between valid and neurotic entitlement. While there is always a feeling of indebtedness when one has been cared for and protected, the child who feels he can never do enough in return requires the therapist's skills to help him to achieve a mature separation. Often, of course, it is the parent who generates undue demands seeming to "harbor the expectation that the devotion and care given by the young parent to the infant and child will be reciprocated and the indebtedness repaid in kind when the parent, having grown old, becomes dependent" (Brody, 1985, p. 26).

As Brody (1985) implies, there is no return to the earlier period of family life. The roles of parent and child cannot be completely reversed. Hence, adult children may need help to understand that they cannot, nor are they expected to, pay back directly to their parents all that their parents did for them. There are, of course, many parents and children who express minimal conflict about the debits and credits of their relationship. The quantity and quality of help is negotiable within a give-and-take atmosphere. This is rooted in the family's history of knowing which expectations are fair and just, and which are not.

Justice

Justice and fairness are interrelated and integral to the concepts of loyalty already discussed. Nagy and Spark (1973) use the powerful concept of justice (which is generally used in a legal sense) because they "feel that it connotes human commitment and value in all their rich motivating power and meaning" (p. 55). In the therapy group of women referred to earlier, the mothers in the group spoke of a recurring theme expressed in a number of different ways by their children: "You didn't love me enough. You loved and yet you didn't love." Intrinsic in all this was a sense of the child's feelings of injustice at not receiving as much evidence of love as he was entitled to, and the mother's feelings of being judged too harshly.

An interview with a mother and her three adult children illustrates a family conflict over an issue of justice. The children were angry and hurt because their mother had not prepared a meal for them in a number of years, thereby giving them a reason for coming to her home. The mother, however, felt that the ledger was unbalanced. She had prepared the meals throughout their childhood and their early years of marriage and she was now, implicitly, telling them that the family ledger could only be balanced with justice if they took turns in preparing holiday dinners. She was adamant about sticking to her "vow," made a few years earlier, that she would never prepare another dinner for her children. It was "unjust" of them to expect this from her. She wanted reciprocity.

In a poignant interview with a more mature and healthier mother and her adult child, the strong commitment of the children emerged early in the session. They expressed the feeling that it was their turn to take care of and protect their mother, listing for her the many credits that she had accumulated through the years of raising them.

Legacy for Posterity

Loyalty, entitlement, ledger balancing, and justice are integral components of the legacy that is handed down from the past. These forces extend beyond the parent–child relationship to encompass the third generation of the grandchildren who represent the link to the future. "Since the reciprocity of parent–child justice is based on a minimally 3-generational context, what remained unbalanced in one generation is expected to be balanced in the next. From the vantage point of the parent, it appears that his child is entitled to more rights if he, the parent, was himself raised with the proper amount of love and consideration—and so the chain continues" (Nagy and Spark, 1973, p. 86).

When parents pressure children to live out their unfulfilled goals, a burdened legacy results. The children's options are these: to remain forever stuck with indebtedness, to estrange themselves completely from their parents, or to force the legacy of unfulfilled dreams onto their children (grandchildren), thereby perpetuating the legacy from one generation to the next.

When a therapist sees a family in distress, it is crucial for him to think through the invisible strands of the legacy. What debits, credits, and merits have been handed down? What balancing needs to be worked through? The key to all of this is an understanding that the parent–child relationship is necessarily asymmetrical. There is no such thing as equality, even though a child may believe that once he has children, he will at last be equal to his parent. Symmetry of the relationship is not the goal. If symmetry is forever sought after, a never-ending legacy of unfulfilled wishes and needs will pass from generation to generation.

Formulating Three Generational Conflicts

"The meaning of person and the nature of inner growth are personal matters—personal things, if you will—which even though they are universal, are at the same time individual. Individuality seems to defy the tools of science, because an individual is a value-laden object not well described simply by a list of the facts of his existence" (Cassell, 1973, p. 1112). The aged, perhaps more than any other group, have been the victims of global rather than individual approaches to understanding, diagnosis, and treatment. Such approaches have led to solutions to the problems of aging which, although sometimes appropriate, stem often from an inadequate recognition of the total problem picture. Solutions have tended to be embodied in referrals to golden age clubs, day care centers, nursing homes, or in overused drug therapy. Halsall (1967) has commented on the need to examine problems more carefully. "Modifying environmental pressures has its part to play, but, after all, the very fact of doing so removes a stimulus to look at the problem in greater depth. Like other social challenges, the problems of the elderly have a presenting crisis, e.g., a request for urgent admission because a relative cannot cope. The urgency of a crisis may well obscure what is, in fact, a complex problem of family and social relationships" (p. 757).

Fortunately, the pendulum has shifted (in social work and psychiatric therapy) from a concrete, task-oriented approach to a dynamic, family approach. By looking beyond the "identified patient" one minimizes the scapegoating of the older individual and, to a degree, lessens the guilt of the adult child who brings the older person for help.

Case Illustration

The following case example illustrates the intergenerational family themes described by Nagy and Spark: loyalty, ledger balancing and entitlement, justice and legacy for posterity. In particular, the case demonstrates the need for ongoing long-term involvement, at various levels of intensity, with each of the three generations.

In working with the elderly, psychotherapists cannot consider problems totally resolved, since the aging process, with ebbing physical strength and weakening defenses contributes to ongoing pressures. It has been the author's experience that therapy for the geriatric group is ongoing. The therapist moves in and out and cases are often not closed. It is not enough to tell older persons and their families to telephone when they are in trouble. The psychotherapist must make the caring and concern of the therapeutic relationship visible by reestablishing contact. A telephone call is all that is necessary. The therapist should understand that the helping process is not syntonic for this generation. Crises can be avoided if one does not take the strict "traditional" psychotherapeutic approach which holds the individual responsible for "asking" for help. "Life-line therapy" simply says to older people and their families—"I am here if you need me." This is not therapeutic omnipotence, but a recognition that older people are exposed to many losses and that they and their children need the reinforcement and support of the therapist.

Family History

Mr. Q. was an 81-year-old man who developed cognitive impairment and aggressive behavior following a series of strokes. While there was a long-standing history of marital friction, a balance had been achieved with Mr. Q. being employed and out of the house. The strokes resulted in his being more vulnerable, easily provoked, and subject to verbal outbursts and physical threats. The family physician recommended a day care program, prescribing social activity as a remedy for Mr. Q.'s difficult behavior. Before the referral could be acted upon, Mr. Q. developed depressive symptoms with suicidal thoughts and was physically aggressive toward his wife. For example, on one occasion, he threw her out of bed following an argument about sex, and on another, he threw her out of the house.

The daughter, an only child, was caught in the middle and saw herself as a rescuer and the protector of both parents. This was not a new role as they had used her, in the past, as a go-between. She felt that the situation was catastrophic and that if she did not take action the result would be bloodshed. In what seemed to be a panic reaction, the daughter ran from hospital to hospital trying to get her father admitted because of his three-day refusal to eat or drink—"his way of committing suicide." Mr. Q. was ultimately admitted to a geriatric psychiatric treatment unit.

Mr. Q. was a robust, handsome man with a warm, open face, friendly smile, twinkling blue eyes, and an affectionate manner. His presenting illness was set against a backdrop of Holocaust trauma in both he and his wife, as well as long-standing marital discord.

He was born in a village in Poland. Little is known about his developmental history. He had minimal education because he did not like school. He was illiterate but with some difficulty had been able to write his name. He spoke Polish, German, and Yiddish, but his English was poor. In his early years he worked in a coalmine. Later he married and had four children. He earned a living peddling his own farm-grown produce; occasionally he went to the large cities to purchase goods for resale in the smaller towns.

When war broke out the family and their relatives were taken to concentration camps. They were in Buchenwald and Auschwitz. The patient's wife, children, mother, and six brothers and sisters were killed. (The patient's father had died before the war.) Mr. Q. was himself saved at the last minute "when the noose was around my neck." The Germans were struck by his robust appearance and that he had proven himself to be a hard worker. The patient's oldest brother died in the concentration camp on the day of liberation. The brother's three children survived and managed to make lives for themselves. Mr. Q. always remained an integral part of their lives even though they were scattered in various parts of the United States while he had settled in Canada.

Mr. Q. was a man of considerable strength, making a new life in a strange country, providing well for his family, and throughout, maintaining a generous outward appearance. While he was described by his daughter as never being intimate in his relationships, he was more sociable than Mrs. Q. and welcomed anyone to his home. The behavior that brought him into the psychiatric unit had never been witnessed before—he raged at

his wife, he wept at his physical and mental decline; he appeared
to relive his earlier losses and spoke of his first wife as "a dia-
mond" and his second wife as "a cow, whore, crazy. . . ." He
dreamed of his first family and felt that he might as well be
"dead." His deep sadness and his behavior toward Mrs. Q. caused
his daughter intolerable pain and anguish. She felt overwhelmed
and utterly helpless in the face of the pain of both parents. It is
significant to note that unlike his wife, Mr. Q. had (as far as we
can tell) achieved a happy adult life before the Holocaust.

Mr. Q.'s physical strength and shrewd business capacity enabled him to set himself up in several businesses where he accumulated sufficient money for the later years. Wife and
daughter stated that he was most successful when he worked on
his own.

Mrs. Q. was petite, on the cute side, with an infrequent warm
smile, but tight and tense in her overall appearance. She was
born in a large city in Poland, the middle child in a family of
seven children. She completed high school. Her father was a
learned, devout, religious man who owned and operated a dry-
goods store. Mrs. Q. emphasized her protected, sheltered early
life wherein she had all the necessities. She never worked. It was
expected that her father would arrange her marriage, as was the
custom. However, Mrs. Q. met her first husband at a local bus
stop and the relationship grew. She convinced her parents that
he had all the proper qualifications. The first bombs of the war
fell on her hometown during the early weeks of the marriage.
Her husband fled to Russia to escape the Nazis but could not
convince her to join him. She stated that she had led a sheltered
life and her parents did not want her to leave. The husband
returned after a few months, malnourished and sexually impotent. Again he fled to Russia but could not bear the separation
and returned. This time a child was conceived. Shortly thereafter,
while trying to flee the Germans, he was killed. Their baby died
of malnutrition at four weeks of age.

Mrs. Q.'s brothers tried to save the family by hiding everyone
in bunkers. When they were caught and brought out into day-
light, Mrs. Q.'s hair had turned gray. Her family all perished in
concentration camps. Mrs. Q. survived the camps by volunteering
to work in a munitions factory. While her friends in the camp
thought she would be killed, she believed that there was such a
risk of death in either case that she would take her chances.

After the liberation, she wandered the streets in Germany.

She was dressed in rags and limped because she only had one shoe. Mr. Q. noticed her wandering in the streets and approached her with a pair of shoes. To this day, this singular event brings a surge of overwhelming emotion within Mrs. Q. He was 45 and she was 31. He clothed her, fed her, and became a significant nurturing figure whom she chose to marry in preference to a younger boyfriend. When friends cautioned her that Mr. Q. was too old, she said that she felt "old too." He offered her the security that she lost when her family was uprooted and killed. Interestingly, for the first few years of their marriage she called him "father." Their daughter was born a year after their marriage. Although she had several pregnancies thereafter, they all miscarried, which she attributed to poor medical care in Germany. There were no more children. Subsequently a relative brought all three to Canada.

Mrs. Q. stated that upon arrival in Canada, the marital relationship, which had been better in Europe, changed. Mr. Q. became obsessed with "making money." He forced her to work and take in boarders while their daughter was placed in a nursery. Although Mrs. Q. wanted to care for her daughter and had hoped she could conceive again, Mr. Q. did not want more children. Later she had to have a hysterectomy, which she again stated was necessary because of the previous poor medical care. For a number of years she worked in a bakery and a paper company and together they were financially successful, with a large car, their own home, and ample savings. An intelligent woman, Mrs. Q. capably managed all their finances. However, socially she appeared isolated and had no close friends.

The only daughter, M., was 36 years old when she brought her father for treatment. At that time she appeared depressed, older than her age, and conveyed an air of sadness. Her overall appearance was unremarkable and colorless. Her face was tense, worn, and joyless. She recalled her troubled childhood during which her parents argued constantly—"each one had to have the last word." While material needs were met, she lacked affection and warmth. For example, she could not remember any words of praise from her parents for achievements, nor could she recall ever going out with them for entertainment. Her memory was of a joyless, bickering household. She was well aware of their Holocaust experiences as her mother had related many of the details. Her mother shared all of her marital and other problems with M. to the point of giving her intimate details. This was very upsetting to M. Her response to her parents' tragedies was to be the "good little girl" and to give no trouble. She was an excellent student and an achiever and she had no memory of the normal pranks or misbehavior that are part of childhood. In conversations with her women friends of today, they told her that they remembered her as "good little M."

M. daydreamed about an idealized marriage. She became attached to the first man she dated, even though she felt he might be a bit too quiet compared to her daydreams. He was kind, considerate, and offered some affection, which she needed. He was an only child whose mother became ill with a progressive disease when he was very young. She died when he reached adulthood. This had an obvious impact upon his formative years when he, like M., felt deprived of affection. Both M. and S. completed university. She is a teacher and he a businessman. They demonstrated a strong sense of loyalty and concern for one another. Unlike M.'s parents, their disappointments with one another did not result in accusatory battles, nor did they recapitulate the pathology of M.'s parents. While M. tended to be overly good and compliant, she was also rewarded. When she began to have long bouts of weeping after the birth of their third child, for example, her husband supported and encouraged her to return to her professional career. In other ways she felt emotionally abandoned. For instance, S. never discussed his work with her; she looked forward to his coming home from work each day, but felt always disappointed and shut out.

Despite the surface awareness of each other's needs, M. and S. displayed little outward affection. S. was described as passive and content to sit at home, while M. was constantly "on the go." She was always doing for others. Desperate for approval, she would never say no or set her own priorities.

Over the past few years, with her father's decline, M.'s own family life took second place. Her three children were acutely aware of her tension every time the phone rang. M.'s conflicts were especially evident in her difficulties with her oldest daughter, P. She moralized on any subject or problem the daughter raised and there was special friction when her daughter asked for those clothes and other items that were in vogue and a fad. She was equally hard on the children she taught. M. was a generous woman but fun and spontaneity had not been integrated into her life-style.

The grandparents' relationship with their grandchildren was

affectionate but strained. Mrs. Q. was generous with them on special occasions, took them on outings, and occasionally let them sleep over. However, she always compared their behavior (fights and squabbles, etc.) to that of M. whom she considered to have been well behaved. Mr. Q., while not a talkative man, took pride in his grandchildren and was warm and affectionate, although he did not play with them.

Formulation of Family Dynamics

Initially, the inpatient psychiatric treatment team was concerned with Mr. Q. who came as the identified patient and whose deterioration opened wide the "Pandora's box of family stresses and strains." Already emotionally vulnerable, his most recent stroke, three years previously, appeared to have been the major precipitant for a breakdown of his defense structures leading to a collapse of ego capacities. He had endured suffering, incomprehensible to anyone who did not experience the Holocaust. During the Holocaust his life was violently ripped apart; he was uprooted from all that was familiar; he witnessed death daily and lived in constant fear of his own destruction. He was totally helpless in terms of saving those dear to him and his survival depended only on his physical strength. The soul or heart that are part of one's being was almost totally destroyed. He had recreated parts of himself in his four children only to have that connection to posterity totally destroyed. A parent who survived, but was unable to save his children, no matter the circumstances, will be forever haunted.

As with many survivors, Mr. Q. had been able to cope well in Canada as long as he was working and maintaining his position as head of his household. His symptoms appeared to be a complex mix of an organic response to his multiple strokes and a psychological response to his profound loss of power and control. He had lost much of his ability to have an erection and was no longer able to write his name legibly as he had been prior to his stroke. The team interpreted his refusal to eat for three days, which had brought him to therapeutic attention in the first place, as a signal of his desperation and a struggle to regain power and control. His behavior was indeed powerful, demanding immediate attention and throwing the family into a state of helplessness. Of equal emotional significance was the patient's unmodified rage at his Holocaust experiences and his intense and entirely unresolved grief at his losses. As long as he was able to maintain a sense of control over his life and his family, he could ward off the full magnitude of his guilt and inability to save his first family. The onset of his physical deterioration, dramatically reawakened the extent of his wartime helplessness and his current incapacity.

Berger (1985) has written about regressive responses in later life in survivors. He states: "That many survivors who managed to create a successful life in the post-war period broke down and exhibited florid symptoms many years later is evidence of the incompleteness of the recovery process" (p. 58).

> Mrs. Q. did not have a normal adult life. She presented as a needy, narcissistic, immature woman to whom life had dealt blows beyond human comprehension. Although massively traumatized by the Holocaust, she retained certain qualities from her prior life such as the expectation that she would always be cared for by a man. Mr. Q. met these needs until his retirement and subsequent illnesses.
>
> Like Mr. Q., Mrs. Q. was a woman with many strengths, some of which manifested in her ability as a manipulator of the environment. She chose her first husband herself when custom required otherwise, and having survived the Holocaust she successfully tackled a new country.
>
> As a couple, the Q.'s, despite their conflicts, raised an accomplished daughter, and managed to maintain a stable and superficially successful unit. Despite the difficulties in their relationship, wherein Mrs. Q. felt forced by her husband into all kinds of situations—working, treating him like a king, sex—it was also obvious that there were many compensations.
>
> These two very different individuals were thrown together because of circumstances beyond their control. While their relationship developed out of survival needs, as it did for many postwar couples, their marriage endured, lasting over 38 years. Together they gave each other strength and made a life.
>
> Because of the Q.'s interrupted lives and their extreme deprivation, they never felt truly secure, nor did they feel loved or desired by the other. Mr. Q. absented himself from the home

for days at a time, working on the road. His main focus was to accumulate money for security and this he felt was his primary contribution. For many Holocaust survivors, material possessions are an apparent reaffirmation of their sense of being alive and secure in the external world. It is also a way of coping with losses. For both Mr. and Mrs. Q., the Holocaust caused overwhelming loss. Mr. Q., however, had an additional burden. Because of his powerful guilt over failing to save his first wife and four children or for not perishing with them, he was unable to fully emotionally commit himself to his second family. Undoubtedly this accounted, in part, for much of the family conflict, especially that component which arose out of his comparisons of his first and second wives.

While the family lived in conflict, it was also a crucial restorative vehicle for Mr. and Mrs. Q. As Ornstein (1981) has said:

parenting is the adult experience that can most fully restore the survivor who has lost his or her original family. The survivor's need for this particular adult experience may be greater than the need for any other creative activity that might have the potential to provide the all-important sense of sameness and continuity throughout the life cycle. In creating a family, whether biologically or otherwise, the survivor experiences himself or herself as capable of creating new life [p. 152].

M. was thoroughly aware of her parents' tragic backgrounds and the need for her to make up for all that they lost. She became a source of replacement and felt that she had the task of replenishing their losses. This was her lifelong burden, her mortgage for all time, the implicit debt which she had to pay back to her parents in order to balance the emotional ledger. She referred to herself as always being "the good little girl." To this day, she seeks constant approval from others, having difficulty setting her own priorities. M. feels she was emotionally cheated. Her parent's constant bickering, for example, had a significant impact upon her since her parents could articulate positive feelings neither for each other nor for her.

Mrs. Q. sees herself as a victim and lives vicariously through M. Her envy and jealousy is apparent in her attitudes to M.'s achievements—a profession, a satisfying marriage, and three children. Mrs. Q. says, "I was in a concentration camp and later wandered the streets in rags." Clearly, M. had to live through her mother's horrendous life while her mother struggled with whether her daughter was truly entitled to happiness.

The legacy M. carries from the Holocaust has affected her own child rearing, particularly with her eldest daughter who is 11 years old. Her daughter, for her part, demands, through acting out, the pleasures in life which her mother never had. This completes a cycle of three generations of women in competition for scarce emotional supplies.

In summary, this was a family unit where split loyalties impacted on three living generations. The unspoken loyalty to the generation murdered during the Holocaust remained in the present, as seen by the joyless home of Mr. and Mrs. Q. They did not feel entitled to joy; it would have been disloyal. Their daughter realized at an early age that her loyalty was best expressed by being well behaved, but she was not entitled to overt emotional understanding from her parents in return. There were too many debts owed to the murdered generation. The grandchildren, particularly the eldest, unconsciously acted out the needs of all concerned for caring and pleasure. There was, however, no justice for any of the generations. The legacy of the dead was emotionally crippling.

Treatment

In order to understand the nature of the treatment interventions, it is necessary to give a brief description of the geriatric psychiatry unit to which Mr. Q. was admitted.

The unit is headed by a psychiatrist whose specialty is geriatric psychiatry. In addition to a complete psychiatric workup that includes individual and family history and a mental status assessment, there is also a routine medical workup by a geriatrician, who is an active team member. Particularly with the elderly, medical and psychiatric problems impact on each other. Staff on the unit utilize a strong team approach: physicians, nurses, social workers, occupational therapists, and health care aides. Each professional brings his own expertise to bear on the assessment process. Who does what, who carries what responsibility for treatment is clearly defined. At the time of admission, it is made clear to the family that they have to participate in the treatment process. The patient is not removed from the context of the family. Patients are expected to dress in their own clothing and to take as much responsibility for self-care as is possible. Individual therapy, group therapy, family therapy, occupational therapy, and recreational therapy are all important modalities of treatment. Psychotherapy is often concurrent with medication and in specific situations, electroshock therapy. As the patient improves, leaving the institution with staff and subsequently going home on weekend passes communicates recovery expectations. Psychotherapy enables older persons and their families to move away from the stereotyped message, "You are old, what can you expect other than permanent institutionalization?"

The comprehensive intergenerational approach to formulating the problems of the Q. family made it clear that the therapeutic journey would be arduous and painful in its early stages. A major task of the therapist was to be able to bear the family's tragedies while not becoming overwhelmed by the impact of aging, the Holocaust legacy, and the intense interplay of complex family forces. The author, who was the family therapist in this case, maintains a paramount belief system which focuses upon the strength, endurance, and incredible survival skills of people. The belief system emphasizes the need to enhance relationships and to nurture growth and development rather than focusing on sickness and pathology. This life-enhancing approach to treatment is particularly relevant in dealing with Holocaust survivors.

Three integrated modes of therapy were the treatments of choice—individual, conjoint marital, and family sessions. The interventions began intensively on a weekly basis, subsequently moving to more infrequent monthly sessions, and finally into a phase of intermittent contact which may be termed review check-ups.

There were four treatment phases: The inpatient phase; the postdischarge family treatment phase for Mr. Q., wife, and daughter; the marital therapy phase for daughter and husband;

and the family therapy phase for daughter, husband, and their three children.

Phase I

The eight weeks of Mr. Q.'s hospitalization served as a period of respite, thereby putting out the fire in Mr. and Mrs. Q.'s relationship. With the tensions reduced, it was possible to establish an alliance with Mrs. Q. and with M. There was opportunity to understand the family dynamics and to integrate this knowledge with the important aspects of Mr. Q.'s medical and psychological functioning.

Mother and daughter were initially seen together, but it soon became evident that joint sessions were counterproductive because of their competition for the social worker. There was an immediate positive transference during the admissions interview when the worker recognized the burden and the pain for all concerned. This opened a floodgate of emotions and tears. The therapist's empathy awakened feelings of being cared for, so often longed for but always frustrated. They could not tolerate sharing the worker, so great was their deprivation. Mrs. Q. emphasized the primacy of her own suffering and seemed unable to understand that M. required her own source of support. This furthered M.'s long-standing enmeshment with her mother. During the weeks of crisis prior to her father's hospitalization, M. had emotionally abandoned her husband and three children in favor of supporting her mother and the crumbling structure of her parent's relationship. However, she paid a continuing emotional price, weeping in the face of their unbearable suffering.

The health care team took complete charge of Mr. Q.'s management. This approach permitted the daughter to step back and begin to receive sorely needed emotional support from the therapist. Additionally, Mrs. Q. had the opportunity to express her painful disappointment that her old age was not turning out to be "the golden years." In acknowledging for the patient the injustice of her life and the fact that both she and her husband had suffered enough, the therapist began to forge a therapeutic alliance which had its initial basis in the confirmation of the reality of the patient's suffering.

Mr. Q.'s management, while based on psychodynamic understanding, focused primarily on supportive measures because of his stroke-related cognitive impairment, his hearing deficit, and his inherent difficulty in expressing his feelings. Although support is sometimes viewed as a simpler mode of therapy, it is, in reality, complex, a process of identifying and mitigating stresses, supporting adaptive strengths, assisting the patient's caretaking environment (Kahana, 1983), and providing direction. For example, the staff took advantage of Mr. Q.'s preserved personality to encourage his love for gardening, and he became a member of the hospital gardening group which enhanced his self-esteem, and helped his wife and daughter to recover some of their more positive and hopeful feelings about him.

The inpatient phase required close collaboration between the social worker, therapist, psychiatrist, nursing staff, occupational therapist, and recreation therapist. While formal marital therapy was avoided, the staff directly intervened to control the angry, hurtful interactions between Mr. and Mrs. Q. As their capacity to relate without the feared "bloodshed" became evident, their daughter's anxieties diminished. Discharge rather than placement could now be contemplated.

A family therapeutic alliance developed with the treatment team as a result of the therapeutic emphasis on the whole family system. Such an alliance is a crucial element in successful therapy of these complex problems.

Once the basic alliance has been launched, the therapist must choose between the alternative therapeutic techniques. In the world of family therapists, there are pros and cons about seeing members separately. For example, Framo (1985) quoting Bowen, maintains "that there are occasions when the therapist can at certain stages in the treatment process, see one family member in family therapy and that this procedure is not individual psychotherapy because the raising of the level of differentiation of one member is oriented toward serving a therapeutic need for the entire family" (p. 180). In the Q.'s case, the therapist decided that the family's interests could be best served by dealing individually with the family members during the second phase of treatment.

Phase II

The second and longest phase of treatment, began when Mr. Q. was discharged home. He was registered in a day care program four days a week which served his needs and provided essential, brief periods of separation for Mr. and Mrs. Q., thereby diminishing their level of destructive emotional intensity.

Although, in many ways, Mr. Q. was not an active participant in the social programs of day care, he was considered an authority in the "growing plants program." This and a variety of other opportunities to enhance his self-esteem in the supportive community of day care, further reduced the devastation of his stroke and helped modify his symptom picture.

Meanwhile, concurrent sessions with Mrs. Q. continued. These were concrete and educational. For example, it took a number of sessions to help her understand that her husband was indeed physically ill. She felt that his behavior was purposeful and that he blamed her for all that was going wrong with him. Mrs. Q. finally began to change when the therapist told her, in session after session, that she was not to respond to her husband's accusations or try to have the last word, which had been the pattern in their marriage. Mrs. Q. did not understand the "last word syndrome" explaining her newfound technique of not responding to his outbursts as "giving him his way." However, as demonstrated by Mrs. Q., it is not important for the client to fully understand everything which the therapist says. If the therapeutic alliance is strong enough, the client will begin to follow advice, even if, initially, it may be for the wrong reasons. The clinician can foster this aspect of supportive and directive therapy by presenting himself as a strong personality and symbolically lending his ego-strength to the patient (Karpf, 1980).

As the patient further allied herself with therapy and began to follow the therapist's advice, it became possible for her to attend to her own needs, especially since Mr. Q.'s day care schedule reduced the necessity for Mrs. Q. to look after him. With "time on my hands" she became freer to talk about her love for reading, housekeeping, and her interest in clothes. Her mood lightened and she smiled more frequently, subsequently being able to relate amusing, warm, and happy memories about her marriage. As her trust grew, she spoke too of her losses, the early years of deprivation, and her strength to survive.

Inherent in this phase of Mrs. Q.'s treatment was the encouragement of her reminiscences and life review (Lewis and Butler, 1977). This is a powerful therapeutic tool which places events in perspective and aids in the reestablishment of self-esteem and a sense of self-cohesion. While painful events are relived in the telling, the sharing of such material lends a humanness to the therapeutic relationship which is crucial for older people. Memories of life events which were fulfilling and which demonstrated courage and strength may be used in the present to encourage continued competency. An additional bonus to such work can be the transmission of family history to younger generations, a process which is often gratifying to the older patient.

A similar but necessarily more concrete approach was used for Mr. Q. when M. was encouraged to put together a family album for him to bring to day care. This concrete form of reminiscence therapy gave him a tangible history to share with pride. Moreover, the family album contained clear evidence that Mr. Q. would be able to live on through his offspring, and that, despite his overwhelming losses, his life would end with a measure of ego-integrity not despair (Erikson, 1950).

While it is often impossible to work through the despair and sorrows of a lifetime, it is possible to find aspects of life that enhance self-esteem and bring integrity to the remaining years.

During the second phase of therapy, M. was seen alone weekly for several months. For a number of sessions, she wept profusely as she related her difficult past, her present pain, and her guilt at "never doing enough." Her loneliness and profound sadness mixed with anger and resentment, emerged, and she articulated her fears of her parents' death. Over and over, she said "we are all we have." Through M. it became clear that the legacy of abandonment was a central theme for the family. The parents had lost all they had as a result of the Holocaust, and now M. felt abandoned by her father's illness, his eventual loss and death, and her growing awareness that one day she would lose her mother. As M. more effectively put her fears into words, she was able to deal more realistically with day-to-day living.

Initially M. felt that she was not entitled to cry as much as she did, or express feelings. The therapist responded by articulating her feelings and acknowledged the valid aspects of her inadequate family support system thereby enhancing the positive transference. With time, M.'s refrain, "I want to do the right thing. I feel for both my parents," diminished and she began to focus more appropriately on her inability to give to herself and set her own priorities. It took her months to accept the fact that she had an hour a week (in therapy) just for herself. In fact, her attendance itself was an important treatment tool.

Gradually, fewer and fewer crises became evident and Mr. Q., his wife, and daughter all coped better with their fears. One of the turning points for M. occurred when her mother apparently precipitated a crisis by trying to force Mr. Q. to take his pills on Yom Kippur, the most sacred Jewish Fast Day. Mrs. Q. fought with her husband, then panicked and phoned M. who went rushing over to her parents' house. Later as she walked with her father to the synagogue, Mr. Q. told her, with great sadness, of his awareness of his decline, the special meaning of this Fast Day, and explained that at day's end he would take his pills. M. was overcome with affection, a feeling she had rarely experienced for her father in those last years. She began to view him as more special and struggled to understand and accept him. Although she began to resolve some of her anger toward her father, she continued to be angry at her mother, a manifestation of her split loyalties. Initially, M. had presented in alliance with her mother accepting that mother was the victim. As her father declined, however, she became confused as to who was the victim. Nagy and Spark (1973) state that "split loyalty, in the sense of simultaneous rejection of one person and devotion to another, can be the source of great psychic pain and a frequent cause of intense jealousy" (p. 132). The "split loyalty" issue was mitigated to some extent by the fact that the therapist also saw Mrs. Q., and was able to help M. understand that her father's illness was a major trauma for her mother.

M.'s powerful feelings of guilt and responsibility for her parent's happiness made it imperative that she come to an emotional understanding that she was *indeed* doing the *very* best for her parents. Satir (1964), has pointed out that children have needs and rights as human beings, and that "it is all right to recognize these needs and meet them in order that you can meet your parents needs in a responsible and loving way" (p. 115). The ability to give to one's self without guilt and still maintain a close and caring relationship with one's parents is an important step in the attainment of filial maturity. "The concept of filial maturity implies that the old relationship with your parents has been worked through, perhaps resolved and that you and your parents forgive each other for whatever caused pain to you both in the past. As a person who has achieved filial maturity you can hold your own, meet your own needs, set proper limits and give real help to your parents without feeling overwhelmed or overpowered" (Goodman, 1980).

With time, therapy induced important basic shifts in M.'s perspective on, and response to, her parents. Gradually she was able to tell her mother, "it hurts me to hear that you two are fighting. You both need each other. I cannot stand it." As she developed further, M. could begin to recognize when she needed to intervene and when not. She said to her mother, "don't pay attention to everything Daddy says. I know it hurts you to hear these things but he is not well. Mom, I know that the terrible things Daddy says are *not* true. You have been a good wife. You are a good mother. You are a good person. Try not to answer him." With direction from the therapist, M. was better able to distinguish what constituted a crisis and began to stop running over to her parents home to see if "either one has killed the other." She established some limits for herself and developed some preventive strategies. For example, she knew that Fridays, Saturdays, and Sundays could be tense times for her parents because there was no day care and they had to be together constantly, so she had them over to her house at least once on the weekends.

"Entitlement" was a crucial aspect of the work with M. She had suppressed her own pleasure-seeking desires from early childhood and recalled feeling unhappy in the day nursery when other children could be with their parents. She always studied hard and received good grades. She rarely had fun with girl friends. She did not ask for special things from her parents. She did not date much. She was a very serious minded young woman. In contrast, M.'s oldest daughter, P. expressed her needs and demanded pleasure. The therapist hypothesized that she was expressing not only an appropriate desire for enjoyment, but also an unconscious rejection of her mother's pleasure-sacrificing stance in life. M. seemed unable to tolerate this aspect of her daughter's behavior. In contrast, the middle child, a daughter, was an extrovert, fun loving, with lots of friends, who managed to get what she wanted without provoking the same intensity of M.'s anger. M. spoke of the differences between the two girls and singled out the older one for criticism. M.'s growing self-awareness and ability to give more to herself, reduced her anger at her daughter. As she began to understand herself in relationship to her mother, she had less of a need to criticize her daughter. Therapeutic techniques were concrete and specific, for example, asking M. to list P.'s demands. Significantly, a number of her demands had to do with the latest fashions in clothing. Analysis of the clothing issue helped M. begin to gain insight. She realized that she was imposing on her daughter what her parents had unwittingly imposed upon her—the strict limitations on gratifications. Moreover, M.'s need for a warm winter coat and shoes emerged. She delayed the purchase yet talked about it frequently. It took some time for her to accept responsibility for meeting her own needs and to relinquish the defensive mechanism of attacking her daughter for expressing those desires which she could not tolerate in herself.

The relationship between M. and P. was a dramatic example of the legacy of the Holocaust, the trauma of the first generation being passed down through the second to the third. Evident in all the family conflict was the essential underlying dynamic question of who was "entitled" to what pleasures in life. Because of their survivor guilt and a need to suffer for those who perished, the grandparents could not allow themselves to have what they might have been entitled to. Because of their own needs, Mr. and Mrs. Q. were rendered ineffective in pursuing a balanced entitlement for their daughter, and she in turn had the same difficulty with her children.

This phase of treatment opened up the intense pain which the Holocaust caused to this family. A discussion of the theory and techniques of approaching such families is beyond the scope of this chapter. For this family, however, the therapist recognized the need to discuss the Holocaust openly. This is not the case in every such family. Mrs. Q. spent many sessions detailing the horrors of the Holocaust experience and emphasizing her own strength in surviving. It was the therapist's important task to tolerate the pain (her own and the patient's) of this extraordinarily devastating experience. There was little attempt to explore prewar life and experiences. Mrs. Q. remembered that time as "happier days." To have "analyzed" these memories would have been a serious blow to the sustaining view she held of her former life. The therapist's compassion and empathy enabled Mrs. Q. to value herself more. In particular, she had a chance to understand the affirmation of life inherent in her daughter and grandchildren.

Phase III

During phase II, the therapist realized that the younger couple (second generation) had to be seen for a number of sessions because both had entitlement problems which impacted on the marriage.

In the third phase of therapy therefore, treatment focused more on the marital problems of M. and S. This phase began over a year after the onset of the treatment program, and involved joint interviews with M. and her husband S., despite S.'s initial skepticism.

The marital sessions opened communication between the couple around their needs and what each felt they could give in response to what they each felt they were entitled to receive.

S. was less verbal than M. in the sessions, however, his concern for her was evident. He revealed that he did not think he could place any limits on M.'s involvement with her parents. Loyalty to one's parents was of major importance for him. This was related to having lived for many years with his mother who had a progressive disease. M. was able to share with S. her awareness of boundaries and limitations. He responded that he did experience his wife as being less depressed in more recent weeks. Both recognized aloud to one another the strong role that the tragedies of their respective parents had played in their lives. It became clear, however, that M.'s depression was not simply tied to her parent's situation, but that it was compounded by her feeling devalued by her husband. S. was unaware of the depth of M.'s feelings. He was a sensitive person but was unaware of the hurtful effects of his unilateral behavior, such as never asking for help, and that he shut her out of his business except for signing legal documents.

The emotional marital conflicts demonstrated how the failure to negotiate earlier stages of growth interferes with the evolution of a mature marital relationship in the offspring. In Framo's (1985) words, "people who do not successfully resolve problems that arise with each step of growth, carry over to each successive developmental stage a series of conditions and handicaps which limit their capacity to relate to others except in the light of their own needs" (p. 158). These two individuals had to assume emotional adulthood prematurely, thus cutting off some of the joys of childhood innocence. The intent of treatment for them was not in-depth marital therapy. The essential goal was to free M. and S. to begin to enjoy their life and perhaps recapture or reexperience some of the lost joys of childhood.

Phase IV

In the fourth phase there were a series of sessions with M., S., and their three children. The focus of these sessions was, in part, education about grandfather's illness. The grandchildren had already participated with their grandfather in day care by attending holiday celebrations. The youngest grandchild, age 7, cried and spoke of his fears and his terrible sadness about his grandfather's illness. He was the spokesman for the family's feelings and the therapist spent a great deal of time encouraging the expression of his feelings. They expressed concern for their grandmother and their mother and shared, for the first time, not just their tension when mother was on the phone with grandmother, but their concern for how sad their mother seemed to be much of the time. M.'s eyes welled with tears. Momentarily everyone was silent and then M. acknowledged their sensitivity and said that indeed she was sad at times but not as sad as before.

Nagy and Spark stress the need for including grandparents in sessions. In this situation, the grandparents were not physically present, but they were in the room. M. was not ready to have them present and while the therapist pressed for their participation, it was not forced. M. still feared "hurting" her mother and felt that her mother was a concrete thinker who would not be able to engage in a meaningful dialogue.

After the initial session the grandchildren sensed an atmosphere where it was all right to speak. M. and S. were a bit uncomfortable and M. in particular gave the children critical looks when they spoke of her moods and anger. However, a dialogue of give and take ensued, and interestingly moved into other areas such as which of the parents disciplined, chores, entitlement to special things, the parents' anger and disappointment with each other, and sibling struggles. Subsequently, without prompting from the therapist, family discussions became more integral to day-to-day events. For example, M. and S. began to set aside time each day to catch up on one another's activities.

This phase demonstrated that involving grandchildren is a great resource in work with the elderly.

> Much that was unknown or unclear about the older person's circumstances may be shared for the first time. This can lead to a new understanding and mutual compassion between the generations. . . . The grandchildren, who may have been carrying the brunt of the negative transference of one or both adult parents, are very eager for a reconcil-

iation with their grandparents. It not only helps free them of the scapegoated or parentified role, but it renews their hope and provides them a model for reconciling their conflict with their own parents [Nagy and Spark, 1973, p. 225].

Mr. Q. died in 1984 after another stroke. Mother and daughter were both present at his death. This was a powerful ending. They felt that he knew of their presence and their caring to the end.

Mrs. Q. gave a piece of gardening equipment to the day care center in memory of her husband. A ceremony marked the event. Members of day care spoke of Mr. Q.'s love and knowledge of flowers and beauty. His grandchildren listened attentively and were obviously moved as they bore witness to "the whole grandfather." Perhaps this tangible evidence of a more positive legacy will help to diminish in them the legacy of the Holocaust.

Currently, therapeutic help is being directed to bereavement work for mother, daughter, and grandchildren. M. goes to synagogue twice a day to say Kaddish (prayer for the dead) for her father. It is M.'s tribute to her father; it is a healing event for her, and surely it speaks to posterity—it gives a message to the grandchildren about parenting, and keeping warm memories intact.

Mrs. Q. is touched by her daughter's commitment and secretly wonders whether this will be done for her. The mother–daughter dialogues may take place once the pain of their loss is eased.

Mrs. Q., in life-review sessions, has come to terms with the positive aspects of her marital relationship. She recognizes that she is lonely and misses this once vital man. Six months after his death she sold her house and moved to a more manageable apartment. She has subsequently been encouraged to join a widows' group. The therapy sessions are now infrequent as she mobilizes her inherent strengths. For the first time she took her grandchildren on a month's holiday. Although she had always spent time with them, this was the most generous amount of time she had spent and an occasion when she was completely on her own and responsible for the three youngsters.

In giving permission to the therapist to tell "their story" so that others might benefit, the family is making a further contribution to posterity.

Conclusion

Because it is healing for all members of a family to see the connecting links between generations, "the family" must be understood in longitudinal and intergenerational terms.

The dynamics of one particular family was examined within the context of Nagy and Spark's complex family accounting system of loyalties, entitlements, ledger balancing, justice, and the legacy to posterity. Each generation was viewed from the perspective of an intergenerational framework.

In describing the family's history, special emphasis was placed on the role of the parent's Holocaust experience in skewing and distorting the family relationships of three generations. Four phases of therapy were described in some detail to illustrate the complex nature, both of geriatric family therapy and three-generational therapy. By taking a life affirming, positive approach to change, the therapist echoed, in her interventions, the family's wish to escape the horror of the Holocaust and live fuller loving and giving lives. While neither finished nor completely successful, therapy clearly aided Mr. Q.'s final months and the emotional growth of Mrs. Q., her daughter, and her daughter's family. Perhaps the legacy of the Holocaust in this family will not be perpetuated for posterity.

References

Berger, D. M. (1985), Recovery and regression in concentration camp survivors: A psychodynamic reevaluation. *Can. J. Psychiat.*, 30:1:54–59.

Brody, E. M. (1985), Patient care as a normative family stress. *Gerontol.*, 25:1:19–29.

Carter, E. A. (1980), The family in later life. In: *The Family Life Cycle: A Framework for Family Therapy*, ed. M. McGoldrick. New York: Gardner Press, p. 207.

Cassell, E. J. (1973), Learning to die. In: *Meeting the Problems of Older People*. The 1973 Health Conference, New York Academy of Medicine. pp. 1110–1118. April 30 & May 1, 1973.

Erikson, E. H. (1950), *Childhood and Society*. New York: W. W. Norton, pp. 231–233.

324   TREATING THE ELDERLY WITH PSYCHOTHERAPY

Framo, J. L. (1985), Rationale and techniques of intensive family therapy. In: *Intensive Family Therapy: Theoretical and Practical Aspects*, ed. I. Bosomenyi-Nagy & J. L. Framo. Hagerstown, MD: Harper & Row, p. 180.

Goodman, J. G. (1980), *Aging Parents: Whose Responsibility?* New York: Family Service Association of America.

Gussow, M. (1983), Review of *Women Playwrights—New Voices in the Theatre* by M. Norman. *New York Times Magazine*, p. 40.

Halsall, R. W. (1967), A social approach to geriatrics. *New Zealand Med. J.*, 66:755–757.

Kahana, R. J. (1983), Psychotherapy of the elderly; a miserable old age—What can therapy do? *J. Geriat. Psychiat.*, 16:1:7–32.

Karpf, R. J. (1980), Modalities of psychotherapy with the elderly. *J. Amer. Geriat. Soc.*, 28:367–371.

Lewis, M. I., & Butler, R. N. (1977), Life review therapy: Putting memories to work in individual and group psychotherapy. In: *Readings in Psychotherapy with Older People*, ed. S. Steury & M. L. Blank. Rockville, MD: National Institute of Mental Health, pp. 199-205.

Nagy, I., & Spark, G. M. (1973) *Invisible Loyalties: Reciprocity in Intergenerational Family Therapy*. Hagerstown, MD: Harper & Row.

Ornstein, A. (1981), The effects of the Holocaust on life-cycle experiences: the creation and recreation of families. *J. Geriat. Psychiat.*, 14:135–154.

Satir, V. (1964), *Conjoint Family Therapy*, 2nd ed. Palo Alto: Science and Behaviour Books, 1967.

11

GROUP PSYCHOTHERAPY WITH THE ELDERLY

Molyn Leszcz, M.D.

Introduction

Many of the contributors to this text have argued cogently for the value and feasibility of the application of psychodynamic, psychotherapeutic principles to the elderly. As clinical experience has broadened with an ever-increasing population of elderly individuals in psychological distress, new models of understanding and therapy have evolved. This chapter will explore some theoretical, clinical, and practical issues in the group psychotherapy of elderly patients. Clinical illustrations from the group therapy of elderly individuals will demonstrate that the specific attributes of group psychotherapy and the psychological requirements of many of the elderly are well matched. A central and organizing concept throughout this chapter will be the value of group therapy in providing a self-esteem enhancing relational matrix for those elderly who respond to their aging with depression, disengagement, and demoralization (Leszcz, Feigenbaum, Sadavoy, Robinson, 1985).

Theoretical Considerations

Some Psychological Perspectives on Aging

The majority of the elderly negotiate their ongoing development and aging with relative calm and success. They are able to review their past life, their successes and failures, and accept their life's unfolding "as something that had to be and that, by

325

necessity, permitted [of] no substitutions" (Erikson, 1950). They face the future without undue fear and as Erikson (1950) suggested, their feelings of wholeness, or ego integrity, predominate over feelings of despair. In contrast, many individuals are overwhelmed by the experience of aging's assaults on their object relationships and sense of self. There is a rupture in the continuity of their sense of self over time. Depression, isolation, and malignant feelings of worthlessness and helplessness replace calmness and comfort. This is exemplified by an 88-year-old man, cognitively intact, admitted to an active care psychogeriatric unit because of a serious suicide attempt. He was humiliated and depressed because of the recent onset of urinary incontinence. He responded quietly to a request to participate in a psychotherapy group on the ward in the following way: "Doctor, what could you want with me there, now? I used to be something, now I am nothing—useless. If you really want to help me you'll get me a gun!" This man was depressed, without doubt, but he was not suffering from a primary affective disorder. As such, his primary treatment was psychotherapeutic in nature.

It is the author's premise that the impact of the narcissistic injuries of aging on the elderly individual's sense of self, determines whether feelings of integrity or feelings of despair will predominate, as well as which approaches a therapist may follow. The issues of reactions to loss and diminishments in self-esteem are central to almost every explanation of depression in aging (Breslau and Haug, 1983). Yet, the very breadth and common sense of this statement can obscure the extreme importance that loss and decline have on the aging individual's psychological functioning and sense of self.

Recent theoretical advances have increased our understanding of these critical, narcissistic issues. As described by Kohut (1977), and Kohut and Wolf (1978), in addition to the developmental line of narcissism leading to object love, there is a separate line of development that leads from immature, to more mature, forms of narcissism. At the heart of these ideas is the concept of the self. This term refers to a central, psychological entity, subsuming the ego, id, and superego. It is the central, composite representation of all of one's experiences, emotions, and aspirations, determining the total measure of oneself. The self is bipolar, consisting of the grandiose self and the idealizing parental imago. The grandiose self reflects the infant's sense of specialness and omnipotence, which matures in time into the self's ambitions, purposes, and sense of self-esteem. The idealizing parental imago consists of the later projections of this infantile grandiosity onto an idealized object, usually the parent. The child is soothed by merging with, and basking in the light of, this idealized object. This too matures, over time, into the capacity to admire others, maintain ideals, and soothe oneself.

In Kohut's model, the child's parents serve as selfobjects. The selfobject is experienced by the self as part of and not separate from the self. The selfobject performs essential functions of psychological maintenance, and in essence completes the self, giving to the self that which the self is unable to provide. This includes mirroring the child's grandiosity, empathically responding to his affective experiences, and serving as an object of idealization to soothe him. The sense of self is initially regulated externally by the selfobject. However, through the selfobject's inevitable, but, hopefully, not too traumatic disappointment of the child, within a nurturing and empathic matrix, the child's disillusionment in the selfobject promotes a healthy shift to a stronger internal sense of self. Moreover, this shift aids the internal regulation of self-esteem maintenance, reducing reliance on external supplies. However, as Anna Ornstein (1981) notes, "Separateness and independence of self and object are relative, and the self, even in its most mature form, is not independent of selfobjects" (p. 445).

Throughout life, the individual can invest activities, endeavors, affiliations and relationships with the self-cohesing function of the selfobject. For example, the man who, 20 years after his retirement, still prides himself on being "the best scissor sharpener in the trade" is commenting that his job, as unprideworthy as it might seem to others, was a credential, and perhaps for him the most important credential, used in the service of maintaining his self-esteem much as Berezin (1977) has commented. The self can be relatively stable and cohesive or it can be vulnerable to fragmentation and empty depression. This depends on how much the sense of self is regulated internally, how much it is regulated "externally," and how much these external regulatory selfobjects or representative activities are in fact available. A sense of self-cohesion or its converse, a sense of fragmentation, are relative. Self-cohesion is experienced as vigor and vitality, with associated feelings of pride and pleasure in the self. The absence of self-cohesion is experienced, conversely, as apathy, worthlessness, and hopelessness, inducing a feeling of inconsolable failure.

If the elderly are conceptualized along a developmental continuum, in which the majority of their narcissistic gratifications lie behind them, while the majority of their narcissistic assaults are present or imminent, then it seems clear that their needs for the affirming, mirroring, and soothing function of the selfobject are as great, if not greater than at any other time in their life (Leszcz, et al., 1985).

Kohut's contributions have also deepened appreciation for the need for therapists to maintain an empathic-introspective stance, attending to the subjective reality of the patient as well as the objective realities. The loss of certain relationships, functions, and talents, needs to be understood in terms of what the patient derived from them. Subjectively this may be quite different from what an objective evaluation would suggest.

The elderly are vulnerable to narcissistic assaults both internally and externally as they age (Cath, 1976; Berezin, 1977; Meissner, 1977; Kernberg, 1977; Lazarus, 1980). This refers to the gradual or sudden loss of one's sense of potency, power, and specialness through illness, forced retirement, and declining health and cognition (the elements of the grandiose self), and the gradual or sudden loss of those idealized objects, such as spouses, friends, colleagues, and affiliations that offered a sense of security and protection. Such losses are even more grievous for the elderly, because the chance for restoration and substitution diminishes with aging. The greater the narcissistic caste to one's adult life, the greater the difficulty aging's decline will bring; the greater the forced change in self-concept, the greater the struggle for self-acceptance will be.

In addition to the primary impact of later life assaults on the sense of self, major problems arise from the secondary defensive elaborations which are aimed at maintaining and protecting the remaining fragile sense of self. Regression, somatization, denial, withdrawal, projection, and rageful devaluation aim at protecting the narcissistically injured person from further trauma. If he can force his caretakers to take care of him, deny his true loss, withdraw from situations that expose his limitations, project the defects as lying outside of him, and demean those who have failed him, his vulnerable sense of self-worth is protected. However, protection comes at extreme interpersonal cost, aggravating social isolation, which further exacerbates the loss of self-esteem. Reverberations can be experienced within the family and external community as well as within the environment of an institutional residence. As more withdrawal from the environment ensues, more investment in the self follows. This is often marked by increasing self-preoccupation and somatization, which also aggravate the interpersonal isolation.

The Role of Group Therapy

Social isolation is associated with depression in the elderly. Murphy (1982), suggested that the absence of a confiding relationship distinguished elderly depressives from normal elderly. In addition, those depressed elderly who do respond well to active biological treatment in hospital, often stop follow-up, and remain isolated and chronically dysphoric after discharge (Sadavoy and Reiman-Sheldon, 1983). At a point when interpersonal connectedness is most critical, it can be least available—both for objective reasons, such as the increasing rate of widowhood (70 percent at age 75) and widowerhood (25 percent at age 75) (Klerman, 1983), and for the subjective psychological factors described above.

For many of the elderly, group psychotherapy is an effective treatment approach, because it specifically addresses itself to relational and interpersonal concerns. Its efficacy has been reported in a variety of clinical settings with a variety of patients. Linden (1953, 1954, 1955) pioneered group treatment of institutionalized women aimed at reversing the clinical picture of "psychological senility"—regressed dependency, morbid self-absorption, and disengagement. He felt this characteristic presentation reflected the elderly's response to their repeated losses and their devaluation by society. Using a flexible approach, including education, humor, go-rounds, and interpretation, his group approach resulted in excellent outcomes as measured by discharge rates. Similar positive outcomes were reported by Silver (1950), Rechtshaffen, Atkinson, and Freedman (1953), Brudno and Seltzer (1968), and Katz (1976).

Others, such as Finkel and Fillmore (1971), Lazarus (1976), and Britnell and Mitchell (1981), described the therapeutic benefits of group psychotherapy in active care psychogeriatric units. Group therapy became an integrated part of the overall assessment and treatment, increasing staff's information about the patients, and providing patients with avenues for problem solving, information exchange, and provision of motivation and hope. In addition, group psychotherapy has been used effectively in retirement homes (Berland and Poggi, 1979; Leszcz, Feigenbaum, Sadavoy, and Robinson, 1985) and in ambulatory settings (Lieberman and Gaurash, 1979; Levine and Poston, 1980). In their study, Lieberman and Gaurash documented positive outcomes from participation in a weekly, nine-month, structured activity and interactional group. Participants showed a reduction in symptoms of anxiety, depression, and obsessions, enhanced self-esteem and communication skills, and an increased use of the present, instead of the past, to bolster their self-image.

Central to all of these approaches was the therapists' awareness of the risk of overestimating the presence of irreversible, organic impairment, while ignoring the functional, reversible components. Coupled with age biases or ageism (Butler, 1975) and a lack of emphasis in psychiatric training on geriatric issues (Ford and Sbordone, 1980), numerous myths have arisen about the inflexibility of the elderly, their unresponsiveness to intervention, and the futility of psychotherapeutic efforts. While it may be understandable that the patients may underestimate their capacities, when "helpers" collude, the synergy of therapist pessimism and patient discouragement can make treatment impossible. In comparison to treatment with younger patients, both in individual therapy and group therapy, modifications in technique and approach may be necessary, but therapy is viable and effective. A variety of different group approaches have been described in the literature, encompassing a broad range of modalities and patient cognitive capacity (Kubie and Landau, 1953; Klein, LeShan, and Furman, 1965).

Clinical Considerations

Three discrete group experiences contributed to the clinical material described in this chapter: an ongoing weekly group for depressed men living in a home for the aged (see Leszcz, Feigenbaum, Sadavoy and Robinson, 1985) a group on an active care psychogeriatric unit that meets three times weekly, and an ambulatory, posthospitalization group composed largely of patients being followed after discharge. Depending on the patient's clinical status, group therapy was a major modality of treatment, or adjunctive to biological, individual, or family therapies. Despite the different settings, certain fundamental principles of treatment overlap.

A central and organizing principle in the conduct of group psychotherapy with elderly patients, is the therapist's responsibility in safeguarding both the psychological integrity of the individuals, and the functional integrity of the group. In addition, the group leadership must be active, supportive, and flexible, to ensure that the group will be valued by its members as enhancing self-esteem and providing a genuine opportunity for interpersonal engagement. Certain technical modifications facilitate these developments. These include fostering group cohesion through increased levels of activity, focusing on integrative operations, combining here and now approaches with reminiscing, empathically confronting projective defenses, and negotiating certain transference–countertransference vicissitudes. Each of these modifications will be explained more fully.

Group cohesion in any setting and with all patients is the single most important group therapeutic mechanism, setting the stage for the utilization of all other group therapeutic factors. In the absence of group cohesion, demoralization and disengagement ensue, and groups usually dissolve. This is especially true with the elderly, whose own sense of despair and futility can be easily projected onto, and accepted by, their peers. The elderly can be as prejudiced about the elderly as the young are, further depleting their available object world. Several group members reported later in treatment, that they were surprised to see that other members of the group were not senile or crazy. Despite substantial feelings of loneliness, they had never greeted each other in the hallway before because they each assumed that they would not be recognized or recalled in the future. Similarly, a frequent initial response to the recommendation of group therapy was, "What would you want with me? What good are a bunch of old, useless people to anybody?" Their one-dimensional view of themselves and their immediate peers as decrepit, often became the first hurdle to overcome. The therapist could often reduce initial resistance by adopting a stance of focusing empathically on the patient's discouragement and the self-protective function of their withdrawal. Although gratuitous encouragement would be experienced as trivializing, realistic therapeutic hopefulness on the other hand need not be concealed.

The group leader must assume the responsibility for actively leading the group, making it a safe, self-esteem supporting milieu. The group cannot be allowed to be a failure-experience for any member and the leader needs to acknowledge each member's exquisite sensitivity to being trivialized or ignored. The leader's activity, support, and invitations to talk and to give and take feedback, set the stage for an interactive group and foster group cohesion. His activating and translating tasks may at times require him to repeat certain patients' statements or get copatients to push each other to talk louder. Go-rounds, and structured exercises such as describing to the group an important past event or present feeling; exercises aimed at increasing empathic awareness of each other by speculating on what other members of the group felt and then checking this out; as well as learning to ask one another personal questions, all serve to maintain an interactive group. At times the leader may need to clarify patient comments in order to safeguard patients from ostracism or scapegoating. It is imperative as well that each person feel that his contributions are valued and perceived to be sensible. The therapist may need to aid this process in those patients in whom anxiety and mild cognitive impairment interfere with lucid expression. Generally, for such patients, giving them more time and clarification results in them becoming more lucid. Conversely, there are times when the therapist and the group may need to confront the defensive purpose of obfuscation.

> An 82-year-old man, Mr. S., partially recovered from a CVA, with some residual dysarthria, attacked the slowness of articulation of another group member, Mr. D., an 88-year-old man. After making hand signs first, implying that Mr. D. was senile, he verbalized, "He's finished, let's forget him." When it was pointed out to Mr. S. that he was writing off a member of the group and assuming he was a lost cause, merely because he spoke slowly (an intervention Mr. D. acknowledged with appreciation), Mr. S. became sad and apologetic. He went on to recount his own frustration in talking, which precluded his participation in many of his former clubs, "Now I'm nothing"; to which Mr. G. warmly responded, "You are a man like we all are—talk—we're listening to you". This led to further elaboration of his difficulties in adapting following his CVA. At the end of that meeting, Mr. S. thanked every man in the group and then proceeded to shake hands with each member of the group and the therapists, reflecting a warm, genuine sense of acceptance.

Devaluation and projection of negative parts of the self—like Mr. S.'s dysarthria—are frequent occurrences in the maladaptive efforts of self-esteem maintenance. In this case, empathic confrontation of this projection, promoted the beginning of some grief work and also diminished the interpersonal consequences of Mr. S.'s continued projection.

An effective way to stimulate interpersonal engagement is through the establishment of an interactive, here and now orientation in the group (Yalom, 1975). A here and now focus is not to be confused with a confrontational approach (Yalom, 1983). In fact, it can be highly supportive and affirming, especially when the therapist, through his empathic understanding of the internal object world of the individual patients in the group, is aware of what requires support. A here and now focus means that all patients are close to the action in the group at all times. Patient communications are shaped to be centripetal, not centrifugal. Patients may need encouragement to address each other, for example, by discouraging the use of pronouns like "he" and "she" and by insisting on face-to-face contact. Healthy interactions can be reinforced by the positive statements of the therapist. This breeds group cohesion (Liberman, 1971).

The encouragement of appropriate life review within the group is an additional component to the here and now approach. As described by Butler (1963, 1974) life review is a normal developmental process of reminiscing and reintegrating the past. It serves adaptive functions for the individual by bolstering self-esteem through the recollection of past successes. This may be of particular value when the future looks discouraging or bleak. In the context of each life review, it is essential to recognize the real importance to each individual, of the details of his life review, despite its occasional rambling quality.

When life review is done in the context of the group, several other benefits arise. The life reviewer takes on additional dimensions within the group and group members come to know him in more depth. As well, the group is able to correct patient distortions and help him organize the life review. Furthermore, the life review can be brought back into the here and now of the group by asking the reviewer and the group to describe how they felt sharing and hearing the life review. This also minimizes the risk to the individual of an excessive preoccupation with the past at the expense of the present.

This process may be most valuable with beginning groups (Lesser, Lazarus, Frankel, and Havasy, 1981) at a time when concerns about self-acceptance and acceptance by others may be greatest. In addition, at the beginning of groups, other group members require more information about each member. The life review may also be valuable at times of regression within the group, when it seems too difficult for group members to maintain a sense of self-integration in the face of ongoing assaults and losses. An introductory question like, "You seem to be feeling really helpless right now, can you tell the group about a time when you felt differently?" often can be enough to elicit reminiscence. In those instances, the life review is integrative to the individual and consequently, through the here and now focus of the group, it is integrative to the group as a whole. "The cathexis of the memories of old pleasures, that is the reworking of old gratifications as if they were an old movie to be played over and over again" (Modell, 1977, p. 49), is a comment which describes the nature and significance of highly valued and sustaining memories.

Not uncommonly, elderly group patients are highly sensitive to any sign that the group is not important to the therapists. Hence, as with inpatient groups and groups with vulnerable, fragile patients (Yalom, 1983; Leszcz, Yalom, and Norden, 1985), the group must be conducted at an inviolate time, in an inviolate locale, with reliable and predictable leadership and free from inadvertent institutional devaluation and competitiveness.

Periods of demoralization and discouragement fluctuate and relate to specific environmental and psychological stresses. As such, they are responsive to psychotherapeutic intervention and are reversible.

In the last inpatient group meeting prior to the Jewish New Year, the group was highly resistant and regressed. Two of the more verbal group members had been recently discharged from the hospital. Yet, neither the discharges nor the impending holiday were acknowledged. Instead, the group was self-devaluing, helpless, and hopeless. Patients were somatically preoccupied and their only interactions seemed to focus on who was in greater distress. The therapists commented on the depression within the group and asked if it might be connected to the unmentioned events. Patients responded to encouragement to describe their reactions to the imminent holiday and the state of the present group. This led to the group members questioning each other about previous holiday celebrations, recalling more gratifying holiday and family times, as well as questioning the therapist about his current plans. The therapist responded to detailed and increasingly enthusiastic questioning, transparently. The process became so lively that at one point one patient told another, "Stop asking so many questions so that the doctor can answer the first ones."

The group's regression was encompassed by connecting the current state of demoralization to intercurrent stresses. It is essential to view these states as reactive and not as fixed and inevitable consequences of aging. This intervention promoted desomatization of their affect and a return to verbalization and interaction. The therapist's transparency served to further vitalize the group as his disclosures deepened their engagement in the here and now. Therapist transparency should always be in the service of the group and the therapist must be cautious in the presence of patients' curiosity and idealization, to monitor his narcissism, and to react appropriately, neither exhibiting himself for his own needs, nor withdrawing from the transferential demands in inhibition.

A well-functioning group provides valuable and needed narcissistic supplies to its members, through its mirroring and affirming of members' strengths, and its empathic awareness of members' weaknesses. The value of group therapy arises not only from the provision of a relational matrix to work through losses and conflict, but also, from the group providing restitution for lost narcissistic supplies. It may serve essential self-object functions (Schwartzman, 1984). As stated elsewhere (Leszcz, Feigenbaum, Sadavoy and Robinson, 1985):

> Those injuries of aging that attack at the level of one's grandiosity, power and potency, can be compensated for by the group's positive mirroring, valuation and empathic connection with others who share the same concerns. Similarly, the loss of objects of idealization, such as spouses and affiliative institutions, can, in part be compensated for by feelings of cohesion, acceptance, presence of the group, and the relationships with the therapists who are perceived to be caring, empathic, powerful and, most importantly, respectful [p. 188–189].

The importance of creating a court of one's peers in which every member counts, cannot be overestimated. The availability of peers who can respond genuinely, "I know what you mean and how you feel," to a person who experiences his world as not wanting to know him at all, can be reparative. Accordingly, ruptures in the relationship of the individual to the group need to be addressed quickly.

Mr. I, a 78-year-old concentration camp survivor, was admitted as an inpatient because of acute confusion and depression. Later he began a group meeting enraged at Mrs. Y., a 74-year-old woman in the group whom he had previously befriended. She had been admitted because of behavioral problems following a CVA that left her aphasic and hemiplegic. Despite her difficulty in talking, she was encouraged to participate in the psychotherapy groups as she was able to comprehend quite well. Mr. I. had spent much energy trying to assist Mrs. Y. on the ward. However, despite his help, she made little progress. His attack was savage and unexpected. Turning to the therapist he said, "Next thing you'll be bringing us bodies from the cemetery to this group—no one gets better here." This was in stark contrast to previous meetings in which he was highly enthusiastic and encouraging. One reaction might have been to be outraged at his attack on the group members and to confront his negativism, which was obviously upsetting the other patients in the group. Instead, the therapist pointed out to Mr. I. that he seemed really angry and discouraged, in contrast to previous meetings—why was that? He responded immediately, "Because they are not getting better!" With identification of the importance to him of the group members getting better, he softened considerably and sadly stated, "Of course, what else is there? I've got to help people get better!" This led to his recalling a recurring dream dating back to the war, in which he dreamt that he was a doctor trying to look after his wife and children but always failing to save them. He then became apologetic to the group and the group's response changed dramatically, from anger at him to compassion, as it tried to comfort him through his obvious pain.

Clearly, Mr. I.'s survivor guilt fueled a reparative wish which had been thwarted by Mrs. Y. The rage that ensued was in response to this disappointment and frustration. Not helping others successfully, infuriated him, and he attacked them for robbing him of a chance to repair them and appease his guilt. His violent overreaction to an objectively small event was an important sign that an old wound was being touched. Addressing this subjective reality led to a period of greater integration for Mr. I. and some grieving over his past losses. Furthermore, once the subjective reality had been addressed, he himself was able to focus on the objective reality and apologize to the group for his outburst.

Attending to the subjective reality of the patient is necessary in order to maintain an empathic connection with those patients whose narcissistic entitlement and defensiveness make them otherwise unpalatable, and evocative of harmful countertransferential reactions. Group therapy is a useful treatment modality for younger patients with narcissistic character disorders (Horwitz, 1980), because of the dilution of intense transference and countertransference reactions and the opportunity within the group for the patient to feel supported by some group members while being confronted simultaneously by others. Gains in interpersonal learning also follow, as members become more aware of how they come across to others, initially within the group, and then more broadly.

Mrs. Z, a 79-year-old depressed widow, presented as the kind of entitled, haughty, and demeaning person who immediately engenders a negative response amongst staff and patients alike. Patients found her greedy and entitled, and staff, demanding and unappreciative. This picture was superimposed upon that of a woman who had been depressed and isolated for many years and who had a hostile relationship with her only son whom she continually devalued for not giving her enough. The manner in which she demeaned and devalued that which she could not have was a way of making it less important to her. As a consequence it made it impossible for her to derive any future benefit from that which she had devalued. This lessened her sadness but augmented her loneliness.

In a group that began with people talking about birthdays and their ages, one member in the group fumbled for another member's name. Mrs. Z. interjected, saying that she believed that no one in the group knew her name. A few people responded affirmatively. When the therapist asked her if she knew anybody else's name herself, she said "No," which led to her saying she was concerned only with what went on inside of her and had no interest in other people. People's problems would only weigh her down and she had enough of her own. She then went on to list a litany of her losses and difficulties, starting with the death of her mother in her childhood and the more recent death of her daughter-in-law seven years earlier. She yelled, "Why did God do this to me, why did he take my daughter-in-law away from me?" An unchecked countertransferential response would have been to focus on her seeming egocentricism and how she focused on her loss exclusively, ignoring her son's loss. However, in this instance, recognizing this woman's narcissistic disturbance, a line of questioning was pursued which led to elaboration of the fact that this daughter-in-law had lived with Mrs. Z. for seven years and had clearly served as a self-sustaining object—someone gratifying and protective, whom Mrs. Z. mothered and, in an introjective way, thereby became mothered herself. As she began to cry about this loss, the other group members supported her need to ventilate and to cry. That they were, in fact, willing to hear and listen to her, surprised and shocked her. Strikingly, however, once this empathic connection was made she was able to give much more to other members of the group, offering assistance to one man to walk down the hallway, and later, complimenting one of the group therapists.

This was the first of many such "bits" of working through. The group's ability to empathize with how frightened and sad Mrs. Z. was feeling—so unrecognized and without her valuable supports—seemed to be the essential ingredient. She gradually became less angry, more sad, and more accessible to copatients. As her anger diminished, she began to get more in touch with her sadness and began to do some grief work while an inpatient. Over the next few weeks she became a valuable and valuing member of the group, utilizing her increased interpersonal awareness to address some of her unfair attacks on her son. A humorous and revealing highlight of her treatment was finally being able to ask her, in the hallway, how she was, and be told, "Fine—how are you?" instead of her familiar refrain, "You could die here, and no one would come!" Ultimately, she was able to leave hospital successfully.

The supportive, affirming group also provides an opportunity for working through and grieving specific narcissistic losses. As Grunes has already noted in chapter 2, "The Aged in Psychotherapy," a young therapist has realistic limits on his capacity to empathize with someone raised in a different culture and 40 years older. Certain comments coming from such a therapist might feel patronizing but not so when they come from a peer. For example, when a 93-year-old man says to a 77-year-old depressed comember in the group, "I know how you feel. I was depressed like you before—I even tried to kill myself once, but don't give up. You have lots to live for, like your family and grandchildren", the younger man listens in a very appreciative, serious way. The immense value of peer support, and affirmation is further illustrated by the following case example.

Mrs. H., a 67-year-old woman, had suffered a CVA four years prior to admission. During the interim she had been living in a nursing home. She had made a partial recovery and was now chiefly impaired by a right-sided hemiparesis. She was able to use her right leg slightly. She was admitted to the hospital because of increasing withdrawal in the home. She had developed a phobic aversion to walking with a tripod cane, and preferred to sit in her wheelchair or to lie on her bed. She spoke in the meeting, "It's crazy, because I want to walk, but as soon as I start to walk all I want is to get back to my wheelchair." A copatient suggested she was not crazy, just ambivalent, "Lots of times we want to do two opposite things at the same time." The therapist asked the group if they could speculate on Mrs. H.'s ambivalence? Why would she want to walk? Why would she not want to? The first question was easily answered. Everyone responded appropriately that she would want to walk because it allows her to get around and it would give her a sense of freedom. Less clear was why she would avoid walking. Mrs. H. responded, motioning with her hand like a bird soaring, "I'm not used to this—I used to run a store all by myself you know, I want to be unrestricted. I want to walk free without this cane. I almost fell recently. I must be a real sight, like some crazy person." That near fall was a clear precipitant and one of the copatients commented, "You're not just afraid of falling and hurting yourself—you're afraid of being embarrassed—of failing." She agreed. Fearing humiliation she had stopped trying, to which the group responded with admiration for her efforts to date. Additionally, it reflected back to her that she didn't look as awkward as she thought. The impact which this group session had on Mrs. H. was unclear until the next morning, when she walked into the group room with her tripod cane and, with some cajoling, walked around in the group room, much to her own and the group's delight. She maintained this improvement, and was soon discharged back to the nursing home.

Coming to grips with real losses and decreased mastery are ongoing struggles for many of the elderly, particularly those who become depressed following a CVA. In the foregoing example, the group became a forum for Mrs. H. to explore the reality of her deficit, as well as to distinguish her organic impairment from her functional one. The benefit this had for her was apparent. Less apparent but equally significant was the group's increased sense of self-worth and effectiveness in being so obviously helpful to the patient.

The help-rejecting complainer poses particular challenges to the group and group therapist. She demands attention in a way that is impossible to ignore, and then proceeds to dismiss every effort at helping her, resulting quickly in group frustration and anger. The therapist may be required to intervene in order to protect the patient from committing "social suicide" by her unrelenting rejection of the group's therapeutic efforts. At the same time, it is essential to protect the group from the guilt that would follow if it extruded the help-rejecter. This is a particularly likely outcome as such a patient becomes an easy target for other patients' projections of their own irreparable difficulties. Stone and Whitman (1977) recommend that the therapist provide an empathic, nondepreciatory recognition of the basic wishes inherent in the help-rejecting complainer. This allows the patient's fundamental narcissistic need to be at the center of the group to be acknowledged, while simultaneously clarifying the patient's maladaptive efforts at getting hostile attention. The therapist can prescribe certain activities in the group for such a patient and proscribe others.

Mrs. W., a 74-year-old widow admitted to the hospital because of depression related to a traumatic brachial plexus injury, infuriated her group with her incessant displays of distress and refusal to find merit in any intervention. It was impossible to ignore her because of her histrionic falling over, even while seated and her exhibitionistic display of her injured arm. She seemed intent on demanding the group's attention and simultaneously demonstrating how incompetent all of the group was in helping her. She was finally approached by the therapist in the group in the following fashion: "It's obvious you feel nothing the group can do for you would help. That's unfortunate, but we hope, though, that'll change. In the meanwhile, you can be of great help to the other group members by your questioning of them and by giving them feedback. The group would like you to stay very much and do that, but only if you can stop talking about yourself because that doesn't seem to be helping you at all." Mrs. W. accepted this offer and although she often needed to be reminded of this agreement, her help-rejecting behavior diminished substantially.

Concerns about death and disability are obviously frequent in this patient population. In fact, the ongoing group of men in the home for the aged has had five deaths in three years. The therapists anticipated that this would be a difficult therapy issue, with their primary fear being that patients' anxieties would be raised counterproductively in response to a discussion of these issues. Surprisingly, however, the group members met the death of peers with sadness but not preoccupation. It was striking that more depressive reactions resulted from the death of the wife of a comember. The men all appeared to be less frightened about dying than about being abandoned. Hence, the ongoing sense of connection within the group, the presence of the group, and the opportunity to talk about death seemed to detoxify death's fearsome quality and diminish apprehension about abandonment. This echoes the experience with groups of cancer patients (Spiegel, Bloom, and Yalom, 1981). As Krystal notes in chapter 5, "The Impact of Massive Psychic Trauma and the Capacity to Grieve Effectively," the presence of a supportive group during a time of crisis and loss is a fundamental element in coping with traumatic events.

Upon being notified of the death of Mr. S., a comember, the initial reaction in the group was disbelief. A patient wondered if it was the same Mr. S. whom he had known for so long, who sat in "this very chair" in the group, pointing to his traditional spot. There was much sadness, needless to say, but the way in which the group worked through the sadness was striking. Unlike previous such unfortunate events, the group was quite willing to talk about its reactions without sign of overstimulation. In fact, in this instance the men were very verbal, and they led the discussion themselves. Mr. B., an 80-year-old isolated widower, stated that he was envious of Mr. S. because "a man who dies no longer has problems to deal with." He was nonetheless feeling very sad, and asked that "we all stand up to say Kaddish," the traditional Jewish prayer of mourning, because of his concern that the deceased did not have family to do that. All of the men stood up for a moment or two, including two who were not able to walk independently, while Mr. B. recited the Kaddish. He went on to describe how a friend of his once told him that the luckiest person in this world is an orphan because he never loses anybody again and never has to grieve. Rather than being met with agreement, this issue was contested quite vehemently by other members of the group, who said that they would much rather have a chance at friendship and lose it, or have a chance of a family and lose it, than never experience it. One of the quieter men in the group echoed this response by agreeing, "Absolutely." As a result of this confrontation with Mr. B., the group, including Mr. B., grew closer together through its mourning and began to talk in more accepting terms of Mr. S.'s inevitable death. He was, after all, a man in his mideighties, they said. They also spoke of the merit of friendship and companionship, not as an antidote to death, but as something that reduces fear and loneliness. Relationships make the threat of death seem, at the same time, both less appealing and less ominous.

In this instance, the men responded to the loss of a peer by drawing closer together, lauding the merit of friendship and companionship. This is a significant shift away from withdrawal and despair. The value of their interpersonal connection and the group's cohesion, despite this obvious group loss, was evident. At other times, following news of such events within the home, the men regularly and spontaneously shared the life review process. Frequent memories focused on their youthful heroics and mastery of dangerous situations. This dynamic was never interpreted, despite this transparency, because of the sense of self-soothing calm associated with this mastery through memory. Insight must never be added to injury (Weinberg, 1976).

In addition to what the therapist does with the group is the important issue of what the group does with the therapist. Countertransferential reactions in work with the elderly are complex phenomena. Authors have commented on multiple sources of therapist difficulty, including the impact of societal prejudices about aging (Butler, 1975) and the limitations in knowledge of the elderly and limitations in the therapist's empathic capacity (Lewis and Johansen, 1982). As well, narcissistic issues within the therapist may be aroused by being confronted with his own limitations in reversing irreversible decline (Levin, 1977) and facing the finiteness of all life. In addition, of course, a variety of idiosyncratic countertransferential reactions may occur, limited only by the intrapsychic world of the therapist.

Two types of countertransferential difficulties arising in group therapy require special notation. These are the therapist's collusion with the patients' demoralization, and the therapist's reaction to the patient's idealization. Collusion gains expression both subtly and blatantly. Subtle manifestations may include a therapist's lack of regard for punctuality or other similar "statements" reflecting unspoken or unconscious biases that the elderly require or deserve less treatment than the young. More blatantly, the therapist may find himself agreeing with patients' expressions of futility, thereby losing his therapeutic perspective. It is imperative, at that moment for the therapist to explore internally the nature of the projections to which he may be responding. Depression, discouragement, and demoralization are not "givens" of old age—rather they are affective states triggered by stresses, losses, and insults. If this collusion cannot be undercut, the therapist's despair or withdrawal will augment the narcissistic injuries already experienced by the group, which have, in all likelihood, induced the therapist's initial sense of despair. Despair in the group can have a cascading effect which can seriously damage the group's integrity.

A different kind of difficulty for the therapist may arise when he finds himself the object of patient idealization. This may arouse therapist anxiety, as his own narcissism gets overstimulated in the face of being unrealistically overvalued. This may arise in response to patients' transferential needs to be dependent upon a powerful and idealized caretaker. These transferential demands are best handled with equanimity by the therapist, neither rebuffed prematurely nor exploited for his own narcissistic needs. This is easier to ensure if the therapist can recognize the idealization as emanating from the needs of the patient, reflecting a wish to be protected and soothed, seeking protection, perhaps, from a threat of death through a magical rescuer (Yalom, 1980; Van der Kolk, 1983). Furthermore, if the idealizing transference promotes patient well-being—if it is sustaining and invigorating and not infantilizing—it is easier to allow it, while keeping one's own narcissism in balance.

Cotherapy may aid in the maintenance of a proper therapeutic perspective amidst the patients' alternating projections of specialness and devaluation. As well, the intercurrent successes and frustrations can be better modulated by a cotherapy team. There are significant stresses on the therapist who works with the elderly, because of the inherent risks of attrition through illness and death. Patient illness and death will need to be mourned by the therapists, as well as the patients, and the peer support of cotherapy may be essential in doing this. As well, male–female cotherapy models may also stimulate a greater wish for engagement amongst the patients (Linden, 1954). Finally, having more than one therapist present ensures that the group will be able to meet despite the therapists' vacations. Continuity is essential to the maintenance of group cohesion.

An outgrowth of the efficacy of the group psychotherapy practiced on the inpatient unit, has been the development of an aftercare group. Patients discharged into the community return one afternoon a week for an informal gathering with other patients and individual medication assessment, followed by a psychotherapy group. A number of spouses of patients have also started attending. Attendance is quite regular, and some patients who were convinced of their intractability while inpatients now pride themselves on their acceptance and presence in this aftercare group. As much as any other measure of effectiveness, the creation and maintenance of a progroup culture amongst these initially resistant patients underscores the value of group psychotherapy approaches with the elderly.

Conclusion

Losses of relationships, functions, and health as a result of the aging processes can impair the ability of some elderly individuals to manage their later years with a sense of calm and ego integrity. Instead, these losses result in diminishment in the sense of self and consequent feelings of depression, futility, and withdrawal. Group psychotherapy is well suited to address these issues, because of its capacity to offer an opportunity for genuine relatedness in a time otherwise depleted of object relationships. As such, for many group members the group may need to be available in an ongoing way, for as long as its members can utilize it. In the face of the increasing likelihood of further loss and decline, this ongoing group presence and affiliation, either in a home or as part of an aftercare program, serves invaluable self-cohesing and integrative functions for its individual members through the restitution of lost narcissistic supplies. Group psychotherapy with the elderly requires modifications in the technique and approach of the leader, in comparison to group therapy with younger patients. Effectiveness is reflected in greater person-to-person engagement and connectedness; diminished morbid self-absorption and an increased capacity to deal with affects verbally; improved participation in home and community activities and greater involvement with the present world in general.*

References

Berezin, M. A. (1977), Normal psychology of the aging process, Revisited—II: The fate of narcissism in old age: Clinical case reports. *J. Geriat. Psychiat.*, 10:9–26.

Berland, D. I., & Poggi, R. (1979), Expressive group psychotherapy with the aging. *Internat. J. Group Psychother.*, 29:87–108.

Breslau, L. D., & Haug, M. R. (1983), *Depression and Aging*. New York: Springer.

Britnell, J. C., & Mitchell, K. E. (1981), Inpatient group psychotherapy for the elderly. *J. Psychosocial Nursing and Mental Health Services*, 19:19–24.

Brudno, J. J., & Seltzer, H. (1968), Resocialization therapy through group process with senile patients in a geriatric hospital. *Gerontol.*, 8:211–214.

*Dr. Leszcz acknowledges with gratitude the cotherapists with whom he has worked: Ms. Elaine Feigenbaum, Mrs. Masha Posen, and Dr. Margaret Dean.

Butler, R. N. (1963), The life review: An interpretation of reminiscence in the aged. *Psychiatry*, 26:65–76.

———— (1974), Successful aging and the role of the life review. *J. Amer. Geriat. Soc.*, 22:529–535.

———— (1975), Psychiatry and the elderly: An overview. *Amer. J. Psychiat.*, 132:893–900.

Cath, S. H. (1976), A testing of faith in self and object constancy. *J. Geriat. Psychiat.*, 9:19–40.

Erikson, E. H. (1950), *Childhood and Society*, 2nd Ed. New York: W. W. Norton, pp. 247–274, 1963.

Finkel, S., & Fillmore, W. (1971), Experiences with an older adult group at a private psychiatric hospital. *J. Geriat. Psychiat.*, 4:188–199.

Ford, C. V., & Sbordone, R. T. (1980), Attitudes of psychiatrists toward elderly patients. *Amer. J. Psychiat.*, 137:571–575.

Freud, S. (1905), On psychotherapy. In: *Collected Papers*, 1:249–263. London: Hogarth Press, 1924.

———— (1914), On narcissism: An Introduction. *Standard Edition*, 14:69–102. London: Hogarth Press, 1957.

Horwitz, L. (1980), Group psychotherapy for borderline and narcissistic patients. *Bull Menninger Clin.*, 44:181–200.

Katz, M. M. (1976), Behavioral change in the chronicity pattern of dementia in the institutional geriatric resident. *J. Amer. Geriat. Soc.*, 24:522–528.

Kernberg, O. (1977), Normal psychology of the aging process, Revisited—II: Discussion. *J. Geriat. Psychiat.*, 10:27–45.

Klein, W. M., LeShan, E. J., & Furman, S. S. (1965), *Promoting Mental Health of Older People Through Group Methods*. New York: Mental Health Materials Center, Inc.

Klerman, G. L. (1983), Problems in the definition and diagnosis of depression in the elderly. In: *Depression and Aging*, ed. L. D. Breslau & M. R. Haig. New York: Springer, pp. 3-19.

Kohut, H. (1977), *The Restoration of the Self*. New York: International Universities Press.

———— Wolf, E. (1978), The disorders of the self and their treatment: An outline. *Internat. J. Psycho-Anal.*, 59:413–425.

Kubie, S. M., & Landau, G. (1953), *Group work with Aged*. New York: International Universities Press.

Lazarus, L. W. (1976), A program for the elderly at a private psychiatric hospital. *Gerontol.*, 16:125–131.

———— (1980), Self psychology and psychotherapy with the elderly: Theory and practice. *J. Geriat. Psychiat.*, 13:69–88.

Leszcz, M., Feigenbaum, E., Sadavoy, J., & Robinson, A. (1985), A men's group: Psychotherapy of elderly men. *Internat. J. Group Psychother.*, 35:177–196.

———— Yalom, I. D., & Norden, M. (1985), Inpatient group psychotherapy: Patients' perceptions. *Internat. J. Group Psychother.*, 35:411–433.

Lesser, J., Lazarus, L. W., Frankel, R., & Havasy, S. (1981), Reminiscence group therapy with psychotic geriatric inpatients. *Gerontol.*, 21:291–296.

Levin, S. (1977), Normal psychotherapy of the aging process, Revisited—II: Introduction. *J. Geriat. Psychiat.*, 10:3–8.

Levine, B. E., & Poston, M. (1980), A modified group treatment for elderly narcissistic patients. *Internat. J. Group Psychother.*, 30:153–167.

Lewis, J. M., & Johanson, K. M. (1982), Resistances to psychotherapy with the elderly. *Amer. J. Psychother.*, 36:497–504.

Liberman, R. (1971), Reinforcement of cohesiveness in group therapy. *Arch. Gen. Psychiat.*, 25:168–177.

Lieberman, M. A., & Gaurash, N. (1979), Evaluating the effects of group changes on the elderly. *Internat. J. Group Psychother.*, 29:283–304.

Linden, M. E. (1953), Group psychotherapy with institutionalized senile women: Study in gerontologic human relations. *Internat. J. Group Psychother.*, 3:150–170.

——— (1954), The significance of dual leadership in gerontologic group psychotherapy: Studies in gerontologic human relations III. *Internat. J. Group Psychother.*, 4:262–273.

——— (1955), Transference in gerontologic group psychotherapy: Studies in gerontologic human relations IV. *Internat. J. Group Psychother.*, 5:61–69.

Meissner, W. W. (1976), Normal psychology of the aging process, Revisited—I: Discussion. *J. Geriat. Psychiat.*, 9:151–159.

——— (1977), Normal psychology of the aging process, Revisited—II: Discussion. *J. Geriat. Psychiat.*, 10:61–70.

Modell, A. M. (1977), Normal psychology of the aging process, Revisited—II: Discussion. *J. Geriat. Psychiat.*, 10:47–52.

Mohl, P. C., & Burstein, A. G. (1982), The application of Kohutian self psychology to consultation-liaison psychiatry. *Gen. Hosp. Psychiat.*, 4:113–119.

Murphy, E. (1982), Social origins of depression in old age. *Brit. J. Psychiat.*, 141:135–142.

Orenstein, A. (1981), Self-psychology in childhood: Developmental and clinical considerations. In: *Psychiat. Clin. of N. Amer.*, 4:435–453.

Rechtshaffen, A., Atkinson, S., & Freedman, J. G. (1953), An intensive treatment program for state hospital geriatric patients. *Geriatrics*, 9:28–34.

Sadavoy, J., & Reiman-Sheldon, E. (1983), General hospital geriatric psychiatric treatment: A follow-up study. *J. Amer. Ger. Soc.*, 31:200–205.

Scheidlinger, S. (1966), The concept of empathy in group psychotherapy. *Internat. J. Group Psychother.*, 16:413–424.

Schwartzman, G. (1984), The use of the group as selfobject. *Internat. J. Group Psychother.*, 34:229–242.

Silver, A. (1950), Group psychotherapy with senile psychotic patients. *Geriatrics*, 5:147–150.

Spiegel, D., Bloom, J. R., & Yalom, I. D. (1981), Group support for patients with metastatic cancer. *Arch. Gen. Psychiat.*, 38:527–533.

Stone, W. N., & Whitman, R. M. (1977), Contributions of the psychology of the self to group process and group therapy. *Internat. J. Group Psychother.*, 27:343–359.

Van der Kolk, B. (1983), The idealizing transference and group psychotherapy with elderly patients. *J. Geriat. Psychiat.*, 16:99–103.

Weinberg, J. (1976), On adding insight to injury. *Gerontol.*, 16:4–10.

Wolff, K. (1957), Group psychotherapy with geriatric patients in a mental hospital. *J. Amer. Geriat. Soc.*, 5:13–19.

——— (1962), Group psychotherapy with geriatric patients in a psychiatric hospital Six Year Study. *J. Amer. Geriat. Soc.*, 10:1077–1080.

——— (1967), Comparison of group and individual psychotherapy with geriatric patients. *Dis. of Nerv. System*, 28:384–386.

Yalom, I. D. (1975), *The Theory and Practice of Group Psychotherapy*. New York: Basic Books.
——— (1980), *Existential Psychotherapy*. New York: Basic Books.
——— (1983), *Inpatient Group Therapy*. New York: Basic Books.

NAME INDEX

Abraham, K., 18, 32
Adams, J. E., 135
Adler, G., 180
Akiskal, H. S., 161
Allerton, C. W., 148
Amory, C., 233-234
Andrulonis, P. A., 177
Archibald, H. C., 124
Atchley, R. C., 278
Atkinson, S., 330
Avorn, J., 61

Bartemeier, L. H., 116, 117
Bartko, J., 273
Bastianns, J., 124
Baum, S. K., 129
Baxley, R. L., 129
Becker, S. S., 139
Beebe, G. W., 124
Belluomini, J., 161
Berezin, M. A., 45-63, 47, 52, 62, 189, 201, 216, 327, 328
Berger, D. M., 309
Bergman, A., 178
Bergmann, M. V., 148
Berland, D. I., 330
Bibring, E., 49, 246, 257
Bibring, G. L., 235, 246, 247, 257
Bloom, J. R., 342
Bohnert, P. J., 82
Book, H. E., 183, 206, 225
Bostock, T., 139
Boyd, H., 114
Breslau, L., 56, 157-173, 159, 192, 201, 208, 326
Breuer, J., 31, 43
Brewin, R., 49
Bridge, T. P., 67, 86
Brill, N. W., 124

Brink, T. L., 82
Britnell, J. C., 330
Brodey, W. M., 160
Brody, E. M., 299
Brudno, J. J., 330
Buckley, P., 267
Buie, D. H., 180
Burnham, D. L., 176, 183
Butler, R. N., 41, 315, 330, 334, 344

Caplan, G., 112-114, 135
Carter, E. A., 323
Cassell, E. J., 301
Cath, S. H., 328
Cavenar, Jr., J. O., 154
Chamberlin, B. C., 135
Chatfield, D., 272
Cicero, 3, 14
Coble, P., 161
Coelho, G. V., 135
Cohen, B. M., 124
Cohen, G., 9
Cohen, N. A., 19, 20
Collins, G., 7
Conte, H. R., 267
Cooper, M. A., 124
Curtis, J., 267

Danieli, Y., 130, 145
Dann, S., 129
David, C., 124
Davis, K. L., 16
DeGrunchy, C., 265
deM'Uzan, M., 124
Deutsch, H., 176, 177
Dewind, E., 139

351

DeWitt, K. N., 266
Dorian, B., 183, 185, 197, 213, 217
Dorsey, J. M., 106
Drye, R. C., 176

Easser, B. R., 206
Eisdorfer, E. H., 67, 86
Eissler, K. R., 143-144, 145
Eitinger, L., 112
Engel, G. L., 99, 102
Erikson, E. H., 67, 102, 110, 178, 315, 326
Erikson, K. T., 115, 118, 139

Fairbairn, W. R. D., 178
Farber, I. J., 135
Feigenbaum, E., 325, 330, 331, 336
Fenichel, O., 33, 40
Fern, D. J., 52
Fillmore, W., 330
Finkel, S., 330
Fish, F., 67
Fleiss, J., 273
Ford, C. V., 330
Foster, G. F., 161
Framo, J. L., 313, 320
Frankel, R., 265, 334
Freedman, J. G., 330
Freud, A., 98, 108, 129
Freud, S., 31, 39, 49, 54, 55, 96, 132, 142, 176, 257
Fromm-Reichmann, F., 37
Frosch, J., 176, 177, 180
Frost, R., 150
Furman, S. S., 331
Furst, S., 98

Gaurash, N., 330
Giovacchini, P., 177
Gitelson, M., 205
Glass, A. J., 135
Glueck, B. C., 177
Goldfarb, A. I., 177, 215, 245, 265
Goodman, J. G., 317
Gralnick, A., 88
Greenberg, M., 114
Greenson, R. R., 210
Greenspan, S. T., 9
Griffin, B., 40

Grinker, Sr., R. R., 176, 177
Grotjahn, M., 265
Groves, L., 265-293, 268
Groves, J. E., 176, 177
Grunes, J., 31-44, 40, 42, 45, 53, 55-57, 58, 265, 339
Gunderson, J. G., 176
Gunderson, E. K., 112
Guntrip, H., 176, 178
Gussow, M., 324
Gutmann, D., 15, 35, 40, 41, 265, 278, 285, 286

Halsall, R. W., 301
Hamburg, D. A., 135
Hamilton, J., 183
Hartmann, H., 228
Haug, M. R., 326
Havasy-Galloway, S., 265, 334
Henderson, S., 139
Herbert, M. E., 86
Herink, R., 46
Hillman, R. G., 139
Hoch, P., 176, 177
Hoff, L. A., 245
Holmes, T. H., 112
Hoppe, K. D., 129-130, 143
Horowitz, M., 266, 267, 270
Horowitz, M. J., 114-115, 122, 131, 134, 135, 139
Horwitz, L., 338
Hughes, R., 48
Hussain, A. H., 139

Jacobson, S., 86
Jacques, E., 195
Jaffe, W. G., 104
Johanson, K. M., 344
Johnson, D. A., 151
Jung, C., 32, 44

Kahana, R. J., 45, 52, 53, 59-60, 233-263, 246, 247, 257, 259, 313
Karasu, T. B., 267
Karpf, R. J., 314
Katan, A., 107
Katz, M. M., 330
Kay, D. W. K., 67, 86
Keller, S. E., 16

Kelly, K., 159
Kernberg, O., 176, 177, 178, 180, 328
King, D., 161
Kjaer, G., 112
Klein, D. F., 177
Klein, H., 151
Klein, M., 69-71, 74
Klein, W. M., 331
Klerman, G. L., 329
Knight, P., 245
Knight, R. P., 176, 177
Kohut, H., 36, 38, 39, 176, 179, 278, 279, 280-281, 326-327, 328
Koranyi, E. R., 117
Kraepelin, E., 86
Krupnick, J. L., 115, 122
Krystal, H., 95-155, 96, 97, 99, 103, 105, 106, 107, 109, 110, 111, 113, 114, 115, 118, 120, 121, 122, 123, 124, 125, 126, 129, 131, 132, 133, 134, 135, 136, 138, 139, 140, 144, 147, 148, 179, 342
Kubie, L. S., 116
Kubie, S. M., 331
Kupfer, D. J., 161

Landau, G., 331
Lawlis, G. F., 272
Lazarus, L. W., 45, 53, 54, 201, 265-293, 268, 278, 328, 330, 334
Lemmi, H., 161
LeShan, E. J., 331
Lesser, J., 334
Leszcz, M., 325-349, 328, 330, 331, 335, 336
Levin, S., 59, 344
Levine, B. E., 330
Levine, M., 259
Levy, D. M., 152
Lewis, J. M., 344
Lewis, M. I., 315
Liberman, R., 334
Lieberman, M. A., 117, 330
Lifton, R. J., 98, 109, 111, 121, 128, 134
Lindemann, E., 152
Linden, M. E., 329, 345
Lister, E. D., 136
Long, D. M., 124
Lutkins, S. G., 111

Mackenzie, T. B., 176
Mahler, M. S., 178
Main, T. F., 176, 181, 183, 192
Malan, D. H., 266, 267, 269, 270
Maltsberger, J. T., 228
Marmar, C., 266
Martin, L. J., 265
Marty, P., 124
Masterson, J. R., 177
Meerlo, J. A., 195, 265
Meerloo, J. A. M., 292
Meissner, W. W., 328
Mende, W., 135
Menninger, K. A., 116
Meyer, M., 112
Meyerson, A. T., 16
Michels, R., 176
Miller, C., 124
Millward, J. W., 177
Minkowski, E., 109, 121
Mitchell, K. E., 330
Modell, A. M., 335
Moeller, T. P., 6
Mohl, P. C., 348
Moore, R. A., 106
Murphy, E., 329
Murray, H. A., 128, 129

McEwan, E., 173, 211, 295-324
McDougall, J., 124
McNiel, J. N., 89
McPartland, R. J., 161

Nagy, I., 295-298, 299-301, 316, 321, 323
Nemiah, J. C., 124
Neugarten, B., 34, 40
Newton, N., 265, 268
Niederland, W. G., 98, 119, 121, 122, 124, 136
Norden, M., 335
Norman, M., 295, 298
Novick, T., 159

Ornstein, A., 309, 327

Papousek, M., 99
Papousek, H., 99
Peak, D., 89
Pfeiffer, E., 265
Pine, F., 178

Plato, 26, 62
Ploeger, A., 135
Ploye, P. M., 183
Plutchik, R., 267
Poggi, R., 330
Polatin, P., 176, 177
Pollock, G. H., 3-29, 6, 9, 11, 12, 20, 25,
    45, 53, 57-59, 187, 216
Poston, M., 330

Rado, S., 100
Rahe, R. H., 112
Raskin, H., 105
Raskin, M. J., 16
Rechtschaffen, A., 266, 330
Rees, W. D., 111
Reiman-Sheldon, E., 329
Richter, C. P., 109
Ripeckyj, A., 265
Robinson, A., 325, 330, 331, 336
Romano, J., 116
Rosenbaum, R., 266
Roth, M., 67, 86

Sadavoy, J., 175-229, 183, 185, 197, 206,
    213, 217, 225, 325, 329, 330, 331, 336
Salzman, C., 48
Satir, V., 317
Sbordone, R. T., 330
Scheidlinger, S., 348
Schleifer, S. J., 16
Schmale, A. H., Jr., 99
Schmideberg, M., 177
Schur, M., 99
Schwartzman, G., 336
Seligman, M. E. P., 109, 111
Seltzer, H., 330
Shatan, C. F., 116, 134
Sheps, J., 177, 215
Shneidman, E. S., 128
Shrout, P., 273
Sifneos, P. E., 124, 126
Silberschatz, G., 267
Silver, A., 330
Silver, D., 176, 177, 178, 183, 200, 206,
    225
Singer, M. T., 176
Smith, J. A., 82
Smith, M., 112

Snyder, S. H., 120
Soloff, P. H., 177
Solomon, G., 134
Spark, G. M., 295-298, 299-301, 316, 321,
    323
Spiegel, D., 342
Spitz, R., 229
Stein, M., 16
Sterba, E., 129
Stern, A., 176
Stern, M. M., 97, 101, 109, 111, 120
Stone, W. N., 341
Stroebel, C. S., 177
Swanson, D. W., 82

Tanay, E., 123
Terr, L. C., 154
Tozman, S., 139
Tuddenham, K. D., 124
Tyhurst, J. S., 154

Ulrich, R. F., 161

Valenstein, A. F., 102
Van der Kolk, B., 114, 345
Venzlaff, U., 128
Verwoerdt, A., 67-93, 89, 91
Vogel, N. G., 177
Volkan, V., 180, 184

Walker, J. I., 154
Wallant, E. C., 128
Weinberg, J., 265, 343
Weiss, D. S., 266
Werble, B., 176
Wetmore, R. J., 140
Whitehorn, J. E., 116
Whitman, R. M., 341
Wild, K. V., 267
Wolf, E. S., 176, 278, 279, 280, 326
Wolfenstein, M., 119, 122, 135
Wolff, K., 348
Wyatt, R. Z., 67, 86

Yalom, I. D., 195, 333, 335, 342, 345
Yerevanian, B., 161

Zetzel, E. R., 53, 103, 106
Zilboorg, G., 176, 177

SUBJECT INDEX

Abandonment, 25, 179
  fears of, 190
Aberrant interactional patterns, 197
Accidents
  predisposing conflicts and, 254-257
  traumatic stress of, 250-257
Acting out, blocking channels for, 190
Adaptation, successful, 8
Adaptive intervention, 257-259
Adjustment reaction, behavior and, 194
Administration on Aging statistics, 4-6
Adult catastrophic psychic trauma, 108-111
Affect
  alexithymia and, 124
  availability of, 141-142
  blocking or anesthesia of, 109, 121
  character disorder and, 183-184
  early verbalization and, 103
  extreme stress and, 117-118
  genetic view of, 99-101
  hedonic quality of, 120-121
  language development and, 103
  psychosomatic manifestations of, 99-101
  role of, 97-98
  survivor psychotherapy and, 141-142
  undifferentiated, 103-104
    manifestation of, 99-101
  utilized as signals, 101-104
Affect tolerance, 97, 104-108, 179
  in character disorder, 215, 262
Affective anesthesia or blocking, 109, 121
Age
  as issue in patient selection for treatment, 34, 289
  psychodynamic concerns and, x-xii
  see also Aging; Elderly
Age bias, vii, x
  in predicting process and outcome of psychotherapy, 34, 289

Ageism, x, vii, 34, 289
Age-specific aspects of therapy, viii-x
Aging
  catatonoid reaction in, 117
  impact of, 184-186
  multiple dynamic systems in, 10
  see also Elderly
Aggression, 129-131
Alexithymia, 124-126
  therapeutic approach to, 147
Alliance with therapist, 215-216
Alzheimer's disease, 239
Ambivalence, 181, 199
American Association of Retired Persons
    statistics, 4-6
Anesthesia, affective, 109, 121
Anger, 102, 260
  survivors and, 129, 131
Anhedonia, 147
Antecedent psychopathology, 17
Anxiety, 283
  chronic, 123-124
  death, 195
  of family members, 238-239
  painful affects and, 101
  pseudophobia and, 127
Anxiety disorder, 283; see also Anxiety
Anxiety states, chronic, 123-124; see also
    Anxiety
Approaches to treatment, xvi
  in character disorder, 208-218
  combined, 22-23
  of massive trauma victim, 137-145
  in stress trauma of injury, 254
  team, xiv, 171-172, 211-214, 313
  therapeutic modalities and; see Therapeutic modalities
Aspiration or hope, loss of, 71
Assessment interviews, 271
Authoritative firmness, 259

Behavioral pathology of characterologically disordered, 175, 196-208
Bereavement, 16
Blocking
  affective, 109, 121
  of channels for acting out, 190
Bodily concerns, 204-206
Brief psychotherapy, xvi, 265-293
  evaluation of efficacy and process of,
    266-268
  case illustration of, 301-323
  clinical illustrations in, 281-290
  clinical observations of process in, 277-
    281
  clinical reports in, 265-266
  conclusions of, 290-291
  findings in, 274-277
  impact of, 279-280
  introduction in, 265-266
  methods in, 268-271
  outcome scales construction and use in,
    270-271
  process and outcome of treatment in,
    283
  reported results in, 266-268
  and terminal illness, 242-244
  theoretical considerations in, 266-268
  of traumatic reaction, 250-254
  treatment in, 271-273
Buffalo Creek disaster, 118, 134

Capabilities, emergence of, 281-289
Capacity for continued growth, 282-290
Caregiver, 183
Caretakers, 157-158, 160
  characterologically disordered patient
    and, 200
  interpersonal pathology between pa-
    tient and, 158, 166-168
  patient's withdrawal from, 206
  reliance on, 191-194
  support of, 171-173
Catastrophe, 7, 113-131
  emotional needs of victims of, 133-134
  terminology of, 109
  see also Massive psychic trauma
Catatonoid reaction, 109, 117
  as primal depression, 119-121
Catharsis, 23
Central nervous system disorders, exag-

gerated helplessness and, 161
Character change through insight and
  maturation, 259-262
Character disorders, xv, 175-229
  behavioral pathology in, 196-208
  case example of, 218-222
  conclusions in discussion of, 226
  conflict over death in, 194-195
  core pathology in, 176
  definition of, 176-177
  depressive withdrawal in, 206-208
  description of symptoms in, 180-181,
    182
  impact of aging and, 184-207
  interpersonal loss in, 186-188
  introduction to, 175-176
  loss of defensive outlets in, 190-191
  narcissistic symptoms in, 201-204
    group therapy and, 338
  pathological interpersonal relationships
    in, 199-201
  physical disability in, 189-190
  psychodynamics of, 177-180
  reliance on caretakers in, 191-194
  somatic preoccupations in, 204-206
  terms of, 177
  treatment for, 208-226
    case example in, 218-222
    cohesive staff team approaches in,
      211-214
    containing and limiting pathological
      behavior in, 209-210
    establishment of working alliance in,
      210-211
    reduction of primitive pathological
      behavior in, 214-226
Character flexibility in character changes,
  262
Character structure, 247-248
Characterologically difficult patient, ter-
  minology of, 176-180; see also Char-
  acter disorders
Children, rights of, 297-299
Chronic conditions, 5
Chronic secondary dysphoria, 160-163
Clarification, group therapy and, 333
Cognition and empathy in therapy, rela-
  tionship of, 36-37
Cognitive and perceptual symptoms, 184
Cognitive constriction, 126

Cognitive impairment, psychotherapeutic work and, 163-166
Cohesive staff team approaches, xvi, 171-173, 211-214, 313
Combined therapeutic approach, 22-23
"Common scoundrel," 176
Communications, interpersonal, group therapy and, 333
Concentration camp survivors; see Massive psychic trauma
Conceptual model for rating scales, 270-271
Conflict
    crisis treatment which mobilized predisposing, 254-257
    over death, 194-195
Confrontation with death, 111
Containing and limiting pathological behavior, 209-210
Contracts, character disorders in elderly and, 213-214
Convalescence, crises in, 250-254
Coping, 111-118
    models for, 114
Cotherapy, group therapy and, 345
Countertransference, xii, 36, 37-38
    group therapy and, 344-345
    survivor psychotherapy and, 143-145
The Course of Life, 9
Creativity, 15-16
Crises in aging, 7, 10, 185-186
    emotional trauma and, 237
    management of, 245-246
        frail elderly and, 246-247
    meaning of, 233
    psychological
        characteristics of, 234-236
        classification of, 236-245
        precipitating factors in, 235
        predisposing circumstances of, 234-235
        symptoms of, 235
    situational, 17
Crisis intervention goals, 245-246
Crisis management, principles of, 245-247

Danger
    recognition of, 118
    submission to unavoidable, 118
"Dead to the world" reactions, 127-129

Death and dying, 186-188, 242-245
    anxiety of, 195
    conflict over, 194-195
    confrontation with, 111
        aftereffects of, 127-129
    fantasies of, 195
    group therapy and concerns of, 342-343
    of parent as crisis, 261
Death anxiety, 195
Death fantasies, 195
Defenses
    denial as, 329
        trauma and, 114, 115
    loss of, 190-191
    splitting of good and bad self in, 180
Demoralization, group therapy and, 335
Denial
    as defense in aging, 329
    trauma and, 114, 115
Dependence
    alexithymia and, 125
    forced, 207
    longings for, therapeutic relationship for men and, 288-289
Depression, 119-121, 326
    chronic, 160-163
    handling of, 340-341
    projection and, 73-74
    secondary to illness, 160-163
    as stage in paranoid psychopathology, 68, 69
    survivor families and, 111, 130
        psychotherapy of, 142
    withdrawal and, 197, 206-208
Depressive affect of survivors, 111
Depressive guilt, projection of, 73-74
Depressive stage of psychopathology, 68, 69
Depressive withdrawal, 197, 206-208
Desensitization, emotional, 259
Development
    crises in, 7, 236-237; see also Development, problems in
    of emotions, 99-100
    late middle age, 286
    normal, 236-237
    postparental period and, 285
    problems in, 7, 236-237
        characterologically disordered pa-

tients and, 178-179
early life, 178-179
Developmental shift in late middle age, 286
Developmental theory, postparental transition and, 285
Disaster syndrome, 119; *see also* Massive psychic trauma
Differentiation, capacity for, 16-17
Disability
  group therapy and concerns of, 342-343
  physical, 189-190
  exaggerated helplessness and, 162
Disasters, studies of, 118-119; *see also* Massive psychic trauma
Discouragement, group therapy and, 335
Discrimination
  capacity for, 16-17
  constriction of, 126
Discussion, life-history, 259
Disillusionment as age specific dynamic theme, xi-xii
Disorders of self, 278-279
Drugs as therapeutic modality, 48-49, 217-218
  in crisis management, 246
  in paraphrenia, 88
Dynamics
  age specific, x-xii
  of friendship, 14
  treatment process and, 33-44; *see also* Psychodynamics, treatment process

Ego strength in depression, 71-72
Elderly
  caretakers of; *see* Caretakers
  exaggerated helplessness of, 157
  mental health problems of, 6; *see also specific problem*
  narcissism of, 157-158
  group therapy and, 336-339
  injuries in, 39-40, 326-329
  see also Age; Aging
Emergency regimes, continuation of, 121-124
Emotional desensitization, 259
Emotional flooding, 197-198
Emotional needs of victims of catastrophe,

133-134; *see also* Massive psychic trauma
Emotional trauma as crisis, 237; *see also* Crises in aging
Emotions
  crises and; *see* Crises in aging
  desensitization of, 259
  developmental line of, 99-100
  flooding of, 197-198
  massive psychic trauma and; *see* Massive psychic trauma
  maturation of, 100
Empathy
  and cognition in therapy, relationship of, 36-37
  reverse, 38-39
Entitlement problems, 297-299, 319
Environment
  crisis management and change in, 246
  manipulation of, as therapeutic modality, 49-52
  therapeutic, 280
Envy, projection of, 74
Establishment of working alliance, 210-211
Ethics, 61-62
Exacerbations of psychosis, 239-240
Exaggerated helplessness syndrome, xvii, 157-173
  chronic secondary dysphoria and, 160-163
  clinical illustrations of, 163-171
  definition of, 157-158
  management and treatment of, 171-173
  theory of, 158-160
Expectations of patient, 209
Explorative psychotherapy, 52-53
Externalization, 268
  exaggerated helplessness syndrome and, 159-160
  of past decathected memories, 42
  refound assertiveness and mastery and, 287

Fairness, 299-300
Families
  anxiety of, 238-239
  dynamics of, 307-310
  supportive network of, 171-173
  working alliance with, 24, 211

see also Family history; Family therapy
Family dynamics, 307-310
Family history, 302-307
  for major affective disorder, exaggerated helplessness and, 161
Family therapy, xviii, 312, 320-323
  integrated modes of, 311
  intergenerational approach to, 295-324
    case illustrations in, 301-323
    conclusions in, 323
    entitlement in, 297-299
    family dynamics in, 307-310
    family history in, 302-307
    formulation of three generational conflicts in, 301
    introduction to, 295-296
    justice in, 299-300
    ledger balancing in, 297-299
    legacy for posterity in, 300-301
    loyalty and, 296-297
Fantasies, death, 195
Fears
  of loss of self, 191
  of return of trauma, 122
Feelings
  of injustice, 299
  of worthlessness, 325
Filial maturity, concept of, 317
Firmness, authoritative, 259
Focal conflict
  resolution of, 281-289
  unresolved issue from early adulthood as, 281-289
Folie à deux, 88-90
Forced dependency relationships, 207
Formulating three generational conflicts, 301
Fostering of socialized living, 259
Freud's *Studies on Hysteria*, 31
Friendship dynamics, 14

Gender differences
  in outcome and process, 277
  in response to brief therapy, 286
Genetic view of affects, 99-101
Geriatric psychiatry unit, 310-311
Geriatric psychotherapy beyond crisis management; *see* Psychotherapy beyond crisis management
Geriatricians, 6

Giving of information, 259
Goals
  of crisis intervention, 245-246
  elderly character disordered patient and, 209
  of psychoanalytic treatment, 21-22
Grandchildren
  family therapy and, 320-323
  legacy of unfulfilled dreams for, 300
Grandiose self, 38
Grief and grieving, 260
  survivor psychotherapy and, 142
  work of, 186-188
  see also Mourning-Liberation
Group cohesion, 331
Group psychotherapy, xviii, 325-349
  central and organizing principle in conduct of, 331
  clinical considerations in, 331-345
  conclusions in, 346
  efficacy of, 329-331, 345
  introduction in, 325
  role of, 329-331
  self-esteem and, 325
  theoretical considerations in, 325-329
  therapeutic approaches in, 329-331
  value of, 325
Growth, capacity for continued, 282-290
Guilt, 260

Hallucinations, 184
Haloperidol, 88
Hate of survivors, 131-132; *see also* Massive psychic trauma
Health care expenses, 6
Health problems, 5-6, 17-18
Hedonic quality of affects, 120-121
Helplessness
  feeling of, 326
  state of total, 120
  syndrome of exaggerated; *see* Exaggerated helplessness syndrome
Help-rejecter, group therapy and, 341-342
Here and now focus, 333-334
History, 36
  family, 161, 302-307
  of psychoanalytic treatment for aging, 31-32
  victims of massive trauma and, 136-138

History taking, 36
  victims of massive trauma and, 136-138
Holocaust, 96, 319, 337-338
  family dynamics and, 307-310
  see also Massive psychic trauma
Hope, loss of, 71
Hopelessness, prejudicial, 32-33
Hyperarousal, 113-114
Hyperstimulation, 113-114
Hypervigilance, 121
Hypochondriacal concerns, 69, 75-79, 197
  preoccupations with, 204-206
  see also Psychosomatic diseases
Hysteria, age and, 31

Identification, projective, 180
Illness
  combined therapy in, 22
  organic, 17-18
  terminal, 242-245
Immune mechanisms, 16
Impact of aging, 184-186
Inconsistency, 181
Individual therapy, xviii; see also Psycho-
  therapy; Therapeutic modalities
Individualized outcome scales
  consistency of, 273
  reliability of, 272-273
  results of, 274-277
Infantile affective responses, 99-100
Infantile psychic trauma, fears of return
  to, 122-123
Inferiority, situations of, 202
Information, giving of, 259
Initiation of therapy, 35-36
Injuries
  predisposing conflicts and, 254-257
  stress trauma of, 250-257
Injustice, feelings of, 299
Inner life of older adult, 3-29; see also
  Mourning-liberation process
Inpatient phase of family therapy, 311,
  312-314
Insight, 248-249
  in character changes, 262
Institutions, 207-208
  staff in, 212
    character disorders and, 183
    team approach and, xvi, 171-173,
      211-214, 313

Insurance third-party payers, 61
Integration, 131-132
  of developmental potentials, clinical il-
    lustration of, 285-286
Intensity of stimuli, 96-97
Intensive individual psychotherapy, 223-
  226
Interdependence with caretaker and aged
  patient, 158, 160, 166-168
Interdisciplinary team, xvi, 171-173, 211-
  214, 313
Intergenerational approach to family
  therapy, 295-324
  case illustrations in, 301-323
    family dynamics and, 307-310
    family history and, 302-307
    treatment and, 310-323
  conclusions in, 323
  entitlement in, 297-299
  formulation of three generational con-
    flicts in, 301
  introduction to, 295-296
  justice in, 299-300
  ledger balancing in, 297-299
  legacy for posterity in, 300-301
  loyalty and, 296-297
Intergenerational conflict, underlying
  sources for, 295
Internalizations of love-objects, 105
Interpersonal pathology between patient
  and caretaker, 158, 166-168
Interpersonal relationships, 200-201, 249-
  250
  group therapy and, 333
  loss and, 186-188
  pathological, 199-201
  symptoms and, 181-183
  unstable, 181
Interviews, assessment, 271
Intrusion on personal space, 207
Isolation, 326
  trauma and, 114, 115

Jealousy, 83-85
Judgment, constriction of, 126
Justice, 299-300

Language, child and, 103
Ledger balancing, 297-299
Life review, 259

group therapy and, 334-335
Life-history discussion, 259
Loneliness, 194
Long-term care, exaggerated helplessness and, 168-171
Long-term psychotherapy, 216-217
Loss
  as age specific dynamic theme, xi-xii
  changing meanings of, 13-14
  defensive outlets and, 190-191
  disillusionment and, xi-xii
  group therapy and concerns about, 342-343
  impact of, 12
  of parent, 261
  physical, 189
  self
    fear of, 191
    sense of, 41-42
  self-cohesion, 180
  of significant other, vulnerability to, 19-21
Love object, 40-41
  internalizations of, 105
Loyalty, family treatment and, 296

Male-female cotherapy models, 345
Manipulation, 194
Marital therapy phase of family therapy, 311, 319-320
Mass disasters
Massive psychic trauma, xvii, 95-156
  adult catastrophic psychic trauma and, 108-111
  affect tolerance and, 104-108
  affects utilized as signals and, 101-104
  aftereffects of, 110, 118-131
    affective blocking in, 121
    aggression in, 129-131
    alexithymia in, 124-126
    catatonoid reactions as primal depression in, 119-121
    cognitive constriction in, 126
    continuation of emergency regimes in, 121-124
    "dead to the world" reactions in, 127-129
    pseudophobia in, 127
    recognition of danger in, 118-119
    submission to unavoidable danger in,
118-119
    surrender pattern in, 119
  conclusions in, 145-148
  coping and, 111-118
  general considerations of, 133-139
  genetic view of affects and, 99-101
  hate addiction and, 131-132
  integration and, 131-132
  introduction in, 95
  mental functions and, 113
  mourning and, 111-118
  psychosomatic diseases and, 104
  specific considerations in, 139-145
  studies of, 135-137
    review of, 96-99
Maturation of emotions, 100
Medical care, crisis management and, 246
Mellaril, 79, 85
Memories
  constriction of, 126
  as pathways to insight and resolution, 249
  pseudophobia and, 127
Mental health problems of elderly, 6; see also specific problem
Models
  characterologically disordered patients and, 178-179
  conceptual, rating scale construction and, 270-271
  coping, 114
  male-female cotherapy, 345
  for treating elderly, xviii
Modulators of rage, failures in development of, 180
Mortal dread, 101
Mourning, 111-118
  of one's eventual death, 195
  outcome of, in posttraumatic states, 132
  for past states of self, 11, 13
  pathological, 11, 12
  process, 11-26
  relinquishing anger and, 131-132
  stage of therapy and, 216
  work of, 115-116
  see also Mourning-liberation process
Mourning-liberation process, 3-29
  abandonment experiences and, 25
  clinical account of, 19-21
  conclusions for, 26-27

crises of, 7, 10
health problems and, 5-6
introduction to, 3-11
multiple dynamic systems of, 10
process of, 11-26
psychoanalytic treatment and, 18-19
  goal for, 21-22
research and, 8-9, 11
significant kinship relationships and, 13-14
statistics of, 4-5
successful adaptation and, 8
see also Mourning
see also Grief and grieving
Multiple dynamic systems, aging and, 10
Mutual selfobjects, 38

Narcissism, 157-158
injuries and, 39-40, 179, 190, 326-329
group therapy in, 336-339
symptoms and, 201-204
Narcissistic injury, 39-40, 179, 190, 326-329
group therapy and, 336-339
National Institute of Mental Health Program on Aging, 9
Navane, 81
Neuroses traumatic, 98; see also Massive psychic trauma
Nostalgia, 23

Object love, 40-41
Object-investments, 105
Operative thinking, 124
Oppressors, massive trauma and, 146
Organic illness, 17-18
paranoid symptoms and, 91

Pain threshold, 104
Pain tolerance, 104
Painful affect, 100-101
tolerance to, 105
Panic-flooding, 197-198
Paradigms of crisis therapy in elderly, 250-262
Paralysis of initiative, 109-110
Paranoia; see Paranoid disorders
Paranoid decompensation
of depression, 69-75
of hypochondriasis, 75-79

progression of, 67-69
see also Paranoid disorders
Paranoid delusions, 184
Paranoid disorders, xvii, 67-93, 239
as associated feature, 90-92
classification of phenomena of, 70
delusions in, 184
depression and, 69-75
hypochondriasis and, 75-79
self-aggrandizement and, 85-86
shared, 88-90
terminal illness and, 92
Paranoid stage, 69
Paraphrenia, 86-88
Parent-child relationship, 297-299
affect tolerance to, 106-107
see also Family therapy
Parents, 297-299
affect tolerance and, 106-107
meaning of children to, 13-14
pressure children to live out unfulfilled goals, 300
rights of, 297-299
Passive longings, men and, 288-289
Past states of self, mourning of, 11, 13
Pathological interpersonal relationships, 199-201; see also Interpersonal relationships
Pathological jealousy, 83-85
Pathological mourning, 11, 12
Patient's interests, 250
Patient-therapist relationship, 268; see also Psychotherapy
Patronizing comments, 207
Patterns of human damage, 135
Peer support, 339-341
Perception, constriction of, 126
Persecutory anxiety, 80
Personal relationships, 249-250; see also Interpersonal relationships
Personal space, 207
Pharmacotherapy, 48-49, 217-218
crisis management and, 246
in paraphrenia, 88
Phenothiazines, 88
Philosophy, 61-62
Physical disability, 189-190
exaggerated helplessness as, 162
Physical illnesses, 17-18
combined therapy, 22

terminal, 242-245
Physical losses, 189; *see also* Loss
Physicians treating older persons, 6
Positive feeling toward therapist, 268
Postdischarge family treatment phase of family therapy, 311, 314-319
Posterity, legacy for, 300-301
Predisposing conflict, crisis mobilizing, 254-257
Prejudice, 33
Primal depression, 119-121
Primary paranoia, 80-90
Primitive pathological behavior, reduction of reliance on, 214-226
Problem solving, constriction of, 126
Process
  clinical observations of, 277-281
  and outcome of treatment, clinical illustration of, 283-285
Productivity, 15-16
A Profile of Older Americans, statistics in, 4-6
Projection, 268
  as defense in aging, 329
  refound assertiveness and mastery and, 287
  self, 40, 41
Projective ecology, 40, 41
Projective identification, 180
Prolixin enanthate, 88
Pseudophobia, 127
Psychiatry unit, geriatric, 310-311
Psychic closing off, 109
Psychic trauma
  catastrophic; *see* Massive psychic trauma
  difficulties in understanding, 96-97
  infantile, fears of return to, 122-123
  meaning of, 97
  terminology of, 98, 109
Psychoanalytic psychotherapy, xv, 9-10, 32-33
  alexithymia as block to, 125-126
  goal of, 21-22
  history of, 31-32
  indications for, 18-19
  therapeutic process initiation in, 35
  see also Psychodynamics, treatment process; Psychotherapy
Psychodynamic concerns, age specific, x-xii

Psychodynamic issues, general, xvi-xvii
Psychodynamics
  paranoid, 67-93
  conclusions in, 92-93
  paranoia as associated feature in, 90-92
  paranoid decompensation of depression in, 69-75
  paranoid decompensation of hypochondriasis in, 75-79
  primary paranoia in, 80-90
  psychosis in, 79-92
  treatment process, 31-44
    case examples in, 34-35
    conclusions in, 42-43
    countertransference and, 36, 37-38
    empathy and cognition in therapy and, 36-37
    history of, 31-32
    initiation of therapy in, 35-36
    loss of sense of self and, 41-42
    love objects and, 40-41
    narcissism and, 39-40; *see also* Narcissism
    object love and, 40-41
    prejudicial hopelessness and, 32-33
    reverse empathy and, 38-39
    transference phenomena and, 38-40
Psychoimmunology, 16
Psychological crisis
  characteristics of, 234-236
  classification of, 236-245
  precipitating factors in, 235
  predisposing circumstances of, 234-235
  symptoms of, 235
Psychological perspectives on aging, 325-329
Psychopathology, xvii
  antecedent, 17
  manifestations of, 65-229; *see also specific behavior*
  three stages of, 67-69
Psychopharmacology, 48-49, 217-218
  crisis management and, 246
  in paraphrenia, 88
Psychosis, 79-92
  depressive, 239
  schizophrenia in later life as, 91
Psychosomatic diseases
  affect and, 99-101, 184
  alexithymia and, 125

concentration camp survivors and, 104, 124

fears of infantile psychic trauma and, 123

hypochondriacal concerns and, 69, 75-79, 197

preoccupations with, 204-206

see also Somatization

Psychosomatic manifestation of affect, 99-101, 184

Psychotherapy

beyond crisis management, 247-250

adaptive intervention using existing character structure in, 257-259

brief therapy of traumatic reaction in, 250-254

character change through insight and maturation in, 259-262

characteristics of crisis and, 234-236

classification of crisis and, 236-245

conclusions in, 262-263

general principles of crisis management in, 245-247

paradigms of, 250-262

predisposing conflict in, 254-257

brief, xviii, 265-293

case illustration of, 301-323

clinical illustrations in, 289-290

clinical observations of process in, 277-281

clinical reports in, 265-266

conclusions in, 290-291

findings in, 274-277

inpatient phase of, 311, 312-314

marital therapy phase of, 311, 319-320

outcome scales construction in, 270-271

process and outcome of treatment in, 283

reported results in, 266-268

theoretical considerations in, 266-268

traumatic reaction and, 250-254

combined with other therapies, 22

long-term, 216

positive indication for, 248

process of, 23-25, 283

proportion of aged seeking, ix-x

psychoanalytic; see Psychoanalytic psychotherapy

reflections on, 45-63

therapeutic modalities and, 47

scientific evaluation of effectiveness, xviii

Psychotic depression, 239

Rage

and devaluation as defense in aging, 329

modulators of, failures in development of, 180

survivors and, 129, 131

Rating scale

conceptual model for, 270-271

reliability of, 272-273

Reactions to aging, statistics in, 4-6

Reactive aggression, survivors and, 129

Recognition of danger, 118

Recollections, 23

Reconstruction, 42

Referrals, 33-34

selection of subjects and, 268-270

Regression

as defense in aging, 329

as response in later life, 308-309

Regressive state of therapist, 42

Rehabilitation, 139

Reinternalization, 42

Relationships

interpersonal; see Interpersonal relationships

selfobject, 38, 39, 40-41, 179, 327

Reliability, rating scale, 272-273

Reliance on caretakers, 191-194; see also Caretakers

Reminiscences, 23

Research, 8-9, 11

Resistance, 260

group therapy and, 332

Resolution of focal conflict, 281-289

Restitution, 42

Retraining methods, victims of massive trauma and, 147

Retreat into despair, 206-208

Reverse empathy, 38-39

Rights of children and parents, 297-299

Role shift in relationships, 15

Scapegoating, 130

Schizoaffective illness, 239

Schizophrenia, 91
Scientific evaluation of psychotherapy effectiveness, xviii
"The Scope for Change in Later Life," xv, xvii
Self
  changes and restoration of, 281-289
  disorders of, 278-279
  loss of
    fears of, 191
    sense of, 41-42
  mourning for past states of, 11, 13
  projection of, 40, 41
Self expectations, affect tolerance and, 106
Self-aggrandizement, paranoia with, 85-86
Self-cohesion, loss of, 180
Self-continuity, 278, 279-280
Self-esteem, 202
  failure of, 179
  impact of therapy on, 278, 279-280
Self-gratification
  affect tolerance and, 105
  possibilities for, 105
Self-healing,
  massive psychic trauma and, 140-141
Self-image, 202
Selfobject relationship, 38, 39, 40-41, 179, 327
Self-psychology, 278
Self-referrals for therapy, 33-34
Self-righting factors, 8
Self-selfobject relationships, 179; see also Selfobject relationship
Sense of self
  aging and, 326-329
  loss of, 41-42
  see also Self
Separation fears, 192-195
Setting for treatment, 24-25
Sexual bimodality, 285-286
Sibling relationships, 14
Significant kinship relationships, 13-14; see also Families
Simultaneous diseases of psychic system, 9-10
Situational crises, 17; see also Crises in aging
Social issues, 5
Social smile, 102

Socialized living, fostering of, 259
Socioeconomic problems, 5
Soldiers, stress and, 116-117
Somatic hypochondriacal concerns, 69, 70-75, 197
  preoccupations with, 204-206
  see also Psychosomatic diseases
Somatic responses to affect, 99-101, 184
Somatization
  as defense in aging, 329
  fears of infantile psychic trauma and, 123
  see also Psychosomatic diseases
Specialized care programs, 171
Splitting, defense of, 180
Spouse, changing meaning of word, 14-15
Staff, institutional, 212
  character disorders of patients and, 183
  education of, 212
  team approaches of, xvi, 171-173, 211-214, 313
Statistics, 4-6
Stimuli, intensity of, 96-97
Strengths, emergence of, 281-289
Stress of traumatic accident, 250-257
Stress management, 112-113
Structure, character disorders and, 211-214
The Studies on Hysteria, 31
Submission to unavoidable danger, 118
Substance abuse, 125
Successful aging, 12-13
Suicidal ideation, 195
Suicide, 197-198
Supportive measures, 258-259, 268
  family and, 171-173
  frail elderly and, 246
  group therapy and, 332
Surgery as crisis, 250-254
Surrender pattern, 119
Survivors and survivor families, 318-319
  aggressive behavior of, 130
  depressive affect of, 111, 130
  family dynamics and, 307-310
  group therapy and, 337-338
  guilt feelings of, 318-319
  regressive responses in later life and, 308-309
Symbiotic enmeshed relationships, 199-200

Team approach, xvi, 171-173, 211-214, 313
Terminal illness, 242-245
Therapeutic approach, xviii, xv-xvi
  age-specific aspects of, xii
  in character disorders, 209
  combined, 22-23
  definition of, 45
  initiation of psychoanalytic, 35; see also Psychoanalytic psychotherapy
  in intergenerational family therapy, 310-323
  in stress trauma of injury, 254
  in victims of massive psychic trauma, 137-139; see also Massive psychic trauma
  see also Psychotherapy; Psychodynamics; Therapeutic modalities
Therapeutic environment, 280
Therapeutic modalities, 47-61
  environmental manipulation in, 49-52
  explorative psychotherapy in, 52-53; see also Psychotherapy
  psychopharmacology in, 48-49, 88, 217-218, 246
  psychodynamic psychotherapy in, 55-61; see also Psychodynamics
  time-limited treatment in, 53-55
Therapeutic perspectives, xv-xvi
Therapeutic role, 280-281
Therapeutic team, xvi, 171-173, 211-214, 313
Therapist
  alliance with, 215-216
  survivor psychotherapy and, 143-145
  see also Countertransference; Transference
Therapy; see Therapeutic approach
Thiothixene, 88
Threatened suicide, 240-242
Time perspective, loss of, 71
Time-limited treatment, 53-55

Transference, 23, 24, 38-40
  beyond crisis management and, 249, 256, 260
  brief psychotherapy and, 280-281
  crisis management and, 246
  survivor psychotherapy and, 143-145
Transition in postparental years, 285
Trauma, psychic; see Psychic trauma
Traumatic neuroses, 98; see also Massive psychic trauma
Traumatic screens, 127
Traumatic state, catastrophic; see Massive psychic trauma
Traumatic stress of accident, 250-257
Treatment; see Therapeutic approach; Therapeutic modalities
Treatment outcome, 273
Treatment team, xviii, 171-173, 211-214, 313
Trust, 26, 110-111

Undifferentiated manifestations of affect, 99-101, 103-104
Unpredictability, 181
Unresolved issue from early adulthood, 281-289
U.S. National Institute on Aging, 8

Verbalization, child and, 103
Victims of catastrophe; see Massive psychic trauma
Vietnam veterans, 134, 145
Vulnerability, 110

War stress, 116-117; see also Massive psychic trauma
Withdrawal as defense in aging, 329
Wolf Man, 54
Work
  of grieving, 186-188
  of mourning, 115-116
Worthlessness, feelings of, 326